THE FATHERS
OF THE CHURCH

A NEW TRANSLATION

VOLUME 141

THE FATHERS OF THE CHURCH

A NEW TRANSLATION

ORIGEN

HOMILIES ON THE PSALMS: CODEX MONACENSIS GRAECUS 314

Translated by

JOSEPH W. TRIGG

THE CATHOLIC UNIVERSITY OF AMERICA PRESS
Washington, D.C.

Copyright © 2020
THE CATHOLIC UNIVERSITY OF AMERICA PRESS
All rights reserved
Printed in the United States of America

The paper used in this publication meets the minimum requirements of
the American National Standards for Information Science—Permanence
of Paper for Printed Library Materials, ANSI z39.48 - 1984.
∞

Cataloging-in-Publication data can be obtained
from the Library of Congress.
ISBN 978-0-8132-3319-2

CONTENTS

INDICES

ACKNOWLEDGMENTS

Many people have given me help and encouragement with this project. I thank all of them. In particular, I would like to acknowledge the constant support of my wife, Joy Trigg, who provided me emotional support and a place to work in addition to catching errors and making helpful suggestions as the work progressed. Along with my friend, Linda Klein, and my sister, Jane Trigg, she also prepared the Index of Holy Scripture.

I also thank my long-time friend, Robin Darling Young, who read through the homilies twice with me as we shared the excitement of encountering the discovery of CMG 314 and who first encouraged me to translate it.

I also owe a major debt of gratitude to Lorenzo Perrone and his collaborators for making CMG 314 accessible in a splendid critical edition. I thank him also for his generosity and support to me, sharing successive digital drafts of his edition as well as his provisional translation of the homilies into Italian.

The eager involvement of my friend, Linda Klein, and my sister, Jane Trigg, helped keep me on task. They worked together to proofread as many as five successive drafts of each homily. They not only checked for style and grammar, but also checked biblical citations and cross-references within the homilies and helped me conform to the publisher's format. With my wife, Joy Trigg, they prepared the Index of Holy Scripture and proofread the General Index.

I thank Mark Randall James, whose forthcoming book on Origen's use of language I cite. He introduced me to the homilies, which he used extensively in the doctoral dissertation that was the basis for that book. He gave me new insights into Origen's use of language and helped me translate musical terminology.

I thank Tim Vivian, who read drafts of this translation from the perspective of a translator and a teacher. He also had a sharp eye for misplaced punctuation and formatting errors.

I thank my son-in-law, Eric Cahanin, for giving me helpful feedback on the introduction.

I also thank Carole Monica Burnett, the editor for CUA Press, who encouraged me at all stages and compared my translation with the original.

Those who provided assistance with this translation have helped me to identify problems and make improvements; nevertheless, for any errors that remain, I am solely responsible.

Almost every one of the people whom I have named here, and others, have encouraged me also by reaffirming my conviction that Origen still has something to say today.

ABBREVIATIONS

Works of Origen

Cels.	*Contra Celsum*
Comm. Cant.	*Commentary on the Song of Songs*
Comm. Jo.	*Commentary on John*
Comm. Matt.	*Commentary on Matthew*
Comm. Rom.	*Commentary on Romans*
Dial.	*Dialogue with Heracleides*
Ep. Afr.	*Letter to Julius Africanus*
Fr. Lam.	Fragments, *Commentary on Lamentations*
Fr. Ps.	Fragments, *Commentary or Homily on Psalm or Psalms*
Hom. Gen.	*Homilies on Genesis*
Hom. Exod.	*Homilies on Exodus*
Hom. Ezech.	*Homilies on Ezekiel*
Hom. Isa.	*Homilies on Isaiah*
Hom. Jer.	*Homilies on Jeremiah*
Hom. Jos.	*Homilies on Joshua*
Hom. Lev.	*Homilies on Leviticus*
Hom. Luc.	*Homilies on Luke*
Hom. Num.	*Homilies on Numbers*
Hom. 1 Reg.	*Homilies on 1 Samuel*
Mart.	*Exhortation to Martyrdom*
Or.	*On Prayer*
Princ.	*Peri archōn (On First Principles)*

Individual homilies translated in this volume are designated by PS followed by the number of the Psalm being commented on, followed by H, then the number of the particular homily on that Psalm (if there are more than one), followed by a period and the section number in the Greek text published in

GCSO13. (For the abbreviation GCSO13, please see below, under "General Abbreviations.") Thus PS77H8.1 is a reference to the first numbered section of the eighth homily on Psalm 77.

Other Ancient Sources

Disc.	Epictetus, *Discourses*
Enn.	Plotinus, *The Enneads*
Haer.	Irenaeus, *Adversus haereses*
Hist. eccl.	Eusebius, *Ecclesiastical History*
Math.	Sextus Empiricus, *Adversus mathematicos*
Paed.	Clement of Alexandria, *Paedagogus*
Philoc.	*Philocalia*
Protr.	Clement of Alexandria, *Protrepticus*
Resp.	Plato, *Republic*
Strom.	Clement of Alexandria, *Stromateis*

General Abbreviations

CMG 314	Codex Monacensis Graecus 314
CMS	Commentariorum Matthaei Series
CSEL	Corpus Scriptorum Ecclesiasticorum Latinorum
FOTC	The Fathers of the Church
GCS	Die Griechischen Christlichen Schriftsteller der ersten Jahrhunderte
GCSO13	Die Griechischen Christlichen Schriftsteller der ersten Jahrhunderte (GCS), Origenes Werke XIII
JTS	*Journal of Theological Studies*
LCL	Loeb Classical Library
LXX	Septuagint
PL	Patrologia Latina (Migne)
Prol.	Prologue
SC	Sources chrétiennes

SELECT BIBLIOGRAPHY

Works of Origen

Harl, Marguerite, ed., with Nicholas de Lange. Introduction, text, translation, and notes. *Origène, Philocalie, 1–20 Sur les Écritures et la lettre à Africanus sur l'histoire de Suzanne.* Paris: Cerf, 1983 = SC 302.

Origen. *Die neuen Psalmenhomilien: Eine kritische Edition des Codex Monacensis Graecus 314.* Edited by Lorenzo Perrone with Marina Molin Pradel, Emanuela Prinzivalli, and Antonio Cacciari = Die Griechischen Christlichen Schriftsteller der ersten Jahrhunderte (GCS) Neue Folge, Band 19, *Origenes Werke* XIII. Berlin: De Gruyter, 2015.

———. *Peri archon.* In *Origenes Werke V, De principiis.* Edited by Paul Koetschau. GCS 22. Leipzig, 1913.

———. *Contra Celsum* and *On Prayer.* In *Origenes Werke I, Contra Celsum I.* Edited by Paul Koetschau. GCS 2. Leipzig, 1899; *Origenes Werke II, Contra Celsum II, De oratione.* Edited by Paul Koetschau. GCS 3. Leipzig, 1899.

Other Ancient Sources

Philo. *On Moses.* In *Philo, Volume VI: On Abraham. On Joseph. On Moses.* Edited and translated by F. H. Colson. LCL 289. Cambridge, MA: Harvard University Press, 1935.

———. *On the Unchangeableness of God* and *On Drunkenness.* In *Philo, Volume III: On the Unchangeableness of God. On Husbandry. Concerning Noah's Work as a Planter. On Drunkenness. On Sobriety.* Edited and translated by F. H. Colson and G. H. Whitaker. LCL 247. Cambridge, MA: Harvard University Press, 1930.

Plotinus. *The Enneads.* Edited and translated by Lloyd P. Gerson et al. Cambridge: Cambridge University Press, 2018.

Modern Scholarship

Bradshaw, Paul F. *Reconstructing Early Christian Worship.* Collegeville, MN: Liturgical Press, 2009.

Clark, Stephen R. L. *Plotinus: Myth, Metaphor and Philosophical Practice.* Chicago: University of Chicago Press, 2006.

de Lange, Nicholas. *Origen and the Jews: Studies in Jewish-Christian Relations in Third-century Palestine.* Cambridge: Cambridge University Press, 1977.

Dively Lauro, Elizabeth Ann. *The Soul and Spirit of Scripture within Origen's Exegesis.* Leiden: Brill, 2005.

Gerson, Lloyd P. *Platonism and Naturalism: The Possibility of Philosophy.* Ithaca, NY: Cornell University Press, 2020.

Gillingham, Susan. *Psalms Through the Centuries: Volume One.* Chichester: Blackwell, 2008.

Grafton, Anthony, and Megan Williams. *Christianity and the Transformation of the Book.* Cambridge, MA: Harvard University Press, 2006.

Grant, Robert M. *Heresy and Criticism: The Search for Authenticity in Early Christian Literature.* Louisville, KY: Westminster/John Knox, 1993.

Hadot, Pierre. *Plotinus and the Simplicity of Vision.* Translated by Michael Chase. Chicago: University of Chicago Press, 1993.

Harl, Marguerite. *La langue de Japhet: Quinze études sur la Septante et le grec des Chrétiens.* Paris: Cerf, 1994.

———. *Le déchiffrement du sens: Études sur l'herméneutique chrétienne d'Origène à Grégoire de Nysse.* Paris: Études Augustiniennes, 1993.

———. *Origène et la fonction révélatrice du Verbe Incarné.* Paris: Éditions du Seuil, 1958.

Jacobsen, Anders-Christian. *Christ—The Teacher of Salvation: A Study on Origen's Christology and Soteriology.* Münster: Aschendorff, 2015.

James, Mark Randall. *Learning the Language of Scripture: Origen, Wisdom, and the Logic of Interpretation.* Leiden: Brill, forthcoming in 2021.

Karamanolis, George. *The Philosophy of Early Christianity.* London: Routledge, 2013.

Kugel, James L. *The Bible As It Was.* Cambridge, MA: Harvard University Press, 1997.

———. *Traditions of the Bible: A Guide to the Bible As It Was at the Start of the Common Era.* Cambridge, MA: Harvard University Press, 1998.

Lehoux, Daryn. *What Did the Romans Know? An Inquiry into Science and Worldmaking.* Chicago: University of Chicago Press, 2012.

Marrou, H. I. *A History of Education in Antiquity.* Translated by George Lamb. Madison, WI: University of Wisconsin Press, 1982.

Martens, Peter. *Origen and Scripture: The Contours of the Exegetical Life.* Oxford: Oxford University Press, 2012.

Nautin, Pierre. *Origène: Sa vie et son œuvre.* Paris: Beauchesne, 1977.

Neuschäfer, Bernhard. *Origenes als Philologe.* 2 vols. Basel: Friedrich Reinhardt Verlag, 1987.

Niehoff, Maren R. *Jewish Exegesis and Homeric Scholarship in Alexandria.* Cambridge: Cambridge University Press, 2011.

———. *Philo of Alexandria: An Intellectual Biography.* New Haven, CT: Yale University Press, 2018.

Pace, Nicola. *Ricerche sulla traduzione di Rufino del "De principiis" di Origene.* Florence: La Nuova Italia Editrice, 1990.

Perrone, Lorenzo, ed. *Il cuore indurito del Faraone: Origene e il problema del libero arbitrio.* Bologna: Marietti, 1992.

———. *La preghiera secondo Origene: L'impossibilità donata.* Brescia: Morcelliana, 2011.

Pfeiffer, Rudolf. *A History of Classical Scholarship: From the Beginnings to the End of the Hellenistic Age.* Oxford: Oxford University Press, 1968.

Rondeau, Marie-Josèphe. *Les commentaires patristiques du psautier (IIIe–Ve siècles).* 2 vols. Rome: Pontificium Institutum Studiorum Orientalium, 1982 and 1985.

Runia, David T. *Philo in Early Christian Literature: A Survey.* Assen: Van Gorcum, 1993.

Seidman, Naomi. *Faithful Renderings: Jewish-Christian Difference and the Politics of Translation.* Chicago: University of Chicago Press, 2006.

Somos, Róbert. *Logic and Argumentation in Origen.* Münster: Aschendorff, 2015.

Stroumsa, Guy G. *Hidden Wisdom: Esoteric Traditions and the Roots of Christian Mysticism.* Leiden: Brill, 1996.

Torjesen, Karen Jo. *Hermeneutical Procedure and Theological Method in Origen's Exegesis.* Berlin: De Gruyter, 2011.

Trigg, Joseph W. *Origen.* London: Routledge, 1998.

———. "The Angel of Great Counsel: Christ and the Angelic Hierarchy in Origen's Theology." *Journal of Theological Studies,* n. s. 42 (1991): 33–51.

———. "What can be Learned by Translating the Homilies?" In Robin Darling Young and Joseph W. Trigg, *Origen's Last Words.* Forthcoming from The Catholic University of America Press.

Wilken, Robert L. *The Land Called Holy: Palestine in Christian History and Thought.* New Haven, CT: Yale University Press, 1992.

Williams, Rowan D. "Origen: Between Orthodoxy and Heresy." In *Origeniana Septima: Origenes in den Auseinandersetzungen des 4. Jahrhunderts,* ed. Wolfgang A. Bienert and Uwe Kühneweg, 3–14. Louvain: Peeters, 1999.

INTRODUCTION

INTRODUCTION

The Discovery of CMG 314

In 2012 the Bayerische Staatsbibliothek in Munich announced a spectacular discovery in its manuscript collection by Dr. Marina Molin Pradel, an archivist on the staff. She had identified twenty-nine Greek homilies in Codex Monacensis Graecus 314 (henceforth CMG 314), a thick twelfth-century Byzantine manuscript, as works by Origen. That announcement also stated that Professor Lorenzo Perrone of the University of Bologna, an internationally respected scholar of Origen, vouched for the identification. Perrone quickly realized that the homilies in CMG 314 could be identified conclusively as hitherto lost homilies of Origen on both external and internal grounds. He knew that homilies by Origen on the Psalms had once existed because a list survives in Jerome's Letter 33 that states how many homilies Origen preached on selected Psalms throughout the Psalter.[1] This list attests to each of the homilies in CMG 314. Nine of the homilies in Jerome's list survived in a fifth-century translation of homilies on Psalms 36, 37, and 38 into Latin by Rufinus of Aquileia (ca. 345–ca. 412).[2] The homilies on Psalm 36 in CMG 314 were clearly the Greek original of four of these. Around 408 Rufinus also translated the first book of an *Apology for Origen* composed by Pamphilus of Caesarea that incorporates a passage from Homily 2 on Psalm 15.[3] We find the Greek original of that passage as well in CMG 314. Extensive excerpts from Origen's nine homilies on

---

1. Jerome, *Ep.* 33.3, CSEL 54, 258.

2. See PL 12:1319–1410.

3. For Rufinus's translation of the first book of Pamphilus's *Apology for Origen*, see René Amacker and Éric Junod, editors, *Pamphile, Eusèbe de Césarée, Apologie pour Origène*, 2 vols. (Paris: Cerf, 2002) = SC 464 and 465.

Psalm 77 in *catenae*, that is, commentaries from the Byzantine period that were compiled by excerpting earlier works, demonstrated the authenticity of those homilies in CMG 314. Excerpts have survived for other homilies as well. Furthermore, Perrone could immediately see that the style and content of the homilies in CMG 314 were consistent with the rest of Origen's surviving work, with which he was deeply familiar.

Excited by the discovery, Perrone quickly began transcribing CMG 314 from the library's website as the first step in preparing a critical edition. That edition, done in collaboration with Marina Molin Pradel, Emanuela Prinzivalli, and Antonio Cacciari, appeared in 2015 as the thirteenth volume of Origen's works in the distinguished Die Griechischen Christlichen Schriftsteller series.[4] Along with the text of the homilies, it contains introductory essays about the manuscript itself by Pradel, about the authentication and dating of the homilies by Perrone, and about what they show about Rufinus as a translator by Prinzivalli. The text itself is accompanied by an *apparatus criticus* and by extensive notes. In the notes Perrone and his fellow editors identify references to the Bible and other ancient literature. They also cite and quote extensively on almost every page from other works by Origen that demonstrate the consistency between the style and content of the newly discovered homilies and the rest of Origen's work. The edition incorporates Rufinus's translation of a passage from Homily 2 on Psalm 15 in a column parallel to the Greek text. In an appendix to the edition, Prinzivalli, the editor of the four homilies on Psalm 36, provides Rufinus's translation of them in columns aligned with the Greek text. Passages of the homilies attested in Byzantine *catenae* are indicated in bold text. The GCS text is the basis of this translation.

In his introductory essay Perrone shows that these homilies are, in fact, the last known work by Origen. In Homily 8 on Psalm 77 Origen states that Hebrew was the original human lan-

---

4. Origen, *Die neuen Psalmenhomilien: Eine kritische Edition des Codex Monacensis Graecus 314,* ed. Lorenzo Perrone with Marina Molin Pradel, Emanuela Prinzivalli, and Antonio Cacciari = Die Griechischen Christlichen Schriftsteller der ersten Jahrhunderte (GCS) Neue Folge, Band 19, Origenes Werke XIII (Berlin: De Gruyter, 2015), henceforth GCSO13.

guage, retained by the Hebrew people alone when peoples were separated by language at the Tower of Babel. Origen states that he had once thought that this division of languages was also the occasion when God assigned angels to each people, reserving the people of Israel for himself. (He, in fact, states this view in *Contra Celsum,* previously his last datable work, written in 249.)[5] Nonetheless, after examining the matter more thoroughly, Origen says that he changed his mind. The distribution of the nations to various angels could not have been accomplished until Jacob had received the name Israel, and it probably occurred when the people of Israel received their boundaries at the conquest of Canaan.[6] Lorenzo Perrone, in his introduction to the critical edition of CMG 314, shows how this statement indicates that Origen preached the *Homilies on the Psalms* after writing *Contra Celsum,* where he had put forth the view that he subsequently abandoned. Because *Contra Celsum* refers to the Millennium of Rome in 248, it had previously been considered Origen's last known work. Perrone points out that this honor now belongs to these homilies, which must have been composed shortly before Origen's arrest and torture during the Decian persecution of 251, which led to his death.[7]

CMG 314 increases from twenty-one to fifty the number of homilies we possess in Origen's own words. Trained stenographers recorded Origen's words as he spoke. Each homily is, effectively, a time capsule, preserving Origen's interaction with a congregation. In Homily 1 on Psalm 67 we see Origen reacting in real time to a statement that had recently been made by a bishop. Sometimes the text makes most sense if we assume that it was accompanied by gestures or spoken in an amused tone of voice. If Jerome's list is correct, Origen preached more than a hundred homilies, covering about half of the Psalms, the first being Psalm 3 and the last being Psalm 149. We do not know why he preached on some Psalms and not others or why CMG 314 contains the particular selection of homilies that it does; some of the Psalms are cited in the New Testament, but most are not.

5. Origen, *Contra Celsum* 5.29.
6. PS77H8.1.
7. GCSO13, 17–25.

Perrone has pointed out[8] one clue that may explain the selection. He notes that seven of the ten Psalms for which we have homilies are among the twelve Psalms ascribed to Asaph, identified in 1 Chr 16.5 as the leader of the choir appointed by David to worship before the Ark of the Covenant in Jerusalem.[9] If Jerome is correct, Origen preached on all but one of the Asaph Psalms. Origen probably counted the Asaph Psalms among the more difficult ones, which he as a teacher had an obligation to explain. (Although he would have known better than to draw an etymological connection, "Asaph" does sound like the Greek word *asaphēs,* "obscure.") Through Asaph, also, these Psalms had a close association with the worship of God in the Temple, the place where, as we shall see, God is present in the human soul. Accordingly, Psalms associated with Asaph might be expected to have particular relevance to the deification of humanity, a pervasive subject throughout the homilies.

Preaching

Origen's surviving homilies in Greek, now much augmented by the twenty-nine in CMG 314, are our earliest transcripts of actual Christian preaching. Ancient Latin translations by Jerome and Rufinus survive of almost two hundred more homilies. He preached all of these after 234, when he took up residence in Caesarea Maritima, the center of Roman administration in the province of Palestine.[10] He had relocated there after having lived his early life in Alexandria, the capital of Egypt and second-largest city in the Roman Empire. He was (probably) born in Alexandria around AD 185 to a well-to-do Christian family. He received a splendid education there in Greek literature and philosophy as well as the Christian Bible. While still in Alexandria, a wealthy layman, Ambrosius, whom he convinced to abandon the

8. See Lorenzo Perrone, "Origen's Interpretation of the Psalter Revisited: The Nine Homilies on Psalm 77 (78) in the Munich Codex," in Robin Darling Young and Joseph W. Trigg, *Origen's Last Words.* Forthcoming from The Catholic University of America Press.

9. See PS76H1.1.

10. In PS36H1.2 below, Origen may be alluding to his summons to the imperial court before he took up residence in Caesarea. See n. 26 below, p. 82.

Valentinian heresy, encouraged him to write and supplied him with a staff of assistants. His Alexandrian writings were mostly biblical commentaries, now largely lost save for two volumes of his *Commentary on John* and his treatise *Peri archōn* (usually translated, *On First Principles*), which presents Christian doctrine as an organic whole, a "body of truth." At Alexandria he also began his massive *Hexapla,* discussed below. Most of Origen's surviving works were written with Ambrosius's help and encouragement at Caesarea, where he had been ordained as a presbyter in 232 and was invited to preach.

We cannot be sure when, during his residence at Caesarea for nearly twenty years, Origen preached his homilies. Presumably we can thank Ambrosius for the team that transcribed them. The identification of CMG 314 showed that an ambitious attempt to reconstruct their chronology by Pierre Nautin in 1977 is untenable,[11] although, as will be shown below, this particular set can now be dated to around 250. The homilies are exegetical sermons, not commentaries. They share a common structure that includes elements of Greek rhetoric. The first numbered section of each homily is normally an introduction, *prooimion,* that often deals with a particular issue related to the Psalm. There follows a line-by-line exposition of the Psalm in which Origen relates each line to the lives of his hearers. The exposition of the last lines on which he comments in any homily is abbreviated and rhetorically heightened to constitute a final exhortation that concludes in a doxology reminiscent of 2 Pt 3.18, usually: "to whom is the glory and the might to the ages of ages. Amen."

As a pastor, Origen warns against typical vices, especially wrath, greed, and sexual license,[12] but his pastoral advice tends toward the specific. He often calls on his congregation to respect and assist those who are destitute (*ptōchoi*). He stresses taking personal responsibility, often making himself the prime example, as when he speaks about neglecting spiritual nourishment[13] or, more tellingly, when he prays that he may not become

---

11. Pierre Nautin, *Origène: Sa vie et son œuvre* (Paris: Beauchesne, 1977).

12. See PS80H.7. On wrath, see also PS75.7–8 and PS77H7.7.

13. See, for example, PS15H1.9.

one of Satan's arrows, causing others to stumble and sin.[14] He encourages his congregation not to be disheartened by their failings but to learn from them and to make steady, even if slow, progress.[15] He also tempers the zeal of some of his hearers for advanced teachings by stressing the prior importance of conduct[16] and biblical knowledge.[17] To bring home what he says, he employs rhetorical techniques such as personification[18] and antithesis[19] and uses examples taken from activities with which his congregation would be familiar, such as acting in the theater,[20] wine connoisseurship,[21] sailing into Caesarea's tricky harbor,[22] or children's wrestling matches.[23] He employs humor as well. His figurative interpretation of Egyptian vegetables and his personification of the senses are deliberately over-the-top.[24] He asks those who resist figurative interpretation if they actually think that the angels have kitchen utensils for cooking manna or a brass section that will play the trumpet of doom.[25] They might try stepping on a cobra, he suggests, if they think that Jesus promised that actual snakes will not harm his followers.[26]

Origen exemplifies a self-confident Christianity that has won over some Jews[27] as well as adherents to traditional polytheistic religion.[28] He differentiates Christian teaching from Judaism, but does not treat Judaism, much less Jews, as a threat. He saw no danger in conceding that traditional Greek religion had a few things right,[29] or any need to guard his hearers against

14. See PS77H8.6.

15. For example, PS36H2.3.

16. PS77H1.5.

17. PS80H2.5.

18. PS36H1.4.

19. For example, PS81H.7.

20. PS81H.3.

21. PS80H1.1.

22. PS36H4.2.

23. Ibid.

24. PS77H4.11 and PS36H1.4.

25. PS77H4.5 and PS80H1.5 referring to Ps 77.25 and 1 Thes 4.16.

26. PS73H3.7, referring to Lk 10.19.

27. PS73H2.1.

28. See PS76H2.6.

29. See PS76H3.2.

idolatry. His concern, rather, is to show that the biblical prohibition of idolatry is still relevant to the idolization of riches or popularity.[30] On the other hand, he makes a point of warning against false teaching, at one point even giving his congregation a lesson in how to detect it.[31] He often mentions three figures: Basilides, Valentinus, and Marcion. All were second-century Christian teachers who anticipated Origen in applying the techniques of Hellenistic literary criticism, known as "grammar," to the Bible.[32] All three explained in different ways how the cosmos was created by an inferior God, whom they identified with the God of the Hebrew Bible. All three taught that Jesus was not a human being descended from David, but an emissary from a higher God. Because Basilides and Valentinus taught that Jesus came to summon back to God a spark of the divine shared by at least some human beings, the two of them are usually classified today as Gnostics. Marcion read Paul to teach that Jesus was the emissary of a good God, previously unknown, who took pity on human beings trapped in a cosmos made by the God of the Hebrew Bible, a God who was just, but not good.

Origen took issue with the way all three and their followers interpreted the Bible. Specifically, they employed their expertise in grammar to argue that the God of the Old Testament, the Creator and Lawgiver of the Jews, is not the same God as the God of the New Testament. They often sought to show that the Bible had been interpolated to incorporate teachings about the inferior God. For Origen, accepting both Testaments as authoritative was the distinguishing mark of a "man of the Church," *ekklēsiastikos anēr*. Origen believed that, just as they denigrated the Old Testament, derived from the God who inspired Moses and the Hebrew prophets, so they also denigrated the goodness of the cosmos that God had created.[33]

Origen shared with Platonists the belief that the beauty and order of the cosmos manifested the divine mind. Of all the her-

30. See PS80H2.3–4.

31. See PS77H2.4.

32. See Robert M. Grant, *Heresy and Criticism: The Search for Authenticity in Early Christian Literature* (Louisville, KY: Westminster/John Knox, 1993).

33. See PS77H1.1, also PS73H2.3 and PS77H2.5.

esies he criticized, Origen seems to have considered Marcionism as the greatest continuing threat. He does not seem to be aware of the teaching of his younger contemporary, Mani, who held views similar to those of Basilides, Valentinus, and Marcion and whose teaching would soon become an attractive alternative to the emerging orthodoxy that Origen identifies as the teaching of the Church. Eusebius, though, cites a passage in an otherwise lost homily of Origen on Psalm 82 that warns against the teaching of Elkesai, in whose sect Mani grew up.[34] Rejecting the marginalization of the Old Testament implied by all of these heretics, Origen insisted that lessons of its sacred history are as applicable to Christians in his or any time as they had been to the people of God in the past.[35]

Grammar

Origen initially takes the approach to the Psalms that is mentioned above as "grammar." Though its roots go back at least as far as Aristotle, this discipline, encompassing literary criticism, achieved full development in Hellenistic Alexandria.[36] The Homeric poems, central to Greek education, stimulated the development of grammar. The Greeks did not themselves know when the *Iliad* and the *Odyssey* were written, though it now seems most likely that they were composed and written down during the seventh century BC. Their language and content filtered down through oral tradition from the vanished Bronze Age Mycenaean Greek culture of the late second millennium BC. Though they are works of literary genius, the Homeric epics posed multiple problems. To begin with, there was no single agreed text. They were written in an artificial and archaic dia-

34. Eusebius, *Ecclesiastical History* 6.38.

35. See PS73H2.3, PS76H4.5, PS77H3.1–4, PS77H4.2, and PS77H6.3.

36. H.-I. Marrou, *A History of Education in Antiquity* (trans. George Lamb [Madison, WI: University of Wisconsin Press, 1982]), originally published in French in 1948, and Rudolf Pfeiffer, *A History of Classical Scholarship: From the Beginnings to the End of the Hellenistic Age* (Oxford: Oxford University Press, 1968) remain the best overall introductions to ancient grammar. On Origen's use of grammar, the indispensable work is Bernhard Neuschäfer, *Origenes als Philologe*, 2 vols. (Basel: Friedrich Reinhardt Verlag, 1987).

lect as distinct from classical Greek as Shakespeare's language is from ours. They also reflected a long-lost society with some beliefs that had come under attack as immoral, notably on the part of Plato. Grammar dealt with all of these problems. Its techniques have never been superseded. When Jews in Hellenistic Alexandria obtained education in Greek culture, they realized that the techniques of grammar, developed for dealing with Homer, could be used just as profitably in the study of the Hebrew Bible, which confronted them with similar issues.[37] Origen, who was himself trained as a teacher of grammar, *grammateus,* followed the example of Philo, whose works he valued, in using the techniques of grammar to interpret the Bible.

It should be borne in mind that the experience of reading in Origen's time was not what it is for us today. Texts had no distinction between capital and lower-case letters, no spaces between words, and minimal punctuation. This meant that reading itself required more skill and effort than it does for us. The books of the Bible had no chapter and verse numbers, although the Psalms were numbered and written in fixed lines like poetry. Books themselves were scarce and valuable because they could be reproduced only one-at-a-time. Even with skilled copyists, flawless reproduction was unlikely. As a result, the grammatical discipline of textual criticism (*diorthōtikon*), today a specialized academic field engaging relatively few scholars, was a normal procedure in Origen's time. In the course of the homilies we see Origen adjudicating between competing readings. In establishing the text of Scripture, Origen faced a challenge beyond what the Alexandrian grammarians faced with Homer: his text was a translation from Hebrew, a language he could scarcely read. The Church used the Septuagint, an ancient translation made by Alexandrian Jews and retained by Christians as they took on an identity distinct from Judaism. In the homilies on Psalm 36, in passages that Rufinus left out of his translation, Origen argues that the translators of the Septuagint found ordinary Greek usage inadequate to convey distinctions in the Hebrew.[38] In one

37. See Maren R. Niehoff, *Jewish Exegesis and Homeric Scholarship in Alexandria* (Cambridge: Cambridge University Press, 2011).
38. PS36H1.1 and PS36H4.1.

of these cases he states that the translators did their work as well as humanly possible, implying that a perfect translation would be impossible.[39]

Though it could not have been for lack of intelligence, Origen never mastered Hebrew.[40] Like most native English-speakers today, most native Greek-speakers in antiquity had little need to learn other languages; Origen, for all his motivation and intelligence, may not have known how to do it. As a result, he had to rely throughout his life on Jewish informants. It also led him to compose the *Hexapla,* an innovative and sophisticated research tool. The *Hexapla* ("sixfold") contained at least six columns that juxtaposed a word or phrase from the Hebrew text with its transliteration in Greek characters, with at least three Jewish translations made subsequently to the Septuagint in order to improve on it, and with the Septuagint text.[41] In Homily 1 on Psalm 77 Origen speaks of the comparison of these versions in order to correct the text as still ongoing.[42] In Homily 8 on Psalm 77 he seems to be doing that: a reading "in some reliable copies" of the Septuagint is to be preferred because it agrees with the other translations and the Hebrew.[43] When Origen finds an obscure word in Ps 75.15, he cites all the versions in the *Hexapla* in what seems to be an attempt to approximate the sense of the original Hebrew by extrapolation.[44] Ultimately, Origen thinks, a perfect translation is impossible because the Hebrew language is, uniquely, the language of converse with and about God.[45]

Once the text itself was corrected, grammar embraced interpretation (*exēgētikon*). This included the determination of the meaning of words (*glōssēmatikon*). In the homilies this process is complicated by the fact that the original words of the Psalms

39. PS36H1.1.

40. See Nicholas de Lange, *Origen and the Jews: Studies in Jewish-Christian Relations in Third-century Palestine* (Cambridge: Cambridge University Press, 1977), 22 and 58.

41. See Anthony Grafton and Megan Williams, *Christianity and the Transformation of the Book* (Cambridge, MA: Harvard University Press, 2006).

42. PS77H1.1.

43. PS77H8.9.

44. PS73H3.1. Something comparable occurs at PS77H9.6.

45. PS80H1.7.

were in Hebrew. Grammar also included historical investigation (*historikon*), the clarification of narrative background such as places, names, and times. A third subdiscipline of interpretation, *technikon*, included what we call grammar as well as the identification of literary devices such as metaphor or hyperbole. The fourth subdiscipline of grammar, judgment (*krisis*), dealt with how the text as a whole formed a coherent narrative or argument. In the course of the homilies we see Origen using all of these disciplines. Origen used all of these methods of interpretation to perform depth soundings of the biblical text; he found philosophical implications even in the use of a demonstrative.[46] Judgment could be exercised in the form of *problēmata kai luseis,* "problems and solutions." In that genre the interpreter discussed "problems" or "difficulties" (*aporiai*) one by one. Originally used for interpreting Homer, Philo used it for the Bible. A teacher might also employ "problems and solutions" as a pedagogical device, a practice Origen engaged in and ascribed to Jesus himself.[47]

A vital aspect of judgment is determining personae (*prosōpa,* singular *prosōpon*). In classical drama, actors wore masks depicting faces (*prosōpa*) of the characters they played. In drama, of course, each character speaks from a particular perspective that colors how we understand what is said. Ascribing the right words to the right character and showing how those words reveal that character's perspective is obviously necessary in drama. Grammarians adopted the term *prosōpon* to indicate the speaking voice in any written work. Identification of *prosōpa* is relevant to most of Greek literature. Plato's dialogues are entirely in direct discourse, and epic poetry and history employ it as well. In the works of Plato, admired as a prose stylist as well as a philosopher, the narrative voice recounting a dialogue is itself the *prosōpon* of a character with a particular perspective.

Identification of *prosōpa* is a concern in understanding the Psalms because, when they employ direct discourse, they rarely identify either the speaker or the person or persons being spoken to. This concern has New Testament roots, as Origen

46. See PS77H8.4.
47. PS77H1.6.

points out in PS15H1.2 below, where he appeals to the witness of all twelve apostles that Psalm 15 is spoken in the persona of Christ. If the Gospels are to be trusted, Jesus himself employed such interpretation at a crucial stage of his ministry, confounding the Pharisees by asking them to explain how Ps 110.1 (in the Hebrew numbering used in modern Bibles) could be spoken in the persona of David (Mt 22.43–44 and Lk 21.41–44). The identification of Christ as a *prosōpon* speaking in a Psalm could be used to gain insight into his character and purposes. Origen identifies the *prosōpon* speaking in the Psalms as that of Christ in the newly discovered homilies on Psalms 15 and 67. The conclusions he draws from that identification bear witness to the fruitfulness of this approach, pioneered by Marie-Josèphe Rondeau,[48] making clear how deeply Origen thought about the Incarnation.

Principles of Interpretation

Insofar as he employed the techniques of Hellenistic grammar, Origen's interpretation differs little from that of many biblical scholars today, who continue to employ them. The interpretation that arises from those techniques, on the other hand, may, initially at least, strike the modern reader as bizarre. James Kugel's *Traditions of the Bible*, even though it is focused principally on early Jewish biblical interpretation, helps us understand why, using techniques still employed by contemporary scholars, Origen reached startlingly different conclusions about the meaning and message of the Psalms. Kugel identifies four assumptions shared by early interpreters of the Bible: 1) that it is a fundamentally cryptic document, 2) that it is a book of instruction of continuing relevance to its readers, 3) that it is totally harmonious and says nothing without purpose, and 4) that it is divinely inspired.[49] We find all of these assumptions operative

---

48. See Marie-Josèphe Rondeau, *Les commentaires patristiques du psautier (IIIe–Ve siècles)*, 2 vols. (Rome: Pontificum Institutum Studiorum Orientalium, 1982 and 1985).

49. James L. Kugel, *Traditions of the Bible: A Guide to the Bible As It Was at the Start of the Common Era* (Cambridge, MA: Harvard University Press, 1998),

in Origen's work. In his case the third assumption is particularly important, since, for Origen, the purpose of any scriptural statement must be worthy of God, not only true and useful, but non-trivial.

All four of these assumptions are implicit or explicit in Origen's exposition of biblical hermeneutics, the fourth book of the pioneering treatise *Peri archōn* (sometimes referred to as *De principiis* or *On First Principles*), the first presentation of Christian theology as a coherent whole. Scripture is a living being in which the divine logos animates human language. Like human beings, it has three components: a body, that is, the human words (*lexeis*) with which it is composed, a soul, and a spirit. The soul and spirit of Scripture always instruct us, the soul giving us instruction about conduct, and the spirit giving advanced instruction in divine secrets (*mustēria*). Normally the body of Scripture, what the words say in ordinary speech, is helpful as well. At times, though, it says something patently false, as in Ps 36.25, "I have not seen a just person forsaken or his seed seeking bread";[50] or silly, as in Ps 73.14, "You have crushed the heads of the serpent. You have given him as food to the Ethiopians";[51] or shocking, as in, for example, telling God in Ps 77.65 that he is acting like a drunkard sleeping off a bender.[52] Such statements are "stumbling blocks," *skandala,* incongruities in the text that the interpreter must explain,[53] even if they have been deliberately incorporated into the biblical text by God to point the way to divine secrets. Even when the words of Scripture say something seemingly unobjectionable, such as, "Sing to God, play a stringed instrument to his name" (Ps 67.5), asking whether such a command is genuinely worthy of God leads to a deeper sense.[54] In these homilies Origen adds a new wrinkle to his interpretation: the body of Scripture can also hide divine secrets in plain sight.[55]

14–19. On early interpretation, see also Kugel, *The Bible As It Was* (Cambridge, MA: Harvard University Press, 1997), 1–49.

50. See PS36H4.3.

51. PS73H2.7.

52. PS77H9.2.

53. See PS67H2.5.

54. PS67H2.1–2.

55. See PS76.H3.2 and possibly PS80H1.7.

Like that of his Alexandrian predecessors, Philo and Clement, Origen's understanding of the Bible was shaped by philosophy, specifically the Platonism of his time.[56] Origen's younger contemporary Plotinus is usually credited with the fusion of Platonism with Aristotelianism and elements of Stoicism referred to as "Neoplatonism,"[57] which achieves classic expression in the *Enneads,* his collected philosophical treatises. Though Origen was a Christian and Plotinus was not, they shared a common philosophical teacher, Ammonius Saccas. Both Plotinus and Origen conceived of the universe as a *kosmos,* a coherent whole ordered by a divine Creator, as described in Plato's *Timaeus.* Philo, whose work Origen knew and admired,[58] had already found the *Timaeus* profoundly compatible with the Mosaic account in Genesis. Because it emanates from God conceived as Being, One, and Good, the cosmos reveals God. For Origen the cosmos embodies the Logos similarly to the way Scripture does and is as worthy as Scripture of close investigation.[59] Plotinus reproached so-called "Gnostics" who denied the goodness of the cosmos.[60] Origen objects to the same thing in the three figures whom he often names together in his works, including these homilies, as heretics: Basilides, Valentinus, and Marcion.[61]

56. On the use of philosophy by Origen and other early Christian authors, see George Karamanolis, *The Philosophy of Early Christianity* (London: Routledge, 2013). Origen cites Philo, though not by name, in PS75H.6.

57. In a series of books culminating in *Platonism and Naturalism: The Possibility of Philosophy* (Ithaca, NY: Cornell University Press, 2020), Lloyd P. Gerson argues forcefully that we should abandon the term "Neoplatonism," a modern term implying a substantial departure from Plato's thought, and return to the older term, "Platonism," for this school of thought. Excellent introductions to Plotinus are Pierre Hadot, *Plotinus and the Simplicity of Vision,* trans. Michael Chase (Chicago: University of Chicago Press, 1993), and Stephen R. L. Clark, *Plotinus: Myth, Metaphor and Philosophical Practice* (Chicago: University of Chicago Press, 2016). For his works, see Plotinus, *The Enneads,* ed. and trans. Lloyd P. Gerson et al. (Cambridge: Cambridge University Press, 2018).

58. See David T. Runia, *Philo in Early Christian Literature: A Survey* (Assen: Van Gorcum, 1993), 157–83.

59. See PS77H1.1 and PS80H2.1.

60. Plotinus, *Ennead* 2.9, which his editor, Porphyry, entitled "Against the Gnostics."

61. Marcion, in particular, got under Origen's skin. See PS36H3.11, PS73H2.3, PS77H1.1, and PS77H9.5.

Both Plotinus and Origen also conceived of human beings as composite. Our bodies belong to the realm of Becoming, the realm of space and time, as opposed to the divine realm of Being. On the other hand, both taught that our *logos* or reason, an attribute of our animating principle or *psuchē*, "soul," has a capacity for giving us access to the God or Being itself. Origen, in contrast to Plotinus, identified what activates that capacity for participation in God as a third component of the human composite, akin to God, the *pneuma* or "spirit." Origen shared with Plotinus the belief that God, identified as Being, is thus the beginning and the end; the realm of Becoming proceeds from the realm of Being, and its goal is the return to the realm of Being through purification.

This pattern of procession and return through purification accounts for Origen's distinctive and controversial theological speculations, enunciated in *Peri archōn*. The human soul, proceeding (or falling) from an original unity with God or Being, preexists its embodiment. Eventually all human beings will be saved; that is, they will return, purified of what caused them to fall, to unity with God. Origen considered these doctrines divine "secrets," *mustēria,* which we can only gradually comprehend as we experience a moral and intellectual transformation achieved through disciplined attention in thought and action. Although they are appropriately discussed only among Christians who have achieved a measure of moral and intellectual transformation,[62] Origen occasionally hints at these secrets. For example, Origen's discussion of an enigmatic statement, "My kidneys have disciplined me" (Ps 15.7b), hints at the preexistence of the soul of the incarnate Christ.[63] Similarly, Origen hints at universal salvation when he interprets "reject to an end" to mean that God's rejection is limited or when he proclaims that sinners have hope for deliverance in a future age.[64]

Origen, like Plotinus, followed Plato in characterizing this process as bringing our soul "into rhythm" with the logos[65] and

---

62. See especially PS76H4.5 and PS80H2.5.
63. PS15H2.5.
64. See especially PS73H1.2 and PS80H2.7.
65. See PS67H2.3.

as attaining "likeness to God."[66] In these homilies, however, as in the rest of his work, Origen differs from Plotinus and non-Christian Platonism in teaching that God's logos had, in fact, come down to be with us and assist us by becoming a human being, Jesus Christ. Though our return to God is always "up to us" (*eph' hēmin*), it is, Origen taught, impossible without such assistance.[67] To provide it, Christ, the divine logos, seeks us out, assuming the multitude of devices (*epinoiai*)[68] corresponding to biblical titles, like "shepherd"[69] and "bread of heaven,"[70] to meet each of us where we are and assist us. Christ is also the model whom we imitate in order to become like God ourselves.[71]

Origen's exploitation of the rich imagery of the Psalms goes well beyond the biblical titles of Christ. Christ not only identifies himself as the light of the world (Jn 8.12) but also tells his followers that they are the light of the world (Mt 5.14).[72] The cosmos itself is an expression of logos, so that natural phenomena like thunder,[73] clouds,[74] lightning,[75] rivers,[76] and springs[77] all have spiritual significance. Origen takes Paul's distinction between an outer and an inner human being (Rom 7.22, 2 Cor 4.16) to imply that the human body and each of its parts, the human life cycle, and every human activity have spiritual significance.[78] This applies especially to the activities that provide human sustenance, not only eating and drinking,[79] but horticulture as well.[80] Wrestling, which probably formed a part of Origen's education, is particularly significant.[81] One activity prom-

---

66. See PS77H8.9, echoing Plato, *Theaetetus* 176A, as well as Gn 1.26.
67. See, for example, PS15H1.4 and PS36H4.1.
68. See PS36H2.1.
69. See PS73H1.3, PS77H8.2–4, and PS77H9.6.
70. See PS77H2.5 and PS77H4.3.
71. See, for example, PS15H2.4 and PS67H1.7.
72. PS67H1.7, PS73H3.3, PS76H1.5, PS77H5.6, and PS81H.1.
73. PS76H4.3.
74. PS77H3.2.
75. PS76H4.4.
76. PS77H3.3 and PS77H7.2.
77. PS73H3.1.
78. See especially PS36H1.4 and PS36H4.3.
79. PS15H1.9, PS77H4.9–11, PS77H5.1–2, and PS80H1.8.
80. PS77H7.4–5.
81. PS36H4.2, PS77H4.4, and PS80H1.3.

inent in the Psalms is music. Commenting on the imagery of the Psalms, Origen likens the human body and its constituent parts to various musical instruments: a drum,[82] a trumpet,[83] or a harp.[84] The mirror image of this symbolism, which embraces aspects of the human relationship with the divine logos, is a symbolism of evil. Origen states that, just as the cosmos could not contain books describing all the deeds of Jesus (Jn 21.25), the same applies to the works of the devil.[85] Thus he discusses an antibridegroom,[86] a sun of injustice,[87] and an anti-panoply,[88] as well as making our body the temple of a false god.[89]

The accounts of sacred history in some of the Psalms on which Origen preached provided the occasion for him to show how a particular biblical story is also our story. All the events recounted in the history of the people of God in the past, including warfare,[90] exile,[91] and return,[92] occur to us now in a deeper, spiritual sense.[93] Sacred geography also, such as the distribution of land to the tribes, has spiritual significance.[94] The Holy Land,[95] and Jerusalem in particular,[96] are sacred because of the Temple,[97] where God is present. The destruction of the Temple confirms, as far as Origen is concerned, that the reality of the Temple was always spiritual. Drawing on the New Tes-

82. PS80H1.4.
83. PS80H1.5.
84. PS67H2.2–4 and PS80H1.4.
85. PS73H1.7.
86. PS67H2.7 (as opposed to Christ as bridegroom in such passages as Mk 2.7).
87. PS67H2.6 (as opposed to the "sun of justice" or "righteousness" of Mal 4.2).
88. PS36H2.8 (as opposed to the "panoply of God" in Eph 6.10).
89. PS80H2.3. See Jn 2.21 and 1 Cor 6.19.
90. PS77H8.9.
91. PS67H2.2.
92. Ibid.
93. See PS73H2.3, PS76H4.5, PS77H3.1–4, PS77H4.2, and PS77H6.3.
94. PS15H1.6 and PS73H2.7.
95. See PS15H1.6 and PS75H.1. On Origen's understanding of the Holy Land, see Robert L. Wilken, *The Land Called Holy: Palestine in Christian History and Thought* (New Haven, CT: Yale University Press, 1992), 65–81.
96. PS67H2.2, PS73H1.2, and PS75H.2.
97. PS77H8.2–4.

tament (1 Cor 6.19, Jn 2.21), Origen teaches that the human body, divinized, can be God's Temple.[98] Just as our body can be the Temple, it is also the Temple's predecessor, the tabernacle or tent (*skēnē*), the earthly tent of which Paul spoke (2 Cor 5.1) and where the divine logos "tented" (*eskēnizeto*) among us (Jn 1.14).[99] The saints, divinized, are tents of witness.[100] Perrone's notes show how this symbolism, which applies also to the Church as Christ's body, is a consistent theme through all of Origen's works, including one of his earliest, his *Commentary on Lamentations.*[101]

What We Learn from the Homilies

CMG 314 opens a window onto Origen's understanding of a book that occupied him throughout his life and also onto how the Psalms took their place at the heart of Christian worship and devotion. The Psalms, considered as a book of prophecy, are clearly central to Christian thought from the earliest time. The Gospels depict Jesus referring the Psalms to himself, and they play a key role in the Epistles as well. In this tradition, Origen interprets the Psalms as prophetic, applying them in these homilies to understand, among other things, the Incarnation of Christ and the necessity for maintaining the unity of the Church. Although there is ample evidence for the use of Psalms as a book of prophecy, there is almost no evidence from the first three centuries of Christianity about the use of the Psalms in worship and devotion.[102] The author of Eph 5.19 urges Christians to speak to one another "in psalms, hymns, and spiritual songs," and Tertullian (ca. 150–ca. 220) mentions

---

98. PS80H2.3.

99. PS15H2.8, PS77H4.10, and PS77H8.7. We find similar ideas in Clement of Alexandria, *Stromateis* 5.6.

100. PS81H.5.

101. For a translation of *Fragments on Lamentations*, see Joseph W. Trigg, *Origen* (London: Routledge, 1998), 73–85.

102. See Paul F. Bradshaw, *Reconstructing Early Christian Worship* (Collegeville, MN: Liturgical Press, 2009), 117–31, and Susan Gillingham, *Psalms Through the Centuries: Volume One* (Chichester: Blackwell, 2008), 24–42.

singing psalms in worship;[103] that is as specific as the evidence gets. It would be hazardous simply to assume, with such meager evidence, that using the Psalms in personal and communal devotion was so pervasive that no one else bothered to mention it.

It is significant, then, that Origen's homilies largely constitute instruction in how to pray with the Psalms. They become a map guiding the believer's spiritual life. Origen is particularly interested in those points where long, sustained effort brings mastery[104] or one breaks through to a new insight.[105] The Psalms remind believers not to be complacent but to remain alert[106] and open to correction.[107] They must guard against turning back when they are making progress,[108] confess their shortcomings,[109] correct their faults,[110] and seek God's favor by cultivating virtuous behavior.[111] They encourage believers that God invites them to call out when they are in distress[112] with complete freedom of speech.[113] They recommend gathering together with other believers to experience Christ fully as the power of God,[114] making themselves strong for spiritual combat by feeding on God's word,[115] and looking to God for victory.[116] In doing so they provide the words we can pray to draw God to us.[117]

The homilies themselves add to our documentation of early Christian worship. Origen clearly indicates that gathering together weekly was the accepted norm and that, as we might expect, many believers did not observe that norm. Origen stresses that this gathering is a vital activity by itself, fortifying the com-

103. Tertullian, *De anima* 9.
104. PS76H2.1.
105. PS36H4.1.
106. PS77H9.1–2.
107. PS77H9.4.
108. PS77H6.3.
109. PS75H.6.
110. PS36H4.2.
111. PS76H1.4.
112. PS80H1.8.
113. PS67H1.2.
114. PS76H2.7.
115. PS77H4.4.
116. PS15H2.6.
117. See PS67H2.4.

munity against its demonic enemies and providing a foretaste of eschatological unity.[118] As actual transcripts, the homilies greatly increase our documentation on early Christian preaching. They are also evidence that preaching was a vital part of worship. By gathering weekly, believers receive regular sustenance by feeding on the divine logos in the homily. The opening passages of two homilies give hints about the conduct of worship. Origen begins Homily 1 on Psalm 67 with a reference to a prayer by the bishop (*papa*) that, it would seem, implied that Origen would be an inspired preacher. In response Origen points out that this promise is yet to be fulfilled and compares it to what he refers to as the congregation's prayer "to dedicate" themselves in the Church. This implies that a congregational prayer of self-dedication was a normal part of worship. He also states that more than one Psalm had just been read and asks the congregation to join him in praying verses of one of them, Psalm 69, that God may assist and protect him as he undertakes to preach. This is an early example of the use of a Psalm for a congregational prayer. It is also evidence of a fairly long reading, longer than the preacher could be expected to expound.[119] The length of the reading is consistent with what we learn from another homily preserved in Greek, the Fifth Homily on Samuel, where Origen asks the bishop which of the four full pericopes that had just been read, constituting our 2 Sm 25–28, he should address.[120] The opening of Homily 1 on Psalm 76 provides another intriguing hint as to the actual conduct of worship. Origen indicates that it was expected that a bishop would compose his own eucharistic prayer, presumably a solemn prayer covering certain conventional topics delivered in his own voice. He speaks of a situation in which an experienced bishop would help out a new colleague by composing a prayer in the persona of the new bishop.[121]

The homilies contain little information about the conduct or theology of baptism and the Eucharist. Origen often employs water imagery without mentioning baptism. Washing is spiritual

---

118. Heb 10.25. See PS67H1.4, PS77H6.3, and PS77H8.2.
119. See PS67H1.1. On the Psalms as prayers, see PS77H4.10 and PS80H1.1.
120. *Hom. I Reg.* 5.1.
121. PS76H1.1.

cleansing.[122] Rivers and springs provide spiritual refreshment.[123] The danger posed by the sea, including the Red Sea, which God broke apart to deliver the Israelites, is the danger of being engulfed in the affairs of ordinary life.[124] The only explicit reference to baptism is, "You have been buried with Christ in baptism,"[125] an allusion to Rom 6.3–4. Origen nowhere refers to eating bread and drinking wine in the eucharist. Biblical imagery of eating bread and drinking wine consistently refer to the assimilation of the preached logos.[126]

CMG 314 also gives us new insights into Origen's life and thought. As discussed, the dating of these homilies is important for the chronology of Origen's life and work. Origen enlivens our picture of daily life in Caesarea and seems to indicate that the Romans had installed a stable on the Temple Mount in Jerusalem. We get new information about the celebration of the eucharist in Origen's time. We learn more about his struggle with what he considered heresies, particularly the teaching of Marcion. We learn how he valued the Hebrew language even as he differentiated Christian teaching from Judaism. We also find that he could speak knowledgeably about wine and about the theater.

The textual apparatus of the twenty-nine homilies supplied by Perrone and his collaborators quotes from multiple works by Origen on almost every page. These quotations, from works written throughout Origen's life, including some of his very first, demonstrate not only the genuineness of the homilies, but the coherence and consistency of Origen's work. They also deepen our understanding of his conceptualization of the human person, of Christ, and of the Church. They are particularly important for his understanding of divinization, including the divinization of the body, as the goal of Christian life. They give us new evidence for understanding better Origen's method of argumentation, his use of rhetoric, and his attitude to the scien-

122. PS67H1.2 and PS67H2.5.

123. PS77H3.1, PS77H6.3, PS77H7.2

124. PS73H2.5–6 and PS77H3.5.

125. PS67H1.6 and PS77H1.7.

126. See PS15H1.8, PS36H1.2 and 4, PS36H3.10, PS36H4.3 and 8, PS73H2.3, PS77H2.5 and 7, PS77H3.4, PS 77H5.1–2, PS81H.1, and, especially, the entirety of PS77H4.

tific investigation of the cosmos. Since the cosmos was created and is continually ordered and sustained by the divine logos, the investigation of the cosmos has comparable status to the investigation of the Bible, composed by the logos.[127]

The homilies also give us important new information about the composition, purpose, and use of his massive *Hexapla,* described above. This in turn helps us understand how Origen regarded the Septuagint. Some in the Greek-speaking Jewish community in Alexandria that created the Septuagint had put forward that it was, effectively, an inspired text on par with the original Hebrew. A Jew of the second century before Christ, the anonymous author of the *Letter to Aristeas* promoted the legend that the translators of the Septuagint were themselves miraculously inspired to produce a perfect translation, making it no longer necessary to read the Hebrew original. Philo, the first-century Jewish writer whom Origen respected (and cites in these homilies),[128] attests to a further elaboration of this legend.[129] Philo used the Septuagint exclusively and did not apparently have access to the Hebrew text.[130] The notion that the Septuagint had effectively superseded the original Hebrew has often been all too simply regarded as normative in the Christian community, including Origen, the one notable exception being Jerome's insistence on "Hebrew truth" dictating his use of the Hebrew for his Vulgate translation into Latin. Some Christians did adopt this position, notably Augustine, who objected to Jerome that he was misguided in seeking to replace the Old Latin translation of the Septuagint with a translation from Hebrew.[131]

---

127. See PS77H1.1. Origen was born at the close of an era when Greco-Roman science saw its most impressive achievements. See Daryn Lehoux, *What Did the Romans Know? An Inquiry into Science and Worldmaking* (Chicago: University of Chicago Press, 2012).

128. PS75H.6.

129. Naomi Seidman addresses the way in which the Septuagint comes to be understood as a replacement for the Hebrew text in *Faithful Renderings: Jewish-Christian Difference and the Politics of Translation* (Chicago: University of Chicago Press, 2006). She does not discuss Origen's perspective.

130. See Maren R. Niehoff, *Philo of Alexandria: An Intellectual Biography* (New Haven, CT: Yale University Press, 2018), 4.

131. See Augustine, *Letters* 28.2 and 71.4.

(Even so, by relying on etymologies from Hebrew, both Augustine and Philo tacitly acknowledged the continuing importance of the Hebrew text.)

It has always been difficult, though, to justify the sheer creativity, labor, and expense that Origen devoted to the *Hexapla* if it is assumed that he regarded the Hebrew text as definitively superseded. Until recently, the loss of the Greek text of most of Origen's work on the Old Testament made it difficult to draw firm conclusions. Origen's principal discussion of the Septuagint is in his correspondence with another Christian scholar, Julius Africanus. Africanus argued that the story of Susanna, contained in the Septuagint but not in the Hebrew, could not be an authentic part of the book of Daniel because it had to have been composed in Greek. Origen's response sought to vindicate the authenticity of the story. Before examining Africanus's arguments in detail, he stated a presumption that passages in the Septuagint but not in the Hebrew should not be set aside, because Divine Providence had so far supplied the Septuagint to Christian believers.[132] He then argued, in detail, that the evidence adduced by Africanus was not sufficient to overturn that presumption of authenticity. Though Origen did not claim that the Septuagint was itself an inspired translation, his defense of the story of Susanna shows that he held it in high regard and believed that Jews might have expurgated the original, inspired text. At the same time, scholars who closely examined Origen's works demonstrated that he preferred textual readings in the Hebrew and the other versions as superior to the Septuagint. Furthermore, they showed that he did not use the *Hexapla* to produce a corrected Septuagint text.[133] Such a use of the *Hexapla* might have been expected had Origen believed that the Septuagint began as a perfect, inspired translation.

The discovery of CMG 314 provides us with more data about how Origen regarded the Septuagint text. The homilies do not mention the *Hexapla* by name but show him making use of it

---

132. *Ep. Afr.* 8.

133. See Pierre Nautin, *Origène: Sa vie et son œuvre*, 344–50; Bernhard Neuschäfer, *Origenes als Philologe*, 1:86–103; and Marguerite Harl, *La langue de Japhet: Quinze études sur la Septante et le grec des Chrétiens* (Paris: Cerf, 1994), 253–75.

and discussing it as a life-long task. In them Origen treats his Septuagint text as a witness to an original (and no longer fully recoverable) Hebrew text older and more authentic than that used by his Jewish contemporaries. These homilies make it clear that, somewhat anticipating Jerome's concept of "Hebrew truth," Origen considered the Septuagint an excellent translation and a vital witness to the Hebrew original, but not an inspired text in its own right. No translation could, on principle, supersede the original Hebrew, because Hebrew is the language *par excellence* for discussing ultimate reality[134] and can only be translated into Greek insofar as humanly possible.[135]

Although the apparatus of Perrone's edition abundantly demonstrates that the homilies are consistent with the rest of Origen's work, we do see him continuing to integrate his thought. Close attention to what Origen considered the "body" of Scripture, the *lexis*, the "wording" in human language that constitutes the Bible, had always been a feature of Origen's thought. In keeping with the principles of interpretation that he had set forth in *Peri archōn*, the immediate sense conveyed by those words ordinarily has a useful message. What the *lexis* says must be interpreted to discover deeper, hidden meanings.[136] In the reference to the "sons of Ephraim" in Ps 77.9, Origen finds this message to be a specific prophecy addressing the Church of his own time. This leads him into a lengthy excursus in which he interprets Hos 6.11–7.16 as a detailed prophecy of his own struggle against heresies.[137] The homilies also suggest that the body of Scripture, its *lexis* or wording, can be highly instructive even when it does not serve as the basis of a higher interpretation. In the case of Ps 73.1, the wording itself of a prophecy can refer to two events at once, in this case the destruction of both the First and the Second Temples.[138] When he comes to "the voice of thunder in the wheel" (Ps 76.19), Origen argues that,

---

134. PS80H1.7.

135. PS36H1.1. See Joseph W. Trigg, "What can be Learned by Translating the Homilies?" in Robin Darling Young and Joseph W. Trigg, *Origen's Last Words*, forthcoming from The Catholic University of America Press.

136. As in the case of "sing to the Lord," PS67H2.2.

137. PS77H2.3–6.

138. PS73H1.1.

rather than rejecting the immediate sense of the wording, one can find in it a reference to the circular movement of the cosmos.[139] Similarly, the immediate sense of the words of Ps 76.17, "the waters saw you and were afraid," indicates that the components of the cosmos are animate, so that the Greeks were not entirely deluded in worshiping nymphs and river gods.[140]

Much as Origen finds intrinsic interest in the wording that composes the body of Scripture, so he finds intrinsic value in the human body. In his homily on Psalm 81 Origen states that it is no marvel that the human spirit can be divinized, since it is akin to God, but it is a marvel that the soul is divinized, since it can sin. Furthermore, he says, it is yet more marvelous that the body can be divinized.[141] He explains what such divinization of the body actually entails when he speaks of the body as an instrument on which we make music for God. Thus, for example, our hands are divinized, becoming God's hands, when we give to the poor, and our ears are divinized when we pay no attention to scandal.[142] In Homily 2 on Psalm 15 Origen identifies the Incarnation of the divine logos as the means by which human flesh comes into the actual presence of God.[143]

As well as giving us new insights into Origen's understanding of the divinization of the human body and the embodiment of the divine logos in Scripture and in the person of Jesus Christ, the homilies in CMG 314 give us insights into Origen's understanding of the Church. What interests him is not church order—who is in charge or who is in or out—but the Church as a gathering of the body of Christ on earth. In Homily 8 on Psalm 77, dealing with a portion of the Psalm that recounts the Exodus, Origen finds the formation of the Church in Ps 77.52: "He brought out his people like sheep; he led them as a flock in the desert." When they were in Egypt, the people were like sheep, scattered about, gathering mud in subjection to Pharaoh. When they were in captivity to Pharaoh, that is, Satan, the people

139. PS76H4.2.
140. PS76H3.2.
141. PS81H.1.
142. See PS67H2.4 and especially PS80H2.1.
143. PS15H2.8.

were isolated and entirely preoccupied with earthly things. When Moses, that is, Christ, has brought them out and has begun to lead them up toward the Promised Land, that is, the presence of God, they are no longer isolated but have become a flock. As a gathered flock, the people are safe from the adverse powers.[144] To stay safe, believers should heed Heb 10.25, "Do not neglect gathering, as is the custom of some." Elsewhere he states that, by the very act of gathering, believers become a new nation[145] and scatter the enemies of God.[146] By the same token, when believers divide, they make themselves vulnerable. Homily 7 on Psalm 77 deals in detail with the parallels between those who set up a separate Kingdom of Israel after the death of Solomon and the heresies of his own time. He makes the point that, even when schismatics have valid objections to the community's leadership, they tend to drift into heresy once the separation has occurred; those who begin by dividing the Church all too easily end by dividing God.[147]

Origen shows little interest in the Church as a structured institution, but regards it as a community of prayer and mutual support, where all see each other's needs as their own because they belong to Christ's one body.[148] In his death and interment, Jesus's bones were never scattered; but when believers fail to gather together, they fulfill the words spoken in Christ's persona, "all my bones are scattered" (Ps 21.15).[149] In four separate homilies Origen states that, because all believers constitute Christ's body, what we do or fail to do for any other believer, we do or fail to do to Christ. By this principle, set forth in Mt 25.31–46, whenever we commit any offense against another Christian believer, we do so against Christ.[150] The Church is one "place" where God dwells because we are all one in Christ.[151] Its gathering in uni-

---

144. PS77H8.2.

145. PS36H1.1.

146. PS67H1.4.

147. PS77H7.2.

148. The angels and the departed also belong to this community and assist us. See *Or.* 12. See also *Princ.* 2.1.2.

149. PS77H8.3.

150. PS15H1.3, PS36H3.12, PS 73H3.6, and PS81H.4.

151. PS67H2.8.

ty is a prefiguration of eschatological unity when God is all in all.[152] At the same time, this side of the final consummation, the Church is only "in part" the body of Christ,[153] participating in the same experience short of perfection in which "we know in part" and "we prophesy in part."[154] This sense that the Church does not experience and cannot expect perfection prior to the eschaton makes it easier for Origen to counsel unity in the face of deficient leadership. In this understanding of the Church he approaches Augustine's understanding of the Church as a *corpus permixtum.*

Another new insight we obtain from CMG 314 is relevant to the large portion of Origen's work—*Peri archōn,* his commentaries on Romans and the Song of Songs, and most of his surviving homilies—that survives only in Latin translations by Rufinus of Aquileia. Emanuela Prinzivalli's essay in GCSO13 and her appendix presenting the four homilies in CMG 314 that Rufinus translated in parallel columns with the newly discovered Greek text enable us to see how Rufinus's translation is a "work of cultural mediation."[155] Like Nicola Pace, who examined Rufinus's translation of those passages of *Peri archōn* that have survived in Greek, Prinzivalli shows that Rufinus genuinely sought to make Origen's work accessible.[156] In his effort to make Origen comprehensible and relevant to readers of a different language living in a different age, he freely adapts the text, sometimes seeking to clarify it with passages taken from other works of Origen, often at the expense of its intellectual subtlety.[157] He simplifies complex arguments and omits passages where Origen dealt with the difficulty of translating Hebrew into Greek. He also modifies passages that might seem doctrinally suspicious. As Prinzivalli puts it, one misses in Rufinus's translation what she calls his *tono zetetico,* the tentative, inquisitive tone in which *tacha,* "perhaps,"

---

152. PS67H1.6. See also *Princ.* 2.1.2.

153. PS15H1.6 and PS67H1.6.

154. See PS67H1.6, PS67H2.3, and PS77H4.9.

155. "Opera di mediazione culturale," GCSO13, 38.

156. See Nicola Pace, *Ricerche sulla traduzione di Rufino del "De principiis" di Origene* (Florence: La Nuova Italia Editrice, 1990).

157. GCSO13, 38.

has a vital function.[158] We now can better evaluate how far we can rely on Rufinus's work.

This Translation

Origen, trained in grammar and in philosophy, treated the biblical authors as if they used language as precisely and subtly as did Plato. Evidently this was the standard that Origen set for himself as well, as his precise wording consistently rewards close attention. In this translation I have tried, where at all feasible, to reproduce his precise use of language. I have resisted the temptation to simplify Origen's long and involved syntax, because I have found that doing so inevitably simplifies his thought. Whenever at all possible, I have used one English word consistently to translate one Greek word. Translations of biblical passages and of works cited in the notes follow the same principles. I have sought to translate biblical passages in a way that reflects Origen's reading of them, as in the case of *ek merous,* "in part," mentioned above, where Origen understood the phrase to mean the same thing in 1 Cor 12.27 as it means thirteen verses later in 1 Cor 13.9, "For we know in part and we prophesy in part." I have kept awkward wording of the Psalms in the Septuagint that was, for Origen, an indication of their cryptic character.

I have struggled to use upper and lower case letters, a distinction that did not exist in Ancient Greek. Origen understood there to be a dynamic continuity between God and creation in a way that was not problematic in the third century but became very much so later. As a result, it is often impossible to tell whether words like "god," "son," and "spirit" have a divine (upper case) or human (lower case) application or both. I do not want my translation to give the false impression that Origen intended either one or the other. I have left one word untranslated as well as in lower case: *logos,* plural *logoi.* "Logos" can mean any number of things, including "speech," "argument," and "reason." The best translation might be "rational discourse."

---

158. GCSO13, 40. In Origen's writing, any sentence containing *tacha* is guaranteed to be interesting.

Origen does not use it to refer to a single "word" as a unit of discourse. Sometimes distinguishing the divine "Logos" (upper case) from other uses of "logos" (lower case) could be appropriate, but there are other occasions where Origen employs what Rowan Williams has called "a characteristic and significant ambiguity" where "logos" can refer "either to Origen's own rational spirit or the divine Logos."[159] Logos, "reason," is shared by all *logikoi,* "rational beings," making them potentially akin to God. When Origen speaks, he anticipates that his own logos, that is, the homily that he is giving, will mediate, in part, the divine logos. By the same token, it can be impossible to determine whether Origen is using "logos" to refer to a biblical passage or to the divine logos addressing us in that passage. Distinguishing between upper case and lower case forces a distinction Origen himself intended not to make.

One reason for using one English word for one Greek word is that Origen's categories of thought do not necessarily conform to ours. As discussed above, in *Peri archōn* Origen sets forth his position that the Bible is the embodiment of the divine logos and may be interpreted at the levels of body, soul, and spirit. Origen ordinarily uses two Greek words, *lexis* and *rhēton,* often in conjunction with the preposition *kata,* "according to," to refer to the body of Scripture. In the homilies Origen consistently distinguishes these words, which he uses in preference to the biblical word *gramma,* "letter." Most translators, starting with Rufinus, have rendered these as "letter" or, when used with the preposition, "literal." The word "literal" is notoriously ambiguous, usually referring to what contemporary biblical scholars consider to be the original meaning or intention of a passage. Origen's usage is more precise and consistent. He uses the grammatical term *lexis* to refer to the actual words of Scripture and *rhēton* to refer to the immediate, intuitive sense of those words. The first two columns in the *Hexapla* are the *lexis* in Hebrew letters and transliterated in Greek characters. The remaining columns translate the *rhēton* of that *lexis.* The *rhēton* is simply what

159. Rowan D. Williams, "Origen: Between Orthodoxy and Heresy," in Wolfgang A. Bienert and Uwe Kühneweg, eds., *Origeniana Septima: Origenes in den Auseinandersetzungen des 4. Jahrhunderts* (Louvain: Peeters, 1999), 8.

the words say, even if it ascribes a "hand" to God or "doors" to heaven. I translate *lexis* as "wording" and *rhēton* as "statement." Understanding the "hand" figuratively as God's power or the "doors" as the virtues belongs to a higher level of interpretation.[160] I translate *epistolē* consistently as "epistle." This is to avoid confusion with the plural form, *grammata,* a term Origen occasionally uses to refer to Scripture as a whole, not just the epistles in the New Testament, as "letters."

I have also maintained the distinction between *penēs,* "poor," that is, "not rich" or "doing manual labor for a living," and *ptōchos,* "destitute." I have consistently translated *zēteō,* the word Plato uses in the sense of "investigate," as "seek," in order to maintain its resonance with Mt 7.7, "Seek and you will find." In Origen, philosophical investigation is the "seeking" that Jesus commended in the Sermon on the Mount. While I maintain the use of male generic pronouns, since they are a feature of Origen's Greek, I translate *anthrōpos* as "human being," since that is the technical term for a composite rational being. Another technical term, *pathos,* I translate as "mental disturbance" rather than "emotion." I translate *mustērion* as "secret" because it is not until the following century that it took on, for Christians, the classical Greek sense of "mystery," an esoteric ritual.[161] "Perhaps" always translates the word that Emanuela Prinzivalli considered[162] characteristic of Origen, *tacha.* "Perhaps" signals the conclusion reached by a philosophical investigation—the "find" in "seek and you will find"—while indicating that all such conclusions must be provisional. I have not been able to find a single word that is adequate to the verb *noeō* and to *nous,* the noun that corresponds to it. "Mind" almost works for both, but I use "understand" or "perceive" and their noun equivalents depending on context. Origen's vivid use of biblical symbolism makes the more concrete, so to speak, "road" preferable to "way" as the normal translation of *hodos.*

160. PS73H2.4 and PS77H4.8. For a fuller discussion, see Joseph W. Trigg, "What can be Learned by Translating the Homilies?" in *Origen's Last Words.*

161. See Guy G. Stroumsa, *Hidden Wisdom: Esoteric Traditions and the Roots of Christian Mysticism* (Leiden: Brill, 1996), 27–45.

162. See GCSO13, 40.

This translation is based on the text of CMG 314, edited by Lorenzo Perrone and his colleagues in GCSO13; occasionally I have consulted Pradel's excellent digital version of the manuscript on the Bayerische Staatsbibliothek website. Notes called for in a translation differ from those appropriate to a scholarly edition and are my own. I have gratefully used many of their citations to other works by Origen. As is appropriate in a scholarly edition, these comprehensively demonstrate the consistency of the newly discovered homilies with the rest of Origen's œuvre, but many of them contribute little to understanding the homilies themselves. I have just as gratefully used over a thousand of the editors' biblical references. I have not repeated citations of the same verse when they are close to each other and have simplified citations to individual segments of the same verse. I have also included additional references of my own in an effort to use the notes to call attention to Origen's methods; to clarify obscurities; to show Origen's intellectual context, particularly in the Platonic tradition; and, occasionally, to draw attention to his legacy. The notes incorporate little of that portion of the editors' apparatus that explains their textual decisions, which I follow unless otherwise indicated.

I have used italics for my translation of the Psalm texts that Origen preached on in order to make it easier to maintain the thread of his homilies. Like the editors of the GCS volume, I have retained the numeration of the Psalms in the Septuagint. These are the numbers that Origen himself knew and used to refer to the Psalms (usually one number lower than the more familiar numeration in the Hebrew Bible). The verse numbers provided in the footnotes when Psalms are cited are also those from contemporary editions of the Septuagint. If these are not the same as those in other editions, they are usually only one number off.

HOMILIES ON THE PSALMS: CODEX MONACENSIS GRAECUS 314

HOMILY 1 ON PSALM 15

OME LETTERS are written on animate monuments, not with ink, but with the spirit of the living God, monuments written not on flat, stone slabs, nor on stone hearts, unyielding to the God's logoi and hard,[1] as the heart of Pharaoh was when it was hardened.[2] But these are written on a heart tender and compliant to the writer and, on this account, a heart of flesh. These letters written on a monument of flesh, when they are holy, cause what is written to have the heading, "monument-inscription." Thus the Psalm that has been read is entitled: "*A monument-inscription to David.*"[3]

If you want to know which Psalms have the title "monument-inscription,"[4] with other accompanying words, learn that they are the 55th, the 56th, the 57th, and after this the 58th and the 59th. This one says "*monument-inscription to David,*" but each of the others has additional words. For example, in the 55th, "To the end, on account of the people put at a distance from the holy ones, to David in a monument-inscription, when the aliens prevailed over him in Gath"; and the 56th, "To the end, so that you may not perish, to David in a monument-inscription on his escape from the face of Saul into the cave." But rather than speaking about things that you can find for yourselves by

1. See 2 Cor 3.3. For "logos" and "logoi," see introduction, pp. 30–31.

2. See Ex 7.3 and 11.9 and Rom 9.17–18. Origen alludes to passages that, taken on their face and as interpreted by Valentinians and Marcionites, seemed to contradict two of his core beliefs: human freedom of choice and the goodness of God. See *Princ.* 3.1.8–14, and Lorenzo Perrone, ed., *Il cuore indurito del Faraone: Origene e il problema del libero arbitrio* (Bologna: Marietti, 1992).

3. Ps 15.1a.

4. The Septuagint translates as *stēlographia,* "monument-writing," the Hebrew *mikhtam,* a word of unknown meaning used only in the Psalm titles Origen enumerates.

reading,[5] we say that the rest have other accompanying indications, besides "*monument-inscription*" in their titles, but only this Psalm has "*monument-inscription*" by itself in the title.

"Do not make for yourselves a monument, which things the Lord hated";[6] but when you understand what this means, you will see that the person entitling Psalms "*monument-inscription*" did not violate the law. Pay attention to the meaning of the law that says, "Do not make for yourselves a monument, which things the Lord hated." If what is written were to be understood simply, it would have said, "You shall not make for yourselves a monument, for the Lord hated monuments," or, "Do not make for yourselves a monument, which the Lord hated." But in this case, after initially referring to "monument" in the singular, he adds a plural, saying, "Do not make for yourselves a monument, which things the Lord hated."

I consider that what is legislated amounts to this: each person who accomplishes anything at all makes for himself a monument. If he should lead a bad life, he makes out for himself a "monument, which things the Lord hated," since, in fact, there is sin on the monument and "the works of the flesh[7] are sexual immorality, uncleanness, licentiousness, idolatry,"[8] and so on. On the other hand, if someone leads a good life, he does not violate the law by making a monument, for he makes a monument, which things the Lord loved. And the epistles[9] of his own monument are a part on which are written things the Lord loved, and his life is a part of a monument, which the Lord loved. Therefore it is not simply that one must not make a monument for himself—otherwise David would be violating the law by writing a monument-inscription—but one must not make "a monument, which things the Lord hated."[10]

---

5. Origen indicates that people to whom he is speaking have their own copies of the Psalms and can read them. See William V. Harris, *Ancient Literacy* (Cambridge, MA: Harvard University Press, 1989), esp. 175–284.

6. Dt 16.22.

7. Since this is a monument in flesh.

8. Gal 5.19–20.

9. See 2 Cor 3.2.

10. Origen argues that the clause "which things the Lord hated" is, in terms of grammar, restrictive rather than descriptive. On the idea of making a monument, compare sculpting one's own statue in Plotinus, *Enn.* 1.6.9 and 1.6.5.

And Jacob honored Rachel, when she departed life, with a monument: "This is a monument for remembrance of Rachel until today."[11] And he was not in any way violating God's law, with which Abraham, Isaac, and Jacob were then living, having, as the Apostle said, been taught it by nature: "Whenever the nations who do not have the law do the law by nature."[12] Abraham thus had done the law by nature, so that before the law had been written in ink, the law of God had been written on his heart. For he was justified by doing all God's enactments, judgments, and commandments as it has been written in Genesis.[13] Jacob, then, also did not violate the law by making a monument as a memorial to Rachel, so that the good deeds of Rachel might be evident to anyone who could look at it. For the present occasion, this is enough to say about the title.

2. Let us see the Psalm itself. The first thing to be said is that the persona[14] in the Psalm is that of our Lord Jesus Christ. In introducing some Psalms, we may or may not speak soundly, identifying the persona of the Psalm as Christ Jesus, depending on whether we find it or we apply it, whether we are enlightened or we guess.[15] In the case of some Psalms, though, including this one, we learn the persona from Scripture. It has been written in the Acts of the Apostles that a passage of this Psalm, "*You will not abandon my soul in Hades, nor will you allow your devout one to see corruption,*"[16] is spoken in the persona of the Savior. Peter, interpreting it together with the other eleven apostles, said: "David said to him, *I have foreseen the Lord face to face through everything; for he is on my right hand, so that I should not be moved. Therefore my heart rejoiced and my tongue exulted. Moreover, my flesh also shall set up*

---

11. Gn 35.20.

12. Rom 2.14. Even if, before Moses, there was no written law, the precedent Jacob set for the acceptability of a monument is still valid.

13. See Gn 26.5.

14. Greek, *prosōpon,* the identity of the voice speaking. See introduction, pp. 13–14.

15. We identify the persona speaking the Psalm, or a portion of a Psalm, when we "find" it after "seeking" through prayerful scriptural analysis ultimately enlightened by God. We misidentify the persona when we apply the identification arbitrarily based on nothing better than a guess. Here, however, Scripture explicitly identifies the persona.

16. Ps 15.10.

a tent in hope, because you will not abandon my soul in Hades, nor will you allow your devout one to see corruption. You have made known to me the roads of life; you will fill me with joy with your persona.'[17] Brothers, I can say to you with confidence concerning the patriarch David that he died and was buried and his tomb is among us to this day. Being a prophet, then, and knowing that God had sworn an oath to him that from the fruit of his loins he would set someone on his throne, he spoke looking ahead to the Christ's arising, that he would not be abandoned in Hades, nor would his flesh see corruption."[18] Explicitly, then, he says in this passage that Jesus would not see corruption and that his soul would not be abandoned in Hades, since he had descended in accord with the plan of salvation; because every region needed the visitation of Christ Jesus, including the place beneath the earth, he descended to Hades.[19] For the one who ascended and the one who descended are the same, so that he might fill all things.[20] But the utterances cited by Peter from the Acts of the Apostles will prove that the Psalm was spoken in the persona of our Lord Jesus Christ.[21]

3. "*'Protect me, Lord, because I have hoped in you,' I have said to the Lord.*"[22] The Savior tells us his own prayer so that, by telling it, he may teach us to pray.[23] For he prayed to the Father, saying, "*Protect me, Lord,*" because the Savior is in want of the Father and because only the God of the Universe wants not and needs no one else. But the Savior, even if he is in want, has a special property: he is in want only of the God of the Universe. But Moses, insofar as he is in want, is in want of God, of Christ, of the Holy Spirit and of the angels assisting and attending him.[24] And to the extent that we are inferior, we are in want even more, no one having the capacity to be aided by God alone. Therefore, if I say that the Christ, the Savior and Wisdom, is in want, do not

---

17. Ps 15.8–11.

18. Acts 2.25–31.

19. See also *Hom. 1 Reg.* 5, one of the few other homilies to survive in Greek, for a fuller treatment of this issue.

20. See Eph 4.10.

21. For a similar issue, see PS77H1.2 below.

22. Ps 15.1b–2a.

23. See Lk 11.1.

24. See Jude 9, Heb 2.2, Acts 7.53, Gal 3.19.

look askance at what I say.[25] I do not say that he is in want in the same way as you are or as anyone is who requires assistance from those beneath God. But I say that he is in want of one, his God and Father, to whom he prayed as he does even now through prophets,[26] and also in the Gospels when he withdrew into deserted places addressing God in prayer as one in want of him.[27]

But if I were ever to wish to pray to God, as if I were in want of God alone, in a similar manner to the Savior, and to address my prayer to God apart from the Savior, I would offer an incomplete prayer. My prayer, if it is to be sent up to God, must be sent up through Jesus Christ, the high priest and guardian of our souls.[28] The Father will not receive the prayer if I address him without employing the high priest, since it cannot reach him unless Jesus Christ offers it. Our Lord, to whom God said with an oath: "You are a priest forever according to the order of Melchizedek,"[29] is saying, "*Protect me, Lord, for I have hoped in you,*"[30] as if he needs the Father's protection, and telling us this prayer and saying what had been said by him to the Lord. He, then, also needs protection; without the fatherly protection I do not know what he would have experienced.[31]

But I can give a different account, more estimable and pleasant to many, of how the Savior says, "*Protect me, Lord, for I have hoped in you.*"[32] For I say that he said this to his Lord and Father

25. Origen is aware that some may take offense at the notion that Christ, being God, is "dependent," *endeēs*. He addresses the same point when commenting on Jn 4.32 in *Comm. Jo.* 13.34.219.

26. When we pray now, making use of the Psalms, Christ is praying "through prophets," i.e., the composers of Psalms. See PS76H1.1 below. In *Or.* 22 Origen states that we can address God as Father in the Lord's Prayer only through our status as sons of God by adoption in Christ. See also the discussion of having faith "in" God in PS77H3.5 below.

27. See Mk 1.35, Lk 5.16, 6.12, 9.18, 11.1.

28. See also *Or.* 15.2, where Origen cites Jn 16.23–24. "Through the high priest and guardian of our souls, Jesus Christ" occurs in Clement of Rome. See *1 Clement* 61.3. See also *1 Clement* 36.1 and 64. Origen often makes this explicit in his own prayers, as in *Comm. Jo.* 1.15.89, where he prays "to God, through Christ in the Holy Spirit" for assistance in interpreting the Gospel.

29. Ps 109.4, Heb 5.6.

30. Ps 15.1b.

31. Or "what he would have relied on."

32. Ps 15.1b.

about those who are his constituent parts. I also say that, just as someone praying about his own body does not pray about someone else, but about himself—for example, if I pray about my head, I pray about myself; if I pray about the constituent parts of my body, I pray about myself—thus, understand with me, the Savior does so as well. Since you are the constituent parts of Christ and, in part, constituent parts, and you are the body of Christ,[33] when he prays and says, "*Protect me, Lord,*" he is speaking about himself as he prays on your behalf. For you are his body, you are a constituent part of him, if you do not wish to be separated from him. The Savior is composite for your sake. You are composite, having a body inferior to the being of your soul and to the nature of your spirit. But my Savior is composite through the Church, insofar as it is his body,[34] about which, when he prays, as for one needing protection, he says: "Protect me, Lord." And therefore, referring to everyone as his body, he says, "When I was hungry, you gave me food; when I was thirsty, you gave me drink,"[35] as if I too were to say, "If you give my body food, you have given it to me; if you give my body drink, you have quenched my thirst."

Thus if we do anything to the body of Christ, the Church, and to the constituent parts of Christ, our brothers, we do them to Christ. In fact, we either behave badly to a believer in Christ—we violate Christ, we insult Christ, we disdain Christ—or we act well, we treat Christ well: we feed the hungry, we give drink to the thirsty. Therefore, do not think that you are liable only to a

33. See 1 Cor 12.27. Origen understands the Pauline phrase *ek merous* to have the same meaning here as it does thirteen verses later in 13.9. We are members, that is, constituent body parts, of Christ "in part." Origen explains in *Hom. Lev.* 7.2: "Let us then see what 'in part' said. I now, for example, am subordinate to God according to the spirit, that is by intention and choice, but as long as 'the flesh has desires against the spirit and the spirit against the flesh' [Gal 5.7] and I have not yet been able to subordinate the flesh to the spirit, I am somewhat subordinate to God, but, in fact, not entirely, but I am subordinate 'in part.' If, then, I could drag my flesh as well and all my constituent body parts into concord with the spirit, then I would be seen to be completely subordinate."

34. See *Cels.* 6.48: "The holy logoi say that the whole Church of God is the body of Christ animated by the Son of God, but believers, whoever they may be, are constituent parts of this body as a whole."

35. See Mt 25.35.

human being for what you do when you treat your neighbor well or poorly; you are actually liable to Christ himself.[36] "If when he sins, a man sins against a man"—says Eli in the first book of Kingdoms—"they may also address a prayer for him, but if he sins against the Lord, who will address a prayer for him?"[37] Do not think that you sin against a human being when you sin against a Christian; when you sin against a Christian, you sin against Christ; when you sin against a gentile, you sin against a human being.

But do not presume that you can sin even against a gentile. Should you sin against a gentile, look at his beginning, how it consists of, "Let us make the human being in our image and likeness."[38] And if you avoid sinning against a Christian and sinning against a human being (by which is understood sinning against all "in the image of the Creator,"[39] including also the angels, thrones, and lordships), what you do no longer constitutes a sin. As long as you avoid sinning against a human being, against a brother, or against one who is in the image of the Creator, you may do what you want to an irrational animal. Slaughter it, sacrifice it, you will not be sinning against an irrational animal. For the nature of sin does not extend to an irrational animal, so that one might say, "I have acted unjustly to an irrational animal, I have defrauded an irrational animal, or I have done something of that kind." "For I shall even demand an account of the blood of your souls from every brother and from every beast."[40] Thus you, a human being, can suffer injustice, but, by nature, an irrational animal cannot suffer injustice.

"*Protect me, Lord*" requires this brief digression.

36. See PS36H3.12, PS73H3.6, and PS81H.4 below.

37. 1 Sm 2.25. On the eight other occasions in his extant writings where Origen refers to this verse, in which the priest Eli laments the sins of his two sons, his emphasis is on the sinner or the act of forgiveness. Here it is on the one sinned against.

38. Gn 1.26. See also Gn 9.6. Origen elaborates them in PS77H8.9 below.

39. Col 3.10.

40. Gn 9.5. The relevance of this passage from God's commands to Noah's sons would be clearer had Origen continued with the next clause, "the one who sheds the blood of a human being, in exchange for his blood shall it be shed, for I made the human being in the image of God." In Second Temple Judaism this prohibition of murder constituted a covenant with Noah, giving divine sanction to natural law. See James L. Kugel, *Traditions of the Bible*, 224–26.

4. But what must be the cause for me to be protected by the Lord? "Because," it says, "*I have hoped in you.*" I am bold to say to the Lord, "*Protect me, Lord,*" because "I have hoped in him."[41] I am bold to say that I must be one concerning whom he says, "*Protect me,*" and that through him I, also a constituent part of him, have hope in God. And we actually do need great protection from the Lord and need it on every occasion. When we are not protected, but are abandoned even briefly, we fall immediately into temptations. Abandoned, we feel, as we have recounted earlier,[42] that the Lord has somehow forgotten us. But one who is tempted will not be forgotten in the end,[43] for: "persecuted, but not utterly abandoned."[44] We require so much protection that he has even commanded his angels concerning him, so that our foot should never stumble over a stone.[45]

We require protection as we walk; for "the Lord's angel camps around those who fear him and delivers them."[46] We require angelic assistance, so we say, "the angel who delivers me from all evils."[47] Why am I speaking about angelic assistance in this passage? Let us look at the whole statement: "The God who nourished me from my youth, the angel who delivered me from all evils, bless these children."[48] What angel delivers from all evils? I, for one, do not believe that Michael or Gabriel or any of the holy angels can "deliver from all evils"; one can scarcely be delivered from one evil, much less from two. Whom, then, am I to seek, who delivers from all evils, but the one who also has au-

41. Ps 15.1b. Since the Savior is the "I" in "I have hoped in him," our promise of protection is grounded in the Savior's hope.

42. Origen conceivably refers to a now-lost homily on Ps 12, which contains the words, "Will you forget me, Lord?" (12.2).

43. See Ps 9.19a.

44. 2 Cor 4.9.

45. See Ps 90.11–12. Note the abrupt shift in pronouns from their second-person original: "concerning *him,* that *our* foot never stumble." The promise made to Christ in his humanity transfers automatically to us insofar as we are constituent parts of his body. Origen makes the same point in CMS 102; it is we who are in danger of stumbling, not Christ. "Stumbling" is a danger in biblical interpretation. See *Princ.* 4.2 and PS67H2.5 below.

46. Ps 33.8.

47. Gn 48.16.

48. Gn 48.15–16.

thority to bless Ephraim and Manasseh? Who is this angel who delivers from all evils? Jesus Christ, who is called by the name "angel of great counsel."[49]

And do not suppose that I degrade Christ by calling him an angel, just as I do not degrade him by calling him a human being, less than the angels.[50] For out of his love of humanity he did not consider being equal to God a thing to be grasped, but to become a human being in his appearance and to humble himself and to become subject even to death, death on a cross,[51] just as it was also a work of his love of humanity toward the angels, that he became an angel. And just as he adorned[52] the race of human beings by becoming a human being, for it would not have been adorned or completed if Christ had not become a human being, in the same way what was lacking in the race of angels the Christ of God adorned by becoming an angel and supplying, by himself, what was lacking in that race. So also the Christ of God adorned all things by becoming an angel, and he adorned all things solely by being a god, since he had been adorned, having been begotten as a god by the paternal Godhead.

5. *"You are my Lord, because you do not have a need for my good things."*[53] There are many gods, as the Apostle says, and many lords,[54] but even though there are many gods, there is for us one God the Father from whom are all things, and we into him, and even though there are many lords, there is, nonetheless, for us one Lord Jesus Christ, through whom are all things, and we through him.[55] And among the many gods, there are also those

49. In the LXX, Is 9.6 reads "angel of great counsel" where the Hebrew has words often translated "wonderful counselor." See Joseph W. Trigg, "The Angel of Great Counsel: Christ and the Angelic Hierarchy in Origen's Theology," *JTS* n.s. 42 (1991): 33–51.

50. See Ps 8.6 and Heb 2.7.

51. See Phil 2.6–8.

52. Greek, *ekosmēsen.* Like the related noun, *kosmos,* the verb suggests both order and beauty. This is how *kosmos* gives us "cosmetic." The cosmos is adorned because it shares in the order and beauty of God.

53. Ps 15.2b–c.

54. 1 Cor 8.5.

55. 1 Cor 8.6.

to whom the logos says: "I have said: 'You are gods.'"[56] But given that there are many lords, this one Lord, whom the Savior also, addressing the Father, named "Lord," has an exceptional property in contrast to the many lords; for the other lords have a need for good things, which their subordinates furnish them, but this Lord alone has no need for the good things of any of those whose lord he is. Therefore, the Savior says, in such a way as to attribute an exceptional property to the Lord, his Father: "*I have said to my Lord, 'You are my Lord, because you do not have a need for my good things.*"[57] Therefore, "*You are my Lord, because you do not have a need for my good things;* by no chance are you in want of them."[58]

I shall start from the way things are here below, so that you may observe what this passage says. The master has a need for a servant's goodness. He needs him to do his job competently. He has a need for his service, since he cannot subsist in human terms without the services he needs, such as farming by a servant, oversight of his household by a servant, or the preparation of nourishing dishes that come through a servant's efforts. The human being who is lord cannot say to the servant, "*I do not have a need for your good things,*" nor can the servant say to the lord (when he is not naming God as Lord), "You do not have a need for my good things," for a human being does need them. Therefore, just as you have understood, in the case of a human being, how the lord has a need for good things of the servant, ascend[59] in logos and you will see that the other lords, about whom the Apostle speaks, have a need for good things. That is what underlies, "The servants of lords go with their own lords."[60]

I say that, unless I am such as to be under the Savior as Lord

---

56. Ps 81.6.

57. Ps 15.2.

58. The "I" in this Psalm is Christ, so the Psalm provides information about the relationship of Christ to the Father.

59. *Anaba,* "ascend" or "step up," is one of the words Origen uses to indicate moving to a "higher," more spiritual, level of interpretation.

60. Servants accompany their masters because the masters may need their assistance. Origen cites this otherwise unknown saying as if it were familiar to his hearers.

or under God as Lord, any other lord of mine does have a need for my good things. The God of the Universe is the only Lord, who hears from the Savior, "'*You are my Lord, because you do not have a need for my good things*'; this is why you are my Lord, because you do not have a need for my good things."

6. So, assuming that you had my need for good things, look at what follows: "*He has made wonders for the holy ones who are in his land.*"[61] The Father does not show wonders to all, but only to the holy ones, and to them not when they are outside of his land, but when they happen to be in his land. If you can ascend onto the genuine land, which God promised, the token of which was this earthly Judea, go ahead and step up onto that one, and you will see to what extent you have not at all reached the land that is truly[62] land, the land that is truly great, the land that is truly flowing with milk and honey; you have not at all come to the inheritance of the gentle that the Savior referred to, saying, "Blessed are the gentle, because they shall inherit the land";[63] you do not at all see the wondrous things of God.[64] Even if you seem to see wonderful things, as did those who saw them on Moses,[65] and as Moses himself saw,[66] you see wonderful things outside of God's land, through a mirror and in a riddle, not the wonderful things person to person.[67]

But seek to see God's good things! Who else arrives in God's land but someone who has come out of the land of Egypt, someone who has become fit, so that his limbs do not fall in the wilderness, someone who is not committing the sins that those who came out of Egypt committed, before they could reach the holy land? If you want to go to the holy land and see God's wonders, become Caleb the son of Jephunneh. Become Joshua the son of

61. Ps 15.3a.

62. In Origen's Platonic outlook, spiritual reality is more "true" than sensible reality.

63. Mt 5.5.

64. Compare this invitation to Augustine, *Confessions* 9.10.24, in which Augustine and his mother ascend inwardly to the "land of unfailing fruitfulness, where you feed Israel forever with the food of truth."

65. See Ex 34.35 and 2 Cor 3.13.

66. See, for example, Exodus chapters 3, 19, and 33.

67. See 1 Cor 13.12.

Nun.[68] Become Eleazar the priest.[69] Become Phineas the zealous one, the son of Eleazar the priest![70] For in that case you would go so that you might see God's wonders in the land.

The logos is about to dare something and to dare something big. The logos could offend a person who is not remaining diligently for the whole observation of the good thing.[71] The people saw God's wonders in the plain of Zoan.[72] So how is it true that *"he has made wonders for the holy ones who are in his land"*? The people saw God's wonders in the wilderness, the events recorded in Exodus, Leviticus, and Numbers. How, then, is it truly exceptional that *"he has made wonders for the holy ones who are in his land"*? But if you evaluate the wonder that came about through Joshua when he had just gotten into the holy land, of which he had to some extent not yet taken possession, you will see that the wonder in the holy land is not comparable to the wonders in Egypt, on the plain of Zoan, and to the wonders in the wilderness. Was there anything in the wilderness so great, was there anything so great in Egypt, in comparison with the wonder performed by Joshua: "Let the sun stand below Gibeon and the moon below the ravines of Ajalon"?[73] What is so very wonderful about the parting of the Red Sea, compared to the wonder when the Jordan was parting, a river flowing with fresh water? And if you are enabled[74] to compare these wonders with wonders, Moses's with Joshua's, you will verify that *"he has made wonders for the holy ones who are in his land."*

68. See Nm 14.26–30. Caleb and Joshua, who trusted that God would give them the promised land, are the only two adults at the time of the Exodus whom God allows to survive forty years in the wilderness and enter it.

69. Eleazar, the son and successor of Moses's brother Aaron, was the high priest who entered the Holy Land with Joshua. See esp. Nm 20.25–28.

70. See esp. Nm 25.1–9.

71. Origen does not specify whether "the logos" here is the divine logos "with God" speaking through the Psalm, the Psalm itself as a divine discourse, or his own logos explaining the Psalm. It dares to say something that apparently conflicts with other scriptural passages in which God showed wonders to the whole people, not just '"the holy ones," and outside the promised land, not "in the land."

72. Ps 77.12, 43.

73. Jos 10.12.

74. "Enabled," that is, by God to do the work of interpretation reserved for those who are spiritual, "comparing" spiritual things with spiritual things. See 1 Cor 2.13.

And just as when you compare one land distribution to another, Moses's land distribution to Joshua's, Joshua's land distribution is much better than Moses's and more divine.[75] For Moses's was beyond the Jordan and took place there, occurring for those who possessed many flocks, the tribe of Reuben, the tribe of Gad, and the half-tribe of Manasseh.[76] No further land distribution by Joshua was produced for them,[77] but Joshua's land distribution took place for the royal tribe of Judah,[78] the tribe of Ephraim,[79] and the rest of the tribes, including the tribe of Benjamin, where God's Temple was.[80] Just as one land distribution differs greatly in comparison with the other, in the same way "*he has made wonders for*" those[81] "*holy ones who are in his land.*"

If you would like to hear another way in which God has shown wonders to those in the land but does not do the wonderful things for those outside his land, understand with me figuratively: the Church is already God's land. If you are within the boundaries of the Church, you enjoy God's wonders, but if you go outside the boundaries of the Church—and you go outside them whenever you stray—you do not taste God's wonders. Therefore, it has been said: "*He has made wonders for the holy ones who are in his land; all his things willed are in them.*"[82]

In whom? Those in God's land. It does not say, "Some of my things willed are in them, but some are not in them." Either, according to the second explanation,[83] all God's things willed are in those who are settled in the Church, or, according to the first and a loftier explanation,[84] all God's things willed are in those who have come to be in the holy land, where he has made won-

---

75. What applies to wonders also applies to land distributions.

76. See Jos 13.8.

77. See Jos 14.1.

78. See Jos 15.1.

79. See Jos 16.5.

80. See Jos 18.11–20. The presence of Judah, from which Christ came, and Benjamin, the location of the Temple, makes Joshua's division "more divine."

81. "Those" holy ones are the ancient Israelites who arrived in the holy land with Joshua, as opposed to us "now," whom Christ addresses as well.

82. Ps 15.3.

83. That is, the figurative interpretation whereby God's land is the Church.

84. The "first" interpretation relates to the land that Joshua entered. A "loftier" interpretation refers to being in the presence of God.

ders his things willed. Now, in fact, in a complete and accurate sense, all God's things willed are not yet in them. That "*all God's things willed*" are not here before they reach the holy land, hear the words: "We know in part, and we prophesy in part."[85] How then can "*all God's things willed*" be in someone who knows in part? "*All God's things willed*" will appear "when the completion comes and what is in part is canceled."[86] Therefore, "*he has made wonders for the holy ones who are in his land; all his things willed are in them.*"[87]

7. Next, something obscure seems to be said here. Pray with us about the obscurity of: "*Their weaknesses have been multiplied; they hasten after these things.*"[88] Whose weaknesses? Of those in the holy land: [that is,] of those who are going to be in the holy land or of those who are in the holy land, since, according to both explanations, *their weaknesses have been multiplied; they hasten after these things.*" If, indeed, power is made complete in weakness and whenever the holy one is weak, then he is strong and the just person flourishes in weaknesses, in outrages, and in tortures, persecutions, and difficult situations,[89] and many are the afflictions of the just.[90] But whenever the weaknesses of the just multiply, those who take the road toward good things hasten toward God, who works together[91] with them so that they may hasten. Therefore, if you want to hasten, taking the road toward the good, do not shrink from flourishing in weaknesses and from being such a person as to say, "When I am weak, then I am powerful."[92] "*Their weaknesses have been multiplied*"—since many are the afflictions of the just—"*they hasten after these things*" among many weaknesses; they hasten after these things.

---

85. 1 Cor 13.9.

86. 1 Cor 13.10. Although the holy land can be interpreted figuratively as the Church, being in the Church does not "now" constitute the complete presence of God. Origen's understanding of the Church is governed by 1 Cor 13, which has hovered behind the entire discussion of Ps 15.3.

87. Ps 15.3.

88. Ps 15.4a–b.

89. See 2 Cor 12.9–10.

90. Ps 33.20a.

91. Origen probably has in mind Rom 8.28.

92. 2 Cor 12.10.

"*I by no means gather with their assemblies because of blood.*"[93] I should gather with those whose weaknesses have been multiplied, who hasten after these things. But as for men of blood, whom the Lord loathes—for the Lord loathes men of blood and deceit[94]—know that, because they are sinners, you are not to gather with them, for "*I by no means gather with their assemblies because of blood.*" One who is going to gather under the persona of Christ must be clean from blood and pollution, from murders, from wounds. About these, evidently, could not the persona of Christ, who gathers with assemblies that are not "of blood," say: "they have been born, not of blood, nor of the will of the flesh, nor of the will of man, but of God" as holy ones?[95]

"*I by no means gather with their assemblies because of blood, nor will I mention their names with my lips.*"[96] Grant that "*their weaknesses have been multiplied,*" that they were saved by God, that "*they hasten after these things,*" and that "*I by no means gather with their assemblies because of blood.*" How is "*I will not mention their names with my lips*" to be interpreted in connection with them? [It is to be interpreted thus:] "I will not be mentioned superficially by those who have been rescued; I will be mentioned in their hearts and in depth." You see how the lips are described as superficial in "This people honors me with the lips, but its heart is far from me."[97] "I will not be mentioned with the lips of those with whom I will gather. I will not be mentioned with the lips of those whose weaknesses have been multiplied and who hasten after these things, but I will be mentioned in their hearts and in their depth."

8. "*The Lord is the portion of my inheritance and of my cup. You are the one restoring my inheritance to me.*"[98] The Savior has two inheritances, on higher and lower levels. God is the one on the higher level, so that he [the Savior] may be helped by him and receive a benefit from the Father. His holy ones are on the lower

93. Ps 15.4c.
94. Ps 5.7.
95. Jn 1.13.
96. Ps 15.4c–d.
97. Is 29.13.
98. Ps 15.5.

level, so that the things most helpful, which he gets from the Father, he may give to those who are being helped. Because the Savior's inheritance appears in these two ways, pay attention to the wording: "*The Lord is the portion of my inheritance and of my cup. You are the one restoring my inheritance to me. My boundary lines have fallen in my strongest, for indeed my inheritance is strongest for me.*"[99] You see, "*My boundary lines have fallen in the strongest,*" not in God, but, if there is one who is very strong and chosen anywhere on earth, my inheritance has fallen there. "Boundary line" is taken from the example of those measuring the earth with boundary lines.[100] The term is found also in Deuteronomy, where the Highest divided nations that dispersed the sons of Adam; he established the boundaries of the nations according to the number of the sons of Israel, and this people Jacob became the Lord's portion, the boundary of Israel, his inheritance.[101] Therefore, my boundary, insofar as it is the measure of the inheritance, fell in the strongest.

You will understand how the boundary lines of Christ are in the strongest by seeing the chosen race, the royal priesthood, the holy nation, the people for safekeeping.[102] For example, look at the land that is Paul's soul, a portion of Christ; will not the Savior reasonably say about him: "My boundary lines have fallen for me in this strongest one"? Add to him the apostles Peter and John. See if you will not also say, "*My boundary lines have fallen in the strongest,*" so that, in each case, you will say: "*My boundary lines have fallen in the strongest.*" If, then, Christ's boundary lines have fallen for him in the strongest, know that, unless you are strongest, unless you are mightiest, unless you are noblest, Christ's boundary has not fallen in you. For indeed, "*my inheritance is strongest for me, the Lord is the portion of my inheritance and my cup.*"[103]

9. We have almost had to neglect the cup! The Lord is the Savior's portion of inheritance and his "cup." We drink the

---

99. Ps 15.5a, 6.

100. Because "boundary lines" are employed by surveying land or earth, as opposed to heaven, the "strongest" must be found here on earth.

101. Dt 32.8–9.

102. 1 Pt 2.9.

103. Ps 15.6b, 5a.

Savior and we eat the Savior: the logos is "living bread, coming down from heaven"[104] and "the true vine."[105] And, doubtless, since we eat him and his flesh—to which he summons us, saying, "unless you eat my flesh"—and since we drink his blood—if we are persuaded by him when he says: "If you do not drink my blood, you will not have life in yourselves"[106]—the Savior undergoes something from us. Still, he remains the complete logos even when we eat him, and he remains complete even when we drink him. Therefore, just as he is himself our nourishment and he is our drink—"this" is even "my blood of the new covenant"[107]—and he promises concerning himself saying: "I will not drink it, until I drink it with you in the kingdom of God,"[108] in the same way he has the Father as his nourishment, and he has the Father as his cup.[109]

For, as one who is drinkable, the Father says, "They have abandoned me, a spring of the water of life,"[110] so that the Father of the blessed one who drinks is his cup. But what must we also say about the one who is drunk? What sort of blessedness do we speak of with regard to the Father? "*You are therefore the portion of my inheritance and my cup.*" About his cup he says: "You have prepared a table for me in the presence of those who oppress me."[111] And the Savior drinks "your cup most strongly intoxicating,"[112] for he is not without want, as I previously said.[113]

And just as food and drink sustain us—bodily food sustains as far as the body is concerned; remove this and we do not live; bodily drink sustains as far as the body is concerned; take that away and we do not live—in the same manner, change the sub-

---

104. Jn 6.51.
105. Jn 15.1.
106. See Jn 6.53.
107. Mt 26.28.
108. Mt 26.29.
109. See Jn 4.32 and Lk 22.42.
110. Jer 2.13.
111. Ps 22.5a.
112. Ps 22.5c. This is the verse that reads, "My cup runneth over," in the King James Version. Here and in PS36H1.2 below, Origen presupposes the notion of a sober intoxication that comes with the experience of God within. See *Comm. Jo.* 1.30.205–8, and Philo, *On Drunkenness* 36.145–52.
113. See PS15H1.3 above.

ject to logos and give the logos to the soul: for "a human being will not live on bread alone, but a human being will live upon every utterance coming out of God's mouth."[114] Give logos, and my soul lives. If you take away logos, the soul dies, for by the elimination of its nourishment, the soul dies. Concerning this it is said: "The soul that sins, that one will die."[115] Every sinful soul has died, since it is not ever nourished by God's logos.[116]

Pay attention, you who neglect keeping the soul continually nourished. It is shameful that you sometimes eat twice a day, even eat three times a day,[117] and all of you eat at least once, but, when it comes to the soul, you do not give it its appropriate nourishment. Prayer is the nourishment of the soul, especially when it makes supplication with the mind also.[118] The teaching logos entering the hearer[119] is a nourishment of the soul, the logos of wisdom and the logos of knowledge.[120] Just as in the case of the body, the logos has disposed that, without nourishment and drink the body dies, so also a soul, if it is not nourished and does not drink, dies the soul's death.

Not understanding this, some say, out of great stupidity: the souls of the unjust completely die. For this, they say, is implied in, "The soul that sins, that soul will die."[121] And [to prove] that the soul dies, they bring to bear sayings, as if we were unaware that it is written that a soul dies, not seeing that the death of a soul is something different, since a soul not living for God has "died." For example, the souls of Abraham, Isaac, and Jacob are living, according to what was said by the Savior: "Do you not recognize what was said by God at the bush? 'I am the God of Abra-

114. Dt 8.3, Mt 4.4.

115. Ezek 18.4.

116. See PS77H4.6 below.

117. *Trisitein*, "eat three times a day," is not otherwise attested in Greek literature. Medical literature in Origen's day cautioned against overeating, especially among those who customarily ate twice a day (Aëtius Amidenus, *Iatricorum libri* 9.13). Origen may have coined the word to denote this extremity of self-indulgence.

118. See 1 Cor 14.15.

119. See also PS81H.1 below.

120. See 1 Cor 12.8. Note how Origen assimilates the divine logos to his own teaching.

121. Ezek 18.4.

ham, the God of Isaac, and the God of Jacob.' But God is not of the dead, but of the living."[122] But the souls of Pharaoh and of the sinners among the Egyptians died, and they died through deprivation of nourishment.

At any rate, so that I may not lose track of the subject, the soul is nourished, and without nourishment it dies. The soul is nourished with its own proper nourishment. It is nourished with Christ himself, and without nourishment it dies. But my Savior and Lord is nourished and drinks: "You are the portion of my inheritance and my cup," he says to the Father. But I often neglect my nourishment, and as often as I have neglected it, in proportion to the neglect, I am either sickened or I have died. But my Savior never neglects his own nourishment, but always keeps watch and is nourished by the Father. If, hypothetically, he were not to be nourished, I do not know what would follow. But the Savior actually is nourished and always nourished by the Father. [123]

Therefore, I will be bold, and I shall ask a thing to be sought in the Apostle, presented as an inquiry for those able to hear Scripture.[124] The Apostle says concerning God: "the only one having immortality, dwelling in light unapproachable."[125] Paul, does the Father alone actually have immortality, but no one else? He would say, "No, since that one's immortality is not something acquired, but it belongs to his nature." Nothing can possibly come about, in God's case, so that he might not be immortal, but the Savior is immortal, because immortality is supplied to him.[126] At any rate, he says that he himself receives it from the

122. See Mt 22.31–32 and Ex 3.6.

123. Origen's principal reason for stressing the Son's continual need for nourishment is to establish that we, when we have become constituent parts of Christ's body, the Church, do not cease to need spiritual nourishment ourselves.

124. The "thing to be sought" (*zētoumenon*) "as an inquiry" (*eis exetasin*) from the ultimate authority, the Apostle Paul, is the scriptural basis for Origen's position that the Son remains in need of the Father.

125. 1 Tm 6.16.

126. Only God the Father "has" (*echei*) immortality by nature, although the Savior, the Son, is immortal. In *Princ.* 1.2 Origen explains that the Son shares the power and eternity of God the Father and exercises authority over all things because the Son eternally derives his being from the Father. By articulating this notion of eternal generation, Origen laid the foundation for subsequent trinitarian doctrine.

Father, to whom he says: "*You are the portion of my inheritance and my cup. You are the one restoring my inheritance to me.*"[127]

In "restoring an inheritance," what does "restoring" mean? If someone can, let him gather from a different place, like "until the times of the restoration of all things of which God has spoken."[128] Now, have my bones actually been restored, each where it fits? For it was out of its fitting place, but in the "rising up," so-called and recorded, a bone is restored to the joint where it fits.[129] If you have understood what is signified by restoration, run back and see with me the original logoi from "*You are the one restoring my inheritance to me.*"[130] See the logoi of restoration also in "until only the times alone of the restoration of all things, of which God has spoken through the mouth of his holy prophets."[131]

In anticipation, I shall explain "*You therefore are the one restoring my inheritance for me. My boundary lines have fallen in the*

127. Ps 15.5.

128. Acts 3.21. Here Origen alludes to his understanding of eschatology, the most controversial aspect of his thought both in his own time and later. The verb translated "restoring," *apokathistōn,* is the basis of the noun *apokatastasis,* "restoration," in Acts 3.21.

129. Origen discusses the resurrection of the body, understood as the body of Christ, in *Comm. Jo.* 10.36.236: "When this rising up of the genuine and more perfect body of Christ occurs, then what are now the constituent parts of Christ, which are dry bones in comparison to what they are to become, will be assembled, bone to bone and fitting-place to fitting-place [see Ezek 37.1–8], for no one of those lacking fitting-places will arrive at the perfect man, at the measure of the stature of the fullness of the body of Christ [see Eph 4.13]."

130. Origen proposes that those who have understood about restoration, presumably those who have studied with him and know the teachings propounded in *Peri archōn,* run back with him to logoi related to beginning. See the ideas expressed in *Princ.* 1.2: "Seeing such an end, when all enemies will be subjected to Christ, when death is destroyed as the last enemy, and when the kingdom is handed over by Christ, to whom all things have been subjected, to God the Father [see 1 Cor 15.24–28], from such an end of things we can view the beginning. For the end is always like the beginning, and as the end of many things is one, so the many differences and varieties of things are from one beginning, which are summoned back by God's goodness, by subjection to Christ, and by the unity of the Holy Spirit in one end, which is like the beginning."

131. By citing the additional phrase, "through the mouth of his holy prophets," Origen indicates that the author of Ps 15 was one of the prophets Peter was referring to in Acts 3.21.

strongest."[132] For he did not say, "my inheritance is strongest," but [there is] a major addition, "for me."[133] "*For my inheritance is strongest for me*": according to me as judge, it is strongest. Not just anyone judges concerning the inheritance, that it is strongest, but I say, concerning the inheritance, that Christ says, "The inheritance is strongest to whom is the glory and the might to the ages of ages." Amen.

132. Ps 15.5b–6a.

133. Because the Psalm is spoken in the persona of Christ, "for me" is "for Christ."

HOMILY 2 ON PSALM 15

ACH OF THE APOSTLES individually is a holy witness, adorned by Christ's spirit, when he interprets something from the old Scriptures and especially when referring it to Christ. For Christ Jesus appointed the apostles, and God was in Christ Jesus.[1] But if "every utterance shall be confirmed from the mouth of two or three witnesses,"[2] whenever two or three apostles interpret Scripture, what is said will appear all the more convincing, since it has been witnessed by three witnesses of such stature. We find something extraordinary in the case of this Psalm, for the things we have read from the Psalm have not been interpreted by two or three apostles alone. For it is written in the Acts of the Apostles that Peter, along with the other eleven apostles, raised his voice, and he used [the words], *"I have foreseen the Lord face to face through everything, because he is at my right hand, so that I will not be shaken. Therefore, my heart has rejoiced, and my tongue has exulted, and my flesh will still set up a tent in hope, because you will not abandon my soul in Hades, nor will you allow your devout one to see corruption."*[3] And he says that David said this, foreseeing Christ in spirit. David in his own generation, submitting to God's will, saw corruption, but the one whom God raised up not only did not see corruption, but his soul also was not abandoned in Hades. See, then, how many witnesses have witnessed that this Psalm is spoken in the persona of Christ. For Christ's twelve apostles said this in one spirit and in unison like a choir. But if I say twelve, it is because when Judas was eliminated,

1. See 2 Cor 5.19.
2. 2 Cor 13.1, Dt 19.15.
3. Ps 15.8–10, Acts 2.25–27.

Matthias took Judas's place. For, in fact, this is written in the Acts of the Apostles.[4]

It is not at all easy for us to explain in a masterful way in terms of the wording how the passage that the Apostles used refers to the Savior, but to clarify the entire Psalm and make it self-consistent in terms of the wording, showing that the persona is that of the Savior,[5] and to teach the things said worthily of the Savior, this, it seems to me, requires the Savior himself, so that we will be enabled to say, when the Lord himself speaks in us, "or do you seek proof of Christ speaking in me?"[6] Just as, on other occasions, your prayers and requests for good things from God have helped us make Scripture clear, let them also come to our assistance now, that God may furnish a logos to us who thirst and ask for enlightenment on matters that need clarity, and that we, through your prayers, even if at first we do not fully understand, may now, enlightened by the logos, present what must be explained in the Psalm with understanding.

2. At the beginning of today's reading, "*I shall bless the Lord who causes me to apprehend,*"[7] Christ is understood according to his humanity. For in the Scriptures you make a distinction: when it says "Lord," it is understood according to his divinity and when it says "Christ," it is understood according to his humanity.[8] Now, in fact, the things spoken by the persona of Christ in the Psalm are understood in accord with his humanity. For "*my flesh shall set up a tent in hope*"[9] is the voice of a human

4. See Acts 1.23–26. Some hearers must have been looking puzzled about "twelve."

5. Having used the apostles' testimony to identify the persona speaking in the Psalm as Christ, Origen faces a far more intractable problem or "thing to be sought" (see intro., p. 32): how to explain the Psalm as something Christ says. His prayer calls for Jesus Christ, the divine logos, to answer the promise "seek and you shall find" (Mt 7.7) by providing a solution through Origen's logos.

6. 2 Cor 13.3.

7. Ps 15.7a. The verb translated "cause to apprehend," *sunetisanta,* implies that God provides "apprehension," *sunesis,* immediate, intuitive understanding, what we might call, "getting it."

8. Acts 2.36 says that the speaker of the Psalm is both "Lord" and "Christ."

9. Ps 15.9c.

being, and *"you will not abandon my soul in Hades"*[10] is the voice of one endowed with a soul. When you find "before the rising of the sun his name will continue in heaven, and before the moon generations of generations, and he will come down like dew on fleece and as drops dripping on the land,"[11] and such things spoken in praise of him, understand his divinity.

Either as "the firstborn of all creation"[12] or as his soul before his body,[13] he now says, *"I will bless the Lord,"* evidently the Father, *"who causes me to apprehend."*[14] Who could be the one prophesied to be saying this except, as I have already said, the human being? This is the one about whom, as well, Isaiah speaks: "There shall go forth a rod from the root of Jesse, and a bloom shall go up from the root, and the spirit of God will rest upon him, the spirit of wisdom and apprehension."[15] If the spirit of apprehension rests upon the one from the root of Jesse, "begotten from the seed of David according to the flesh,"[16] the one born of the seed of David according to the flesh well says, *"I will bless the Lord who causes me to apprehend."*[17] For "the firstborn of all creation," the "spirit of counsel and might,"[18] has been united to the Savior understood according to the humanity, born from the seed of David according to the flesh. And thus, he says, having taken

10. Ps 15.10a.

11. Ps 71.5–6. This verse describes the descent of the divine logos.

12. Col 1.15. That is, as the divine logos.

13. That is, as his human soul. In Origen's understanding of the human person as set forth most fully in *Princ.*, but also in *Dial.* 136–140, a human being is composite (*sunthetos*), consisting of spirit, soul, and body (as stated also in PS15H1.3 above and in PS77H6.2 below). The spirit is every person's capacity for God. The soul is the basis of rationality. The soul preexists the body. Human souls have fallen from an original unity with God and eventually receive bodies, the instruments God provides them to work out their redemption. In the Incarnation, God's logos became united with a complete human being: spirit, soul and body. The basis of this unity is the soul of Jesus, one soul that did not fall with other souls, but stayed with God's logos (see *Princ.* 2.6).

14. Ps 15.7a.

15. Is 11.1–2. This prophesies Christ's humanity because his capacity for apprehension (see note 13 above) comes to rest on him. By contrast, the divine logos is eternally God's wisdom.

16. Rom 1.3.

17. Ps 15.7a.

18. Is 11.2.

part in the union, "*I will bless the Lord who causes me to apprehend.*"

3. The voice of this one is also speaking in what follows, requiring grace from God for clarification, which says, "*yet also until night my kidneys have disciplined me.*"[19] It is not obvious how Christ's "kidneys" "disciplined" him. And once it is explained how his kidneys disciplined him, why do they do so "until night"? His "kidneys" do not simply "discipline" him, but his kidneys discipline him "until night." I do not actually know of "kidneys" being employed by those outside the logos to refer to matters of understanding or skill as they are in Scripture; in Scripture, when God examines hidden things, he examines hearts and kidneys.[20] And perhaps he examined the kidneys because he searches and examines things still laid up as seeds in the soul that have not ascended to the heart.[21]

Indeed, these kidneys, not the bodily ones, are so designated on the analogy of "heart." We are not, after all, supposed to understand that what is "blessed" is a bodily organ that we see even among animals lacking logos, when it is said that the heart is "pure" and that "the pure in heart" are "blessed."[22] I say that the one who said, "*You will not abandon my soul in Hades*"[23] came to humanity with these kidneys. They have an analogy to the "purity" of the heart, the roots and the beginnings of ways of thinking that discipline the soul of Jesus. So, if I had said something analogous about the human soul, it has in the kidneys the ways of thinking and the seeds of rationalizations before they arise in the heart. These already exist potentially within. They are either the worse kind, for anyone who sinned did the evil act

19. Ps 15.7b.

20. See Ps 7.10; Jer 17.10 and 20.12.

21. Origen's presentation of the "kidneys" as the source of ideas and actions beneath the threshold of awareness resembles contemporary discussions of the adaptive unconscious. See, for example, Timothy D. Wilson, *Strangers to Ourselves: Discovering the Adaptive Unconscious* (Cambridge, MA: Harvard University Press, 2002).

22. Mt 5.8. Elsewhere in his work, elaborating on the Pauline concept of a contrast between an outer and an inner human being (see 2 Cor 4.16 and Rom 7.22), Origen finds inner, non-bodily analogs for all parts of the human body. See *Comm. Cant.* Preface and *Dial.* 144–67.

23. Ps 15.10a.

from such a seed, or the better kind, after the good deed seems to have come about as a result.

If, then, you understand what has been delivered to me about the kidneys, see Jesus's soul coming down from heaven, "for no one has gone up into heaven, except the one who came down from heaven,"[24] not the "Son of God," not the "firstborn of all creation,"[25] but the "son of a human being."[26] Seeing with me that soul, which "did not consider equality with God something to be grasped, but emptied itself, taking the form of a slave,"[27] and understanding with me that soul, see it accumulating opinions and thoughts, and storing them, not in the heart but in the kidneys, so that out of the kidneys they may ascend to the heart. See with me the soul of Jesus coming, wearing non-bodily kidneys, faculties that discipline and direct, through which, visiting with us in that soul, it did not know sin,[28] did not sin, and did not speak sinfully as a human being.

I would not marvel if someone were to refer to the firstborn of all creation what is written about the Savior's not having sinned. For someone to marvel at something like that would be like marveling that the God who made heaven and earth[29] did not sin, unaware that it is not God's nature to sin. As it was not the nature of God's logos to sin, the firstborn of all creation could not sin. But the commendation of Jesus for not sinning—"who did not sin nor was deceit found in his mouth"[30]—refers to the human being. And if it said, "the one who did not know sin was made sin for our sake,"[31] do not hear this about the firstborn of all creation, but about the one who did not know sin, Jesus's soul.

24. Jn 3.13.

25. Col 1.15.

26. Jn 3.13. Origen argues from Scripture that Jesus's soul existed before he was born. This preexistent soul explains, to Origen's satisfaction, how Jesus Christ could be fully human and, at the same time, wholly without sin. See *Princ.* 2.6.3.

27. Phil 2.6–7.

28. See 2 Cor 5.21.

29. See Ps 133.3.

30. 1 Pt 2.22.

31. 2 Cor 5.21.

All of us have known sin;[32] we say in a secret way,[33] "I was conceived in lawless deeds, and my mother conceived me in sins,"[34] and I do not know in what sorts of lawless deeds and sins.[35] But that one who did not know sin, the Father made sin for our sake, sending him from heavens to earth on our behalf. And he came having on the kidneys things actually disciplining him and reminding him, not just disciplining, but, as it is set forth in Scripture, "*until night my kidneys disciplined me,*"[36] the "night," that is, of this life. For "night" is here, concerning which it is said, "The night has progressed, the day approaches, let us walk about decently as in the day."[37] And since it is night, this life is dark. For see: "Consider that our wrestling is not against blood and flesh, but against the rulers, against the authorities, against the cosmic dominators of this darkness, against the spiritual matters of wickedness in the heavenly places."[38]

It also says, then, "*until night my kidneys have disciplined me*"; not only were they disciplining me and reminding me of what ought to be done, but also things coming into the night of this age, into the darkness "*my kidneys have disciplined me. I have fore-seen the Lord face to face through everything, because he is at my right hand, so that I may not be shaken.*"[39] Jesus's human soul says: "*I have foreseen the Lord face to face.*" What "lord" was that? Does it say that the Father or that "the firstborn of all creation" was always

32. Origen taught that all souls, save the human soul of Christ, have fallen to some extent before becoming embodied (*Princ.* 1.4–5 and 2.8). Jesus's human soul was free to sin in its preexistent state, but chose instead to cleave to the divine logos. The rest of us, having fallen, enter into life with a predisposition to sin. This is Origen's way of explaining how Jesus could be fully divine and fully human and also without sin. He is prepared to come into the cosmos.

33. When we say the Psalm, we utter the words "in a secret way," *mustikōs*, because the origin of human sinfulness in the falling away of preexisting rational beings is not explicitly stated and can only be discovered by reading the Bible spiritually.

34. Ps 50.7. This refers to sins that our soul committed before being born. They are unknowable, but influence us. See *Princ.* 3.1.22.

35. In contrast to Jesus, all of us say that we are born as sinners.

36. Ps 15.7b.

37. Rom 13.12–13.

38. Eph 6.12.

39. Ps 15.7b–8.

present with him? But why do I say "present"? Instead, say "united," so that the human being is no longer one thing and the firstborn of all creation something else. If "union" makes you stumble, hear as encouragement a treatment for your stumbling and an apostolic encouragement: "The one who cleaves to the Lord is no longer two, but is one spirit."[40] If the one who cleaves to the Lord is one spirit, do you not want the soul that does not sin, the one that voluntarily came down, the one that did not consider equality with God a thing to be grasped, to become one spirit and to become one with the firstborn of all creation? I have, then, foreseen my Lord, since my kidneys have disciplined me until night.

4. *"I have foreseen the Lord face to face through everything"*—not sometimes and sometimes not—*"but through everything face to face, because he is at my right hand."*[41] For help was always present in the most honorable and right-handed place of the soul; either the Father was present or the firstborn of all creation was present, united with the soul, so that the soul might say *"so that I may not be shaken."* So that, if the soul had not foreseen the Lord face to face through everything, because he is at the right hand, it might have been shaken. For, as far as regards the soul's nature, it can be shaken.

Some say, not understanding the true logos concerning a soul, that the soul is a "middle thing";[42] the body belongs to things below; the spirit belongs to things above. And they say that some are soul-natured, not seeing that, according to a certain logos, different from the one that we often speak, all hu-

40. 1 Cor 6.17. On the union of divine and human in Christ, see especially *Princ.* 2.6.3–5.

41. Ps 15.8b.

42. This is a position Origen associates with Valentinians. Origen uses the term for the top note of the lower octave in Greek music, analogous to Middle C in our music notation. It was originally the term for the middle string of a lyre, the string that made that note. The implication is that, like a string that plays one note, the soul has its own distinct character differentiated from the spirit above it and the body below. Origen rejects this understanding. "Soul" represents the capacity of a rational creature either to rise or to fall. See especially *Princ.* 1.5.3 and 1.8.2. Where some see distinct natures, Origen sees a continuum with potential either for improvement or for deterioration.

man beings first became soul-natured on account of the soul, and after becoming soul-natured on account of the soul, being soul-natured before sin and before being set straight, so that I say in a bolder way, through sin they become earthy, through excellence they become spiritual, so that to be soul-natured is not to be earthy—for they become earthy by falling—nor is to be soul-natured spiritual, for one becomes spiritual by being set straight.

"*I have foreseen the Lord face to face through everything, because he is at my right hand, so that I may not fall, therefore my heart has rejoiced,*"[43] since "*my kidneys discipline me until night.*"[44] Since "*I have foreseen the Lord face to face through everything, because he is at my right hand, so that I may not fall, therefore my heart has rejoiced,*" therefore "*my tongue has been glad,*" therefore "*my glory has been glad,*"[45] as if, had it not been for what was first mentioned, what is added would not have occurred.

When you hear Jesus saying these things, hear Paul as well, ordering you: "Be imitators of me, as I also am of Christ."[46] Whose imitator must I become? Is it the firstborn of all creation? Wisdom? Logos? Truth? Or am I, as a human being, ordered to become the imitator of the human Jesus, so that I may imitate his humanity? I do not say that it is unfeasible to imitate his divinity, for ascending I progress and by God's grace I achieve the ability to imitate the divinity of Christ—if it is actually possible to imitate the divinity of Christ. The same is true of the God of the Universe: "Become perfect, as your Father who is in heaven is perfect,"[47] and, "Be holy, because I am holy, the Lord your God,"[48] and again, "Be perfect before the Lord your God."[49]

We, then, having also become imitators of Christ, will endeavor to say as much as the humanity of Christ says. For that is why he says this, so that we may have some pattern. And we shall

43. Ps 15.8–9a.
44. Ps 15.7b.
45. Ps 15.9.
46. 1 Cor 11.1.
47. Mt 5.48.
48. Lv 11.45.
49. Dt 18.13.

imitate, and let us say: "*I will bless the Lord who causes me to apprehend,*"[50] so that we may also say, "*my kidneys have disciplined me until night.*"[51] For we have come, having certain beginnings of good things in the kidneys, and when we are cultivating the seeds of good things that we have borne, through these seeds that we have, they are said to be in the kidneys.

5. You shall understand such things, if you are enabled to hear and distinguish spiritual things by spiritual things.[52] But thus the wording has: "Whenever nations that do not have the law do the things of the law by nature, they, not having the law, are a law to themselves, who show forth the work of the law written in their hearts, since their self-awareness bears witness."[53] And perhaps such things written are written in the heart. When they are written, hear: when I am an infant,[54] they are not written for me in the heart, but when we begin to be able to receive God's law in the heart, this also is written, not with ink, but with the spirit of the living God,[55] since the seeds have already been stored in the so-called "kidneys."

Words applicable to bodies are applied to the powers of the soul, in a manner analogous to their usage in reference to the body. For example, the eyes of the soul are said to be enlightened by God's commandment,[56] homonymous[57] to the eyes of the body, since the eyes of the body perform a function analogous to the eyes of the soul. The eyes of the body see bodies and colors, and the eyes of the soul see things understood by the mind. So also ears of the soul are mentioned as homonymous to the ears of the body.

If, then, a heart of the soul were to be mentioned as homonymous with the heart of the body regarded as the governing

---

50. Ps 15.7a.
51. Ps 15.7b.
52. 1 Cor 2.13.
53. Rom 2.14–15.
54. See 1 Cor 13.11.
55. 2 Cor 3.3.
56. See, for example, Ps 18.9.
57. "Homonymy," when one word means at least two different things, is a grammatical concept to which Origen attached considerable importance. See especially *Philoc.* 14. See n. 22 above.

faculty,[58] understand with me that it is a heart analogous to the soul's eyes and ears. Thus if you hear of the soul's "kidneys" being examined by God, hear "of the soul" on the analogy of eyes, ears, and heart, for God does not examine either the bodily heart or the bodily kidneys. And just as the heart has the governing faculty when it comes to the body—it thus says: "You shall love the Lord your God out of your whole heart"[59]— so something analogous to what happens in the kidneys happens in the soul's kidneys. Seeds take shape in the kidneys, and the male has these around the kidneys and thus becomes fertile.[60] So the fertile soul has the powers of spiritual seeds in the soul's kidneys. For the soul that has seeds around the kidneys sows, if it merits the holy blessing and beatitude and does nothing meriting the curse that says: "There will not be among you any unproductive or barren."[61]

Hearing, then, the human being who says as the Savior, "*I will bless the Lord who causes me to apprehend. Yet also until night my kidneys discipline me,*"[62] say this also yourselves. But say as well: "*I have foreseen the Lord face to face through everything.*"[63]

For the Lord also dwells in you, if you wish, *through everything.* Become his imitator like Paul, and you will find that the Lord is always in you. For you also will say: "It is no longer I that live, but Christ lives in me."[64]

"*I have foreseen.*" I have eyes that see the Lord being always before me. When is the Lord before me? The Lord is before me when I keep God's law: "Attach these logoi to your hands,

---

58. The heart was believed by ancient medical writers, including Aristotle and Galen, to be the seat of the intelligence.

59. Dt 6.5.

60. Because of their connection with the urethra, kidneys were mistakenly thought to be part of the human reproductive system.

61. Dt 7.14. This passage may have been the best Origen could think of to make his point. It is actually a blessing, but, since the blessing is conditioned on keeping the commandments, a curse of sterility is implicit for those who fail to do so. Perhaps Origen is referring to a passage that he had recently explained in some other context.

62. Ps 15.7.

63. Ps 15.8.

64. Gal 2.20.

and they will be unshakeable before your eyes."[65] Thus I have foreseen my Lord, the logos. Who is blessed in this manner, so that he serves no one but the logos and says: "*I have foreseen the Lord face to face through everything, because he is at my right hand, so that I may not be shaken*"?[66] If you dishonor God's logos, the logos will be on your left; if you dishonor, it will be so. If you honor God's logos, God's logos will be on your right. Because Judas dishonored God's logos[67] and he put him on the left, he therefore received the curse that says: "May the devil stand at his right hand."[68]

6. But if someone[69] hears Scriptures as a whole, that person can respond to me concerning these things and offer cases, until God gives a supply of the spirit of wisdom[70] resolving the difficulty and settling the case. For one who can more deeply hear what is said will ask: "Let the devil be at Judas's right hand? You are making a statement that could offend me, because the devil belongs 'to the left' and the Lord belongs 'to the right' of the just. So let just persons, imitating Christ, say, '*I have foreseen the Lord face to face through everything, because he is at my right hand, so that I may not be shaken*.'[71] What will you say about the scriptural wording in Zechariah concerning Jesus the great priest, for it is written there: 'The devil had stood to his right, to oppose him'?"[72]

But come, Christ; visit, God's logos. Explain to me[73] and to those who genuinely want to listen, how the devil stands at Je-

---

65. See Dt 6.8 and 11.8.

66. Ps 15.8.

67. This could apply to those who dishonor God's logos speaking through Origen.

68. See Ps 108.6. That is, in Origen's interpretation, the devil replaces Jesus for Judas when Judas rejects Jesus.

69. "Someone" is an attentive listener. Origen is encouraging such persons to ask questions and to put their case to him, and, in the process, he is teaching them how to approach a difficulty in interpretation.

70. A conflation of Phil 1.19 and Is 11.2.

71. Ps 15.8.

72. Zec 3.1.

73. The difficulty of explaining how the devil could be on the right is sufficiently great to inspire a prayer. Implicitly, should Origen offer a convincing explanation, the hearer can infer that Christ is speaking through him.

sus's right, since the devil was already at the right of the one he was opposing; or when he was opposing him, he was already opposed; he was already standing. But when Jesus still wrestles, having put on soiled clothing,[74] my sins, before he takes them off, then the devil stands at his right hand when he was opposing him, but when he took off the soiled clothing, my sins—for he took them off and put on the robe[75]—then, when he put on the robe, the devil no longer stands at his right hand to oppose him, but stops. Perhaps then, as long as the wrestling lasts, the devil has not just "stood" on the right, but "stood to oppose." But when you are victorious, you expel him who was opposing you from your right, and then Christ comes on your right hand, and you say: "*I have foreseen the Lord face to face through everything, because he is at my right hand, so that I may not be shaken.*"[76] For this reason, "*because he is at my right hand,*" "*my heart has rejoiced.*"[77] Let us do such things, so that Christ may come on our right and God's logos and our hearts may rejoice, for when the logos is present, a heart rejoices.

7. "*Therefore, my heart rejoiced and my glory exulted.*"[78] In the Acts of the Apostles we find this written, not this way, but also "and my tongue exulted,"[79] instead of, "*my glory exulted*" here. The other versions[80] all have "*my glory exulted.*" I am going to take a risk and say that what the apostles had said is not in conflict with the prophetic logos, but there has either been a scribal error, when someone did not understand "*my glory has exulted*" and substituted "my tongue has exulted," or, if someone does not want a scribal error to have occurred, let him interpret it in a plainer way.

"*My glory has exulted,*" but the tongue is my glory. For the

74. See Zec 3.3.
75. See Zec 3.4, Rv 1.13.
76. Ps 15.8.
77. Ps 15.9a.
78. Ps 15.9a–b.
79. Acts 2.26.
80. Origen deals with a discrepancy between the reading "my tongue" in Acts and "my glory" in the Psalm, where he follows the "versions" he has assembled in the *Hexapla,* which all, in this case, accord with our received Hebrew text. On the *Hexapla* see introduction, pp. 12, 24–26, 31.

tongue of a wise person, since he is glorified by tongue and by logos, is a glory. And just as the glory of an athlete is his excellent body, of a physician it is medicine, of an artisan it is the hands, so the glory of a wise person, when he is saying divine and holy things, is his tongue, so that "glory" and "tongue" are not different things, but "glory" and "tongue" are the same. Pray for me, even if I am unworthy, that, out of his love and yours, God may give me tongue and glory, so that my tongue may be glorified by God and by human beings. For my tongue will be my glory, if you have been heard. The writer of the Acts of the Apostles substituted "my tongue has rejoiced," understanding that "glory" and "tongue" are the same.

8. "*But still my flesh will set up a tent*[81] *in hope.*"[82] My Lord Jesus says this. His flesh first set up a tent in hope, for he was crucified and awoke on the third day, becoming the firstborn of the dead.[83] Once he arose, he was taken up into heaven and brought up from earth an earthly body, so that the heavenly powers were surprised, since they had never seen this spectacle, flesh ascending into heaven. Concerning Elijah, it is written that "he was taken up *as* into heaven"[84] and concerning Enoch, "God transported him,"[85] but "to heaven" is not mentioned. Before my Lord Jesus Christ no one ascended into heaven.[86] Let anyone who wants, take offense at my language. I am venturing to say that, because he is firstborn of the dead, so he also was the first to bring flesh up into heaven. Therefore, the powers are surprised at a new story, because they see flesh that has ascended into heaven and say, "Who is this who has arrived from Edom"—that is, from earthly things—"with red clothing"—they see the traces of blood and wounds—"from Bozrah"—from the

81. See introduction, p. 20, on "tent" and setting up a tent.

82. Ps 15.9c.

83. Col 1.18, Rv 1.5.

84. 2 Kgs 2.11. With "as," Origen's Septuagint Bible implies that Elijah was not necessarily taken up to heaven, but that something like that happened. The conjunction "as" does not occur in our received Hebrew text.

85. Gn 5.24, Heb 11.5. The statement is ambiguous. It does not say that Enoch was bodily transported to heaven.

86. Jn 3.13. See Lk 24.51 and Acts 1.11, which do not actually say "ascended," but "was borne up."

flesh—"so beautiful in a strong robe? I discuss with strength. Who is this?" And no one else answers about him but himself. "With strength I discuss justice and judgment of salvation." Again they inquire: "Why is your clothing red and your garments as if from a trodden wine press full of a trampled thing?" Next, as a conqueror conquering with the body, it says: "and of the peoples no one is with me, and I have crushed them, led them together, and trampled them into the earth."[87] Then the powers remembered[88] the plan that had been spoken of by the prophets[89] concerning the logos of the Savior, and they say: "I have remembered the Lord's mercy, the Lord's excellences, in all those things the Lord has given us in return."[90]

This is on account of "*my flesh will set up a tent in hope.*"

In hope? In how great a hope? Not because he arose from the dead here, for that would be something modest,[91] but it was hope because he has been taken up into heaven, because the powers are speaking. Not only did they speak, but some, serving as escorts, even accompany him in: "Lift gates, your rulers, and be lifted up, age-long gates, and the king of glory shall enter." But other powers respond: "Who is this king of glory?" Then the escorting powers say: "The Lord, mighty and powerful, the Lord mighty in wars." Then the arrayed virtues say: "Lift gates."[92] He is very big; your gates do not have room for the Christ: "Lift gates, those who are ruling you, and be lifted up, age-long gates, and the king of glory will enter. Who is the king of glory? The Lord of powers, he is the king of glory." He is the one who says: "*but*

87. Is 63.1–3. The proposed etymological connections between "Edom" and "earth" and between "Bozrah" and "flesh" are at least possible in Hebrew.

88. I follow a suggestion of Richard Bishop, reading the manuscript of CMG 314 as *eith' hupomimnēskontai*, "then they remembered," rather than *ei oupō mimnēskontai*, "if they had not yet remembered," in GCSO13 since that makes better sense of the passage.

89. The heavenly powers get their information about the divine plan as we do, through the prophets.

90. Is 63.7.

91. An earthly resurrection "here" would have been a "modest" or "moderate" (*metrion*), and not unprecedented, achievement for God's logos, the embodied power of God.

92. Ps 23.7–10. See PS77H4.8 below, which suggests that Origen interpreted the words *hoi archontes humōn*, "those ruling you," to refer to the virtues.

still my flesh will set up a tent in hope, because you will not abandon my soul in Hades."[93]

The soul alone had gone down into Hades, where only souls were. If, in fact, only souls were here and the living being were not composite, a composite would not have come here.[94] From which it follows that they go astray who say that the Savior did not visit humanity as a composite, but taking up a body similar to the transcendent being of his logos, rather, the same being as the logos, and that this soul was the same as the being of the logos.[95] These indeed eliminate the kindness of him who puts on a composite human being and says: "*my flesh will set up a tent in hope, you will not abandon my soul in Hades.*"[96] Wherever, then, the bare souls were, the soul descends alone; wherever the composite living being was, the composite went with a soul.

If in descending, he had descended also to the angels—for he came from the summit of the heavens—perhaps he was formed in accord with the place. And just as in this life he was transformed before those who ascended with him to the mountain and appeared most glorious,[97] he would have been formed in descending from the Father. Since "in the beginning was the logos, and the logos was near God, and the logos was a god,"[98] in descending from the Father he did not remain the same as he

93. Ps.15.9b–10a.

94. The logos became incarnate, a composite of body and soul, "here" on earth, because such living beings exist here.

95. Such persons claim, that is, that the logos was not incarnate as a human being.

96. Origen here states, with regard to the entire human person, the fundamental Christological principle that Gregory of Nazianzus received in the formula that he stated in his so-called "Theological Epistles": "For what is not assumed is not healed, but what is united to God, this is also saved" (Gregory of Nazianzus, *Epistle* 101.32). See also Origen, *Dial.* 7, "They eliminate the salvation of the human body by saying that the Savior's body is spiritual."

97. Mt 17.2, Mk 9.2–3, Lk 9.29.

98. Jn 1.1–2. I have translated this verse unconventionally in order to convey Origen's reading. The Greek language employs the definite article with what we would call proper nouns, including names. In his *Commentary on John*, written while he was in Alexandria, Origen discussed this passage in detail. See esp. *Comm. Jo.* 2.2.13. Origen argued that the evangelist deliberately used *theos*, "god," without the definite article, *ho*, to distinguish the divinity of the logos from *ho theos*, "God." We find this distinction between God as *ho theos* and God's logos as *theos* without the article in Philo. See *On Dreams* 1.229–230.

was at first "in the beginning near God." For the lower regions did not have room for him, but, just as for me he became a human being, so alongside some he became an angel and alongside some a throne, a lordship, a ruler, a power,[99] and alongside each the Lord becomes what each can take in.

Then what do I say? Even today the logos is transformed. Paul and Timothy do not see him in the same way. Paul, as opposed to Timothy, sees him glorious, transformed into what is most divine. Timothy sees his glory less fully. When you understand less fully than the latter, you will see a lesser form of Jesus appearing to one who is lesser. But if someone is completely sinful, he completely fails to see his glory, but sees him "not having form or beauty, but his form dishonored, abandoned among the sons of human beings."[100] They see him a human being, not a human being unbeaten, but "beaten."[101] If you are beaten, you see him beaten; if you are not beaten, you see him not beaten. If you are unblemished, you will see him show himself unblemished to you. It is not because he is ever blemished himself or ever beaten himself. He bears our infirmities and suffers pain for us, and we reckoned him to be in pain, beaten, and in distress.[102]

This suffices for *"you will not abandon my soul in Hades."* For it must happen that he would come to be among souls with a bare soul.

9. *"Nor will you allow your devout one to see corruption."*[103] Scripture uses the word "see" in a peculiar way to mean "come to be in a condition," as in: "Who is the human being who will live and will not see death?"[104] Thus one who dies "sees death"; one

99. See Col 1.16.

100. Is 53.2–3.

101. Is 53.3–4.

102. Is 53.4. Seeing Christ "not having form or beauty" is appropriate for beginners in the Christian life. Later, having progressed, believers see him in glory. Thus he states in *Comm. Matt.* 12.30: "If you were enabled to comprehend figuratively the differences of the logos, when a proclamation is proclaimed in foolishness to those who believe and when it is spoken in wisdom to the perfect [see 1 Cor 2.6], you will see in what manner the logos has the form of a servant for those who are being introduced, as if they were to say, 'We saw him not having form or beauty' [Is 52.2], but to the perfect he comes in the glory of his Father [see Jn 1.14]."

103. Ps 15.10b.

104. Ps 88.49a.

being corrupted "sees corruption"; one who is not being corrupted "does not see corruption." This usage is similar to that concerning "knowledge" in customary scriptural usage. How do I speak about knowledge except by saying, "who did not know sin, was made sin on our behalf"?[105] Customary usage, to be sure, employs differently the term "knowledge of sin." The ordinary person is aware of what sin is, but Scripture "knows" differently. If, then, the one who has sinned knows sin, and the one who has not sinned does not know sin, it is evident that the one who knows Christ knows justice; the one who knows injustice is unjust; the one knowing injustice knows it, but he does not know Christ; he does not know justice, and all those who know sin do not know justice.

This concerns "*Nor will you allow your devout one to see corruption,*"[106] for it is necessary to examine together what is said peculiarly, contrary to the customary usage of ordinary people.[107]

10. "*You have made me know roads of life.*"[108] His humanity says, "*You have made me know roads of life.*" For the humanity ascends the roads of life, especially the road in heaven. This composite of the body, about which we have spoken these things, says: "*You have made me know roads of life.*" But perhaps it also speaks about you.[109] For he refers everything in you to himself, to you, I say, being a body that is a part of him, to make known roads of life, not "a road of life," but "roads of life"; not "roads of lives," but "roads of life." For life is one thing, and there are many roads leading to it: primary, secondary, tertiary, and last.[110] A primary road, the road by way of elements, leads to this life; if you

105. 2 Cor 5.21.

106. Ps 15.10b.

107. Origen discusses his digression to speak about the distinction between the ordinary usage and that of Scripture. We ordinarily speak of "being aware" or "knowing" something, but in scriptural usage we know by participation in what we know.

108. Ps 15.11a.

109. These words, like the rest of Psalm 15, are spoken in the persona of Christ; here it is Christ's humanity, the human composite assumed by the divine logos when he comes down to be with us, that says these words. These words are especially appropriate, not so much to Christ, who is himself the road, but to those believers who constitute his body, the Church.

110. Origen compares these roads of life to the Roman road system.

wish, Moses speaks a primary road. The elements, the law as a pedagogue, stewards, guardians,[111] all these are roads of life, but roads of life that do not lead at a short distance to life. For as many roads lead to the imperial city, some at a close distance, some at a farther distance, so some lead at a close distance, and some lead at a farther distance to "the life," who said, "I am the road."[112] But the one saying, "I am the road" leads to the God and Father of the Universe.

After this is "*You will fill me with rejoicing with your persona.*"[113] And concerning this it must be said, because the truly joyful things, of which Christ is full, have come to be from the fatherly persona contemplated by him. And he fills him with joyful things and especially what is referred to as his persona, the very thing that is a delight in his right hand,[114] which extends the right hand to Christ and the holy ones. Before arriving at the end, one does not completely comprehend the delight in the right hand of God, to whom is the glory and the might to the ages. Amen.

111. See Gal 4.1–4. Moses speaks a primary road, because the logos as road is embodied in the Old Testament. This passage is obscure.

112. See Jn 14.6.

113. Ps 15.11b. The final words "with your persona" can also be translated "with your face." See introduction, pp. 13–14.

114. Ps 15.11c.

HOMILY 1 ON PSALM 36

N DIVERSE and varied ways God, speaking in the proph-
ets,[1] sometimes teaches unspeakable and secret matters
in what is said, sometimes announces in advance about
the Savior and his visitation, and sometimes it is also possible
that he treats our behavior. As we approach each passage, we try
to set forth its distinct content. When they prophesy things that
are to come, when the content consists of secrets, when a passage is concerned with behavior, and thus here, as we begin the
Thirty-sixth Psalm, we find that the whole Psalm is concerned
with behavior; it is treating our soul, rebuking our sins, and recommending that we live according to the law.

Let us look at how the first passage reads: "*Do not make jealous
among those who do evil or be jealous of those who do a lawless act,
because they will swiftly be withered like grass and they will fall swiftly
like vegetables of new growth.*"[2] It teaches us through this to do two
sorts of things: first, not to make jealous among those who do
evil, but next, not to be jealous of those who do a lawless act.
Then it says what the consequence is for the one who makes
jealous among those who do evil: to be withered like grass and
to suffer this not slowly but swiftly; and the consequence for the
one who is jealous of those who do a lawless act: to fall like vegetables of new growth.

One must comprehend, then, what distinguishes "make jealous" from "be jealous."[3] The Greek wording is not ordinarily
employed either in literary or in colloquial Greek, but it seems

1. See Heb 1.1.

2. Ps 36.1–2.

3. "Be jealous" is a common word, *zēloō*. "Make jealous" is *parazēloō*, the same
verb stem with the addition of the preposition that, when attached to a verb, can
mean a number of things including "beside," "over," and "amiss."

to have been forced into service by translators wanting to translate the Hebrew statement and to set forth, as far as possible for human nature, the distinction between "making jealous" and "jealousy."[4] In order, then, to understand the unconventional signification of "*not make jealous among those who do evil*,"[5] we must gather terminology from many passages, for thus, by comparing spiritual things with spiritual things,[6] we shall be enabled to see what is indicated by "*not make jealous among those who do evil.*" It is written in the Song[7] in Deuteronomy, "They have made me jealous because of one who is not God; they have made me wrathful by their idols, and I shall make them jealous on account of one who is not a nation, with a nation[8] that lacks understanding; I shall make them wrathful."[9] But also in the Apostle, "Or will you make the Lord jealous? We are not stronger than he is, are we? All things are possible, but not everything is expedient."[10] Gathering the statements of these three passages, Deuteronomy, the Apostle, and the Psalm before us, we shall find what is signified by "*Do not make jealous.*"

Well, then, one who incites someone to jealousy would make him jealous. In the matter of usage, as it were, if one needs to take examples from human behavior, this bears mentioning:

4. The term *parazēloō* occurs only in the Septuagint and authors who cite the Septuagint. Origen suggests that the Septuagint translators coined the word, since he does not recollect its use in Greek literature.

5. Ps 36.1a.

6. See 1 Cor 2.13. Origen considered Paul's "comparing spiritual things with spiritual things" to assert a fundamental principle of Alexandrian grammar. "To clarify Homer from Homer" would entail finding the meaning of a word by a close comparison with other usages of that word in the Homeric corpus. See Bernhard Neuschäfer, *Origenes als Philologe*, 1:276–83.

7. The Song of Moses.

8. Origen also does not seem to have been aware that the same word in Greek, *ethnos*, which ordinarily translates the Hebrew word *goy*, the word that comes to mean "gentile," actually translates two different Hebrew words in Dt 32.21: namely, the word normally translated "people," *'am*, in the phrase about making jealous; and the word *goy* in the second, about making angry. Paul quotes the Septuagint translation, not differentiating the words, in Rom 10.19. The discussion of the Jews in Rom 10 was probably in Origen's mind, even though he does not explicitly refer to it. See also n. 16 below.

9. Dt 32.21.

10. 1 Cor 10.22–23.

there are some nasty, immoral women, dissolute in their inclination, who, unsatisfied with secrecy when they indulge in dissolute behavior, want it to be known even to their lovers' wives that their husbands are with them, wanting this to be known for this reason: so that they may kindle jealousy among them against themselves and disturb the other households. If you have understood the example of the woman who arouses jealousy in a spouse, you will understand that to arouse jealousy in someone and to kindle someone to jealousy is what it means "to make jealous." Because this is what is signified, he repeats it in the wording just cited from Deuteronomy: "They have made me jealous with one who is not God."[11] Because our God is a jealous god,[12] and jealous on the analogy of a husband who is jealous toward his own wife as a consequence of caring for her and being attentive to her, on the analogy of a husband not willing to put up with a wife's licentiousness, therefore it must be said that the sinner arouses jealousy, as it were, in God. One must hear all of these things in a very loose sense, like references to God's wrath, sleep, or sorrow, since the sole thing to be understood is how each of us represents God to himself. They, then, have "made me jealous"; they have moved me to jealousy; they made me jealous by worshiping what are not gods. Do you see what comes next? "By their idols."[13] That is, they excited me to anger by serving idols. "And I will make them jealous of what is not a nation."[14] For because only Israel were my people, and, being the only one, they were not jealous of my love of any other people, I will make them become jealous, and I will awaken jealousy in them by choosing a people without understanding alongside them, giving that people laws and making a covenant with them.

See if "they have made me jealous of what is not a god; they have made me angry over their idols, and I shall make them jealous of what is not a nation; I will make them angry over a nation without understanding"[15] does not amount to this: if you

11. Dt 32.21a.
12. Ex 20.5, Dt 5.9.
13. Dt 32.21b.
14. Dt 32.21c.
15. Dt 32.21.

see a Jew not at all moved by gentiles,[16] seeing their idolatry but neither hating their idolatry nor shunning them, but roused to hatred at a Christian, understand that the prophecy has been fulfilled that says, "I shall make them jealous of what is not a nation." For we are not a nation; a few of us from this city have believed, and others from other cities. We are in no way a nation. In the sense that the Jews were a nation and the Egyptians were a nation, in no way were Christians a nation, but gathered here and there from the nations. "I," then, "shall make them jealous of what is not a nation; I will make them angry over a nation without understanding."[17] From not being a nation, we have become a nation. We have become a nation from not being a nation, and the beginning of our calling occurred when we were not a nation, but gathering together has made us become a nation. And at the same time, those whose nation together rejected the visitation of Christ were made angry. Thus the prophecy from Deuteronomy was fulfilled.

But would the Apostle even say, "Or will we make the Lord jealous? We are not stronger than he is, are we?"[18] He says these things in the logos concerning sacrifice and idolatry; do we want to make the Lord jealous in eating things sacrificed to idols and to arouse his jealousy as Jews aroused jealousy in him on account of idolatry? Do we want to act in the same manner? If we were to arouse jealousy in someone, when we are stronger than the jealous one, incited by us to jealousy, we would not have taken much thought about what might occur, but if we were to bring about jealousy in someone stronger than we are, we bring about consequences for ourselves. Take, for instance, the example of the woman that I used just now. Let us say that one making another jealous is the wealthy mistress of a household and the one who is provoked to jealousy is some servant who counts for nothing. Even when she is moved to jealousy, she [the servant], not being stronger than the one who is making her jealous, has to put up with the aggravation. But if someone

16. *Goyim* can be either "nations" or the individuals who constitute those nations, "gentiles."

17. Dt 32.21.

18. 1 Cor 10.22.

makes a stronger woman jealous, for instance, a slave who does that to her mistress, she arouses anger, and she brings about consequences to herself, because the mistress of a household, when made jealous, can seek satisfaction.

The Apostle, then, wanting to turn us away from food offered to idols, says, "Or will you make the Lord jealous? We are not stronger than he is, are we?" If we make him jealous, are we able to endure his jealousy? If you ever see a man who does evil, see to it that you do not do anything to arouse jealousy against yourself. For being evil, he will not spare you when you do such things unintentionally for which he becomes jealous of you. For instance, if you want another example to understand what is said, perhaps that blessed man Abel acted at a bad time. He had made a sacrifice to God, but he provoked Cain to jealousy; he provoked to jealousy someone who would do evil to him. "And" because he provoked to jealousy someone who would do evil to him, "Cain rose up on Abel his brother and killed him."[19] Let us also look at what happened concerning David and Goliath and its effect on Saul. Because David came out of the line of battle and killed Goliath, girls came out and said, "David has killed in his ten thousands and Saul in his thousands."[20] If David had made this happen, he himself would have been provoking jealousy among those who do evil,[21] namely Saul. But in this case, it was not by his advice that the girls began to raise up the hymn and say, "David has killed in his ten thousands and Saul in his thousands."

For what it teaches us is something like this: the human race is prone to jealousy and is quickly aroused to that mental disturbance. See to it that you do not do such things as to make an evildoer jealous of you, since he plots against you out of hatred to kill you, so that all manner of evil will befall you, so that the same saying applies: "*Do not make jealous among those who do evil or be jealous of those who do a lawless act.*"[22] Do not incite someone else who is an evildoer to rise up against you because he is jeal-

---

19. Gn 4.8.
20. See 1 Sm 17.49–51 and 18.7.
21. See Ps 36.1.
22. Ps 36.1b.

ous of you, nor, on your part, be jealous of those doing a lawless act. How, then, being human, would he be jealous of someone doing a lawless act? For if, according to this, he should do a lawless act, a human being would be jealous of the one doing a lawless act either because of things that come about for the one doing a lawless act or on account of something that came about; sometimes someone is moved to be jealous of someone doing a lawless act. But I say it is something like this. Let there be someone who is rich through a lawless act and changes from being destitute to having great possessions; then his destitute neighbor, seeing him raised up so far off the ground as to be rich, is jealous to be rich himself. He is not jealous because he does a lawless act, but because he is rich. But it follows from being jealous of the man wealthy from a lawless act to be jealous of someone doing a lawless act, and he does a lawless act. But we, human as we are, need such commandments, for often, seeing those promoted to wealth or having come to worldly fame or having taken a noble marriage, we consider it remarkable, not seeing that he is rich from evil deeds or is famous because of sins or initiated the supposedly good marriage out of licentiousness, and we are jealous of making a similar marriage ourselves or of being entrusted ourselves with an honor similar to the honor for the one who received it for wickedness.

2. When we do such things, we are jealous of those who do a lawless act. Remember that the evildoers of whom we are jealous *"will swiftly be withered."*[23] If you also are jealous of them, you will swiftly be dried up. But keep in mind that, if you are jealous of those *"who do a lawless act,"* you will quickly *"fall like vegetables of new growth."* How, then, will those who do evil, of whom one ought not to be jealous, *"swiftly be withered like grass"*?[24] Hear Isaiah teaching you to despise worldly glory and all the fleshly pleasures. For he says, "All flesh is like grass and all its glory is as a flower of grass."[25] Look at the glory of the flesh: those who reigned were favorable to us thirty years ago. Their glory

23. Ps 36.2a.
24. See Ps 36.1–2.
25. Is 40.6.

was, as it were, a flower, but it was quenched; it was withered.[26] Certain others were rich; they came into honors; they walked about puffed up by the promotions they had received. These passed away, because they were withered like grass. "All flesh is like grass, and all its glory is as a flower of grass." But you, who have never come into the flesh's flower or loved the flesh, but loved God's logos and progressing in him, hear what endures for you: "but God's word stays to the age."[27]

He beautifully likens evildoers to grass, when he could have said a thousand things more. And here is a beautiful demonstration of this: grass is feed for livestock; in the same manner those who do evil are the feed of human beings when they misuse fame, wealth, good luck, and, so to speak, eat them up like grass.[28] And just as the just eat Paul, when he is bread—for not only is the Savior bread,[29] but also Paul, for it is written, "we all are one bread,"[30] and, as it were, imitating the Savior in being bread, Paul becomes nourishing to those who hear him—so the illustrious ones of the world are feed to the many and flatter them.[31] *"Because they will swiftly be withered like grass and they will fall swiftly like vegetables of new growth."*[32] Vegetables of new

---

26. This could be a reference to the reign of Alexander Severus, who became Roman Emperor in 222 at the age of 14 and reigned until 235. His mother, Julia Mammaea, who acted as regent at the beginning of the reign and seems to have retained power effectively, summoned Origen to Antioch for his teaching (*Hist. eccl.* 6.21) shortly before Origen settled in Caesarea. According to Eusebius, his successor, Maximinus Thrax, who overthrew Alexander, persecuted Christians because of their prominence in his predecessor's entourage (*Hist. eccl.* 6.28). Origen's *Exhortation to Martyrdom* was occasioned by this persecution. Christians at Caesarea would have remembered Origen's illustrious association with the imperial court.

27. Is 40.8.

28. It is not the fame and wealth that are likened to grass, but those famous, wealthy, and lucky people who serve as models of behavior for others. They fill those who "eat them up" rather than being nourished on substantive teaching like that of the Apostle Paul.

29. See Jn 6.35.

30. See 1 Cor 10.17.

31. The righteous imitate Paul and feed on his teaching. The righteous eat bread, the proper nourishment of human beings, while the many eat "feed" fit only for irrational livestock.

32. Ps 36.2.

growth bloom for a short time, and immediately fall. Such are those who do a lawless act.

Since "*as vegetables of new growth*" is repeated, we want to explain these vegetables, which differ from those about which the logos says, "but the one who is ill eats vegetables."[33] Accordingly, the river of the Egyptians is a water coming from below and watering "as a garden of vegetables."[34] The Egyptians are not a tree, not a vineyard, but the Egyptians are vegetables of new growth that swiftly wilt. And the Scripture in Exodus concerning the scourges shows the Egyptians swiftly collapsing like vegetables of new growth. And because Ahab was going to grow such vegetables in Naboth the Jezreelite's vineyard, Naboth chose to die rather than to allow his vineyard to be cut down by Ahab, when he said, "Let it be a garden of vegetables for me."[35] And he did this as a just man, in order not to allow the vine to be cut down by the lawless one.

But a vine is also in the hearts of us who believe in God, and a vineyard "in a horn in a rich place,"[36] and it is said against those hearing divine logoi: "I have planted you a fruitful vine entirely genuine."[37] Ahab, then, comes seeking to cut down this vine and to plant Egyptian vegetables[38] there, but let us imitate Naboth the Jezreelite and die rather than allow the genuine vines to be cut down from the fields of our souls, for the fields of the souls of just ones have a blessed vine. Therefore, it is said to Jacob by Isaac, "See, the odor of my son is as the odor of a full field that the Lord will bless. And God will give you from the dew of heaven and from the richness of the earth much grain and wine."[39] It is, then, a good thing to have vines and to dig a trench and to make a vat in it and to gather from the vines and to press out the grapes and to drink wine from the vineyards

---

33. Rom 14.2.

34. Dt 11.10.

35. See 1 Kgs 20.1–16.

36. Is 5.1.

37. See Jer 2.21. This is said "against," *pros,* those who hear it, because it is an oracle of judgment and one that may apply to those who listen to Origen.

38. See PS77H4.11 below.

39. Gn 27.27–28.

of Sorech,[40] so that we may say, "Your cup is the most strongly intoxicating."[41]

3. It is said here that those doing a lawless act will swiftly fall like vegetables of new growth, and after these things, because it says what it must not do, that is, "*Do not make jealous among evildoers or be jealous of those doing a lawless act,*"[42] then it says what to do, "*Hope in the Lord, and do kindness.*"[43] Do not provoke, so as to arouse jealousy among evildoers; do not practice such things so that, by being jealous of those doing a lawless act, you will be withered, but rather hope in the Lord and despise fame, wealth, and worldly goods. "*Hope in the Lord,*" but if you hope in the Lord, do not have any other hope, but hope from doing kindness.

"*Hope in the Lord and do kindness.*"[44] What is kindness? It is one of the fruits of the spirit, as the Apostle taught, saying, "The fruit of the spirit is love, joy, peace, long-suffering, kindness, goodness."[45] "*Do kindness,*" as if he said to a field, "Make this fruit," and, "Make that." Thus to you as one who hears the divine lessons, the logos says as if to a field, "*Do kindness and set up a tent on the land and be shepherded in its wealth.*"[46] Do not become like dried up grass; do not become like a wilted vegetable, but hope in the Lord and do kindness and set up a tent in the land. What sort of land? "The seed fell on the good land."[47] "*Set up a tent on the land.*" Become a farmer of land as Noah planted a vineyard—he farms the land in himself and is shepherded in its wealth—not so that you might set up a tent in such a land, for God does not want to be rich from the fruit of this land,[48] but

40. See Is 5.2. The Septuagint translation of Isaiah does not translate the obscure Hebrew term *sorēq*. Origen was apparently unaware that the same word had been translated in the Jeremiah citation above as *karpophoron*, "fruitful."

41. Ps 22.5. See PS15H1.9, n. 108 above. See also Origen, *Hom. Jer.* 12.1.

42. Ps 36.1.

43. Ps 36.3a.

44. Ibid.

45. See Gal 5.22–23.

46. Ps 36.3.

47. See Lk 8.8.

48. I.e., "this" land of Israel promised to the Hebrew people, in which Caesarea arguably belongs, but see PS15H1.6 above.

he says that my soul, if it is honorable,[49] is a good land. What is falling on good land bears fruit. It says, then, "*Set up a tent on the land*"; always be occupied with your own territory and inhabit your own land, so that you may be shepherded in its wealth, because "whatever a human being sows, that he will reap, because the one sowing in the flesh will reap corruption from the flesh, but the one sowing in the spirit will reap age-long life from the spirit."[50] If, then, you set up a tent on the land, you will be shepherded in its wealth. As sheep shepherded in the green shoot concerning which it is said, "In a place of new growth there he set up a tent for me,"[51] in the same manner also you, if you have comprehended this, will be shepherded in the wealth of your land, so that each of us may be shepherded, supplying from what he farmed.

4. "*Take enjoyment in the Lord and he will give you the requests of your heart*."[52] It is the usage of Scripture to introduce two human beings, employing in each case the same words that designate what pertains to the other, but I say what pertains to the worse even in relation to the better, and almost everything that pertains to the worse the better has also.[53] The lesser, this bodily one, eats, but there is a certain food also of the inner human being, about which it is said, "A human being shall not live upon bread only, but upon every utterance proceeding through God's mouth."[54] There is also a certain drink of the inner human be-

---

49. Origen here uses a pair of adjectives, "beautiful and good," *kalos kai agathos*, that, in Greek usage, described a free man of the privileged class. The linked adjectives do not imply a specifically Christian moral ideal and only occur together once in the New Testament, in Lk 8.15, a passage to which Origen is alluding here. Origen used them together in a positive sense, however, as did Philo and Clement of Alexandria. Origen had argued (in *Cels.* 3.63, where he found support in Plato, *Laws* 4.716.63) that being *kalos kai agathos*, properly understood, was best exemplified in Christian humility.

50. Gal 6.7–8.

51. Ps 22.2.

52. Ps 36.4.

53. The "outer human being" of our ordinary experience corresponds to a better "inner human being" (see Rom 7.22 and Eph 3.16). This is a principle of biblical interpretation that Origen expounds in greater detail in the *Comm. Cant.* Prol. and in *Dial.* 16.

54. Dt 8.3, cited in Mt 4.4.

ing, for we drink from the spiritual rock following,[55] and we drink the spiritual and holy water. There is a clothing of the outer human being. There is also a clothing of the inner human being. For if one is a sinner, one has put on a curse as a garment,[56] but if one is just, he hears, "Put on the Lord Jesus Christ[57] and put on bowels of mercy, kindness, humility, gentleness, long-suffering."[58] And why must I say the things of the inner human being are homonymous with those of the outer? A soldier has the whole armor according to the outer human being, and the soldier according to the inner human being puts on the whole armor of God in order to be able to stand against the devices of the devil.[59]

After many examples we come to the passage at hand, so that we may see what is shown by, "*Take enjoyment in the Lord, and he will give you the requests of your heart.*"[60] Just as it is possible for the outer human being to be nourished without actually enjoying it—it is possible also to enjoy, and the rich do enjoy—so also for the inner human being it is possible to be nourished only, and it is possible to enjoy as well. For someone only hearing exhortatory logoi is nourished, but the one dedicating himself to the interpretation of the law, to the narration of the prophets, to the solution of evangelical parables, to the clarification of apostolic logoi, the one who dedicates himself to these things enjoys the Lord and does not eat only as much as required for nourishment.[61] It teaches us, then, to enjoy the Lord. In fact, God, wanting us to have spiritual enjoyment from the beginning, planted the paradise of enjoyment[62] and it is graced with the "torrent of enjoyment" about which it says, "You drink them."[63] And enjoyment is in store for those who have lived well; despising bodily enjoyment, they will receive spiritual enjoyment. If you want to

55. 1 Cor 10.4.
56. See Ps 108.18.
57. See Rom 13.14.
58. See Col 3.12.
59. See Eph 6.11.
60. Ps 36.4.
61. Compare PS77H4.7 below.
62. See Gn 3.23.
63. Ps 35.9.

be persuaded about this from Scripture, there were a certain rich man and a destitute man in the same place, and the rich man took bodily enjoyment. The destitute man did not take bodily enjoyment but passed life in misery. The destitute man who took no enjoyment departed to the breast of Abraham, so that he might take enjoyment, and he was refreshed. The one who took enjoyment also departed. He went to the Gehenna of fire, as it was written in the Gospel.[64] The one who took fleshly enjoyment lacked good things. No one can take pleasure both in the flesh and in the spirit, but he either takes enjoyment in the flesh, so that he is deprived of enjoyment with Abraham as the rich man was, or he does not take enjoyment, but feasting on the bread of affliction[65] he eats as the destitute man did, there; after his condition changes from what it was here, he takes enjoyment. *"Take enjoyment in the Lord, and he will give you the requests of your heart."*[66]

Yet you will understand more clearly *"take enjoyment in the Lord,"* seeing the Lord and understanding that the Lord is "justice,"[67] the Lord is "truth,"[68] the Lord is "wisdom,"[69] the Lord is "sanctification."[70] If you take enjoyment in speculations of wisdom, if you take enjoyment in works of justice, you have fulfilled the command that says, *"Take enjoyment in the Lord."* And, fulfilling it, you will receive what is next, *"and he will give you the requests of your heart."*

It adds a necessary addition, not simply saying "your requests," but *"the requests of your heart."* You will understand what is said if, personifying each of the constituent parts of the body, you see how, by nature, it makes requests. Indeed then, the eye, if it had a voice, would say to you, "I request light; I request to see colors appropriate for me and pleasant to me. I flee from seeing colors that are confusing to me and inappropriate for me to see." If the hearing had a voice, it would say, "I request

64. See Lk 16.25–26.
65. Dt 16.3.
66. Ps 36.4.
67. See Jer 33.16 and 1 Cor 1.30.
68. See Jn 14.6.
69. See 1 Cor 1.24 and 1.30.
70. See 1 Cor 1.30. See PS36H2.1, n .3 below.

a melodious sound, a pleasant sound, but I do not request one that is harsh and unpleasant to me; but I flee it." Thus if the taste had a voice, it would say, "I request sweet things. I flee bitter things. I flee what does not please me but makes me sad." So also the touch, if it had a voice, would say, "I request to touch smooth things, to touch delicate things, to touch soft things, but I do not request to touch fire or rough or scratchy things." Why am I giving these examples? If you understand that there is an appropriate request for each of the senses and an aversion appropriate to its constitution, look at your heart, where your understanding is, where your governing faculty is, so that you may see what function the heart has for you and what the heart requests. As the eye requests light, as the smell fragrance, as the hearing melody, so the heart, the understanding, requests thoughts; it requests rational arguments; it requests intelligent things. If, then, you take enjoyment in the Lord, God will give you the requests of your heart.

5. After this it says, "*Reveal to the Lord your road, and hope in him, and he will do.*"[71] "Everyone who acts contemptibly hates the light and does not go to the light, so that his works may not be reproved, but the one doing truth goes to the light."[72] Accordingly, since the one who acts contemptibly hates the light and, insofar as it is up to him, hides what he does, that he acts contemptibly, so that he may not be reproved; he conceals his road and, as it were, puts a veil over it. If someone in this crowd sees such a thing to be the case, if any one of you somewhere among those being instructed and one somewhere among those of little faith becomes aware of himself as having committed fornication and wants the fornication not to be known, does he not, I say, cover up his road or hide it? It is evident that he covers up his road, the one he traveled. And yet the one who actually is temperate and bold when it comes to having lived well does not want to hide his own road, but he wants to make it manifest, so that it is manifest, not to human beings, so that he may not store up a payment from human beings,[73] but to make it manifest to

---

71. Ps 36.5.
72. Jn 3.20–21.
73. See Mt 6.5.

God. Therefore, it is said, *"Reveal to the Lord your road,"* not simply, "Reveal your road." Should, then, you be aware of contemptible actions on your part, do not hide them by not confessing, but by confessing, *"Reveal to the Lord your road, and hope in him, and he will do"*[74] what remains and cure you from wounds, which you have done to yourself by the sin.

6. If you reveal to the Lord your road and hope in him, understand what he will do for you: *"He will display your justice as light and your judgment as the noonday."*[75] Your justice, practiced by you in hiding but revealed to God, God will display as light and establish you as a just one who has been enlightened by the light of justice;[76] he will make a show of your light of justice to the heavens.[77] If one must speak in such terms, he will make his boast of you and say, "The justice is the light of my son who has received the spirit of adoption."[78] This light was hidden, since the one doing justice was not vainglorious, and, not being vainglorious, he hid his own justice in revealing his road to me. But I disclose and make evident the work of justice of my son, but also I make his legal decision as the noonday.[79] For all things that the just one judged have become not simply as light, but as the light of noonday, when the light is abundant at midday and when from dawn until dusk the sun is giving the peak light, the light of noonday. If you become honorable,[80] God will disclose your justice as light, and he will disclose your legal decision as the noonday, or he will disclose the judgment concerning you according to justice, and he will disclose the legal decision that he has concerning you as noonday. Having comprehended these things, may we beseech God, that he help us become such persons, both that our justice may be disclosed by him, God, as light and that the legal decision by him concerning us may be as noonday and as a bright and as a peak light in Christ Jesus, to whom is the glory and the might to the ages of ages. Amen.

74. Ps 36.5.
75. Ps 36.6.
76. See Mal 4.2.
77. Origen takes the promise to be eschatological. See Dn 12.3.
78. See Rom 8.15.
79. By divinization, we manifest God's light as Christ did.
80. *Kalos kai agathos.* See n. 49 above.

HOMILY 2 ON PSALM 36

HEN THE LOGOS is giving an order and saying, "*Be sub-ordinate to the Lord,*"[1] it is necessary to unfold and present by the logos, who, on the one hand, is subordinate to the Lord, and who, on the other hand, is not subordinated to him. Just as "not everyone who is saying to me, 'Lord, Lord,' will enter the kingdom of the heavens, but the one doing the will of my Father in the heavens,"[2] so not everyone who is saying that he is subordinate to the Lord, simply by saying so out loud, is doing this. To be truly subordinate to the Lord is characterized by works.

You will understand what is said when you gain knowledge of the Lord's devices.[3] The Lord Jesus Christ is justice.[4] No one who acts unjustly is subordinate to Christ, justice. The Lord Christ is truth.[5] No one is subordinate to Christ, the truth, who lies or holds false teaching. The Lord Christ is sanctification.[6] No one is subordinate to Christ, sanctification, when he himself is profane and defiled. The Lord Christ is peace.[7] No one is subordinate to Christ who is hostile or bellicose, unable to say, "I was peaceful with those who hate peace."[8] Therefore, in another

1. Ps 36.7a.

2. Mt. 7.21.

3. Greek, *epinoiai*. These are the various devices by which the divine logos meets the needs of fallen rational beings. Origen most fully discusses *epinoiai* in *Comm. Jo.* 1. See Trigg, *Origen*, 103–49. See also Marguerite Harl, *Origène et la fonction révélatrice du Verbe Incarné* (Paris : Éditions du Seuil, 1958), especially pp. 121–38.

4. See Jer 33.16 and 1 Cor 1.30.

5. Jn 14.6.

6. 1 Cor 1.30.

7. Eph 2.14.

8. Ps 119.7.

Psalm, understanding such a thing, the prophet says to his own soul, "Unless my soul were subordinated to God, because my patient endurance is from him."[9]

But as concerns "subordination," it does not at all signify this here, and, on the other hand, it does not mean the equivalent in other places. So when you read in the Apostle: "When all things are subordinated to him, then the Son himself will be subordinated to him who has subordinated all things to him,"[10] hear "when all things are subordinated to him" in a manner worthy of Christ's own subordination.[11] It must be, then, that, when all things have been subordinated to Christ, so that, with all things subordinated, he might present all things as an offering to the Father, then he is to be subordinated. For if something like this is not to be understood in that passage, something impious will be understood by those who have not grasped what is written: "When all things are subordinated to him, the Son himself will be subordinated to him who has subordinated all things to him." And one of those who do not understand will ask: "If the Son will be subordinated to the Father when all things have been subordinated to him, is the Son, then, not actually subordinated to the Father?[12] Even as we pray to be subordinated as soon as possible to the logos, has he not yet been subordinated?" But look at his great love of humanity and kindness: he does not

9. Ps 61.6. That is, I am able to be peaceful by participating in the logos, who is peace.

10. 1 Cor 15.28.

11. By "comparing spiritual things to spiritual things" (see PS36H1.1, n. 6 above), "subordination" (*hupotagē*), understood worthily (*axiōs*), implies the eschatological hope of assimilation to the divine logos, that is, divinization, not simply being subject to him. The model is the subordination of the Son to the Father in 1 Cor 15.28. In *Comm. Jo.* 6.57.296 Origen states that if we understand being subordinate to Christ "in a manner worthy of (*axiōs*) the goodness of the God of the universe, we will understand 'lamb of God removing the sin of the cosmos'" (Jn 1.29). See also *Princ.* 3.5.7.

12. Interestingly, in light of later criticisms of Origen for having a "subordinationist" understanding of Christ's relationship to the Father, putatively inconsistent with equality of the persons of the Trinity proclaimed by post-Nicene orthodoxy, what Origen would consider impious (*asebes*) is not the belief that Christ is subordinate, but the prospect that he might not be subordinate to the Father.

reckon himself subordinated, as long as there is anything not subordinated to the Father. He will count himself among those subordinated and be bold to say, "I am subordinated to God," when all things prove to be subordinated to the logos.

No one sinning is subordinated to the Lord. And even we, at the time of the sin, are not subordinated to the Lord, and we sin subordinated to Satan. The divine logos promises that "a spirit of power and love and restraint"[13] will come to exist among the just. But there is something opposite to power, something opposite to love, and something opposite to restraint; one having the opposites is not subordinated to the Lord. The opposite of power is powerlessness and weakness; the opposite of love is hatred; the opposite of restraint is licentiousness. No one having any of the things opposed to the just-mentioned good things is subordinated to the Lord, but, at the time of the impure behavior, one is subordinated to a spirit of sexual immorality, having abandoned being subjected to the spirit of restraint. At the time of hatred, speaking logoi of wrath or desire or anger, one is not subordinated to the spirit of gentleness. Therefore, looking at our whole life as a struggle between subordination to Christ and to those opposite to Christ, let us try to put up a struggle by prayers and by logoi[14] and in every way, so that we may never be subordinated to the devil and to evil, but that every practice and every logos and every reckoning of ours might bear the stamp of subordination to the Son of God.

But, granted that I have been subordinated to the Lord, what do I do concerning earlier occasions? On earlier occasions I was not subordinated to the Lord when I sinned. Once I have been subordinated, let me beg, let me beseech God concerning past sins. I must not beg concerning sins before I am subordinated to the Lord and have abandoned sin, for to ask for forgiveness of sins while still being in sin is utterly irrational. I often recall having said that supplication is the preeminent prayer concerning sins, whenever the one praying is enabled to say that he has abandoned sin in the past, "Do not remember our old lawless

13. 2 Tm 1.7.

14. The Psalms themselves constitute logoi that one can use in the struggle against the vices.

deeds."[15] "Be subordinated," then, "to the Lord," and, being subordinated and no longer sinning, beseech him concerning things that are no longer so.

2. "*Do not make jealous one who is prospering on his road, a man breaking the law.*"[16] It delineates what occurs in human affairs. For often, if we see an unjust person prospering and enjoying what would be considered good luck, we risk being caused to stumble when it comes to breaking the law, and we say: "Of what use is it to be just? The just are oppressed, but this person, even though unjust, has good luck; this person, though unjust, is rich; he is praised; he can do big things." Souls that are unsound when it comes to faith say these things concerning those who prosper in their road while breaking the law.

Because these things have come about and have been spoken concerning those who break the law and prosper in their lawless deeds, jealousies are generated of that variety, but perhaps also of a divine variety, for there comes about a certain jealousy even on the part of the divine according to what is said by the Apostle and according to what is said in the great song of Deuteronomy: "They have made me jealous on account of one that is not God."[17] The Lord comes to be made jealous by us. Let us not move the Lord by blaspheming. It must be reckoned that this age belongs to those who do not have any other hope. They prosper in it and have what are reckoned to be good things. "Our age" is not this one; we set sail to another age of life,[18] and "our age" is following this one. And it is not possible to have good things both in this life and in that one. For if someone has them in this, there, as one reproached, he will hear, "You took possession of your good things in your life."[19] But if one does not have them here, it is heard that one took possession of bad things in this age. Therefore, as things are, he is encouraged to be like Lazarus: "*Do not make jealous one who is prospering on his road, a man breaking the law.*"[20]

---

15. Ps 78.8.

16. Ps 36.7b.

17. See Dt 32.21 and 1 Cor 10.22.

18. Compare the "boat of this life" in Plato, *Laws* 7.803b.

19. See Lk 16.25.

20. Ps 36.7b.

3. Then, teaching about the disturbance that does not trouble some only, while not others, but, I venture to say, all human beings with the exception of someone perfect (should someone perfect be found), the logos is teaching: "*Put a stop to wrath and abandon anger.*"[21] For, considering all the passions, some do not occur in many people, and even people who happen to have them reject them. For example, ordinary people are cured from many deeds done out of licentiousness, and many who are making progress have even rejected them as well as many actions done out of greed, so that it is possible to find people who, while not perfect, are not greedy. One could say the like about many evil deeds. But this one wretched passion, wrath, burns up even those who seem to be thoughtful. Therefore, Solomon says in Proverbs: "Wrath destroys even the thoughtful."[22] Do not marvel, it says, if wrath enkindles the stupid, the evil, and the faithless, when wrath often moves even the one who is actually thoughtful. And it is possible that this is the sin of those who convey wood, hay, and straw into the building process.[23] It is necessary to "*put a stop*" on account of that fire concerning which it is written: "the fire will put it to the proof."[24] It is evident that it will last until the wood of wrath, the hay of anger, the straw of logoi of such passions are consumed. "*Put a stop,*" then, "*to wrath and abandon anger*"; for example, do not implement it or be moved by it, but abandon it. But we, despising what is said, abandon gentleness, but we do not abandon wrath. Let us take charge of ourselves as even prescribed in Deuteronomy,[25] so that, little by little, by being wrathful to a smaller extent, we may come to this: to be moved to wrath to such small extent that we achieve a state of not being disturbed by it at all. "*Do not make jealous,*" then, "*so*

21. Ps 36.8a.

22. Prv 15.1. See below PS75H.8 and PS81H.7. Origen shares in a Greek tradition that considered anger to be the most dangerous and intractable of human mental disturbances. See William V. Harris, *Restraining Rage: The Ideology of Anger Control in Classical Antiquity* (Cambridge, MA: Harvard University Press, 2001).

23. See 1 Cor 3.12.

24. See 1 Cor 3.13.

25. Emanuela Prinzivalli (GCSO13, 131 n. g) suggests an allusion to Dt 13.18, an exhortation to keep all the commandments.

as to have evil treatment."[26] Do not so move another to jealousy that you sin and are treated in an evil way because you moved another to jealousy.

4. "*Because those who do evil will be obliterated, but those who endure for the Lord, they will inherit the land.*"[27] It is apparent what things evil consists of: evil is a particularly bad thing alongside the remaining sins, so that, marvelously, the logos says that "sinner" is one thing and "evil one" another. "He will smash the shoulder of the sinner and the evil one."[28] And it says that the devil is not just a "sinner" but an "evil one," for the Savior, teaching us to pray, says that in the prayer we also ought to say, "deliver us from the evil one."[29] Some[30] have defined "evil" to be not unrelated to willful bad conduct. To act badly out of ignorance is one thing; to do so, as it were, because one is overcome is another; but to want to do badly is something different, namely "evil," and, because of this, he is called "the evil one." Upbraiding us, then, the Savior says: "If then you, being evil, know to give good gifts to your children."[31] And according to God in Genesis, the heart of human beings is inclined toward evil every day.[32] But "*those who do evil will be obliterated, but those who endure for the Lord, they will inherit land.*"[33] There is another land, which is called by some "Antichthon."[34] That is the one called "good" according to the Scriptures, "flowing with milk and honey,"[35] which the Savior promised to the gentle, saying, "Blessed are the gentle, for they shall inherit the land."[36] This is not "land," but "dry land," just as, again in the case of a certain heaven, this is not "heaven,"

26. Ps 36.8b.

27. Ps 36.9.

28. Ps 9.36.

29. See Mt 6.13.

30. Origen may have in mind Aristotle, *Nicomachean Ethics* 3.5, which argues that depravity (*mochthēria*) is voluntary.

31. Mt 7.11. The evil must be voluntary, and not due to ignorance; otherwise, we would not know to give good gifts when we choose to.

32. Gn 6.5.

33. Ps 36.9.

34. Aristotle, *On Heaven* (86.5), ascribes the postulation of Antichthon to Pythagoreans. In Origen's time the word could refer to the Southern Hemisphere.

35. See Ex 3.8, Dt 26.9.

36. Mt 5.5.

but "firmament."[37] For God knows a distinction between "firmament" and "heaven" or "heavens" and a distinction between "dry land" and "land." We strive on the basis of a promise of a genuine heaven, so that it is not called "heaven," but "firmament," nor is the true land called "land" but "dry land."

Who will inherit land? "*Those who endure for the Lord.*"[38] Perhaps we endure for one who is "endurance." For it is written, "And who now is my endurance? Is it not the Lord?"[39] And just as the Savior is "wisdom," he is "logos" as well; he is "peace"; he is "justice"; so he is "endurance."[40] And we become just by participation in him;[41] we become peaceable by participation in him; we become wise by participation in him; so we also become patient by participation in him. We have participation in the entire saving action of Christ, from whom it is possible to draw and to take patience, justice, wisdom, and all things that Christ is said to be in the Scriptures. So it is said, "*Those who endure for the Lord, they will inherit land.*"[42]

5. Yet next it asserts a secret beyond my hearing, beyond my tongue, and beyond my understanding. And it says something either about all sinners, or about one sinner. On this account it speaks of a "sinner" in the singular, because "*yet shortly the sinner will not even exist.*"[43] For shortly from the present time will be the completion and the fire chastising sinners after the completion that will make the sinner be no longer. How will the sinner be no longer? Let someone who can make an examination do so.

Only "*yet shortly the sinner will not even exist, and you will seek his place, and you will not find.*"[44] Not only will the sinner no longer exist, but even his place will no longer be. But what is the place

---

37. See Gn 1.8–9.

38. Ps 36.9b.

39. Ps 38.8.

40. See 1 Cor 1.24, Jn 1.1, Eph 2.14, 1 Cor 1.30. The Greek word *hupomonē* can be translated "patience" but always carries a connotation, not just of waiting, but of sticking it out in adverse circumstances. *Hupomonē* is the virtue of martyrs. "Endurance" is the closest English word.

41. On "participation" in justice, see PS67H1.10, n. 133 above.

42. Ps 36.9b.

43. Ps 36.10a.

44. Ps 36.10.

of a sinner? Things passing away! Heaven and earth will pass away with sin as it passes away, and the place of the sinner will pass away and no longer be. Let us hasten to do things that do not pass away, so that they may not pass away with things that pass away. For if we commit a sin that passes away, we shall pass away, but if we do justice that does not pass away, we shall not pass away, but we shall stay along with the justice that stays. We do, then, either things that pass away or things that do not pass away, and we are responsible ourselves for either passing away or not passing away. What does God do, if we have things that pass away? Does he not say to us, "Is not my hand strong to save, or was my ear too dull to hear? But your sins make a separation between me and you.[45] You will, then, seek his place and not find."

There are created things that have come to be on account of sin, and there are things fashioned that have come to be on account of sin for the benefit of those pure from sins. Do not marvel: there are even sinners on the land! This firmament came about so that it might separate the sinful deeds from the just deeds. Thus I hear: "Let there be a firmament in the midst of the water, and let it be a divider between water and water,"[46] between the sinless one praising God above the heavens and the water below the firmament, the water against which is our wrestling.[47] The former waters even see God; the latter, which is the abysses, the multitude of water, does not see God. For it is written, "The waters have seen you, God; the waters have seen you and feared; the abysses were disturbed."[48] The abysses, over which there was darkness, do not have peace, according to what has been said, "darkness was over the abyss,"[49] to which the demons go out as a suitable place because they have been disturbed and they make disturbance happen. For they begged that he not command them to go out into the abyss.[50]

6. *"But the gentle will inherit land."*[51] To those from Valentinus's

45. See Is 59.1–2.
46. Gn 1.6–7. See PS73H3.1 below.
47. See Eph 6.12.
48. Ps 76.17.
49. See Gn 1.2.
50. See Lk 8.31.
51. Ps 36.11a.

party and those of certain other heresies who suppose that the Savior says what was not said in the old Scriptures, we learned from one of the elders[52] to present this as an argument against them in teaching. For see in what is said in the Gospel, "Blessed are the gentle,"[53] what was already said through David by the same spirit which was also in Christ. For the Holy Spirit, which was later in our Savior, was present earlier. "*The gentle will inherit land.*" The prophecy adds to what is written in the Gospel; not only will the gentle inherit land, but "*they will also delight in fullness of peace.*"[54] Bodily, earthly, and fleshly human beings delight in getting drunk, and they delight in foods destroyed by the belly that is itself destroyed,[55] even though destroying that is not what they intend at the time; but, instead of these delights, which they despise, the holy will delight in fullness of peace. The delight is peace, and not a small peace, but fullness of peace, which the logos promises to be in the days of Christ. For the fullness of peace will be in the days of Christ, "until the moon is restored."[56] And those who hear "*will also delight in fullness of peace, put a stop to wrath, and abandon anger*"[57]—the gentle, that is—will "*inherit the land and delight in fullness of peace.*" And it must be known that wrath and peace are diametrically opposed to each other. Wherever there is wrath, there is no possibility of gentleness. Wherever there is gentleness, there is no possibility of wrath. Wherever there is, then, gentleness, there is a delight of fullness of peace. For the gentle will delight, inheriting peace, and the gentle will delight, inheriting the land in fullness of peace.

7. Next, "*the sinner watches closely the just and grinds his teeth on his account.*"[58] Just as light and darkness are naturally opposed, so is the sinful person to the just. And if you should ever see someone hating a just person, do not hesitate to say about the one who hates him, that he is a sinner. If you should see some-

---

52. This could be a reference to Clement of Alexandria, who refuted Valentinians.

53. Mt 5.5.

54. Ps 36.11b.

55. See 1 Cor 6.13.

56. Ps 71.7.

57. Ps 36.8a.

58. Ps 36.12.

one persecuting one who understands well, do not hesitate to say about the one persecuting that perhaps he is not only a sinner, but an evil one.

"*For the sinner watches closely the just and grinds his teeth on his account.*" "Grinds his teeth" is not to be heard as referring entirely to the body, if this possibility is ever produced by the sinner's opposition to the just; see arguments of evil intent, guile, and silence—as to voice, but also a scream in the heart as it deliberates evil against the just—because "grinding his teeth against them" is fulfilled. But when the sinner does these things against the just, "*the Lord will laugh at him, because he sees in advance that his day will come.*"[59] For he sees the day of the sinner coming, because the sinner will no longer exist.[60]

8. "*Sinners have brandished a sword. They have strung their bows to bring down the destitute and poor.*"[61] Not all sinners have a bodily sword, but maybe, just as there is a "whole armor of God" and a "breastplate of justice" (and a "blade of the spirit" and a "shield of faith" are mentioned),[62] so there is a whole armor of the devil that a man who is a sinner puts on. But seeing the whole armor of God, setting its opposite over against each named piece of equipment in the whole armor, you will see the whole armor of the devil, and you will recognize that both soldiers, God's and the devil's, put on the breastplate. The breastplate of justice is from the whole armor of God, but there is also a "breastplate of injustice." And there is a "helmet of salvation," and the sinner also puts on a "helmet of destruction." There is a certain "equipment of the Gospel," and there is something opposed to it; "their feet run to injustice,"[63] so their footwear is evidently equipped for sin. There is a "shield of faith"; there is a "shield of unbelief." Just as there is a "blade of the spirit," there is a "blade of the evil spirit." This is what sinners brandish. Let us put away the arms of sin, which the Apostle refers to as "arms of

---

59. Ps 36.13.

60. The one who is now a sinner will no longer be one. See PS67H1.9 below.

61. Ps 36.14.

62. See Eph 6.11–17.

63. Is 59.7a: "their feet run to evil" shows that there must be an equivalent on the devil's side to the "preparation of the Gospel," the footwear in the whole armor of God, which enables sinners to "run."

injustice,"[64] and take up the "arms of justice on the right hand and on the left."[65]

"*Sinners,*" then, "*have brandished a sword*"[66] because they have sin at hand and are ready to do it, not hiding the sword of the evil spirit in a scabbard of sin, when sinners brandish a sword. Thus also they draw their bows. And the just also have a bow; they have arrows, and Christ Jesus is their arrow—"he has placed you as a chosen arrow."[67] Likewise, sinners have arrows. Their logos is an arrow: it holds the poison of sin; it wounds one who is not fully armed. If the sinner's arrow is able to reach me, it is apparent that I have not made use of the shield of faith.

"*They have,*" then, "*strung their bows to bring down the destitute and poor.*"[68] Sinners know that they cannot bring down a rich person; therefore, they do not even start to deal with him, but every plot is against the destitute, just as the lion lying in wait lies in wait to capture the destitute.[69] Therefore, since "the ransom of a man's soul is his individual wealth, but a destitute person does not experience threat,"[70] let us be rich in logos,[71] in wisdom, in good works,[72] casting off the wealth of sin, so that we may become invulnerable and impervious to plots from the arrows of the evil one, quenching them all with the shield of faith, through Christ Jesus our Savior, to whom is the glory and the might to the ages of ages. Amen.

---

64. Rom 6.13. The word Paul uses here and in the passages alluded to in the note below is *hopla*, the individual pieces of armor or "arms" that together constitute a whole set of armor, a "*panoplia.*" Origen sets out to establish here that, although the Bible does not explicitly refer to a *panoplia* of the devil, we can infer its existence from references to individual items. This constitutes an ensemble that we "cast off" when we put on the whole armor of God, an action that, according to Paul, is the equivalent of "putting on Christ" (Rom 13.14, also Gal 3.27).

65. 2 Cor 6.7. See also Rom 13.12–14.

66. Ps 36.14a.

67. Is 49.2. Origen takes up this theme in more detail in PS76H3.5 below.

68. Ps 36.14b.

69. See Ps 9.30.

70. Prv 13.8.

71. See 1 Cor 1.5.

72. See 2 Cor 9.8.

HOMILY 3 ON PSALM 36

E WERE STARTING to speak recently about the swords and bows of the impious and about the whole armor of God, and that all human beings are armed, all human beings, that is. Now I add what was missing in the logos.[1] Those capable of not sinning and of making amends—for children cannot make use either of the whole armor of God or of the whole armor of the devil—and, on the other hand, those who are sinning in speaking, acting, and thinking or those who understand what is fitting and accomplish it, these all have, when they sin, the whole armor of the devil and the arms of injustice; but when they act well, the whole armor of God. Each of the items in the whole armor of God was mentioned, from which we step onward in the logos to distinguish, by contrast, each item in the whole armor of the devil.

"*Sinners have,*" then, "*brandished a sword,*"[2] and we have received information concerning the sword of sinners and the blade of the just. For, in fact, the Apostle said, "And the blade of the Spirit, which is an utterance of God."[3] Accordingly, if the Spirit, which is the utterance of God—for the utterance of God is spiritual—is the blade of the just, it is apparent that the adverse spirit and the utterance of sin is the blade of the sinner. Indeed, the sinner, to the extent that he stays silent, has this utterance or spirit, as it were, in a scabbard, as someone would hold a sword in his scabbard; but when unsatisfied with the mere possession of evil—for it must restrict and withhold it from action, either because of being attacked or to prevail in an encounter—he brandishes the sword.

1. See PS36H2.8 above.
2. Ps 36.14a.
3. See Eph 6.17.

And if you want to understand by an example how sinners brandish a sword, notice gentiles fighting and saying despicable utterances to each other with wrath and strife. For then you will apply the wording to them, and you will say, "*Sinners have brandished a sword.*" But if I, who am said to be faithful, open my mouth in confused logoi, blasphemies, back-biting, false testimony, and other things so as not to prove myself just and so that I am condemned, even I, although termed a faithful person, brandish the sword as a sinner at the time of committing such sins.[4]

It is good, then, not to have a sword of sin, but, next best, having one, is not to brandish it, but to make it stay idle. For something surprising comes about from not brandishing the sword of sin; it does not just rust and grow dull, but even wears down, for when the sword of sin is idle, it finally disappears.[5] For it is appointed by the Lord for sin to disappear. If, then, we are blessed by not engaging in sin or brandishing the sword from its sheath, we shall destroy the sin and have no need of fire, of the chastisement of darkness, of those things in a threat as being laid up for those who have lived badly. But if we do not hear monitory and healing logoi, it is apparent that fire remains for us, so that we may come to the fire where every work is proved. For, as regards each work, the fire will prove what sort of thing it is. "If someone's work remains after being tested, he will receive a reward," and so on (so as not to repeat the whole passage).[6] Should Paul go to the fire, nonetheless, Paul will hear, "If you go through fire, the flame shall not consume you."[7] Should Peter come to the fire, nonetheless the fire will not touch him. But should there be any sinner, he goes like Paul and Peter to the fire, but he does not pass through the fire as Paul and Peter do. And just as the Hebrews had gone into the Red Sea and the Egyptians went into the Red Sea, but the Egyptians were

---

4. "Brandishing a sword" is a gesture of anger. Origen consistently teaches that when Scripture rebukes sinners, one should first look at oneself.

5. Being slow to anger is biblical (e.g., Prv 16.32 and Jas 1.19) and Stoic advice; according to Seneca (*de Ira* 2.29), "the greatest cure for anger is delay."

6. See 1 Cor 3.13–14.

7. Is 43.2.

drowned in it,[8] in the same way as the Egyptians, we shall be drowned in the river or lake of fire,[9] when we hold sinful actions under Pharaoh's command; as the Hebrews did, we shall pass through, with walls of fire standing to our right and to our left; if, hearing God's logoi, we are faithful to him and to his law, we shall also follow the pillar of fire and the cloud of light.[10]

2. "*Sinners,*" then, "*have brandished a sword, they have strung their bow.*"[11] The Apostle did not name "bows," but, when he described the whole armor, he did not say God's bows, so that from opposites—as we had done earlier—we come to the bows of sinners. I seek, then, a Scripture offering me indications for the interpretation of "they have strung their bows." I find[12] such wording in the Psalms: "See, the sinners string a bow; they prepare arrows in a quiver to strike down the well-disposed of heart in a moonless night."[13] Like a quiver, the heart of the impious has been filled with poisoned arrows. Each, in accordance with his particular sin, supplies arrows. Next he readies arrows "in a quiver to strike down." Where? "In a moonless night." For these bowmen are not in light, but in darkness. And whom do they shoot? Those "well-disposed of heart." It is apparent at the same time that the logos is not about human sinners, but about powers.[14] These, actually, want "to strike down the well-disposed of heart on a moonless night." Therefore, as many as want to be well-disposed of heart watch night and day, for these have made ready to strike them down. These have made ready bows and arrows to strike down, so they, always on watch, guard their own heart.

8. See Ex 14.21–29.

9. See Dn 7.10 ("river of fire") and Rv 20.14 ("lake of fire"). The connection between the crossing of the Red Sea and the Christian journey and between Pharaoh and Satan must have seemed so obvious to Origen that he could move effortlessly from the one to the other, perhaps because the "lake" of fire already suggests a body of water.

10. See Ex 13.22.

11. Ps 36.14.

12. See Mt 7.7.

13. Ps 10.2.

14. Actual human beings would not try to shoot someone down "in a moonless night," since they could not aim at anyone in the dark.

3. Now perhaps I am finding something new in the passage, so that I may not be constantly using these, but, by the renewal of the mind[15] concerning first things, the next ones may be found.[16] I say that, just as the Savior is God's arrow—according to the saying, "He has placed me as a chosen arrow"[17]—and on the analogy of the Savior as God's arrow, Moses and the rest of the prophets, the apostles of Christ, the just—wounded by the chosen arrow, so that those who are wounded say, "I am wounded by love"[18]—so, on the analogy of the chosen arrow, the antichrist would be the arrow of the evil one, but on the analogy of the arrows under Christ, there would be arrows of the evil one, for example: the "false prophets,"[19] the "false apostles."[20] I even say that all the just, being imitators of Christ,[21] are God's chosen arrows, serving human beings for benefit and salvation. So, in fact, all sinners are arrows of the devil. If, then, a sinner does something against you or says something against you, pity that person for making himself available, so that the evil one may use him as an arrow against you. Meanwhile, guard yourself, and take up the shield of faith, so that you may be enabled to quench "all the fiery arrows of the evil one."[22]

And perhaps I can, on the evidence of the exposition furnished,[23] apply it to "So that you may be able to quench all the fiery arrows of the evil one." See a woman scheming against you, if she is not a fiery arrow, having fire in her mouth, so that she may talk and burn you, having fire in her hand—for it touches

---

15. See Rom 12.2.

16. Possibly an allusion to 2 Cor 5.17.

17. Is 49.2. See PS76H3.5 below.

18. See Song 2.5. See Catherine Osborne, *Eros Unveiled: And the God of Love* (Oxford: Oxford University Press, 1994), 52–85, for a discussion of this topic in Origen and its relation to Platonic understandings of eros.

19. A common New Testament term, as in Mt 7.15, though it does not occur in Paul's epistles.

20. See 2 Cor 11.13. The ability to express himself in actual biblical terminology whenever possible reassures Origen that he is on the right track in his analogies.

21. See 1 Cor 11.1.

22. Eph 6.16.

23. This is the exposition that was "furnished" when Origen, relying on Jesus's promise, "found" it after "seeking" it from God. See n. 12 above.

you and wounds you—fire in her whole body, in her whole soul. Thus if you see someone moved to wrath against you and goading you to sin, see him as a fiery arrow of the evil one, sharp and destructive from the devil's bow against you. And if you see another doing anything whatsoever so that you will be goaded into evil, so that you will be induced to sin, see in a sensible manner that these are all arrows of the evil one.

God's arrows are few, but the evil one has many arrows: the peoples, whole armies, whole cities are arrows of the evil one. Would that the evil one has reached no more to make arrows of them! But I now fear even for those here, for myself, that at some time the devil may use me to make others stumble, that he may want to use me against the souls of human beings. For one who is caused to stumble is wounded, apparently caused to stumble either because of a false brother or because of a gentile; but is he wounded by someone, or by the fiery arrow that the devil sent out from his own bow?

And just as God placed his bow in the cloud,[24] so that a storm would cease and a flood might not be produced, so, by reverse logic, the evil one makes use of a bow, not so that a storm may cease, but so that tranquility may cease from a soul and that he might quench peace and awaken war and make a storm. If you see one beset and distressed by passions, do not hesitate to say that the devil has taken his bow; he has let loose an arrow against such a person, so that he might wound those who are well-disposed of heart; but those completely armed with the whole armor of God are not wounded.

4. "And sinners," then, "*have brandished a sword; they have strung their bow to strike down destitute and poor.*"[25] I spoke earlier about the destitute and poor; they especially strike down the destitute and the poor. And it can be interpreted in a second way. It did not suffice "*to slay the well-disposed of heart*";[26] there is also a plot against "the well-disposed of heart." On the analogy of the well-disposed of heart, the delivery of an interpretation for the destitute and poor must be sought. Maybe, then, the des-

---

24. See Gn 9.13–16.
25. Ps 36.14.
26. Ibid.

titute and poor are brothers of the well-disposed of heart. For the destitute are those called blessed by Jesus, about whom he said, "Blessed are the destitute, because the kingdom of God is yours."[27]

"*Sinners,*" then, "*have brandished a sword, they have strung their bow to strike down destitute and poor, to slay the well-disposed of heart.*"[28] If you look at someone caused to stumble, and you see him to have been overpowered by sin, you see that that person has been slain and his blood flows, for his life-giving power has been destroyed. And if it is said in Genesis, "I will require the blood of your souls from every brother and from every beast,"[29] do not reckon that it is said about such blood as much as about intelligible blood. For when you cause someone to stumble and the blood flows out of the one caused to stumble and his life-giving power is destroyed as it flows out, the blood will be required from the brother. And why from a beast? When a faithful person causes you to stumble, the brother is the one from whom the blood is required; your brother is the one spilling your blood. Therefore, it is said, "from a brother's hand I shall require the blood." When, nonetheless, a wild, wicked, and opposed power, even a human being alien to the faith of Christians, wants to harm you and has been able to spill the blood of your soul, it is a beast from whom the Lord next requires blood; it is not, in fact, first from a beast, but first from a brother that the blood of a brother was spilled, but that spilled blood is required.[30] You see also in Ezekiel that a certain "look-out" is said to be placed by God's logos, and it says that the look-out, if he does his task, is not liable for the blood of someone who has sinned after hearing him, but if he does not do what he is ordered, it says that he is liable for the blood of the someone who is lost: "I will require his blood from the hand of the look-out."[31] Therefore, let all

27. Lk 6.20.

28. Ps 36.14.

29. See Gn 9.5, which establishes that the blood is life-giving power for which both beasts and human beings are held responsible for spilling or wasting.

30. The first blood spilled in the Bible is that of Abel, which God requires from his brother, Cain. Christians must first take care not to cause each other to stumble, before blaming demons or those outside the faith.

31. Ezek 3.18.

fear that anyone's blood should ever be required from us. The look-out has all the more reason to fear, since the prophet says about him in particular: "I will require his blood from the hand of the look-out."

I have said these things to cover "*strung their bow to strike down destitute and poor*."[32] It was necessary to resume the interpretation and say a deeper thing after saying a simpler thing. "*To slay the well-disposed of heart*" made it necessary to set forth the one slain whose blood spills or the one liable for his blood.

5. But let us see what will come about for those sinners and those who use the devil's sword and the bows of the evil one: "*Their sword would enter into their own heart, and their bows would be broken*."[33] This opposing spirit, this evil logos, which the unjust brings forward in a human manner "*to slay the well-disposed of heart*," then comes to the one who has inflicted a wound in a manner analogous to what becomes of something spoken by the just. What is said? Say,"your peace will bend back to you."[34] Thus if the sword of the impious wants to slay the well-disposed of heart, but the well-disposed of heart takes care of himself, their sword will enter into their own heart, and so also the bows will be broken.

6. "*A little is better for the just beyond much wealth of sinners*."[35] Speaking about the sinner, it adds to the teaching about the sinner, so that, when we see it, we may be protected against being sinners, and it says this: "*A little is better for the just beyond much wealth of sinners*." The wording by itself holds something useful for the more naïve, which we shall present first, but it also has something said secretly for those knowing how to hear Scripture deeply. The simpler goes like this: the just and the unjust make a living, and both just and unjust take thought about how to obtain what they need; but the just do not seek property so much as justice,[36] and they either do not make a living, where

32. Ps 36.14.
33. Ps 36.15.
34. Lk 10.6.
35. Ps 36.16.
36. Mt 6.33 informs Origen's discussion of giving the kingdom of God priority over making provisions for livelihood. Clement of Alexandria makes a similar argument in *Paed.* 2.120.2.

they have an opportunity to acquire unjustly what they need, or they make a living without injustice, so that they tinge their livelihood with justice. Of course, the unjust paying no thought, any of them, to what is just, have, as a whole, been inclined to acquire as much property as they can without seeking as to whether they gain it well, whether it is with justice, whether it is so done that they may remain without reproach in Christ's judgment. And by strictly seeking this, for the sake of possession, but not for justice, they accept it as a possession that injures. Of two outcomes, having a small share with justice and a large one with injustice, the small one is better for the just beyond much wealth of sinners, since, on the whole, the possession comes from injustice. I reckon this is why the Savior, as Savior, said, "mammon of injustice" in, "Make friends for yourselves from the mammon of injustice."[37]

These things address the statement as it stands, but let us also see what has been held in reserve. Those of us who seem to be occupied with logos have most need of it and, again, the simpler of those who have believed. There are some who, in the course of life, have been educated in the education[38] of the cosmos and have known extensively the learning of this age, so that the wording is preeminently for their benefit, because it is not stupid; but if one is a lover of logos, sometimes it is possible to find such people filled with all bad things, being rich in this expressive logos, being rich in learning, being poor in justice, and poor in good deeds. In fact, I often know orators, teachers of literature, and those who give promise of philosophy and dialectic who are not only idol-worshipers, but also persons who sleep with boys, frequent prostitutes, and commit adultery. But it is possible to see someone acting[39] as a member of the

---

37. Lk 16.9. "As Savior," Christ alerts us that wealth usually comes from injustice.

38. *Paideia,* the course of learning prescribed for the Greco-Roman elite.

39. An actor, *hupocritēs,* the word that gives us "hypocrite." An actor in Origen's time would be a mime, playing his role by actions rather than by words. In the Gospels this word is used negatively of those who are "putting on an act." Clement of Alexandria uses the word in a neutral sense, as it appears to be used here, in *Protr.* 1.1.3. See PS81H.3 below.

Church, faithful, but in some manner stupid: he cannot open his mouth,[40] but he fears God. Held in custody[41] by fear, he does not sin, but holds back from sins, while the wise man of this world does not hold back. Accordingly, comparing these to each other, the logos says, "*A little is better for the just beyond much wealth of sinners,*" so that the wisdom of this age[42] would be the wealth of sinners, in which human beings of this age are wealthy. But "*a little for the just*"—because it is possible for the just with a few utterances or none at all to make a presentation by the logos—"*a little is,*" then, "*better for the just beyond much wealth of sinners.*"[43]

If someone actually were enabled both to have wealth and not to have the wealth of a sinner, but to have no small wealth of a just person, someone rich in good works,[44] but destitute when it comes to logoi, would still be labeled "just" because of beneficial intention and the works he had been enabled to perform. If, then, "*a little is better for the just beyond much wealth of sinners*"[45] should be said in figurative language, do not reckon that figurative language of "*little for the just*" goes so far as to include every logos; for what place would there be for "in all logos and in all knowledge"?[46] But this comparison, "*a little is better for the just be-*

---

40. Presumably, the simple believer "cannot open his mouth" because, unlike the educated person, the "stupid" believer has nothing to say that anyone would listen to.

41. *Paidagōgoumenos*, like *hupocritēs* above, echoes Clement of Alexandria. The *paidagōgos* was a servant charged with accompanying a child and keeping him out of trouble. In Gal 3.24–25 Paul spoke of law as having the role of a *paidagōgos* before the coming of Christ. Clement ascribes the role of *paidagōgos* to Christ, the divine logos, who reforms the morals of new Christians, infants in the faith. At this stage of Christian life, fear is the only effective motivation: "For fear guards those who cannot bear the liberty of adoption from acting outrageously" (Clement of Alexandria, *Paed.* 3.45.1). For Clement, as for Origen, growth in Christ eventually replaces fear with love as a motivation. Clement associated this level of Christian life with faith, which growth will replace with knowledge (*gnōsis*). See, for example, Clement of Alexandria, *Strom.* 2.9.45.1–2 and *Strom.* 7.7.57.4.

42. See 1 Cor 2.6.

43. Ps 36.16.

44. See 1 Tm 6.18.

45. Ps 36.16.

46. When it comes to logos, "a little" is good, but much more is even better. Origen must assume that his hearers will remember that the Corinthians have

yond much wealth of sinners," is between the unbelievers of this age and those who are believers, but stupid. Above both is the wealth of the just when it is "much." Perhaps the rich man Abraham is a token, but the riches of Paul were no longer a token, because he said concerning others, "you have been enriched in all logos and in all knowledge," while he himself was far richer, and also told others to "be rich in good works."[47] Paul, then, was rich in every logos and in every knowledge and in every good work. "In all logos" means something like this: he[48] had a logos in Genesis, in Exodus, in Leviticus, in Numbers, in Deuteronomy, and so on, both in the old Scriptures and in the gospel ones. That person was rich "in all logos." For it is possible for someone to be rich, not in every logos, but in some one logos. For example, someone is sufficiently furnished with the gospel Scriptures, but untrained in the law. This person is rich in one logos, the one related to the gospel, if such were possible.[49] If someone is rich in furnishing the law, but not so rich when it comes to the apostles, that person is not rich in every logos, but in every legal logos. If someone is actually prepared in all the Scriptures, so as to be ready to give a logos concerning all the Scriptures and to live according to the true logos in all the Scriptures, such a person is rich in every work and every logos. It is concerning this wealth that "his personal wealth is the ransom of a man's soul."[50] But, being a destitute person when it comes to the opposite destitution, he is not subject to the warning: "*A little is better for the just beyond much wealth of sinners.*"[51]

------

been "*enriched* in all logos and in all knowledge," so that 1 Cor 1.5 provides a scriptural basis for understanding "wealth" in a figurative sense to include intellectual capital. See *Cels.* 7.21 for a further discussion of riches.

47. 1 Tm 6.18. Abraham's wealth was a token (*sumbolon*) of intellectual wealth, but Paul's wealth was the thing itself.

48. Grammatically, the antecedent of "he had" must be Paul, but Origen knew that Paul could not have known the New Testament we have. Paul is still the model for the believer who now knows the whole Bible.

49. Origen hesitates to allow that one can master the New Testament without knowing the Old.

50. Prv 13.8. "Personal" is *idios*, "pertaining to oneself."

51. Ps 36.16. By positing that Scripture distinguishes two kinds of wealth and poverty, Origen reconciles passages that value wealth with ones that caution against it.

7. "*Because the shoulders of sinners will be broken.*"[52] Who can take a stand on the wording, even if he were forced to by stupidity? A few of the things written can disturb even the utterly lowly and one who does not want to step up from the letter; they can abash those who have a preconceived bias: "*the shoulders of sinners will,*" then, "*be broken.*" Does the holy person threaten witnesses, or even actual sinners, that their shoulders will be broken, and say, in another passage, "Break the shoulder of the sinner and of the evil one"?[53] Does it indeed say this because this shoulder[54] of the sinner is broken? But we do not, in every case, see this occurring; everything except this comes about. But if you were to see the force and power of the impious person broken, so that he cannot extend his hand—for it is broken—to a good deed, you will see "*the shoulders of sinners are broken,*" and the one who breaks the shoulders of sinners is the devil. For he breaks and intends to do this, when God's soldiers, being noble, have their shoulders broken. This can clarify "*because the shoulders of sinners will be broken.*"

When it comes to "Break the shoulder of the sinner and of the evil one" spoken in a prayer to God, the logos also requires another explanation; nonetheless, even there someone who has intelligence will not eliminate the interpretation delivered earlier. For someone will say that, just as the devil says to the Lord, "Send forth your hand and touch all that he has, he will surely bless you to your face,"[55] and he receives the approval and Job says, "The Lord's hand is touching me,"[56] so the one who can clarify how these things are said in Job will also be able to clarify the statement of the prayer that says, "Break the shoulder of the sinner and of the evil one,"[57] and what was delivered concerning "*shoulders of sinners will be broken.*"[58]

---

52. Ps 36.17a.

53. Ps 9.36.

54. Origen was probably pointing here to his own shoulder. See PS77H8.4, n. 35 below.

55. Jb 1.11.

56. Jb 19.21.

57. Ps 9.36.

58. Ps 36.17a. Origen's point seems to be that the devil is going to be doing the actual breaking even when we ascribe the action to God. See PS77H9.1 below.

8. *"But the Lord supports the just."*[59] The weak require support, but every human being is weak; every human being, insofar as it is up to him, falls down. Therefore, then, it is written, "the Lord supports the just." In another Psalm, "the Lord supports all those who fall and sets straight all who stray."[60] Let us just stay awake and watch, if we are ever aware that we are about to fall, and let us pray to God, and he will send the logos supporting us.

9. *"The Lord knows the days of the blameless, and their inheritance will be to the age."*[61] According to the Scriptures, as we have often observed and said, the Lord does not know all things, but only those that are good, for he does not know evil things, as they are unworthy of his knowledge. We adduced, "If someone among you is a prophet or a spiritual person, let him recognize the things I write you, that they are of God, but if someone does not know, he is not known."[62] We were also familiar with, "but now, knowing God, or rather being known by God."[63] We have added, "The Lord knows those who are his, and let everyone who names the name of the Lord depart from injustice."[64] But, in any event, may it be found that the impiety of sinners is known, because, actually, it is completely known as good! But if this does occur, the Lord does not know the days of sinners, but those of the blameless, for the days of the blameless merit the knowledge of God.[65]

59. Ps 36.17b.

60. Ps. 144.14.

61. Ps 36.18. Without remarking on the discrepancy, Origen follows the reading we know from the Hebrew text, rather than that in the LXX, which has "roads" for "days."

62. 1 Cor 14.37–38. We find this citation to make the same point in *Hom. Gen.* 4.6.

63. Gal 4.9. We can only know God or be known to God to the extent that we are united with God. Like knows like. See *Comm. Jo.* 19.24.

64. 2 Tm 2.19.

65. What we perceive as evil, God knows as good because all that happens belongs to the divine plan. Dante expresses this knowledge symbolically in the rivers of the Earthly Paradise (*Purgatorio* 28.127–32 in the light of *Paradiso* 9.103–5). As Vittorio Montemaggio puts it in *Reading Dante's* Commedia *as Theology: Divinity Realized in Human Encounter* (Oxford: Oxford University Press, 2016), 171: "Following immersion in Lethe and Eünoè what changes is not what one remembers but the way one remembers it.... The condition of beatitude

It is possible, then, to say simply that the days of the just in this age are the days of the blameless. For each of us makes the day for himself either elegant or evil; for someone sinning, on the one hand, his day is "the day of a sinner," but for someone acting correctly it is a "day of a just person"; so the same day is, for me, a day of a sinner when I sin, but to the just person a day of a just person when he acts correctly: "*The Lord knows the days of the blameless.*"[66] I move in the logos to what is genuine and spiritual, and I say, "These days are evil according to the saying, 'The days are evil.'"[67] But good days are something else; these are "*the days of the blameless.*" The Lord knows these, "*whose inheritance will be in the age.*"[68] For the just will inherit the promises in those days into the age.[69]

10. "*And they will not be put to shame in an evil time.*"[70] The time of judgment is called evil because of the multitude of sinners, because of the large number of those being punished. The just, then, are the only ones who will not be ashamed in an evil time, when the resurrection occurs and some rise to life, but some to reproach and age-long shame.[71] But the just have something else: "*in days of famine they will be fed.*"[72] The first thing to do is to explain the days of famine. In fact, God threatens somewhere through the prophet and says: "Days are coming on the earth, and I shall send out a famine upon the earth, not a famine of bread or a drought of water, but a famine of hearing the logos of the Lord, and they will go about from east to west to hear the logos of the Lord, and they will not find."[73] Has it not therefore become a famine that there are none who speak the logos

---

is such that earthly limitations are not seen as faults but as that in and through which the person providentially comes to be at one with God."

66. Ps 36.18a.

67. Eph 5.16.

68. Ps 36.18b.

69. To the extent that they are sinless, the righteous already experience God's eternity.

70. Ps 36.19a. "Time" here is *kairos,* "time" in the sense of "a crucial season or moment." "Time" as "duration" is *chronos.*

71. Dn 12.2.

72. Ps 36.19b.

73. Am 8.11–12.

of God? For example, now among the Jews there is a famine. Where are the prophets? Where are the wise? Where are the diviners? Where are the commanders of fifty? Where are the wise counselors? Where are the wise listeners? The Lord has taken all these away from the Jews and from Jerusalem.[74]

Even in our case, there is a fear that a famine may be perceived. For, as it seems to be the case for the many at a bodily level, even among those who read the law, there occurs a famine in the days of sinners, and prosperity in the days of the just. Thus if, hearing the things said, you do what is commanded, there will not be lack and famine, but God will give, not just one, but two or more clouds, so that "if it should be revealed to someone sitting down, the first may fall silent."[75] Would that there should come to be many unashamed workers, those who rightly divide the logos of truth,[76] so that one cloud would make room for another, and one living cloud would say to another, "I yield to you, now give your rain," and then that cloud, after giving its rain, would yield to yet another cloud. For just as in the parable concerning the people of the vineyard, as it is written in Isaiah,[77] God orders the clouds not to drench the vineyard, and God will command the rain, so there is an apprehension that we as well, even if we are constantly drinking from the clouds that God gives us, may not bear fruits appropriate to the logoi, but put off what is said to the future, so that even now he will command the clouds not to drench the vineyard with rain. And the intelligent person at that time will sit and be silent, because it is an evil time.[78] This will serve to introduce "*even in days of famine they will be fed.*"[79]

74. See Is 3.1–3.

75. See 1 Cor 14.30. Here, as in the rain prayer in PS73H1.1, Origen counts on his hearers to be familiar with clouds as a symbol of inspired teachers. This symbolism is spelled out in PS76H3.3–4 below and in *Hom. Jer.* 8.3–5. Impressed that Paul needs to instruct charismatic speakers with messages from God instructing them to take turns, he compares the situation in the Corinthian gathering to what we experience at a bodily level when an incoming weather front brings one rain-bearing cloud after another.

76. See 2 Tm 2.15. "Unashamed" echoes the Psalm.

77. See Is 5.1–7.

78. Am 5.13.

79. Ps 36.19b.

I want, then, speaking about the genuine, worse, and spiritual famine, to present how the just person is fed in days of famine. I receive the story about Elijah. There was a famine in the days of the prophet Elijah, when the heaven was closed for three years and six months and the people were famished, but Elijah did not starve, because an angel nourished him and he was carried by the strength of that food forty days and forty nights,[80] because ravens, when they came, brought bread to him in the morning and meat in the evening.[81] And again, after he drank water from the watercourse, he went to Zarephath in Sidon to a widow woman in a time of famine, and, because he was just, he did not experience want in a famine, but an abundance of nourishment came about everywhere for the just man. In the same time there was a famine for sinners, but for Elijah, since he was just, there was no famine. So, accordingly, should a famine ever occur—let it stay away—for the whole Church, the just does not experience famine, for the intelligent person, engaged in reasoning, training, being concerned with the law of the Lord day and night,[82] and conducting himself according to the logos, enjoys spiritual nourishment as did Elijah, according to the story, in a time of famine.

The just, then, *"shall not be put to shame in an evil time, and in days of famine they shall be fed."*[83] Someone will say that *"in an evil time"* refers to the present time, because the days are evil, so that God will even deliver us from this present evil age, but on the analogy of *"they shall not be put to shame in an evil time,"* referring to the place of judgment, so someone will also explain *"in days of famine they shall be fed."* The Savior says somewhere, "The night is coming when no one can work any longer,"[84] and speaks about what is after this age, at the time of punishment of the impious: night will set in, and no one can work any longer, but each one can be nourished then from the works that he has gathered. So, then, in days of famine, in an evil time, when sinners are being punished, the just will be fed. For as in the desert those

80. See 1 Kgs 19.8.
81. See 1 Kgs 17.6.
82. See Ps 1.2.
83. Ps 36.19.
84. Jn 9.4.

who belonged to the people gathered manna on six days and on the sixth day they did not gather for one day, but sufficient food for the following day as well, and each ate from what he had gathered on the sixth day: thus, as it were, on the sixth day, the visitation of my Lord Jesus Christ, the time of his suffering, the time of the divine plan for this age, on this sixth day let us gather a double portion of manna, so that it may be sufficient for us, nourishing us now and when the Sabbath observance of the people of God would be left behind. If we do not gather a double portion, sufficient for the present and sufficient also for the age to come, in days of famine we shall not be fed.

But when the just are fed in days of famine, "*sinners are destroyed, but the enemies of the Lord, just when they glorify themselves and are lifted up, are disappearing even as smoke disappears.*"[85] The logos teaches us not to seek the worldly glories, for, even as they are being glorified, all those glorified on the road of this age, even as they are being lifted up to consulates, governorships, and magistracies, are disappearing as smoke disappears. And consider the first things and the earlier times, if, when they were lifted up then, they disappeared like smoke. For example, then, the enemies of the Lord, even as they are glorifying themselves and being lifted up, are disappearing as smoke disappears, but the friends of the Lord, when they appeared to eschew honors for themselves and to be humbled before human beings, they have been lifted up; they have been brought higher. For everyone who humbles himself will be lifted up, as, conversely, everyone who lifts himself up will be humbled.[86]

11. What follows requires explanation: "*The sinner borrows and will not pay back, but a just person is merciful and would give.*"[87] Again, if we take the statement as it stands, it is false, for many sinners borrow silver and pay back with interest, while they make provision for themselves and make a profit by means of the silver that they have borrowed. But the prophet made a declaration, saying, "*The sinner borrows and will not pay back.*" But if you consider who it is who is lending and who is borrowing,

85. Ps 36.20.
86. See Mt 23.12.
87. Ps 36.21.

and you were to seek a sinner borrowing and not giving back, you will see how the sinner borrows and will not pay back. For example, if Paul is teaching and listeners are present, Paul is lending, but the listeners are borrowing the approved silver in the mouth of Paul. But if the one borrowing is just, he will give back with interest and say, "You have given me one sum. See, I have made ten sums." If he is just: "You have given me one sum; see, I have five. You have given me five talents; see, I have ten. You have given me two. Look, four." But if a sinner pays, he does not return what he borrowed, but he squanders everything that he borrowed.[88]

All of you are borrowing now. These are the loans; these logoi are the silver. "The oracles of the Lord are pure, refined silver, proven, cleansed for earth seven times."[89] If I teach badly, my silver is unproven, according to what is said: "Your silver is unproven."[90] If I teach well, my silver—not mine, but the Lord's— is proven. I am allowed to lend the Lord's silver, but I am not allowed to lend my own. Who, then, lends what is his own? Who lends what is the Lord's? It is allowed to lend the Lord's silver, but not one's own. If you should see Valentinus fashioning logoi and teaching what is his own, say, "That man is lending what is his own and falls under a curse." The same applies if you see Basilides, if you see Marcion. But if you see someone speaking, not what is his own, but what is God's, and daring to say truly, "Or do you seek proof of Christ speaking in me?"[91] know that such a person lends, not what belongs to him, but what is the Lord's. Because, then, he has given the sum or he has given the five talents and the two and the one, and the Lord Jesus Christ—for he is also the master in the parable—says to them, "Go and do business until I return."[92] He exhorted them to lend the Lord's property. Would that I also lend the prophets,

---

88. See Mt 25.14–30 and Lk 19.11–27. The weight Origen gives this parable here and elsewhere in his writings helps to account for the sheer volume of his work.

89. Ps 11.7.

90. See Prv 25.4. Origen was speaking at a time when Roman currency was continually being debased.

91. 2 Cor 13.3.

92. Lk 19.13.

that I lend the Gospels, that I lend the apostles, and that, in lending, I should not be a sinner, so that I may not be punished, but as a just person I can return with interest from my conduct the capital of the logoi I have heard.

"*The sinner,*" then, "*borrows and will not pay back.*"[93] If you should borrow what concerns temperance, give back what concerns temperance. If you should be a sinner, you borrow, but without giving back. If you borrow what concerns justice, give back what you hear about justice through action; but if you are a sinner, you borrow what concerns justice, but without giving back. It is better not to borrow to begin with, especially what is from the Lord's treasure, than to lose the king's property. "*The sinner borrows and will not pay back, but the just has pity and would give*";[94] he does not merely lend, but he has pity and gives.

12. "*Because those who are blessing him will inherit land, but those who curse him are obliterated.*"[95] The just, then, blessing the Lord will inherit land, the good land, the land that has no legal boundaries. For this one is not great, but they shall inherit that one flowing with milk and honey.[96] They shall inherit that one, where the good and genuine things are, for those blessing the Lord will inherit land, but those cursing him will be obliterated.

There is no ordinary danger in cursing a just person and reviling the just person. Those blessing the Lord will inherit land, and those cursing the just will be obliterated. For the Lord says to the just, "I shall be an enemy to your enemies, and I shall oppose your adversaries."[97] There is a danger, then, for us of final destruction when we put a curse on the just, when Jesus in that day,[98] regarding the just person who has been reviled, is not merely going to say, "When I was hungry, you did not give me food," but also, "I was in trouble, and you reviled." And someone who reviled will say, not being aware that he was reviling Christ, "Lord, when did I revile you, Christ, the Son of God?"

93. Ps 36.21a.

94. Ps 36.21.

95. Ps 36.22.

96. See Ex 3.8, Lv 20.24, Nm 13.27, Dt 6.3, and so on.

97. Ex 23.22.

98. See Mt 25.31–46. Origen also applies this principle in PS15H1.3 above and PS73H3.6 and PS81H.4 below.

But Christ will answer and say, "When you reviled this person, when you spoke ill of that person, you were reviling me." And you ought to have understood that this follows from, "Nourishing this person, you nourished me. Giving this person a drink, you gave me a drink. When you clothed the naked, you clothed me. When you reviled this person, you reviled me. When you blessed this person, you blessed me." Therefore, let us beseech God for this, that God will give us the grace always to bless the just and never open the mouth in sin against them, so that we may never be obliterated, but that we may be made just in Jesus Christ, to whom is the glory and the might to the ages of ages. Amen.

HOMILY 4 ON PSALM 36

"*Y THE LORD,*" it says, "*the strides of a human being are straightened.*"[1] The wording "strides"[2] is not customary among Greek-speakers, either among those who speak stupidly or among those who are precise about their wording; likewise, the translators selected it, when it is the only word that has the same force as the [Hebrew] wording, intending to be faithful to the original Hebrew and that one reading the Scripture should ascertain what is signified by the word "strides." And it is not only here that we find the wording "strides"; even in this Psalm itself it still said once more: "*The mouth of the just person will care about wisdom, and his tongue will speak judgment; the law of his God will be in his heart, and his strides will not be tripped.*"[3]

But we find the wording also in the Seventy-second Psalm thus: "How good is God to Israel, to those upright in heart. But

1. Ps 36.23a.

2. Greek, *diabēmata. Bēma* (plural, *bēmata*) means "step." The corresponding verb, from the same root, is *bainō*. The addition of the preposition *dia*, meaning "through" among other things, turns *bēma* into an unfamiliar, new word. By contrast, the verb *diabainō* ("step through" or "cross") is common and was occasionally used by such writers as Philo and Clement of Alexandria to refer to crossing over into a higher realm of consciousness. As in PS36H1.1 above, Origen, claiming that the translators must have used an uncommon word (or coined a new one) in order to preserve a particular Hebrew usage, seems to have discussed an issue of translation without actually referring to the original Hebrew. If we assume that the LXX was translating the Hebrew text that has come to us, *diabēmata* translates two different words in Psalm 36, and the four instances he cites translate three unrelated words in Hebrew.

3. Ps 36.30–31. From PS36H5, which is not in CMG 314, but survives in Rufinus's Latin translation, we learn that Origen interpreted this verse eschatologically as a description of the just person who will come to see God "face to face" (1 Cor 13.12).

my feet were almost shaken, my strides were nearly spilled."[4]
But if "my strides" come about from "stepping through," and
the same understanding[5] is present, the same grammatical construction[6] of wording is in another passage, in Exodus, when
Moses saw the flame of fire and the angel and the bush that was
not burned up. For he said, "Stepping through, then, I shall see
what this great sight is."[7] I have received a means to understand
the passage as far as possible, reading an explanation of what
the speaker intends to say in "stepping through, then, I shall
see what this great sight is." He spoke, relating the statement
referring to the place,[8] because the great sight cannot be seen
by someone who has been halting in the ordinary things of life,
but perception must step through and step over the things of
the cosmos to come to be in the better position and in contemplation of intellectual matters, so that it may be enabled to
comprehend the great sight.

That person, then, said these things, actually the statement
referring to the place, but we, praying to commend a wise human being and add to him,[9] see concerning the place such

4. Ps 72.1.

5. Greek, *nous,* which can also be translated "mind" or "perception."

6. The grammatical construction (*schēmatismos*) is a compound word, formed
by using a preposition as a prefix.

7. Ex 3.3. Origen quotes the passage using *diabas,* "stepping through," a participial form of *diabainō.* The LXX does not use the verb *diabainō,* but a participial
form of the verb *parenchomai,* "go aside," that corresponds to our Hebrew text.
Either Origen is citing a variant reading, now lost, from the *Hexapla,* or he misre-
membered. In *Hom. Gen.* 12.2 (in Rufinus's translation) Origen refers to Ex 3.3 to
explain that when Rebecca "went aside" to question God (Gn 25.22), she did not
go from one place to another, since God fills all things and is not in any particular
place. She did the same thing Moses did when he said, "I shall step aside" at the
burning bush. Moses did not actually go to a different place—he was already at
the bush—but stepped mentally into a higher level of awareness.

8. *To kata to topon,* "the statement concerning the place," is the dialogue
with God, who tells him that the "place" where he "has been standing" is "holy
ground" (Ex 3.5).

9. See Prv 9.9. Origen often makes the point that virtues like wisdom are not
all or nothing. An example is his commentary on the words "so that you may
believe" in Jn 13.19: "Hear 'so that you may believe' as if it had the same force
as 'act so that you may believe, maintaining your faith and having no motivation
to change it.' And if, in fact, faith were not large in size or great in its extent,

things as this. Each person taking the road in virtue first makes progress; then he strides upon it in such a way that, in making progress, he actually "steps through," continually straining forward and forgetting the things that are behind.[10] And by stepping through, he, as it were, steps over the first obstruction of evil, and, stepping over some sins and becoming no longer involved in them, straining to the things ahead, he becomes involved in smaller sins—for I will concede that in this logos there are also lesser evils—and comes to be involved in smaller and limited evils.[11] And this is to step through according to God's logos, up to the point when, stepping through, he has stepped through evil and the effects of evil, and then he will, according to Exodus, see the great sight. No one who is still dealing with evil and has not yet stepped through it will be able to perceive the great sight. What, then, would the great sight be, if not seeing God with a pure heart?[12] What would the great sight be if not God's wisdom and logos,[13] his Christ, whom no one can

---

Paul would not have said, 'even if I have all faith' [1 Cor 13.2]. For just as the perfect person, who has all the virtues, having received each of them perfect, has perfect wisdom and perfect temperance as well as piety and all the rest, so one would say of one perfect in the virtue of faith that he had all faith. I say this on the understanding that an imperfect wisdom, temperance, piety, or any other virtue is not spoken of in the strict sense of the term, but by extension, so that those who are making progress in each virtue are so termed homonymously with perfection. It is in this way that someone who sins in some things so as to need reproof—but who does not hate, but loves the one who reproves—is called 'a wise man,' as it is written: 'Rebuke a wise man, and he will love you' [Prv 9.8]. In the same way someone is spoken of as 'a wise man' even though he is receptive to different principles of wisdom, further ones that he does not yet have, so that it is also said: 'Give an opportunity to the wise man, and he will be wiser' [Prv 9.9]. At any event, we have arrived at these conclusions, demonstrating that someone who is already believing is receptive to learning something, so that he may believe again and add to belief by the addition of things learned" (*Comm. Jo.* 32.15.176–182).

10. See Phil 3.13. Origen had already developed the idea of continual *epektasis* (straining), which Jean Daniélou considered the distinguishing characteristic of the mystical theology of Gregory of Nyssa (see *Platonisme et théologie mystique* [Paris: Aubier, 1944], 309–26).

11. The image seems to be a landslide obstructing a road.

12. See Mt 5.8.

13. See 1 Cor 1.24.

know, unless the Father reveals him to him?[14] What would the great sight be, other than the Holy Spirit?[15]

But perhaps, since there are many great sights, in Exodus it is written, "stepping through, then, I shall see this great sight." In order to distinguish it from other great sights, it says, "I shall see this great sight."[16] But what was that great sight, the one that he beheld by stepping through, but an angel? One who understands an angel's nature and takes note of how all that is recorded concerning them [angels] has been said, even including "who makes his angels spirits and his ministers flames of fire,"[17] one comprehending the logos of the briar bush and comprehending the angel seen in the flame of fire on the bush has seen a single sight, less than greater sights that Moses will see later. For Moses saw this great sight, but he did not stop at this great sight. Read the whole book of Exodus and see that he sees a second great sight, perhaps greater than the first, and again he sees a third sight, while he comes to the greatest of the sights, entering into the darkness, where God was.[18] And if you want to observe a still greater sight, look at the proclamation: Moses alone approaches God; the rest do not approach.[19] This was the greater sight.

Again, on the subject of Moses, pick from Scripture the sights of Moses, and you will see still greater ones: "If," he says, "I found favor with you, manifest yourself to me"; after many great sights, "I would see and know you."[20] And there God says to him, "Place yourself in the opening of the rock"—but the rock was Christ[21]—"so that you may see through a narrow open-

14. See Mt 16.17.

15. The notion of Father, Son/logos, and Spirit, in that order, as successive "sights" calls to mind the same series in Gregory of Nazianzus, *Oration* 31.26.

16. Speaking of "this" sight implies that it is not the only one.

17. Ps 103.4.

18. See Ex 19.16–20.

19. Ex 20.21.

20. See Ex 33.13.

21. See 1 Cor 10.4. Gregory of Nazianzus makes the same connection in *Oration* 28.3, as does Gregory of Nyssa in *Life of Moses* 2.244. Gregory, like Origen, depicts the progression of Moses from one vision to another as progress in personal transformation.

ing"—since he was still going to observe many things, as he was receiving preliminary training by what was observed through the opening—"and you will see what is behind me, but my face will not be seen by you."[22] You will also find other great sights on the part of Moses in Numbers and again in Deuteronomy.[23] Why, indeed, do I investigate "stepping through" and have not yet come to "*the strides of a human being are straightened*"?[24] This explanation is now furnished: each stride, then, often makes it possible to observe some sight. For God gives a reward to the one who steps through each evil; therefore it is marvelously said, "Desiring wisdom, maintain commandments, and the Lord will bestow her upon you."[25]

There are many strides, then. Step through illicit sexual activity. Step through adultery. If you would be more blessed, step through wrath, step through gloom, step through greed. To the extent that you do not step through these but stop in them, you will not see a great sight, being blinded, lamed, by not stepping through. We have, then, other feet that step through mentally, so that, striding so as to step upon the road that is called "I am the road,"[26] we may arrive at God. There are, then, many strides of heaven, the strides that are straightened by the Lord. It is not enough for a human being wanting to step through from a personal choice, unless the Lord straightens the strides. For it is possible for someone who wants to step through, to step through, not directly though, but to walk in such a way as to stride through sideways and crookedly.

If you see those who have fallen from the truth in worldly philosophy, who understand many things, do not hesitate to say that they step through and have made strides—not ones that have been straightened, but ones that have been bent, turned to the right or to the left. If you see those in the heresies wanting to step through in a stupid way and not being satisfied with

---

22. See Ex 33.22–23.

23. See Nm 8.4, 12.6–8, 24.4, and 24.16.

24. Ps 36.23a.

25. Sir 1.26. "Marvelous" because counterintuitive: one does not achieve wisdom (the sight) by seeking it directly (through deeper teachings) but by walking on the road (keeping the commandments).

26. Jn 14.6.

mere faith, understanding something deeper but not true, see that these have made strides, but those strides have not been straightened by the Lord; but, if I must speak boldly, their strides have been bent by the devil and have become bent. But, as for us, if we actually want both things, to step through and for our strides and motion to be straightened, let us move to step through, and, as we perform this activity, let us pray that our strides may be straightened by the Lord.

2. Here, then, it says, "*By the Lord the strides of a human being are straightened, and he will want his road; whenever he falls, he will not be wrecked,*"[27] but in what follows it is no longer spoken simply about a human being, as it is here in "by the Lord the strides of a human being are straightened," but is spoken more about the just person who has something more than an ordinary human being. For "*a mouth of a just person is concerned about wisdom, and his tongue will speak judgment*"[28]—not of a "human being" but of a "just person"—"*the law of his God is in his heart, and his strides will not be tripped up.*"[29] In the one place the human's strides are straightened; in the other, the just person's strides are not tripped up, "*because the Lord supports his hands.*"[30] In another Psalm—I say the Seventy-second—"My feet had almost slipped; my strides were nearly wasted."[31] Assuming that this very thing holds in such a manner, understand, then, from me someone stepping up and progressing in the ascent, then slipping and going down and destroying the progress of his ascent. Do not hesitate to say, "The strides have been wasted." For just as, in another situation, wine or oil or any such thing is wasted, so the strides of the person progressing already in stepping through are wasted, because he looks behind him.

If you want to hear who it is whose strides are wasted, not just from an ordinary example, but from Scripture, hear that Lot's wife stepped through, and, by stepping through, she went out from Sodom, so that she was traveling to the mountain on which

27. Ps 36.23–24a.
28. Ps 36.30.
29. Ps 36.31.
30. Ps 36.24b. LXX has "hand."
31. Ps 72.2. *Exechuthē,* "wasted," can also mean "spilled."

she was ordered to ascend, but because she acted contrary to the command of God saying, "Do not look around to the back or stop in all the surrounding country; save yourself to go to the mountain, so that you might not be taken away with them,"[32] and she turned around and her strides were wasted and she was destroyed, for she remained as a pillar of salt.[33] If you want another example in what manner the strides of some are wasted, hear the Savior saying, "No one putting hand to the plow and turning back is well disposed for the kingdom of God."[34] For someone puts hand to the plow, and, having put it on, he has plowed, he has gone forward, for he must thoroughly perceive the furrows, but the one turning back "wastes his strides"; he has wasted what he seemed to have done well concerning the plow.

Come also to another uncomfortable story, so that you may know how the strides of some are wasted. A multitudinous people went out of Egypt and stepped through the Red Sea, and there was progress for them as they stepped through the Red Sea, but some fell in the desert, wasting greater or lesser strides. But should you as well ever hear about someone who has been for three years among those progressing in chastity, for five years in temperance, for ten years in agreement with the logos, then, after this, should you learn that such a person has been overcome, committing sexual immorality or doing some other sin, do not hesitate to say that his strides have been wasted. And just as a pilot directing a boat, having already approached through many stades,[35] is overcome by an adverse wind and has not been able to face it and has returned backwards because of the wind's impact, the ship's strides have been wasted; in the same manner you as well, when you turn back while straining for things ahead,[36] if you sin, you waste your strides.[37] So that you may be put in fear of wasting your strides, hear the Lord speaking by means of Ezekiel: "The just person, if he turns back from

32. Gn 19.17.
33. See Gn 19.15–26.
34. See Lk 9.62.
35. A stade is one eighth of a mile, the ordinary Greek unit of distance.
36. See Phil 3.13.
37. Getting into Caesarea's artificial harbor could be tricky.

his just deeds, all his just deeds that he has done shall not be remembered."[38] We pray, then, Lord, that you would straighten our strides and that our strides may not be deflected and that, by stepping through, we may see the great sights in proportion to our stride.

When "*the strides of a human being are straightened*" by the Lord, then "*he will want his road.*"[39] The wording is ambiguous, for either the Lord wants the road of the one who has been straightened in strides and approves it, not wanting the road of impious persons or wanting the road of those going sideways and stepping through without straightness, or he whose strides are straightened by the Lord wants the Lord's road, tasting, when his strides are straightened, the sweetness that corresponds to the road in which he has been straightened by the Lord, and, "*he will want his road. Whenever he falls, he will not be wrecked.*"[40] "*Whenever he falls*" does not concern the just. The logos concerns a human being who is not yet just, since he can fall; nonetheless, "*Whenever he falls, he will not be wrecked.*" I want to furnish the difference between falling and being wrecked. Let us take an example from those wrestling and falling in athletic contests and those who are wrecked or completely wrecked after falling. Those in athletic contests have sometimes fallen in the first, but they have won the three matches because the contest does not consist of just one wrestling match. In their case you would say at a bodily level that they have fallen but have not been wrecked, since they have gone on to win after falling. If you have understood the example, step over in the logos to what follows: if you see a human being who has been overcome and, after being overcome, does not give himself over to licentiousness, to all unclean activity, and to greed, but stands back up, bearing in mind the Scripture, "lest the one who falls not stand back up or the one who turns aside not turn back."[41] Woe to those turning aside in a shameless rejection, says the Lord.[42] If, then, you see

38. See Ezek 3.20.

39. Ps 36.23b.

40. See Ps 36.23b–24a.

41. Jer 8.4. If it is possible not to stand back up, then it must logically be possible to do the opposite.

42. See Jer 8.5.

someone, after falling, standing back up and being revived by standing back up and accepting the blame after the failure and making amends after falling and living well, say about such a person that it is true that, "*whenever he falls, he will not be wrecked.*" But if you see someone, after falling, refusing and saying, "I have fallen, I am destroyed, the sins are in me, I no longer have hope of rescue," and you see that person becoming an apostate from God, that person has fallen and has been wrecked.

It is good, then, for an athlete not to have fallen and good for an athlete, if I may use such terms for the sake of an example, to be "ungraspable" and "unthrowable." But if you are not able to become such an athlete, but you have fallen, do not be wrecked, but stand back up. For they are lamented who, when they fall and, after sinning, feel no pain and give themselves over to every sin; but those who are not like that, since they have hope, are not lamented by the just to such an extent because of their sins. Therefore, the Apostle does not just say, "and I shall lament some of those who have already sinned"; but look at the addition: "and not having changed their minds regarding the uncleanness, sexual immorality, and licentiousness that they have practiced."[43] It is a good thing, then, among athletes to be found blameless and undefiled, even if they are not always among those who have overcome but are among those who overcame later. And, while we are still on the subject of athletes, because Scripture uses them for examples, it is possible to say that someone who has been overcome among children has overcome among youths, and one who has been overcome among youths has been crowned among men. And the Apostle says, "no one is crowned unless he competes by the rules,"[44] and, "so I strike, not as one beating the air."[45] Another example is to become as Jacob was, who said, "God, who nourished me from my youth."[46]

It is a good thing to become one who never falls, but, even

---

43. See 2 Cor 12.21.

44. See 2 Tm 2.5.

45. 1 Cor 9.26.

46. Gn 48.15. Jacob is included among the athletic examples of Scripture, not just because he wrestled with an angel (Gn 32.24–30), but also because he was born with a hold on his twin brother (Gn 25.26).

if you have fallen in contests with children, compete as a youth and win there. And if you fall in that contest, the blows administered to those who are overcome as children, as well as to someone worsted as a youth, will assist you. Recover the crowns when you are a man. There are many and various correspondences between games and Christianity: "Our wrestling is not against blood and flesh, but against the rulers, against the authorities, against the cosmic dominators of darkness, against the spiritual matters of wickedness in the heavenly places."[47] Among such adversaries one must be up to the contest, and one must win. What man can do this? What blessed, holy, and priestly man? Daniel, who was prophesying from his childhood, who was rebuking elders as a child and was honored with assignments from God.[48] This is possible for that holy, divine, and blessed man Jacob, such a wrestler that he was supplanting his brother Esau in the womb. But if you cannot become someone such as they are, become the next-best athlete.

This accounts for "*whenever he falls, he will not be wrecked, because the Lord supports his hand.*"[49] And so that a human being's strides may step through and be straightened alongside the Lord and so that he may not be wrecked when he falls, he needs the Lord again. For when do we ever not need the Lord? For because of this he shall not be wrecked: "*because the Lord supports his hand.*" The wording is ambiguous; is it his own hand the Lord supports, not allowing it to be wrecked, or does he hold the hand of the one who wrestles and is about to be wrecked, so that he may not completely fall on his face and lie flat on the ground?

3. "*I was born younger and have grown old, and I have not seen a just person forsaken or his seed seeking bread. All day the just person is merciful and lends, and his seed will be a blessing.*"[50] Someone just taking away an initial impression of this passage of Scripture supposes that this was said by David in a situation when he had

---

47. Eph 6.12.

48. In this Daniel resembles Christ. See Lk 2.41–51. Stories of Origen's own amazing precocity (see Eusebius, *Hist. eccl.* 6.1–2) would probably have been familiar to those listening to him.

49. Ps 36.24.

50. Ps 36.25–26.

grown old and had passed his youth and was saying, "I am an old man now, but I once was born younger, and nonetheless through so much time I have not seen a just person forsaken," and so on. But we, knowing that there is an analogy between the age of the body and that of the inner human being, knowing that someone is a child inside, an infant, younger and a youth, older and an old person, and seeing that he is not at such a level of maturity in bodily years, Abraham was old enough in his inner humanity that he had despised infantile things,[51] and he had stepped in his strides through youthful things. Before Abraham, in fact, those more superannuated than he were not called "elders"; he was the first to be entitled an "elder" on account of virtue,[52] as we pray to be termed "elders" on account of virtue and disposition, not on account of the position in which we are placed,[53] for if one is not someone within who can hear "elder" as Abraham did, reared to a good old age, it is not possible for us to be entitled "elders" by God.[54]

Since, then, we know the age according to the inner human being of a child, a young man, or an old man, therefore we say that the perfect[55] says such things as the Apostle Paul taught, saying: "When I was an infant, I spoke as an infant, I thought as an infant, I reasoned as an infant; but when I became a man, I despised infantile things."[56] I do not hear the Apostle saying this simply about bodily age, but since, as soon as a person believed, he was a baby in reasoning, initially craving guileless milk,[57] and understood the Scriptures as an infant, thought about the Gospel as an infant, reasoned as an infant about interpretations of

51. See 1 Cor 13.11.

52. Greek, *presbuteros* (Gn 24.1 LXX). By Origen's time this had become the accepted title for an order of Christian ministry.

53. Origen was an elder/presbyter in the church at Caesarea (*Hist. eccl.* 6.23.4).

54. The title of "elder" in the Church does not guarantee spiritual eminence, but being entitled "elder" by God, as Abraham was. In *Princ.* 4.24 elders are those who have "grown gray through thoughtfulness."

55. Greek, *teleios,* which can also mean "mature."

56. 1 Cor 13.11.

57. See 1 Pt 2.2.

Scripture; then, progressing in age as an imitator of Christ,[58] who progressed in wisdom and in age and in grace with God and human beings,[59] he has despised infantile things, no longer reasoning as he reasoned when he was an infant. Therefore, he says, "When I became a man, I despised infantile things."

Understand with me that something like this was the case with David when he said, "*I was born younger,*"[60] as if he were saying, "I became an infant according to the inner human being, and have grown old." For if he had not been someone who grew old, he could not have prophesied, for it is for an old person to prophesy. For if you were to see a younger person prophesying, do not hesitate to say that that person was an elder according to the inner human being and was prophesying because of that. When, in fact, Jeremiah heard, "Before you formed me in the belly, you knew me; and before I left the womb, you consecrated me, you appointed me a prophet to the gentiles,"[61] the young man replied, then, and said, "I do not know how to speak because I am a young man."[62] But the one who had bestowed the grace not to be a young man, but an elder according to the inner human being, said, "Do not say, 'because I am a young man.'"[63] If that is not how "do not say, 'because I am a young man'" is understood, does it hold any sort of logos? He was a young man in age; his body was youthful. "Do not say" was the truth because he is a young man in body, but the Lord knows what he says because he has given his logoi into his mouth "to uproot, dig up, and destroy, and to build and to plant."[64] Since this logos was present in his soul, it did not allow his soul to be that of a young man; therefore, he says, "Do not say, 'because I am a young man.'"

And David, then, as we have explained, was younger, but he was no longer a younger person, because he prophesied and because he spoke these things that were worthy of the holy

58. See 1 Cor 11.1.
59. See Lk 2.52. Christ is a model of spiritual growth.
60. Ps 36.25a.
61. Jer 1.5.
62. Jer 1.6.
63. Jer 1.7.
64. See Jer 1.10.

documentation. Therefore, he says, "*I was born younger and have grown old*"—if he grew old, he had once become younger—"*and I have not seen a just person forsaken.*"[65] If you hear this bodily, it is false. For many just persons have been forsaken; but if spiritually, you hear it truly. For example, if you consider being forsaken by becoming destitute, being forsaken by becoming ill in body, being forsaken by going around in deserts on account of persecution, the just have been forsaken. "They have gone around in sheepskins and goat hides, cheated, oppressed, maltreated, wandering in deserts, mountains, and caves and in the holes of the land."[66] Nonetheless, if they were in a desert void of human beings, there was a multitude of angels with them. When Elisha was in a desert void of human beings, but, as he was fleeing in a desert void of human beings, he was with an army of angels. For it is written, "Lord, open the eyes of this your servant and let it be seen that more are with us than there are with them." And "he saw the mountain full of horses and chariots of fire."[67]

The just, then, is never alone, but I shall say something quite surprising: the perfect person is not with one angel or with two, but with whole armies. But if you need something from an abundance of examples, Jacob, as long as he was with Esau along with his father and mother, not fleeing him, he was not with an army of holy angels; but because he came to be in a desert and was out alone in Mesopotamia, he fell asleep, and when he rose up he said, "The place is called 'squadrons.'"[68] And, there, one who seemed to be alone in human terms saw, not a squadron, but holy squadrons. This, to my way of thinking, addresses "*I have not seen a just person forsaken,*"[69] for he is not forsaken in spiritual matters. And I am not diminished, forsaken, when I have needs in bodily things; I have spiritual things. It is possible for me, when I am bodily forsaken, to speak those apostolic boasts: "Up to this present hour we hunger, we thirst, and we have been naked, we are tossed about, we have no place to stay,

---

65. Ps 36.25.
66. See Heb 11.37–38.
67. 2 Kgs 6.16–17.
68. Gn 32.2. Origen appears to have confused this story with Gn 28.11–12.
69. Ps 36.25b.

we labor, working with our own hands," and it is possible for me, when I am forsaken bodily, to say, "When reviled, we bless; when persecuted, we put up with it; when slandered, we bless."[70] But, since I am not forsaken, "I am content in illnesses, in outrages and shortages, in persecutions and constraints, on account of Christ."[71]

There are, then, two kinds of forsakenness: the bodily, which does not hurt us, and the forsakenness of the soul, which is destructive. To the extent that we are rich in good works, we are helped not to be forsaken. Therefore, it is even said, *"I have not seen a just person forsaken or his seed seeking bread."*[72] Again, if you hear "his seed" as referring to bodily descendants, often the seed of the just does seek bread. In fact, Ishmael, when he and his mother were escaping Sarah, thirsted as well.[73] And Esau came from the field wasted away so that he gave away his firstborn status for one mess of boiled lentils.[74] But also the apostles, as we have attested, boast of being in hunger, thirst, and nakedness. One must, then, understand *"I have not seen a just person forsaken or his seed seeking bread"* in a manner worthy of the spiritual Scriptures.

Accordingly, the seed of the just would be his disciple, who receives the seeds of salvation. For example, if you pray for me, so that I become just and that I receive more grace, logos, and wisdom daily and a logos of knowledge; so, would that the logos, as a seed entering the souls of you hearers, form you when Christ is formed in you,[75] so that it would be a seed of logos of a just person. On the one hand, then, *"I have not seen a just person forsaken or his seed seeking bread."*[76] For by all means the seed of the just does not seek bread because he already has it through the just ones, from whom he has received a seed, the power of

70. 1 Cor 4.11–12.

71. 2 Cor 12.10.

72. Ps 36.25b.

73. See Gn 21.15–17.

74. See Gn 25.30–34.

75. See Gal 4.19. Origen suggests that, thanks to the prayers of his hearers, he may receive a logos of wisdom that, in turn, will enter their souls and form them in Christ.

76. Ps 36.25b.

divine bread. But if someone should say in response, on account of those who seem to be hearing the just Paul or Peter and then sinning, he will say to you that sinners were not the seed of the just. And just as sinners were not seed of Abraham, therefore it was said, "If you were Abraham's children, you would have done the works of Abraham."[77] Thus those who seemed to be hearing, but were not hearing, were not seed of Paul, but they seemed to have rejected Paul's logos from their souls. Thus Judas was not a child of Christ, since surely after the sop Satan entered into him and before Satan [did this], the devil had inserted into his heart that he should betray the teacher.[78] We have, then, the solution to the supposed objection to, "*I have not,*" then, "*seen a just person forsaken or his seed seeking bread.*"

To be a "seed" can even be a certain wording in what follows.[79] Here, on the one hand, it will appear to have a forced explanation, but, on the other hand, in what follows this has an explanation; but what is returned no longer has a similar meaning to the explanation, but would seem to be forced. One person will say that "seed" in this Psalm is spoken in two senses, but someone else will try to demonstrate that the forced interpretations are not forced. It is said, furthermore, in what follows, "*and the seed of impious ones will be obliterated.*"[80] And it is evident that the seed of impious persons is not bodily obliterated, but it also reappears as a just person before the Lord and says prophesying, "May he curse that day, the one who is going to take in hand the big sea-monster."[81] But the seed of the just will never

77. See Jn 8.39.

78. See Jn 13.27. Origen discusses Judas's disposition in *Comm. Jo.* 32.19.240–249.

79. The text of CMG 314 is not fully intelligible here, probably because a scribe failed to follow Origen's argument. He finds a complicated way to argue that "the seed of the impious will be obliterated" must be "forced," that is, interpreted to mean something it does not actually say, but in such a way as to avoid coming right out and saying that it is false.

80. Ps 36.28b. Origen argues that his explanation of "seed" as "disciple" rather than "descendant" may seem "forced," or "contrived," but only his explanation makes sense of the passage as a whole. This is because, in the second passage, "seed" cannot mean "descendant"; if it did, it would be patently untrue, since the descendant of a wicked person can, as in Job's case, be outstandingly righteous.

81. Jb 3.8 (LXX). Origen believed that this passage, not found in the received

be obliterated according to this interpretation of "*nor his seed seeking bread.*"[82] The logos does not require nourishment, for he always has it for himself nourishing him.[83]

4. "*All day the just person is merciful and lends.*"[84] All day the just person is being merciful; all day he is lending. He devotes his time to nothing but lending. From a multitude of money, from dawn until dusk, he lends, but it does not say this: if someone who is just opens a bank and has money, he lends it.[85] And this is what is said in Deuteronomy and Exodus, for I suppose that it is said in both books: "Lend to many nations, but, as for you, do not borrow."[86] But it is obvious that, if I have the approved money and I always gather more money from God's treasures and storehouses, from the treasures of wisdom, of knowledge, and I have the five talents that have become ten, and I have the two that have become four, always having more approved money in the soul, being merciful all day, all day I now lend to such with such things. But I am not even just; pray therefore that I may become just, and that, when I have become just, I may lend you funds of justice that have been furnished by justice itself, so that they may be just funds.

But let them not be—as is possible to say of funds—funds raised unjustly and wickedly from groans, from injustice, from sorrow, from theft and greed, but just funds from the personal property of just husbandmen, funds that have distressed no one.

Hebrew text, constituted a prophecy of Christ, who would "take in hand the big sea-monster," Satan. This means that Job is not just a righteous man, but also a prophet, since only a prophet would have such insight into the divine plan. Following Jewish traditions incorporated into the LXX and in an apocryphal work, the *Testament of Job*, Origen identified him with Jobab (Gn 36.33–34), a king of Edom. This makes Job a "seed of the impious," that is, a descendant of the notoriously impious Esau, whom God hated even in the womb (Mal 1.3 and Rom 9.13) because of sins that he had committed before being embodied. See *Princ.* 2.8.3 and 3.1.22.

82. Ps 36.25b.

83. See Jn 4.32.

84. Ps 36.26a.

85. The righteous person lends, but the Scripture does not say that he or she is a banker.

86. See Dt 15.6 and Ex 22.25. Israel is commanded to lend its teaching about the law to many nations, but not to borrow their idolatry.

So it is possible to say about money and about power, including the power of logoi, that there are some just funds, such as were the funds of the apostle Paul, but there are some unjust funds, such as were those of Valentinus and Basilides.[87] (Actually, those two did not have funds, or, if they did have funds, their funds were unjust.) Pray, accordingly, that our coinage may be funded from justice and that you may borrow without risk and that we may not hear, "You should have put your money in the bank."[88]

5. "*I was born younger and have grown old, and I have not seen a just person forsaken or his seed seeking bread; all day he is merciful and lends.*"[89] Above is said, "*The sinner borrows and will not pay back,*"[90] but here the just "*all day is merciful and lends.*" See the diametrical opposition: one of them—the sinner, I say—not only does not lend, but when he borrows he does not pay back; but the other lends, and not just once or twice, but "all day" of his lifetime "*the just is merciful and lends, and his seed will be for blessing.*"[91]

6. "*Shun evil,*" learning these things, "*and do good and set up a tent for an age.*"[92] Do not set up a tent for five or ten days or even after receiving that number of years, but let your tents be age-long. You will do this, if you do not make things that are seen your goal, but things not seen, since things seen are temporary, but things not seen are permanent.[93]

7. "*Because the Lord loves judgment and will not abandon his devout one.*"[94] How does the Lord love judgment? God loves nothing ill-judged. He does not act without judgment, but hear the one who says, "*He makes all things with counsel and judgment.*"[95]

8. "*With counsel,*" because "the Lord will not also abandon his

87. See introduction, pp. 8–10.

88. See Lk 19.23 and Mt 25.27. Origen refers, in the first person, to "our coinage" because, by profiting from his words, Origen's hearers will vindicate his investment of his teaching in them. All concerned will thus avoid God's words of condemnation.

89. Ps 36.25–26a.

90. Ps 36.21a.

91. Ps 36.26.

92. Ps 36.27. On the verb translated here as "set up a tent," *kataskēnou,* see introduction, p. 20.

93. See 2 Cor 4.18.

94. Ps 36.28a (LXX, "his devout ones").

95. See Prv 31.4.

devout ones, they will be guarded for an age,"[96] since "they will set up a tent for an age."[97] For that reason they will be guarded for an age. For the guard in which they will be guarded will take place in the present on account of the age to come. Perhaps there is also some secret in this passage, because if you understand the whole age, it is impossible for a human being worthy of that age to fall for that whole age. But if something can be produced when that age is fulfilled, we shall know about such a thing; besides, "*a seed of an impious one shall be obliterated,*"[98] and, "*just ones shall inherit land*"[99] that the gentle inherit, the good and great land, and "*they shall set up a tent for an age in it,*"[100] and not only for an age, but for an age of an age; so much has been returned to the just person. For, because of a just person's years, he receives not an age instead of days, but an age of an age. But I say that if he should encourage virtue and love of humanity, he will arrive at glorifying God for ages of ages. Amen.

96. Ps 36.28b.
97. Ps 36.29b.
98. Ps 36.28d.
99. Ps 36.11a.
100. Ps 36.29b.

HOMILY 1 ON PSALM 67

E is a disciple of the one who said, "Learn from me, because I am gentle and lowly in heart."[1] While speaking in a more measured way about himself, he ascribes to us better things not belonging to him. As his disciple, training in gentleness, he spoke as one "humble in heart." For he knew that "everyone humbling himself will be lifted up."[2] But I heard what was said, not as referring to things as they already are, but as the fathers heard: Jacob hearing the blessing of Isaac, the twelve patriarchs hearing the blessings of Jacob. For these blessings did not yet exist for the fathers, but they were prophesied of future blessings. As in the instance when you are praying to dedicate [yourselves][3] in the Church, the things spoken about us by the *papa*[4] will also be a prophecy. They are a prophecy rather than things that already belong to us. For I know that they have not yet come about.[5]

Since I am persuaded that every logos without Christ's presence in the speaker is empty and from earth,[6] but it is impossible for a heavenly logos[7] to visit us apart from the Father God

1. Mt 11.29.

2. Lk 14.11. The context is unclear.

3. The Greek is obscure. Origen is probably referring to the prayers of self-dedication to good works that were a regular part of Christian worship. See Justin Martyr, *First Apology* 65.1, and Pliny the Younger, *Ep.* 10.94.7. The word *epididonai* ("dedicate" or "give over") may have been suggested by Jacob's blessing of Naphtali (Gn 49.21).

4. *Papa*. Origen testifies that this word, which came to mean Pope, originally applied to any bishop.

5. Origen appears to be reacting to a glowing introduction by a bishop.

6. See 1 Cor 15.47 and 1 Sm 3.19.

7. See Clement of Alexandria, *Protr.* 1.2.3 and 1.5.4.

who sent him,[8] therefore selecting one Psalm containing a prayer from those read, I would pray it by itself before the explanation of the appointed Psalm read.[9] And I would like all of you, praying together, to say it on my behalf, while I am saying it for myself: "God, attend to my assistance. Lord, hasten to assist me. Let those who seek my soul be ashamed and show respect. Let those who first wished evil to me turn around backwards and be disgraced"—not in some future time, but —"right now. Let those be turned around who say to me"—wanting to exult when bad things occur, that they pray may come about for us—"'Aha, aha.'"[10]

Let these things come about for them.[11] I pray on your behalf that such a logos may be given, as to delight and gladden you. I would therefore say: "'May they be delighted and gladdened'[12] on your behalf today through Christ speaking in me,[13] 'Let them rejoice and let them be glad, all who seek you, and let them always say, May the Lord be magnified.'"[14] Let them say, "be magnified," so that both in the logos given to me the Lord may be magnified, and may the Lord also be magnified in works in us and in all of you.[15]

Let those "who love your salvation"[16] say this: "As for me, I am

8. See Jn 17.18 and 20.21, 1 Jn 4.14.

9. This suggests that at least one neighboring Psalm, Psalm 69, had been read along with Psalm 67, on which Origen was appointed to speak. We find something similar at the beginning of Origen's homily on 1 Sm 28, where Origen asked the bishop which of three self-contained passages read to discuss.

10. Ps 69.2–4. Origen's running commentary demonstrates how to apply and pray a Psalm.

11. "Those who wish evil" would include spiritual adversaries and, possibly, human adversaries as well. Origen cites Eph 6.12 ("our wrestling is not against blood and flesh …") seventeen times in the course of these homilies. We do know that Origen's views provoked opposition during his own lifetime. Perhaps, supported by the bishop, he is rallying the Christian community to his side. On the other hand, this may be little more than a rhetorical technique to gain his hearers' attention and good will.

12. Ps 69.5a. Origen continues to apply Psalm 69 to his hearers. They are no longer praying, since the Psalm is in the third person.

13. See 2 Cor 13.3.

14. Ps 69.5a–b.

15. The Lord is magnified when speech (logos) is accompanied by works.

16. Ps 69.5c.

aware that I am destitute, that I am poor: 'God, help me. You are my help and deliverance, Lord. Do not take your time.'"[17] Please pray together, that the one who promises, saying, "When you talk, I will say, 'I am present,'"[18] even as I am saying these things, he would say, by power and presence, "See, I am present." This will be a sign that he is speaking, when you recognize by fruits[19] not only human beings, but also logos: if a logos should be given, explaining, "*Let God rise up, and let his enemies be scattered, and may those who hate him flee before his face; as smoke vanishes, as wax melts before the face of fire, so may sinners be destroyed before God's face, and let the just rejoice, let them be glad before God, let them be delighted for joy.*"[20]

2. It must be known first that it is the custom in Scripture often to use imperatives in place of conditional statements.[21] And this is found often. It suffices to cite the place in the Gospels where, when our Savior is teaching us to pray, he does not teach us that we should order God around, but that we should use imperatives to express a conditional meaning. For it is said: "Our Father, who is in the heavens, let your name be hallowed, let your kingdom come, let your will take place,"[22] instead of, "may your name be hallowed, may your kingdom come, may your will take place."

Thus if these things are said as imperatives, we hear conditional statements instead. For no one gives orders to God; no one says in his case, "Let God rise up," but prays and says, "May God rise up, and may his enemies be scattered, and may those who hate him flee before his face; as smoke vanishes, as wax

17. Ps 69.6b–d.

18. Is 58.9.

19. Mt 7.16.

20. Ps 67.2–4. Origen turns the opening of the appointed Psalm into a challenge.

21. Using a verb in the imperative or command form ("let God arise") implies that one is addressing someone of equal or inferior status. The optative ("may God arise")—a separate mood in Greek grammar with a full set of verb forms alongside those in the indicative, imperative, and subjunctive moods—is a more respectful way to address a request to a superior. Origen sets forth a hypothetical revision in which optative verb forms replace imperative forms.

22. Mt 6.9–10, using verbs in imperative voice.

melts before the face of fire, so may they be destroyed." But now it actually made a conditional statement openly and clearly: "so may sinners be destroyed before God's face, and let the just rejoice"—instead of "may they rejoice"—"let them be glad"—instead of "may they be glad"—"before God, let them take"—instead of "may they take"— "their fill of joy."

Someone[23] bolder than I am may say that these things may even be spoken as imperatives. For if masters have received a command from Christ speaking in Paul[24] "to allow yourselves fairness and equality toward slaves,"[25] and the good master allows equality with slaves, why is it inappropriate for someone who has been ordered by God, and has received orders, to be confident about observing those orders with a certain freedom of speech, by giving an order reciprocally when praying to God? And he will encourage such behavior with other statements written about these things and will say: "I make some requests of the Lord our God, trusting the one who says, 'Everyone who asks, receives.'"[26] Thus, then, just as we ask from God, God himself is recorded as, of his own accord, not maintaining the dignity of God, as one might ordinarily expect, but as asking something from us, for God is, as it were, if I may use such a term, humble-minded, asking from us what it is written that he asked. But what did he ask? Hear it in, "And now, Israel, what does the Lord your God ask of you but that you fear the Lord your God, that you walk in all his ordinances, and that you love him and worship your Lord God from your whole heart and from your whole soul?"[27] Thus, since he asks of us, so we also ask from him,

23. Origen is said to have presented sound arguments diffidently in order to encourage his students to develop and exercise their own critical judgment (see the *Address of Thanksgiving* 7.104, traditionally attributed to Gregory Thaumaturgus). Here he seems to be employing that technique as a preacher.

24. See 2 Cor 13.3.

25. Col 4.1. When Christ, speaking in Paul, tells masters to allow their slaves the extraordinary privilege of treating them as equals, Christ effectively extends that privilege to us. Other sayings and actions confirm that this was Christ's intention. Such equality enables us to exercise *parrhēsia*, "freedom of speech," with God. A compound of words that mean "all" and "say," *parrhēsia* is the privilege of being able to say anything to someone in authority without fear of retribution.

26. Mt 7.8, Lk 11.10.

27. Dt 10.12.

receiving freedom of speech to command him, if we keep his commandments.

For commanding God is not a greater thing than becoming his heir. Commanding God is not a greater thing than becoming a joint heir with Christ himself.[28] Commanding God is not a greater thing than the eminence of the Son of God, assumed when he came to be in the midst of human beings, not as a diner, but as a waiter,[29] one who serves.[30] Commanding God is not a greater thing than the Son of God's stripping himself and laying aside his garments and taking a towel and girding himself with it and putting water into a basin and washing the feet of his disciples.[31] But it is possible with reference to the one who is washed and who understands that he is cleansed by being washed, and even hopes to receive a portion of him by being cleansed, and speaks in the imperative to him,[32] not because we are worthy to give orders, but because God's charity[33] and the indulgence toward us are great. For let us hear: "Beloved, if the heart does not condemn, we have freedom of speech with God; and whatever we ask, we receive from him,"[34] as John says in the Epistle; only then let our heart not condemn, but let consciousness have freedom of speech towards God.

And so that we might be still more persuaded about freedom of speech, which God wishes the human being to have toward him, I shall put in evidence the very thing that is, perhaps, a greater thing than giving orders to God, which is that the judge is going to be judged in the same way as I am. Therefore, a human being says: "So that you may be justified in your logoi and you may prevail when you are judged,"[35] which those who have

28. See Rom 8.17.

29. Origen uses a play on words: "not as a diner," *anakeimenon*, "but as a waiter," *diakeimenon*.

30. See Lk 22.27.

31. See Jn 13.4–5. Origen's extensive commentary on this passage survives in *Comm. Jo.* 32.

32. See Jn 13.8–9.

33. *Philanthrōpia*, "love of humanity," the preferred term for the gratuitous love of God in Origen and other early Christian authors.

34. 1 Jn 3.21.

35. Ps 50.6 (Rom 3.4). The verb is ambiguous; Origen takes it to mean,

not understood have turned into "when I am judged." What do such persons do to other passages where it is written: "The Lord himself will come to judgment with the elders of the people and with his rulers"?[36] But if this does not yet provide clear evidence that the judge is judged as if with you, hear "Come and let us be rebuked, says the Lord."[37] The Lord has permitted you to speak with freedom of speech to him, if you imagine that you can rebuke him for being slow about his provision and say such things with freedom of speech. This is clear from "Come and let us be rebuked, says the Lord." And it is in accord with "the spirit of adoption,"[38] and, "you are no longer a slave, but a son,"[39] and your father is God and your brother is the Lord, who said, "I shall pass your name to your brothers," or rather, "My brothers, in the midst of the Church I shall hymn you."[40] Is it astounding for a son to have freedom of speech towards his father, not being ashamed of the spirit of adoption, when he is commanded by the father, to command the father in return, thinking that he has a right to do so about the things he wants?

This on account of "*Let God rise up.*"

3. For it must be sought when God rises up and when he sleeps. For the divine Scriptures say such things concerning him in ordinary usage, but it must be understood how such things are recorded. Concerning his sleeping, someone says, praying, in the Psalms: "Rise up. Why are you sleeping, Lord? Why have you turned your face away? Have you forgotten our destitution and our oppression?"[41] Concerning his sitting: "Show yourself, seated upon the Cherubim, opposite Ephraim, Benjamin, and Manasseh."[42] Concerning God's standing, he himself says to Moses: "But you, stand together with me."[43] And concerning

---

"you [God] are judged," but it could be construed to mean "you enter into a dispute." In the original Hebrew, God is doing the judging, not being judged.

36. Is 3.14.

37. Is 1.18.

38. Rom 8.15.

39. Gal 4.7.

40. Ps 21.23.

41. Ps 43.24–25. The LXX actually says "wake up" rather than "arise."

42. Ps 79.2–3.

43. Dt 5.31.

walking, in Genesis it is recorded that, after the transgression, Adam heard "the Lord God walking in the garden in the afternoon."[44]

But in relation to these passages it must be known that, on the one hand, God, insofar as he is by himself, is inalterable and unchangeable and always the same and holding steady. Therefore, we say about created things, "the heavens will be destroyed," but about him, "but you remain," and again, concerning products of craftsmanship, "and all like a mantle they will be worn out, and like a wrap you will roll them up, and like a mantle they will be exchanged";[45] but concerning God, who never wears out but always stays new, "but you are the same, and your years do not vanish." And I trust him who said through the prophet, "I am your God, and I have not changed."[46] Inasmuch, then, as, in himself, the God of the Universe is inalterable, unchangeable, and not to be transformed, on account of you, human being, transformations, as it were, may be spoken of regarding him, becoming for each as it is appropriate to become for each.[47]

Paul, on the one hand, then, as a human being who had become, through love and charity, what the person being benefited needs, says: "I have become a Jew for the Jews, that I might gain the Jews; to those under the law as one under the law, in order to gain those under the law; to those without law like one without law (being not without God's law, but subject to Christ's law), that I might gain those without the law; to the weak I have become weak, that I might gain the weak; to all I have become all things, so that by all means I may save some."[48] On the other

---

44. Gn 3.8.

45. Ps 101.26–27. The LXX has "like a wrap you will exchange them." Origen cites this passage as it appears in Heb 1.12.

46. Mal 3.6.

47. Origen held the Platonic view (see *Phaedo* 78d) that God, identified as being, does not change. On the other hand, we experience God's changelessness as inexhaustible plenitude. See also PS73H1.3 and PS74H.6 below. Divine condescension or accommodation (*sugkatabasis*), adapting to encounter us as we are, is fundamental to Origen's biblical exegesis and theology. See PS77H9.1 below.

48. 1 Cor 9.20–22.

hand, as whose imitator does Paul do this? I am bold and say "of Christ,"[49] who became weak for the weak, so that he might gain the weak. And "the weakness of God is stronger than human beings"; not only is the weakness of Christ, who was crucified out of weakness, stronger than that of human beings, but the Apostle dared to speak in an entirely extraordinary and risky way; when speaking to hearers who do not know what they are hearing, he says: "The foolish thing of God is wiser than human beings."[50]

God's weakness certainly does not exist in truth, but, because of our weakness, the so-called "weakness of God" releases us from all our weakness. But just as there is not, when it comes to the truth, a foolish thing of God, on account of "the foolish things of the world, which God has chosen,"[51] he says that the foolish thing of God is wiser than human beings. Thus then, as God is in truth inalterable and unchangeable, but on account of us, when he is said to be sitting, he is, as it were, sitting in judgment on someone. For he himself would not be standing before the one being judged![52] "Books were opened, and a tribunal sat," and it sits because it is judging. But for the holy and blessed person, to whom the words "the one believing in me is not judged"[53] are fitting, he does not sit, but he has stood up. Therefore, the one who is standing says to the one who is now worthy to stand with God, "You stand here with me."[54] But because for the overseer[55] unworthy of the providence and love of God, "the one who neither slumbers nor sleeps when he guards Israel"[56] sleeps, and if that one should have a change of heart, for whom God sleeps, it says, "and the Lord awoke like one who sleeps, like a powerful man and befuddled with wine";[57] so he also "rises up."[58]

49. See 1 Cor 11.1.
50. 1 Cor 1.25.
51. 1 Cor 1.27.
52. Dn 7.10.
53. Jn 3.18.
54. Dt 5.31.
55. Or "bishop" (*episkopos*).
56. See Ps 120.4.
57. Ps 77.65. See PS77H9.2 below.
58. Throughout this passage Origen argues that "rising up" (from sleep) has

This on account of "*Let God rise up.*"

4. We also see "*Let his enemies be scattered.*"[59] There are two principal gatherings, that of the devil on the one hand and that of God on the other, and it is impossible for both of these gatherings to be gathered together. When the gathering of the devil is gathered, understand the gathering either of the hostile powers[60] or of the heterodox, concerning whom it is said, "I have hated the gathering of evildoers."[61]

Whence a logos necessarily emerges about gathering: that those who neglect gathering,[62] those who do not hear the one who says, "He who does not gather with me, scatters me,"[63] those who do not hear, "Do not neglect gathering, as is the custom of some,"[64] do not commit just one sin, because they scatter when they are not gathered and welded together in common prayers, but they sin a greater sin. For each of those who are not gathered, by so choosing, gathers himself with the gathering of evildoers, as, again, each of those gathered, by his own choice,[65] but gathering as Christ teaches, saying, "He who does not gather with me"—for we should gather with him—each, then, of those so gathered, scatters the gathering of the evil one, and for those so gathered God does not lie down, but rises up. Therefore, it says, "*Let God rise up and let his enemies be scattered.*"[66]

Someone[67] hearing will say, "You have spoken about two

---

the same status as other language denoting human activity—sitting, standing, sleeping, suffering a hangover—when applied to God. This language does not apply to God, but to human beings in relationship to God. Gregory of Nazianzus appeals to this principle in *Oration* 31.25.

59. Ps 67.2b.

60. This is Origen's normal term for demons.

61. Ps 25.5. Although the word translated "gathering" is *sunagōgē*, the word for a Jewish gathering or gathering place for worship, Origen avoids that connotation here. Instead, he takes *sunagōgē* to be synonymous with *ekklēsia*, "assembly" or "church." The same word appears in the "gathering of gods" of Ps 81.1, interpreted below in PS81H.1. See also PS77H2.7, n. 91.

62. See Heb 10.25.

63. Mt 12.30.

64. Heb 10.25.

65. Or "to the extent that it is up to himself," *to hoson eph' heautōi.*

66. Ps 67.2.

67. "Someone," the attentive listener, notices that Origen is speaking at length about a subject, i.e., gathering, that is not actually mentioned in the reading.

gatherings, but what has been written is not about gatherings, but about God." Yes, the introduction begins well with God, because, in fact, for a holy gathering to occur, God must rise up, because the gathering of sinners is actually dissolved when God arises, but the gathering of the just is gathered. See, as things have been said concerning sinners, in the same manner it is said also concerning the just, after needing to descend to sinners, when God stands up, the just have the appropriate feelings. For it is written, "and let the just be glad, and let them rejoice before God, let them be delighted for joy."[68] Each of them is not glad by himself, but gladness is common to all those who are holy, "for the heart and soul of all the believers were one."[69]

Allow this passage, in ordinary usage, to refer to the God of the Universe and, in accord with the leading explanation, let *"Let God rise up, and let his enemies be scattered"* be restored to him.[70]

5. Since I know the Savior and my Lord is a god—"In the beginning was the logos, and the logos was near God, and the logos was a god"[71]—I say, especially because in Hebrew the first article is not employed,[72] that it could be read as "Let a god rise up, and let his enemies be scattered." For before the Savior suffered, "the kings of the earth stood by, and the rulers were gathered together against the Lord and against his Christ."[73] After his rising up, those gathered together were scattered and fled before his face, and they vanished *"as smoke vanishes and wax melts before the face of a fire."*[74] So they were destroyed, defeated first by Christ's death, second by his rising up[75] and life.

But someone[76] hearing, especially someone who is sharp

68. Ps 67.4.

69. Acts 4.32. The use of a plural in the Psalm, expressing a joy held in common, implies that the righteous are, in fact, gathered.

70. Origen allows that the god referred to can be the God of the Universe, but will offer an alternative explanation, applying it to the divine logos.

71. Jn 1.1. See n. 98 on PS15H2.8.

72. Origen correctly points out that Hebrew does not employ an article with its word for God. As we shall see, this grammatical point opens a different and deeper interpretation of the Psalm.

73. Ps 2.2.

74. Ps 67.3.

75. *Anastasis,* resurrection.

76. See n. 67 above.

and can search all things, even the deep things of God,[77] will say, "Did not our Savior, being a god, rise up from the dead especially because he was a god? Very well then, a god died and death could not contain a god." On the contrary, did he not himself teach that what dies is a human being? For he said to those scheming against him: "Now you seek to kill me, a human being who has spoken the truth to you, which I heard from the Father."[78] For he even had known that there was something human present because what they sought to destroy was not the truth, not the life, and not the rising up,[79] for the rising up will not allow death, but the rising up is the only begotten of God. To say that life died involves a contradiction automatically, for the Lord said, "I am the life." How, therefore, do you say that "*let God rise up*" fits the Savior? For if God rises up, see how the logos implies the opposite; it would be a necessity to speak in contradiction to Scripture and say, "If God rises up, God has died."

In fact, then, we can, receiving from the Father himself the presence of the logos, solve the puzzle we are seeking to solve. Let us pay careful attention to the things said by the blessed Paul about rising up: "What is sown in corruption does not awaken in corruption, but in incorruption; what is sown in dishonor does not awaken in dishonor but in power," and why is it that "what is sown soulish[80] does not awaken soulish, but spiritual"?[81] Why is it marvelous that what died, since a human being is subject to death, was a human being, but what rose up, on

---

77. See 1 Cor 2.10.

78. Jn 8.40. See *Comm. Jo.* 19.2.6.

79. See Jn 11.25.

80. *Psuchikos*, "soulish." As Origen understood Paul (and probably as Paul understood Paul), human beings are a composite of body, soul, and spirit (see PS15H1.3 and PS15H2.10 above and PS77H6.2, n. 52 below). The two terms *psuchikos* and *pneumatikos* distinguish between human beings who live by their soul, apart from God, and those who live by their spirit, in faithful relationship with God. In the Vulgate, *animale* nicely corresponds to *psuchikos*. English has no such word. Because German does not either, Luther used *natürlich* to convey the general sense; William Tyndale and English translators after him have usually translated *psuchikos* as "natural." "Natural" would misrepresent Origen's careful attention to biblical language, since Paul does not introduce the concept of "nature" and in his usage the adjectives reflect the nouns from which they are derived. David Bentley Hart uses "psychical" (*The New Testament: A Translation* [New Haven: Yale University Press, 2017], 323 and 349).

81. See 1 Cor 15.43–44.

the analogy of the soulish rising up as spiritual, was no longer a human being but a god? The one who rises up was a human being, since a human being dies, for he is a mortal animal. Having died, he will be mortal again. But if he is not mortal, but stays deathless—"death no longer lords it over him"[82]—evidently being deathless, he is no longer a human being, but the one who has arisen is a god.

And why should I say this about the Savior? For these things, indeed, await you, the one believing in God, the one accepting Christ Jesus. You die a human being, but you awake a god. If you no longer die after you have been awakened, you no longer fall; you are no longer tested as you are now tested. If you were a sinner, now it is said to you: "I have said, you are gods and all sons of the Most High, but you die as human beings, and as one of the rulers you fall."[83] Then you will no longer be rebuked with "you die as human beings." For you remain a god, and it is said to you: "I have said, you are gods and all sons of the Most High." And the rest will still fit you: you do not die, nor do you fall, but you have stood with him, a god who always stands, when therefore our Savior rises up; when he dies he is a human being, but when he awakes, a god.

6. "*His enemies are scattered*":[84] first, those gathered together against the Lord and against his Christ[85] until, second (and now), Christ rises also with each of those rising up, "for we have been buried with Christ through baptism,"[86] and we rose up together with him. And when one rises together with the one who died to sin, when one rises together, I say, with Christ, his enemies are scattered,[87] those who first were gathered together for their own part no longer are together, for they are scattered.[88]

---

82. Rom 6.9.

83. Ps 81.6–7.

84. Ps 67.2.

85. Ps 2.2.

86. Rom 6.4.

87. See Rom 6.10. Christ's enemies, the demonic powers renounced in baptism, are scattered when we rise together with Christ, because those who "rise together" in baptism constitute the Church, gathering back into unity the souls isolated by sin from one another as well as from God.

88. In *Hom. Jer.* 12.3 Origen discusses social isolation as a punishment that

And he who once said, "Come, let us go down and confuse their tongue there,"[89] and is coming down toward you if you rise up from the dead, now says, "Let us confuse, let us scatter the enemies of the one who accepts death to the cosmos, the one who receives the ability to rise up for God."

The enemies of God have been scattered twice already, in the first complete[90] rising up of Christ and in the Savior's rising up in each, when "we walk in newness of life."[91] And [I am] saying a third interpretation, for the logos has urged us to give a third interpretation as well, commanding through Solomon to write down God's letters three times, for he says: "And you shall write them down three times, in counsel and knowledge in order to answer true logoi to those who question you."[92] I know another rising up of Christ's body. "You are Christ's body and members partially"[93] and the head, some of the blessed, cannot say to the feet, other human beings, I do not need you.[94] But look at, as it was said, the many members of Christ.[95] I see this body, all those who have fallen asleep, "in the voice of an archangel and in God's trumpet"[96] rising up at one turn of the scale so as then to say that the Church rises up, Christ's mouth and body, and Christ rises up to be in the whole body as at that time he was in that body, so that he will no longer only be the rising up[97] according to our Father's earnest,[98] but a rising up of the

---

God metes out to sinners to lead them to repentance. It is comparable to exile, a dreaded form of punishment in the ancient world.

89. Gn 11.7.

90. "Complete" or "general," *katholikēn*, may refer to the rising up of body, soul, and spirit together in the person of Christ, or it may possibly refer to the original foundation of the Church.

91. Rom 6.4.

92. Prv 22.20–21. See *Princ.* 4.2.4 on this threefold interpretation. The third interpretation is spiritual and deals with a divine secret, final unity in God.

93. 1 Cor 12.27.

94. See 1 Cor 12.21.

95. See 1 Cor 12.12.

96. See 1 Thes 4.16.

97. See Jn 11.25. Origen treats each title of Christ as a way in which Christ is present for the redeemed. At the final resurrection, Christ will no longer be *anastasis*, "rising up" or "resurrection," in the way he is now, partially and as an earnest, for baptized Christians.

98. "Earnest" is a commercial term for a partial deposit guaranteeing full

dead according to the completion of the gift, when the perfect has come,[99] the rising up together of Christ's whole body. And then Christ comes in the rising up and will be in his own body, not partially,[100] when Christ thus rises up god in the whole body when it has risen up,[101] and then his enemies will be completely scattered, then those who have become enemies will vanish like smoke in chastisement; as smoke vanishes, they will vanish.[102]

7. And "*as wax melts before the face of fire, so sinners will be destroyed before God's face, and let the just rejoice*"[103] is made complete in one explanation concerning the smoke and the wax; I do not suppose three interpretations are bestowed; the logos makes an orphan.[104] For sinners are spoken of as smoke, because when there is fire and when there is light, there is smoke, being a byproduct of fire and a byproduct of light; I find the fire in "who makes his angels spirits and his ministers flames of fire,"[105] and the angel appeared to Moses in the fire of a flame.[106] I seek also

---

delivery in the future. Origen identifies Jesus's resurrection from the dead after his crucifixion, which Paul refers to as the "first fruits" of the resurrection (1 Cor 15.20 and 15.23), with the Spirit as a guarantee of eventual resurrection, referred to as "first fruits" (Rom 8.23) or "earnest" (2 Cor 1.22 and 5.5). Origen apparently counts on his hearers to recognize the "earnest of the Spirit" in 2 Cor as an earnest of the resurrection. See *Hom. Ezech.* 2.5: "The just, rising again, say, 'We have been buried with Christ in baptism, and we have risen again with him' [Rom 6.4]. Because, just as we have received the 'earnest' of the Holy Spirit [see 2 Cor 1.22], which we shall receive in fullness 'when that which is perfect has come' [1 Cor 13.10], so it is thus the earnest of the resurrection, because no one among us has yet been raised in the complete resurrection."

99. See 1 Cor 13.10.

100. See 1 Cor 12.27 and 13.9. Origen understands the same phrase, *ek merous*, to mean the same thing in adjacent chapters. David Bentley Hart (*The New Testament,* 342–43) agrees with Origen.

101. The gathering of the Church as Christ's body is thus a prefiguration of eschatological gathering when God will be all in all. See *Princ.* 1.6.1.

102. Ps 67.3. Enemies have vanished when they are no longer enemies. See PS67H1.9 below.

103. Ps 67.3–4.

104. This sentence is obscure and may not have been transmitted correctly. It appears to apply to an issue of interpretation. In Origen's threefold interpretation of Scripture, the first level, the plain sense of the words, may be untrue. The passage is not about actual smoke or wax at all. See *Princ.* 4.3.

105. Ps 103.4, Heb 1.7.

106. Ex 3.2. This non-material smoke must come from a non-material fire, the fire of Ps 103.4 and Ex 3.2.

the light. I trust in the Lord, who says to me: "You are the light of the cosmos."[107] Perhaps also the angels themselves, when they chastise, are fire, but when they minister matters of blessedness and salvation, they are, instead, the light of those who hear, "You are the light of the cosmos."[108] And do not be amazed if the angels are both of these things, when the God of the Universe himself is said to be both light and fire. To sinners our God is fire, devouring all wickedness.[109] But to the just God is no longer fire, but light, "for God is light, and there is no darkness at all in him."[110]

Accordingly God is light and fire; but the angels, it is bestowed that they are fire and light. And how are the just light and fire? It is said in the Gospel that Christ is the genuine light.[111] I shall propose that he is also fire. The Savior himself said, "I have come to cast fire on the earth, and I wish that it were already kindled."[112] The just are imitators of Christ. Christ has need of the fire also, so that earthly things may vanish. Accordingly he[113] prays, as one who is good, that he should kindle this fire: would that the fire would come concerning which the Savior prayed, saying, "Would that it were already kindled in me," so that, going forth, this fire might burn all the thorn and burn it entirely, for it knows not to set fire to threshing floors or ears of grain or a plain.[114]

107. Mt 5.14. Now Origen finds non-material light.

108. See *Comm. Jo.* 1.12.75 on angels as evangelists.

109. See Dt 4.24 and 9.3, Heb 12.29.

110. 1 Jn 1.5.

111. See Jn 1.5.

112. Lk 12.49.

113. That is, the believer who imitates Christ.

114. See Ex 22.5. Origen cryptically alludes to his teaching that a fire that the believer has prayed for is one of self-purification, which can be painful but is not punitive or destructive. In speaking of "lamb who takes away the sin of the world" in Jn 1.29, Origen says: "Sin is not taken away from all by the lamb without their suffering and torment until it is taken away. For thorns are not just sown in, but in many cases have become rooted in the hands of those who become inebriated through evil and have lost sobriety according to the saying in Proverbs, 'Thorns grow into the hand of a drunkard' [Prv 26.9]. Why, then, is there a need to speak of how much difficulty is occasioned for the one who allows such things to grow into the body of his own soul? For the one who has allowed vice so deep into his own soul that it becomes ground bearing thorns must undergo surgery by the logos of the living God, sharper than any two-

Yes, we have light and fire, which smoke accompanies, for the impious and sinners are a byproduct of the just; not according to an essential logos have they been made such. For the essential logos wanted them to be light as well; it meant them, as the logos had been bestowed, to be fire. Because they had fled from being light and they did not want to be fire, for that reason they have become smoke. Therefore, as smoke vanishes, they vanish.

8. The equivalent must be said regarding the wax. For honey is the essential work of bees, and Solomon said: "Go to the bee and learn how she is a worker,"[115] and, "Four things are wiser than the wise: the ants, the locust, the bee, and the conies, a nation not strong."[116] Yes, the bee makes honey as its essential work, but wax is a byproduct of the essential thing, honey.

But I want to understand, says one hearing me, how the bee makes honey and the generation of a honeycomb follows. Our Savior and Lord of all the prophet bees and of all the apostle bees is, as some call him, the *essēn,* king of bees.[117] He is in charge of the supply of honey. And Moses bee, Isaiah bee, Jeremiah bee, or the rest of the prophet bees have made honey under the direction of the *essēn,* this being the essential work for the king bee and the bees. The just among those hearing the law and the prophets are the honey; the sinners among the hearers have become wax. And when you come to Christ's appearance and you see the apostolic bees and you understand the gospel writings and you see the presence and teaching of Christ, do not hesitate to say that he has made the Church honey, but a byproduct has come about in the generation of such a great honey, the wax of the heresies, the wax in between the just.[118]

And if Christ had not come, there would be neither honey

---

edged sword [Heb 4.12] and more active and more burning than any fire. And in such a soul there must be sent the fire that finds thorns and, because of its divinity, will stop at them and will not break out on threshing floors, or ears of grain, or a plain" (*Comm. Jo.* 6.58.297–98).

115. Prv 6.8.

116. Cf. Prv 30.26–30 LXX.

117. In antiquity and as late as the 16th century, many thought that the bee in charge would have to be male; see Shakespeare's *Henry V* 1. 2.190.

118. Wax was seen as impure or false. *Akeraios* in Greek, "simple" or "sincere," as the Latin *sincerus,* from which we get our word, means "without wax."

nor wax, the heresies, the sinners among us, those who say, "In your name we have eaten, and in your name we have drunk, and in your name we have thrown out demons," but he says to them, "Get away from me, I never knew you,"[119] for he never knew that wax, the byproduct that was generated with honey, except that *"as smoke vanishes, they vanish; as wax melts before the face of fire, so may sinners be destroyed before God's face, and let the just rejoice."*[120]

Still, what I am saying about Christ also applies to the creatures of the God of the Universe. He has made the essential things, but their byproducts have been produced by evil like wax and smoke. Cain was smoke, but Abel was light.[121] Shem was fire, but Ham and Canaan were smoke. Shem was honey, and Japheth was light. Two are blessed for having become light from the light of Noah and honey from his sweetness. But since sinners vanish like smoke and melt like wax, therefore "cursed be Canaan, he will be a houseboy for his brothers."[122] Someone wishing sinners not to be produced effectively says that the just should not have been produced.

9. Let, then, those who hate the God who rises up flee before his face,[123] for insofar as they are arrayed against God and stand against him, they have not fled from before God's face, but when they are defeated by God's divinity, they flee before his face. An equivalent to those fleeing before God's face is found in what is written about Cain, who, after his sins were complete, went away from God's face.[124] Because the Lord's face is upon those who do evil and he will utterly destroy their memory from the earth,[125] therefore those who do evil flee from God's face, but should they flee, as wax melts before the face of fire, so may sinners be destroyed before God's face.[126]

---

119. Mt 7.22–23.

120. Ps 67.3–4.

121. See Gn 4.2.

122. See Gn 5.32.

123. See Ps 67.2.

124. Gn 4.16.

125. Ps 33.17.

126. The righteous rejoice, not over the punishment sinners undergo, but those who were sinners have, like the righteous themselves, been delivered from sin.

When such things come about to those who hate God and to his enemies, the just rejoice. For until the impious die, they do not have a return for their sins, nor do the just have a return for their joy. For whenever sinners vanish like smoke and melt like wax, insofar as they are sinners, not only do the just rejoice over themselves, but also over the vanishing of smoke and melting of wax. For they see a good thing coming about from the vanishing of smoke and melting of wax. Perhaps also, seeing such a thing coming about by means of the fire that was going to melt the wax in order that only the honey would be left, the Savior said, "I have come to cast fire on the earth, and would that it were kindled already."[127]

It seems reasonable to me in the logos to get rid of a stupid assumption of the brothers who sometimes say mindless things about sins. For they suppose that it is possible for one who remains a sinner to be saved and for God to give judgment regarding the stench brought about by sin that it will be saved, not seeing that such a thing is impossible. For they, on their part, say that God can toss in with the good fish even the rotten, guilty fish that have fallen into the net,[128] not seeing that this is not reasonable, to make the net impure, not to take the good ones out clean so that the bad ones will not be mixed in with the good.

Such persons would seem to want to store up the chaff in the granary.[129] For what is the difference between putting the bad fish along with the good and storing the chaff in the granary, and for the smoke not to vanish but to be saved with the light, so that where there would be salvation, there would be smoke and evil, and wherever honey would be, there would be inedible wax, which is not sweet? For conduct is the sweetness of the just person, and God's logos makes everything sweet in him, so, "How sweet are your oracles in my throat."[130] His conduct is sweetness; what a sinner does is bitter. But if they are bitter and therefore taste bitter to the one who is, in a strict sense, just, it is

127. Lk 12.49.
128. See Mt 13.48.
129. See Mt 3.12, Lk 3.17.
130. Ps 118.103.

clear that in the opposite case, the good deeds of the just taste sweet, so that in his own logoi the just person prays concerning himself, "May my dialogue be made pleasant."[131]

10. Therefore, when these things happen to sinners, "let the just rejoice." Let us become just so that we may rejoice. Do not consider becoming just [as] something simple and plain, for justice is Christ. "He became wisdom by God's doing, and justice, sanctification, and redemption."[132] It is not possible to be just without participating in Christ, and if someone supposes that he is someone just outside the faith, one of two possibilities applies: either the gentile participates in Christ, or, if he does not participate in Christ, he is not just. Which do you want to demonstrate, that a gentile participates in Christ? But this is incongruous.[133] A conventional person says, "Let me and everyone who believes in Christ participate in Christ, so that it may be said about me, 'We have become participants in Christ.'"[134] The gentile does not even consider participating in Christ, but if he does not participate

131. Ps 103.34.

132. 1 Cor 1.30.

133. Origen's use of *apemphainetai*, which I have translated "is incongruous," can mean either that such a conclusion is absurd or that it is simply surprising. Perhaps Origen deliberately does not make it clear whether he excludes the possibility that a gentile may participate in Christ without being aware of it. He knew that he was using Platonic terminology when he said that one who "participates," *metechei*, in Christ participates in justice. See Plato, *Republic* 5.472b–c: "But if we were to discover what sort of thing justice [*dikaiosunē*] is, shall we right away deem it fit that the just man must not differ from it, but in every way be the same sort of thing that justice is, or shall we be content, if he should be something as close as possible to it and participate [*metechēi*] in it to a greater extent than others?" He probably knew as well Justin Martyr's position: "We have been taught that Christ is the firstborn of God, and we have already indicated that he is logos in whom all the human race participates [*metesche*]. And those who are living with logos are Christians, even those who were considered godless, for example, among the Greeks Socrates and Heraclitus and those similar to them …" (*First Apology* 46). See also Justin Martyr, *Second Apology* 10.

134. Heb 3.14. Origen's convoluted and qualified language may be deliberately obscure in order to maintain the ambiguity noted above. The ordinary person, or, as above in the text, a "conventional person" (*ho polus*, Origen's way of referring to only one of *hoi polloi*) wants to be spoken of as part of the "we" in "we have become participants in Christ." At the very least, it is more important for him to affirm that one must be genuinely righteous, as Christ is, in order to be a Christian than to suggest that one should be a Christian in order to be righteous.

in Christ, he does not have unfeigned justice. For in distinction from feigned justice, it is said in Proverbs, according to the Seventy, "And in proverbs you will understand true justice and straight judgment."[135] For if there were not a justice that appears so, but is not true, it would not have said, "you will understand true justice"; just as there is a genuine light different from the one that is not genuine, so there would be a more genuine justice alongside the one that is not true.

The just, therefore, those who participate in Christ's justice, will rejoice and be glad. And "they will be glad" does not suffice, for only "they will be glad" is not good, unless you take the next phrase, since it is necessary. And what is that? "They will be glad before God." Surely it is a blessing[136] to be glad before God. But with "to be glad before God" is to be delighted for joy. Then we shall be delighted, if we come together in the same place. "For see, what a good thing and a delightful thing it is for them to settle together as brothers."[137] Then we shall, in a strict sense, settle together, because now we are not really settling, for our quarters now are tents,[138] and I travel until I come to the house of God in the sound of gladness, the house of those who make holiday.[139] And should I go to the house, I shall be delighted in the house of God. Therefore, it is said, "One thing have I asked of the Lord, this I shall seek, that I may settle in the house of the Lord all the days of my life, that I may behold the delightfulness of the Lord and examine the temple of his holiness"[140] in Christ Jesus, to whom is the glory and the might to the ages of ages. Amen.

---

135. Prv 1.3. By referring to the Seventy (i.e., the Septuagint) Origen signals that "true" does not appear in the Hebrew. Given Origen's high estimate of Hebrew (see PS80H1.7 below) this admission may be a hint that an argument based on the LXX alone is not strong.

136. See Ps 132.3. "Blessing" (*eulogia*) is a common word, but its use here indicates that Origen is already moving toward Psalm 132.

137. Ps 132.1. A verbal similarity, the Greek root *terp* shared by the words I have translated "delight" and "delightful," brings the entire Psalm (132), in which Origen appears to see a reference to an eschatological fulfillment, into conversation with Psalm 67.

138. See 2 Cor 5.1–5, which hearkens back to the wanderings in the wilderness of Exodus and Numbers. See *Hom. Num.* 17.4.

139. Ps 41.5.

140. Ps 26.4.

HOMILY 2 ON PSALM 67

T IS NOT possible to do the things commanded by God or by Christ or the Holy Spirit in the divine Scriptures without first having perceived what is said. Often, however, we seem to perceive things that we have been commanded; but when we examine and investigate whether or not what is commanded befits the one who commands and whether it exemplifies a sublimity befitting God as the speaker, we do not find that at all in such a command. Accordingly, the logos himself summons us by "seek and you will find,"[1] and to seek even concerning what we earlier seemed to have understood, so that, then, by seeking we will actually find in the commands of God something worthy[2] of the one who commands and that is brought about not just by any chance person, but only by such and such great persons who do the other great and divine commands of God.

Just as, then, the commandments concerning martyrdom are not to be carried out by everyone, but by those having great love, the love toward God, "the never-failing love toward God that covers up all things, believes all things, hopes all things, endures all things, that never fails,"[3] so in many cases we will

---

1. Mt 7.7.

2. That a passage, to be correctly interpreted, must be worthy of God is a basic principle for interpreting the Bible. Thus in preaching on Jer 13.12, "And you shall say to the people, 'Every jar shall be filled,'" Origen states: "What the prophet is commanded to say by God must be worthy of God, but it appears that it is not worthy of God when we stay with the letter, so that another person hearing the letter would say, 'These letters are foolish'" (*Hom. Jer.* 12.1). See also *Princ.* 4.2.1. On "great commandment," see Mt 22.34–40 and possibly Mt 23.23–24.

3. See 1 Cor 13.7–8. Origen expects his hearers to recall 1 Cor 13.3, which refers to the futility of "handing over my body" if I do not have love.

find that it is for someone great in God to do what God has commanded.[4] And there must be sought in every commandment the intent of the one who commands and the magnitude of love, so that, being empowered by that love and enlightened by the genuine light, we may perform what is commanded with understanding.

2. But what, indeed, is the intention of this introduction? Listen. The beginning of today's reading was a command. The logos said: "*Sing to God, play a stringed instrument to his name. Make a way for him who has trod upon the sunsets. His name is the Lord.*"[5] I seek therefore whether it was the God of the Universe who commanded this, or Christ, or the Holy Spirit, because nothing else may be understood in "*Sing to God*" than a modulation of the voice, which among us is done, rather, by musicians and those who have made it their business to train their voices in both projection and quality through some sort of voice exercise and voice training.[6] I therefore seek to discover whether the logos intends something only like that or intends this commandment first for the simpler as something useful to them by some logos, as we shall establish shortly and also, no less, a second meaning having a greatness worthy of the one commanding, which can be seen in "*Sing to God, play a stringed instrument[7] to his name.*"

First, indeed, the logos professes the statement to have some-

4. Origen was the son of a martyr, risked martyrdom by continuing as a Christian teacher during a time of persecution in Alexandria when he was a young man, and, not long after saying these words, would undergo torture rather than forswear his faith (Eusebius, *Hist. eccl.* 6.2 and 6.39). He wrote *Exhortation to Martyrdom* to his patron, Ambrosius, in which he stated Christians should accept death rather than worship other gods, even if it were done insincerely and under compulsion. Doing so would be a serious sin, endangering their relationship with God. This position accorded with the consensus of Christians in the third century. Here, surprisingly, he appears to modify that position. The implication of his words here, in which he refers to Paul's apparent statement that martyrdom is futile when it is not motivated by love, would be that the command to accept martyrdom applies only to the spiritually advanced.

5. Ps 67.5.

6. It is difficult to see how Origen would have considered singing an action for trained specialists if he were accustomed to congregational singing. Perhaps intoning or chanting the Psalms did not count as "singing."

7. *Psalate,* "pluck," implies playing a stringed instrument.

thing valuable,[8] and it is necessary to establish this to begin with. We know indeed that we all as human beings need relaxation, and it does not do for our governing faculty to be constantly tense, nor that we should become fervent continually. Those outside the faith seek relaxation in disorderly pastimes and pouring themselves out in jollity and in bawdy songs, and they take their own feelings as themes in their songs. Sometimes they sing love songs, at other times paeans and hymns to the gods that accord with their own superstition, and yet again they take their own gloom for themes, so that they sing dirges in accord with their melancholy; at other times they take marriages as their theme, from which come wedding songs.

But in our case, the logos wanted to divert the soul of believers from gentile songs toward better, godly, ones, so that by the substitution of things seemingly of the same genre, but better, he might withdraw the soul from desires expressed in those things. And the logos says, "Do you want to sing and use a song with an erotic theme? Learn that there is also a truly divine heavenly love in the Song of Songs. You want to sing wedding songs? Learn about the divine marriage, according to the Gospel, of the son of the king, a marriage to which you were invited.[9] Understand the bridegroom, identify the bride, and do not just sing a song, but a special one; just as something can be a holy of holies,[10] so sing the Song of Songs. But does he want you to lament, with the odes and laments suitable to you when you were a gentile? Learn that now there is for you a blessedness of those who mourn."[11]

Understand, then, what you must lament, look at your Jerusalem, seek your own return there,[12] say, lamenting, "How did the

8. Although, in Origen's understanding, we need to look beyond the command to sing for something more worthy of God, our first obligation is to examine if the statement (*to rhēton*) as immediately understood has something valuable to tell us. See *Princ.* 4.2.8: "For it was appointed to make even the covering of spiritual things—I speak of the bodily aspect of the Scriptures—not unhelpful in many passages and able to improve the many, insofar as they accept it." Origen may have had in mind 2 Tm 3.16.

9. See Mt 22.2.

10. See, for example, Ex 29.37.

11. See Lk 6.21.

12. The events in the history of Israel trace out the events for each individual soul. See especially the homilies on Psalm 77 below.

city sit alone; she that was full of peoples, ruling in the country districts, was subject to tribute. Weeping, she wept in the night, and her tears were on her cheeks";[13] and so on, lamenting your own arrival in Babylon, saying, "On the rivers of Babylon, there we sat and wept,"[14] and what follows. And see how your lamentation may be helpful to you, teaching you to seek the same fatherland and to comprehend the secrets concerning it and to lament until you return to the city constructed with precious stones, not inanimate ones, for you are to be "living stones constructed, a spiritual house, into a holy priesthood to offer spiritual sacrifices acceptable to God through Jesus Christ."[15] If, then, you will lament your exile from Jerusalem and understand that being present in the body you are absent from the Lord,[16] having been made one by God you will be a crystal stone, a stone of the enclosure, a selected stone, a sapphire stone, and whatever other precious stones are mentioned, of the ones that constitute the Jerusalem in heaven.[17] Turning around toward God and saying, "as our fathers created false idols,"[18] take up the hymns to the God of the Universe; transform the style of your singing and playing a stringed instrument toward something more reverent, more discreet, more helpful.

This suffices concerning the statement, *"Sing to the Lord,"* because, in and of itself, it has something useful.

3. Since the marvelous Apostle has suggested to me, writing in a certain Epistle text "in part,"[19] as power is supplied to me, I shall attempt, starting from there, to suggest how also something deeper can be understood in *"Sing to the Lord, play a stringed instrument[20] to his name."*[21] Paul says, "speaking to yourselves in psalms, hymns, and spiritual odes, singing and play-

---

13. Lam 1.1–2.

14. Ps 136.1.

15. 1 Pt 2.5. Applying the secret meanings of Scripture to their own lives turns believers, all of them (see PS77H8.9 below), "into a holy priesthood."

16. See 2 Cor 5.8. Our present embodiment is an exile from the realm of being, since the body locates us in space and time, the realm of becoming.

17. See Is 54.11–12 and Rv 21.19–20.

18. Jer 16.19.

19. See 1 Cor 13.9–10, 12.

20. See n. 7 above.

21. Ps 67.5.

ing a stringed instrument in your hearts to God."[22] Here in the Epistle he names "psalms, hymns, and spiritual odes." Elsewhere he says "by grace singing in your hearts."[23] If one relies on the wording in these passages, I do not know if it can be established how the heart sings in a way that would be distinct from just speaking. For when it comes to using the voice, I see a distinction between speaking but not singing, on the one hand, and singing but not speaking, without musical accompaniment, on the other. And it seems that if I speak, I need some distinct excellence in speaking, but if I sing, so that I may sing well, I require music and professional skill in rhythms and notes. Also, it will be necessary for me to know the names of tunes and notes, about which musicians, rather than I, speak.

If, then, it is possible both to sing in the heart and, otherwise, just to speak in it, and it is a different thing to sing in the heart as opposed to simply speaking, on account of "for our spirit in our hearts shouts and sings, 'Abba, Father,'"[24] it must be examined what it means to sing in the heart. There is in us another voice besides the sensible voice, a mental one, and, knowing that this one is heard only by God, the logos says: "The spirit shouting in our hearts." But perhaps if it is said, "with my voice I have shouted at God,"[25] the logos is not speaking about the sensible voice. For God has no need, whenever I speak, for me to shout at him, since the sound of the voice itself, so long as it comes through flesh, wind, and blood, is an impact of air.

But we have another voice, and, so that I shall name it for what it is and persuade the hearer, I shall say that this is the voice of a pure mind.

I need, then, mental music bringing into rhythm[26] the voice of the mind; I need spiritual, not sensible, voice practice. And

22. Eph 5.19.

23. Col 3.16.

24. See Rom 8.15 and Gal 4.6. Since shouting is speaking loudly, Scripture mentions a speaking voice in the heart as well as a singing voice.

25. Ps 3.5.

26. Music is such an integral part of Greek education, particularly in the Platonic tradition, that education, particularly in conduct, can be called "bringing into rhythm." (See, e.g., Plato, *Phaedrus* 253b, *Protagoras* 325a, *Laws* 2.259d.) See also Plotinus, *Enn.* 6.9.8, which uses the image of a *choros,* a dancing choir.

where do I learn that? Who are the teachers of this music? David played a stringed instrument; he used instruments. The narrative says that a certain person was a musician;[27] why is the word not applied to David? Perhaps the translators were being cautious because the word sounds like "Muses,"[28] but the object of thought clearly is that David had received this skill and ability. I will speak in a more ordinary way without being cautious, since we understand what music is. But David is often a model of our Savior, and he made for himself an instrument of ten strings or of as many strings as the structure had, but the great musician David—the one "capable with the hand," for this is how his name is translated,[29] moving on from "David" to the one "capable with the hand," concerning whom the prophets prophesied that he would rule the people[30]—went into [human] life and constructed for himself a great, many-stringed instrument for himself, the Church. When for each of us this logos is bringing the mind into rhythm and applying order to the movements of the mind and to the voices of the mind as if they were voices of music, we can keep the commandment that says, "Sing to the Lord." With such an understanding the Apostle could say, "singing and playing a stringed instrument in our hearts."

Whenever the mind does not think out of tune about Christ or discuss out of rhythm[31] about the God of the Universe, but sees what it should concerning him and discourses on God with appropriate knowledge, it expresses, if I may employ such a term, both the tightening of the voice that comes about in his severity and the relaxation that comes about in his kindness. And, whenever, as it makes a proclamation about God, it is enabled to make a combination of the tuning with measured rhythms and heavenly tunes, then he sings similarly to the heavenly bodies;[32] he sings in the heart and plays a stringed instrument to God.

27. See 1 Sm 16.17–23.

28. The Muses, who give their name to "music," were worshiped as goddesses.

29. This specious etymology appears elsewhere in Origen's works.

30. See 1 Sm 9.17.

31. Origen echoes Sextus Empiricus: "The science of music is what is in tune and out of tune, in rhythm and out of rhythm" (*Math.* 6.38).

32. The music of the spheres. See Plotinus, *Enn.* 2.9.16.

How, "similarly to the heavenly bodies"? As it is written, "The heavens set out in detail the glory of God."[33]

But we have read in the Revelation of John how there are certain holy festivals according to the prophet and apostle John—for as a prophet he recorded the Revelation—and angels celebrate holding harps and playing a stringed instrument, and some celebrate singing the ode of Moses, God's servant.[34] I think, because the whole purpose of the Revelation is spiritual, in which was written, "the one having ears, hear what the Spirit says to the churches,"[35] the things concerning both the song and the psalms are clarified in a spiritual way, for all of us must sing to God, learning the spiritual music and wishing to sing to him. As now we hymn "in part," we sing "in part," when the complete comes, as we shall no longer "prophesy in part," and we shall no longer "know in part but know completely,"[36] so, with the holy angels, archangels, thrones, and lordships, we shall hymn God. And this will be our work in the coming age: to sing with the hearts, to see God with pure hearts[37] and, if there is anything analogous to these, to do that as well.

And let us try, then, to sing differently, and not simply sing, but sing to the Lord. In order that I raise my voice to the Lord, I will need to learn the sound in which the Lord rejoices and the tunes that delight the Master. Just as if I had the opportunity to sing to a king, I must know what sort of tunes the king likes so that I will please the king when I sing, and if I am going to sing in the theaters of some town, I will need to know the tunes familiar to peoples and cities; in the same way, if I am going to sing to the Lord, I must know the tunes that gratify the Lord so that, when the Lord is the audience, I may sing to God.

4. It is good to "sing to God," and this is, to be sure, the first good thing, but the second good thing is to "play a stringed instrument to his name"; for to the extent that "God himself" differs from "his name," to this extent "singing" differs from

33. Ps 18.2.
34. Rv 15.3.
35. Rv 2.7.
36. 1 Cor 13.10.
37. See Mt 5.8.

"playing a stringed instrument." Therefore, Scripture applies the greater expression, singing, to God himself, and the lesser expression, playing a stringed instrument, not to God himself but to his name. And it does not say, "sing to the name of the Lord," but, "to God," and says, "play a stringed instrument," not "to the Lord," but "to his name." But so that the difference between singing and playing a stringed instrument may be perceived, I come back to the sensible, for sensible things become a ladder towards understanding greater things. Therefore, the whole Scripture speaks in sensible terms, so that we may step up on them to spiritual things. And if Scripture had not spoken the law sensibly, we would not have originally been able to say, "For I know that the law is spiritual."[38] Accordingly, singing requires the voice alone, but playing a stringed instrument also requires an instrument. The instrument is a certain psaltery, and its singing is very clear, but the psaltery as an instrument is not able to return the clarity of the human voice, but the instrument, as it were, imitates, to the extent that it can, the clarity of the human voice. When in fact you want to achieve an understanding of the difference between singing and playing a stringed instrument, look at yourself, insofar as you are distinct from the body, and you understand "singing." And understand your body—for you know its resurrection—and see "playing a stringed instrument."[39]

If in respect to our present subject matter, you were to request a different perspective on the distinction between singing and playing a stringed instrument, we would say that, on the one

38. Rom 7.14.

39. On the body as a musical instrument, see also PS80H1.4 and PS80H2.1. According to Aristotle (*De anima* 407b), Pythagoreans taught that the body was a musical instrument (*organon*), in this case a flute, played by the soul. We also find this understanding of the body as a stringed instrument that the human mind plays and the contrast between such playing on an instrument (bodily activity) and singing (mental activity) in Plotinus, *Enn.* 1.4.16, where he likens the human body to a lyre. In Plato, *Laches* 188d, Socrates is praised as a musician who, rather than playing an instrument, has made his entire life harmonious. See also Plotinus, *Enn.* 3.3.5. Clement of Alexandria (in *Protr.* 1) wrote that "the Lord fashioned a human being as a beautiful, breathing instrument according to his own image."

hand, in those things you understand correctly about God and in those things in which you discourse on God well, you sing to him, but in those things that you have to perform through the movements of the instrument, what is for you a spiritual psaltery—the body, I say—you play a stringed instrument to God. The person skilled in playing a stringed instrument does not strike the strings discordantly, but knows timing and fingering, and when he may strike the top string or the one beside it, when the bottom string, when to strike the highest one, even when it gives the lowest tone. Thus someone who knows how to play a stringed instrument with this psaltery brings it into rhythm with God's logos and knows when to move the hand string and when to move the foot string so that he may walk in duty, so that he may do what is proper. He knows when he should give his eye to seeing, so that the eye may not see out of tune[40]—but the person who sees a woman to lust after her[41] sees out of tune— and the ear never accepts or hears anything out of tune. But what does the ear do when someone violates the commandment that says, "You shall not accept empty hearsay,"[42] so that this[43] string, the mouth, may never sing out of tune? But this string, the mouth, sings out of tune when we speak an idle saying, concerning which it is written, "You shall give a logos about it on the day of judgment."[44]

There is a way to use the belly string in tune, when we eat and drink to the glory of God,[45] and to use it out of tune, when we perform such things out of gluttony, so that "whose god is the belly"[46] refers to us. You can complete the series. It is appropriate in demonstrating these matters to maintain silence about the specifics involved in the rest of them. And because "Do"— the Apostle enjoins—"everything in the name of Jesus,"[47] there-

40. In Greek the word for "musical tune," *melos,* also means "part of the body." To sing "out of tune" (*ekmelōs*) entails being "dismembered" from the body of Christ.

41. Mt 5.28.

42. Ex 23.1.

43. Origen was probably pointing to the parts of the body as he named them.

44. Mt 12.36.

45. 1 Cor 10.31.

46. Phil 3.19.

47. Col 3.17.

fore it must be understood that he says "*sing to God*" about better things, but "*play a stringed instrument to his name*"[48] about what has been said, as has been demonstrated, playing a stringed instrument by means of the body.

5. Through the instrument, the psaltery, we shall grasp a third commandment. What does the logos command us? "*Make a road for him who rides on the sunsets, the Lord is his name.*"[49] In Isaiah it is written, "Cast away the stones from the road, and make a road for my people,"[50] and, taking this as an example, we shall pass on to the clarity apparent to me—and given to me through your prayers—of the statement designated for explanation.

An acceptable road builder tries to remove stones of stumbling[51] from the road, so that those who journey may do so without stumbling; so it is written, "Cast away the stones from the road, and make a road for my people."[52] And this is written so that, from what is sensible, someone may understand how one who is teaching people removes stones from the road. For whenever he resolves all the seeming stumbling blocks and obscurities in order to make the Scripture safe and delivers to those who listen the healthy logos, he removes stones from the road; whenever he overturns contrary initial impressions suggested by the wording and evens out the Scripture in clarity—for the whole Scripture is the road leading to salvation—then he fulfills the commandment that says, "Cast away the stones from the road, and make a road for my people." This will suffice to explain the stumbling stone.[53]

Just as it is possible—as we have explained[54]—to make a road

48. Ps 67.5.

49. Ps 67.5b.

50. Is 62.10. Quoting from memory, Origen reverses the order of the two phrases.

51. See Rom 14.13, 1 Cor 8.9.

52. Is 62.10.

53. Ibid. See also Is 8.14, Rom 9.33, 1 Pt 2.8. Origen cites this passage in *Princ.* 4.2.9 and *Hom. Jer.* 19.1, where he argues that God places such "stumbling stones" deliberately on the "road," the divine logos embodied in Scripture (see intro., p. 15), so as to alert interpreters to seek deeper meanings.

54. *Apodedōkamen*, "as we have explained," also suggests, "as we have furnished." Origen has not only explained what the Bible means by clearing stones from a road but has just done what he describes.

for a people, so also it is possible to make a road for God when he is willing for our sake to walk about in this location, the land lying opposite to the paradise planted by God in the east;[55] it is possible to make a road: "*Make a road for him who rides on the sunsets, the Lord is his name.*" And since "*for him who rides on the sunsets*" might seem irreverent,[56] because it is the opposite of the sunrises, and someone might be on the point of misconstruing, therefore the Scripture made the needful addition, "the Lord is his name"; so that you might take courage—should it seem, at the time, irreverent to say, "the Lord has ridden on the sunsets"—it is declared that the Lord rides on the sunsets, where Adam was expelled from paradise.[57]

Why, then, "*make a road for him who rides on the sunsets*"? The Lord seeks a road within you, so that he may not only dwell in you—this is not the only thing that he has promised you—but walk around in you.[58] He therefore seeks a road in you for walking around, just as he seeks a house so that he may dwell in you.[59] Then build a house for the Lord, and endeavor also to reflect spiritually as a spiritual person what has been spoken by the prophet and to speak it with nearly the same standpoint as he did: "For remember David, Lord, and all his gentleness, how he swore an oath to the Lord, he vowed to the God of Jacob: 'If I step up into the bed made up for me and give sleep to my eyes, slumber to my eyelids, and rest to my temples, until I find a place for the Lord, a tent for Jacob's God,'" not lying down until you find a place for the Lord, where you may build him a house.[60] He seeks in order that what was promised might be fulfilled, saying, "I shall dwell in them."[61]

Do not give sleep to your eyes and slumber to your eyelids, until you make a road for the one who wants to walk around in you. Why make a road for the God who wants to walk around in

---

55. See Gn 2.8.

56. "Irreverent" because one would expect the devil to ride on the sunset, since it is the opposite of the sunrise, associated with Christ.

57. See Gn 3.24.

58. See Lv 26.12.

59. See 2 Cor 6.16.

60. Ps 131.1–5.

61. 2 Cor 6.16.

you? The Lord walks around on clean places; the Savior makes festival on places that have been swept. Sweeping the place is equivalent to what happens with rich people. Whenever the rich have walkways in their houses, there are some people charged with maintaining the place for walking, and with sweeping, cleaning, and washing it, so that the walkway may be more pleasant for the master. So also you must comprehend that you have walkways in yourselves.

If you want to learn about these walkways from Scripture, hear Solomon saying, "Do not be drunk with wine, but converse among yourselves and converse on walkways."[62] Seeing, then, these natural walkways, constructed so that God may walk around on them, notice that on account of malice they are full of many unclean things, many stumbling stones, many stinking sins; "for my wounds stink and putrefy"[63] is spoken about the nature of sins. Seeing, then, the walkways filled with stinking sins and stumbling stones, understand what is meant in "make a road for the one who rides on the sunsets": make a road for God.

For he seeks to walk about in you and is observing that, when he seeks a place, he does not find one, seeing thorns and not wanting to walk on thorns. For whenever he sees pleasures dominating you and observes you distracted by worldly wealth, whenever he sees worries in you, he sees thorns on the walkways and he seeks other, cleaner walkways and abandons you. For God cannot walk in such walkways. But worries, pleasures, and wealth are thorns according to the interpretation of the parable of sowing in Luke.[64]

6. Next, another interpretation of sunsets will be recounted. In the beginning, when you made a way for God, God was walking in you when you were not yet perfect, not yet coming on the

---

62. Prv 23.31 (in the LXX, where this proverb against drunkenness is fuller and saltier than the Hebrew of the Masoretic text). The word for "walkway" is "*peripatos*." Origen would have expected the word to recall the Peripatetic school of philosophy, so called because its founder, Aristotle, taught as he walked around with students.

63. Ps 37.6.

64. Lk 8.14.

sunrise, not yet genuinely bearing the image of the heavenly;[65] he rides you while you are still in the sunsets. But do not take it for granted that when God rides on the sunsets, he always stays on the sunsets. In the beginning of this Psalm it is written, "*Sing to God, play a stringed instrument to his name, make a road for the one who rides on sunsets, the Lord is his name.*" But at the end of this Psalm, "*Kings of the earth, sing to God, play a stringed instrument to the Lord who rides upon the heaven of heaven on the sunrise.*"[66] If I must speak boldly, he makes himself ride on the sunsets contrary to his own nature.

Perhaps the logos in these things can be hinting enigmatically at something deeper, because there must be produced the setting of another sun and the rising of another sun. And the beginning of God's riding is produced in you, when the opposite sun to the "sun of justice"[67] sets. If you are perfected and the sun of justice is produced in you, the Lord rides on you, no longer simply at the sunsets of that light, but on the heaven of heaven at the sunrise. To show this from the Scripture is not out of place, but necessary. Perhaps some of those hearing will stumble at what is said. If it is possible, when a sun has come to set, for the Lord to ride on the setting of that sun, I say of course that the law holds the shadow of good things that will be produced,[68] and if someone is deriving as much help as possible from it, he [the Apostle] says concerning the law: "We know that the law is spiritual."[69] It is written in the law concerning many unclean persons that they will be unclean until evening and that as long as the sun rises on them they are unclean.[70] If the sun sets and it becomes evening, then they become clean: the Lord rides on the sunsets. For in the lifting up of the law, when you interpret it as spiritual, it is possible to speak about a sun that makes someone unclean, whom the Lord releases from uncleanness when the sun sets. Whenever someone is unclean,

65. 1 Cor 15.49.
66. Ps 67.33–34.
67. See Mal 4.2.
68. See Heb 10.1.
69. Rom 7.14.
70. See Lv 11.25–28, 11.31–32, 11.39–40.

of course, pay attention to this: Satan, transformed into an angel of light,[71] is a sun. But I was bold to say that he is a sun with an adjective, "a sun of injustice," I say. For if there were not another sun, it would not have been said of the Savior, "to those fearing his name the sun of justice will rise." For if "sun" without any adjective was a good thing, the adjective was great that says that the one rising on those who fear God's name is not simply "sun" but "of justice." If you still want to see an example of how the sun of injustice rises on certain people, look with me at those who are relying, as if on the true light, on the logos of heresies, and look with me at the heretic saying, "I am not in a night, but in a day." Looking at the logos in him, do not shirk from naming him a sun of injustice: "he has spoken injustice against the height, he placed his mouth in heaven."[72]

7. The Lord, then, rides at the beginning on the sunsets, but hear what has been written on the sunsets and the one who has ridden them in this way. First let all things set in you that were considered, in your opinion, enlightening, and were magnified and admired by you. Let avarice set; let teachings foreign to the truth set; let sexual misconduct set, which you considered useful and good for pleasure, so that the Lord may ride on you when you have made sunsets of the opposite things and have made a road for him, and he will come to be, not just dwelling in you, but also walking around.

"*Make a road,*" then, "*for the one who rides on sunsets; the Lord is his name. Rejoice before the father of orphans and judge of widows.*"[73] Is God actually the father of all orphans, including those both of the gentiles and of the wicked? For there are orphans wickedly, orphans who are living in the worst way. Is God actually both God and judge of all widows? It is indeed written that he is the father of orphans and the judge of widows. What sort of widows are they? They must not be reverent ones, but those who live badly in widowhood. But if you understand who the father is from whom you ought to be orphaned, if you understand who the husband is whose death must be prayed for by the rever-

71. 2 Cor 11.14.
72. Ps 72.8b–9a.
73. Ps 67.5c–6a.

ent soul, you will see how God is the father of orphans and the judge of widows.

John says in an Epistle that everyone who sins is born of the devil.[74] Therefore, it is said by the Savior, as it is written in the Gospel concerning sinners, "You are from the devil as a father, and you wish to do the desires of your father."[75] Allow this so-called father, the devil—your father, if you sin—to die. But when he dies, is that when you die? What difference does it make to you if, when he dies, he does not live to you even if he seems to live to others? I am encouraged in this from what the marvelous Paul says about the devil, "God will presently crush Satan under your feet."[76] To me Satan is no longer; to me Satan is crushed, when I no longer sin; but since he is already crushed under our feet, so that he may not still be wrathful and may not trouble us again, let us beseech the one who crushed him, that he may crush him now, too.

For it is likely that Satan has been provoked to wrath and raises his head as a serpent and threatens us and makes many designs against us, but the Lord scatters his designs. Therefore, for the just person, he is crushed by God, and, indeed, he has been smashed down under the feet of the just person, who treads on him, not just receiving the authority to walk on him, but making use of it. For the Savior said: "I give you authority to walk on snakes and scorpions and every power of the evil one, and nothing will harm you."[77] But we, if we actually are disciples of Jesus, have received that authority. Nonetheless, someone having it does not always use the authority, but blessed is the person who receives the authority and makes use of it, walking on snakes and scorpions and on every power of the evil one. For take courage; nothing will harm you. If the devil's being crushed by the just is understood, even though he is not crushed for another human being, because that person is still unjust and does not merit the devil's being crushed by God for him and falling beneath his feet, it will be understood what it means for

74. 1 Jn 3.8.
75. Jn 8.44.
76. Rom 16.20.
77. Lk 10.19.

the devil, as father, to die to the one who must thus become the devil's orphan.[78]

Let us get to an image of this matter in the Gospel from which you will understand how the text conserves not so much the statement itself as an elevated one. When someone approached the Savior, he said, "Allow me first to leave and bury my father."[79] And since the logos was spiritual to the Savior, and when he heard bodily things, he did not speak bodily things, as is evident from many instances; therefore, when he answered, he said to him, "Let the dead bury their own dead,"[80] and would not allow him to go and bury his father. As far as the statement goes, what occurred is unreasonable. What harm would it be for him to do his duty and then come back, to bury his father and to return to the teacher two hours later?[81] If someone intends to do and to keep the statement in these matters on all occasions, that person must learn that he is not obligated to bury the one whom Jesus calls father. For we, the living disciples of Jesus, have not been permitted to bury those whom the Savior speaks of as the dead: "Let the dead bury their own dead." And since one who touches a dead person is tainted and becomes unclean,[82] therefore he wishes us not, if the father should die, to touch him using burial as a pretext. I suppose therefore that the orphan is understood as someone whose father is God, according to what is written, *"Rejoice before him, the father of orphans."*[83] For such a thing is said in the Forty-fourth Psalm concerning the Church from the gentiles figuratively called "daughter": "For hear, daughter, and see and bend your ear, and forget your people and your house and your father, because the king has desired your beauty."[84]

I know that you love Abraham and do not want to hear anything ill of him, but when you are paying attention to Scripture,

---

78. Origen needs to show how the devil can be dead to one person without being dead to everyone.

79. Mt 8.21.

80. Mt 8.22.

81. Origen is aware of Jewish funeral customs.

82. See Nm 19.11.

83. Ps 67.5–6.

84. Ps 44.11–12.

you will be puzzled that even he once had the devil as his father before he was given his title by God.[85] So that he might become worthy of the title, he first heard this commandment: "Leave your land and your kinsfolk and the house of your father and go to the land that I shall show you,"[86] and Abraham did according to what God commanded him. And we cannot become children of Abraham unless we do his, Abraham's, works. For the Savior said, "If you are children of Abraham, do the works of Abraham."[87] Therefore, one must examine all the works and do them. But the first work one must do is, "Leave your land," if you are going to be the son of father Abraham, and next, "your kinsfolk, and your house, and your father," so that you may hear from God, "and go to the land that I shall show you."

Here is written, "*Rejoice before God, the father of orphans and judge of widows,*"[88] but in another Psalm, "he will lift up the orphan and widow."[89] And just as he lifted up Jeremiah,[90] so he will lift up the orphan, so he will lift up the widow; therefore, become an orphan according to what has been said and no longer be subject to such a father.

But also let us look at "*judge of widows.*" Just as there are both a Christ and an Antichrist, a genuine light[91] and the one who is transformed into an angel of light,[92] so there are a bridegroom and, if one has to make up a word,[93] an "antibridegroom" equivalent to the Antichrist. Christ, then, is lawfully wedded to the human soul; but the devil [is wedded] unlawfully, and he schemes to become its bridegroom, so that he may make it corrupt. So, once, he wanted to corrupt Eve. So, once, he wanted to corrupt the church of the Corinthians, just what the Apostle was afraid

85. See Gn 17.5, where Abraham receives his name. Kugel, *Traditions*, 245–47, discusses Abraham as the first monotheist.

86. Gn 12.1.

87. Jn 8.39.

88. Ps 67.5–6.

89. Ps 145.9.

90. In *Paraleipomena Jeremiou* (4 Baruch) 9.3, Jeremiah refers to his imminent death as being "lifted up" by God.

91. See Jn 1.9.

92. 2 Cor 11.14.

93. "Antibridegroom" occurs nowhere else in extant Greek literature.

of, wanting to heal the church when it was liable to be corrupted, so that he said, in case the church should hear his logoi, "I fear that, as the snake deceived Eve by his craftiness, your understanding may be corrupted from the simplicity in Christ."[94] Let your soul, then, become a widow of that unlawful and vile husband, so that God may judge just things in you and lift you up, a soul when it has become a widow of such a husband; may the God—about whom it is written, "he will lift up the orphan and widow"—lift you up.

8. The rest of this passage is "*God in his holy place.*"[95] God, whom neither heaven nor earth contains—for all creation is smaller than the creator—when he chooses, becomes spatially present; he becomes spatially present in a holy place, for wherever a place is defiled and profane, God cannot be there. What, then, is the holy place? That place, concerning which the Apostle tells you, "Do not give a place to the devil,"[96] concerning which Solomon says to you, "If the spirit of one having authority rises upon you, do not cede your place."[97] But Judas had given a place to the devil, so that "with the sop Satan entered into him."[98]

God, then, is in his holy place. And if you choose, I will begin from the first place and go through all of them, each place[99] of God. And I say that Christ is the first holy place for God; therefore, speaking as a place of God, he says, "The Father is in me."[100] For if he has promised to dwell in you,[101] if he has promised to walk about in you,[102] how would he indwell there, unless in wisdom, in truth, in justice, in life, in resurrection?[103]

---

94. 2 Cor 11.3.

95. Ps 67.6b. The stumbling block in this statement is the ascription of a "place" to God; God has no spatial location.

96. Eph 4.27. Origen asks "what" the place is, not "where" it is.

97. Eccl 10.4.

98. Jn 13.27.

99. Origen avoids using "place" in the plural. He takes advantage of Greek grammar to put the singular noun *topon*, "place," in apposition to *panta*, "all," in the plural.

100. Jn 10.38.

101. See 2 Cor 6.16.

102. See Lv 26.12.

103. These are *epinoiai*, "aspects" or "devices." See PS36H2.1, n. 3 above.

I cannot discuss all the things that Christ is in those in whom the Father dwells, as in a house, in which he walks around, as in a place.[104] And the Holy Spirit is a place of God, and the whole army of holy angels are places of God. Thus the Church also is a place of God. It is well, then, that the Scripture does not say "places of God," but all are "a place" of Christ, for we many are one in Christ.[105]

"*God settles the single ones*[106] *in a house,*"[107] a house, in fact, about which the Savior says, "In my Father's house are many dwelling places."[108] But let us look at the "single"; to the extent that we still sin, we are multiple,[109] and we have various changes, now having an expression[110] of anger on our face,[111] but at another time an expression of sorrow, possibly also an expression of fear and cowardice, at another time an expression of pleasure, the irrational arousal of the soul. There is another expression on the face, that of greed, and there is also an expression of sexual license. Why do I even need to list the multitude of infinite expressions of evil? The wicked person is multiple, but the just, as an imitator of God,[112] is single. As God is always the same, about whom I say,

104. God walks around, not "in" a place, but "as in" a place.

105. Stumbling block removed: God's "place" is to be fully present to believers. See n. 95 above.

106. The "single ones" (*monotropoi*), have only one *tropos*, "turn," "mode," or (here) "expression." Origen understands them to be "single" in the sense of "fully integrated" or "one," by virtue of their union with God, not "solitary." See *Comm. Jo.* 20.27.239: "But I consider if being established in the truth [Jn 8.44] is not something one (*hen*) and uniform (*monoeides*), but not being established in it is variegated (*poikilon*) and multiple (*polutropon*)."

107. Ps 67.7a.

108. Jn 14.2. The word translated "dwellings" can also be translated "singles" (*monai*).

109. *Polutropoi,* having many modes or expressions. To any educated Greek, this word, *polutropos,* would recall the first line of *The Odyssey.* In that line Emily Wilson translates it as "complicated"; see Homer, *The Odyssey* (New York: W. W. Norton, 2018), 105. In Greek tragedy, Odysseus is usually a devious villain.

110. *Tropos,* "turn."

111. "Face" (*prosōpon*) can also refer to the masks used by actors, which display various emotions. Greco-Roman art took an interest in facial expressions and often sought to convey emotional states as vividly as possible.

112. See 1 Cor 11.1.

"But you are the same,"[113] and as God says, "I have not changed,"[114] in the same way the imitator of God, the son of God, is single and always the same.

Therefore, according to me the Son of God is every virtue, and many virtues are not many substances, but all the virtues are one. And Greeks have been glutted with many virtues, so that they might participate in them,[115] but Christ suffices for us in place of all of them, for he is the all, so that when imitating him I become single, and I will dwell with God's single ones in the house of God in Christ Jesus, to whom is the glory and the might to the ages of ages. Amen.

113. Ps 101.28.

114. Mal 3.6.

115. Nonetheless, Plotinus taught that no virtue can be perfected without the presence of all the other virtues (*Enn.* 7.2.9). See Lloyd P. Gerson, *Aristotle and Other Platonists* (Ithaca, NY: Cornell University Press, 2005), 242–74. See also PS36H4.1, n. 9 above.

HOMILY 1 ON PSALM 73

ET US BEG for rain, the spiritual rain: that God would command the spiritual clouds to shower rain upon our souls and that we might not sprout thorns, so that we might not be discredited and near to a curse, but might bear an acceptable crop and fruit yielding a hundredfold.[1]

So, the Seventy-third Psalm has been read, urging us by its inscription to pay attention, since the Psalm requires the understanding of the hearer because it is not immediately obvious; it is inscribed, as is the case in other Psalms as well, "*of understanding, of Asaph*"[2]—because the Psalm is no longer inscribed "of David," but "*of Asaph*" and because he is prophesying in the Psalms inscribed to him. He has displayed the affairs of Jerusalem, seeing that Asaph prophesied—and tells, as to the statement, what occurred to the people after the captivity. For "*Why, God, would you reject to the end? Has your wrath been provoked against the sheep of your pasture? Remember your gathering, which you created from the beginning,*"[3] and what follows, fits, as far as the wording goes, the events after the captivity.[4] Someone might say that it fits not only those events, but also those after the visitation of our Savior, when his blood, by their [the people's] testimony, was coming on them and their children;[5] the captivity happened, and the things mentioned occurred: "*with an ax and a*

1. Origen adapts Heb 6.7–8 and adds a further botanical allusion from Lk 8.8.

2. Ps 73.1a. On Asaph see introduction, p. 6.

3. Ps 73.1b–2a.

4. Origen's interpretation of the Babylonian captivity here is entirely consistent with that of one of his first works, the *Commentary on Lamentations* written about thirty years earlier.

5. See Mt 27.25.

chisel they shattered their doors"[6]—that is to say, of Jerusalem and of the people—for according to the statement can it be fitted otherwise and to the things recorded after Christ's appearance? But let us see, even with regard to the wording, how disciples of Jesus Christ and those who can say, not only concerning the law, "We know that the law is spiritual,"[7] but concerning the prophets as well, "We know that the prophets are spiritual." Let us try to explain each of these, which are also capable of being explained doubly to our soul, in one case secretly and above us, so that whenever the enemies arrive and shatter the doors of our soul and do everything recorded here, as the logos will present ...[8]

2. The prophet, then, raises a question and says, "*Why, God, would you reject to the end?*" That is, for what cause do you reject your people and expel them? The simpler will say that sins are the cause, for these are the cause of God's rejecting those whom he has gathered together; thus, if we do not plan to be rejected by God, we should not sin. But someone looking to some extent more deeply will say that the cause for the people's being rejected is their rejecting Christ.[9] And certainly God had more reason to reject the people after Christ's visitation and the outrages he suffered. When had they suffered for so long a time? When had Jerusalem been so bereaved? When was the altar so idle, because sacrifices and offerings were no longer presented on it?

But someone else, who understands about Adam, will say that he rejected Adam because of sin and pleasure-seeking, and, just as in Adam we all die, even in Christ we shall all be made alive;[10] thus in Adam all have been exiled, and in Christ God restores us all. You will make a connection with the parable in the Gospel;

6. Ps 73.6b.

7. Rom 7.14.

8. Presumably the phrase should be filled out by words to the effect of "we shall know what is happening and what to do about it." Because both the First Temple and the Second Temple were destroyed, Origen raises the possibility that Asaph's prophecy may apply to both. His interest, though, is the spiritual interpretation, in which Jerusalem is the presence of God to the human soul.

9. Origen suggests that the ordinary interpretation can be deepened by looking at the text in relation to Christ.

10. 1 Cor 15.22.

God rejected the person going down from Jerusalem to Jericho, and, since he rejected the one who wanted to go down, therefore he fell among robbers, so that, if he had not been rejected by God, he would not have shown up in the hands of robbers.[11] We must see also about God's rejection especially through the addition of "*to the end*," for the Scripture is saying, "*Why, God, would you reject to the end?*" Because there is a measure to the rejection with which God rejects someone.

You will understand the same principle from bodily things; it is possible for me to reject[12] someone from myself to a greater or lesser extent, so that the two of us stand more or less together or he is rejected to an end, so that he is rejected to such an extent that there is no longer room for him to be rejected, such as a place at the edge, so that there is no place for him to be rejected.

If you have understood the bodily example, move with me in logos on the intention of the Scripture; and see with me that someone who has made the mistake of sinning once, that sin being a slight fall, is rejected by God as little as befits a small sin, so that he comes to be a little distant from God, but if he adds to the sin, not just in number but in magnitude, someone who has sinned that way is rejected yet more by God. And to the extent that we sin, to such an extent God rejects us from himself and from his oversight. But if the sin reaches such an extreme that we could not fall any farther, God rejects us to an end and it is no longer possible for anyone to be pushed away farther.[13]

11. See Lk 10.30. We may find this "blame the victim" interpretation of the parable implausible. For Origen the imagery of Jerusalem as site of God's inner presence, towards which we move up, is so basic that a neutral interpretation does not occur to him. Origen explains the parable in more detail in his homily on the passage, *Hom. Luc.* 34.4, where he ascribes it to an "elder." He also refers to it elsewhere (*Comm. Cant.* Prol. [p. 70 in GCS], *Hom. Jos.* 6.4, and *Comm. Matt.* 16.9).

12. *Apōtheō*, the verb here translated "reject," also carries its root meaning, "push away." The addition of "to an end" enables Origen to understand God's rejection, not as something total, but as calibrated distancing. In his *Commentary on Lamentations* (*Fr. Lam.* 78) Origen cited this verse from Psalm 73 to make the same point about Lam 3.31: "Because the Lord does not reject to the age." See also PS75H.7 below.

13. Compare Plotinus, *Enn.* 1.8.7: "Since the good is not the only thing, there is a necessity for a departure on its part, or, if one should wish to say it thus, always a retiring or separation, the last thing, after which nothing else whatsoever can still be produced: this is evil."

That according to the measures of sins God rejects each person from himself and his oversight, the Psalm will testify: "Reject them according to the multitude of their impieties."[14] But just as in proportion to the manner of their change of heart, God summons some back from rejection, if a complete change of heart and reversal have occurred to the highest degree, God summons him back from an earlier rejection to an end, so that he may say (the one who is recalled, that is), "My soul has clung back again to you."[15] The causes for our being rejected from God or God's summoning us more or less are up to us, just as he summoned Moses, saying, "Let Moses alone approach God, but do not let the rest approach."[16] And therefore he summoned him, saying that since Moses had not made himself predisposed to the rejection that all human nature has experienced,[17] he was summoned and approached God. We do not see with the eyes of the body how far from God or how close we are to him; and we cannot tell at any given distance from him, if we could be still farther away when our sins had reached the end or if, by a change of heart, we could become close to him. For this reason we scorn how far we are from God and do not make an effort to be close or to avoid being distant; it is necessary to see that these things are grasped by the eyes of our mind. And someone who is sinning distances himself from God according to what is said: "See, those distancing themselves from you are destroyed."[18] And again the just person clings to God by means of justice and virtue: "It is good for me to cling to God."[19]

3. "Why" is common to both phrases: "*Why would you reject?*" and "*Why has your wrath been provoked against the sheep of your pasture?*"[20] It seems to me that [the psalmist is] wanting to present God in the prayer, as much as possible, as favorable to those who have sinned. It has said that his wrath has not been produced

14. Ps 5.11.
15. Ps 62.9.
16. Ex 24.2.
17. Presumably the rejection experienced by Adam and Eve when they were expelled from the Garden of Eden.
18. Ps 72.27.
19. Ps 72.28.
20. Ps 73.1.

against human beings, because they are, as it were, sheep: "Take into account their intellectual capacity;[21] those against whom you are angry are sheep of your pasture. Put the powerful to a powerful test, but the little one is deserving of your mercies. *'Why, then, God, would you reject us to the end? Has your wrath been provoked against the sheep of your pasture?'*" It is necessary to see how the sheep as well as the pasture are God's, for there are certain sheep of God's pasture. It is written in the Gospel, "I am the door; if anyone enter in through me, he will be saved and enter in and out and find pasture."[22] What, then, is the pasture and the pasture of sheep? The holy Scriptures are the pasture, the law is the pasture, the prophets are pasture, the Gospels, the apostles. If you are not pastured on these, you will perish by famine. Let us enter into this pasture, and it is the Lord's task to shepherd us, so as to say: "The Lord shepherds me, and nothing will lack for me, in a place of new growth; there he sets up a tent for me."[23] What sort of thing is the new growth? The flourishing of new perceptions.[24]

4. "*Remember your gathering,*[25] *which you acquired at the beginning.*"[26] The people from the gentiles say: "How did God acquire us as his gathering from the beginning?" The visitation of Christ Jesus at the consummation of the ages is not a beginning, at which God acquired us. Presently the Jew says, "The logos is not speaking about you when it says, *'Remember your gathering, which you acquired at the beginning,'* but about me, for God acquired me from the beginning." I would speak to the latter, who seems to retort to me, saying, "I am the one whom God acquired at the beginning, by the timing of my call." And I shall retort to you likewise, because you have not truly stayed the same from the beginning: "When did God acquire you as a friend? When

---

21. In *Comm. Jo.* 1.27.190, the divine logos is "shepherd" for the simple-minded.

22. Jn 10.9.

23. Ps 22.1–2.

24. Christ as shepherd encounters those who do not use their intellectual capacities and helps them develop those capacities.

25. *Sungagōgē*, then as now, the normal term for a Jewish gathering for worship. On the ambiguity of the term, see PS77H2.7.

26. Ps 73.2a.

the people came out of the land of Egypt, when he redeemed it from the hand of slavery and from Pharaoh. Then see that your beginning is not found to be from the times in Egypt, but are there not ten generations to Noah, are there not ten to Abraham, are there not ten to Moses? You cannot, then, be at the beginning in the times of Moses, but if you force the point and say that it was in the times of Abraham, that is not the beginning, for there are twenty generations to Abraham from Adam; from Abraham the seed according to the flesh has a beginning, so I grant you that."

Neither when you say, "Why at the beginning?" nor when the naïve and simpler people on my side say, "Why at the beginning?" do we hear why "at the beginning": "Those whom he knew before, he recognized before, and those he recognized before, he chose before, and those he chose before, he called, and those he called, he justified, and those he justified, he glorified."[27] When God knew before, he knew before in the beginning and acquired by his foreknowledge everything that was going to be produced by him, and this is what is said in *"Remember your gathering, which you acquired at the beginning."* And I say this, being economical with the logos,[28] for I know the beginning at which God acquired each of us; I know that this beginning is animate, is alive, and says: "God acquired me, the beginning of his roads, for his works."[29] Christ is the beginning;[30] he acquired at the beginning, from Christ, who is the real beginning and the real end, the real alpha and omega.[31]

5. *"I shall redeem a rod of your inheritance."*[32] The captives, his family, are redeemed. God, then, has redeemed a rod of his inheritance; that is, giving ransoms he has redeemed the scepter of his inheritance and his kingdom. For we were subject to en-

27. Rom 8.29–30.

28. "Managing the logos" entails not divulging matters that some are unprepared to hear. Origen is alerting those familiar with his thought to the relevance of the cosmological speculations in *Princ.*

29. Prv 8.22.

30. See *Comm. Jo.* 1.17.101–102. On the word *archē*, "beginning," see PS73H2.6, n. 62, and PS77H7.2, n. 28 below.

31. Rv 21.6.

32. Ps 73.2b.

emies, and those enemies were the devil and his angels. They were the ones who had taken us as captives, and they did not intend to release us without ransoms. And the Savior did not at all intend to compel the devil; he did not take more than his share for us when we had been captured, but he said to the devil, "I want to redeem the captives whom you have taken. What do you want to take as a ransom, in order to give to me the captives you have taken?" But he answered: "I want to take your blood; let your blood be poured out. Die. If you die, when your blood has been poured out, I have the ransoms; I give back those you want to take."[33] Christ, my Lord and my Savior, being a lover of humanity, poured out his blood and bought us with his precious blood. For we have been redeemed, not with perishable gold and silver, from our patrimony of empty turning back, but by the precious blood of Christ, the blameless and immaculate lamb.[34] "You were bought with a price,"[35] is a good saying; do not become slaves of human beings. A great price, then, has been given, so that we might be redeemed, and on account of this price my Lord Christ Jesus, since he is justice, since he is sanctification, since he is wisdom, since he is truth, so he is also redemption.[36]

Since such great ransoms have been given for us, if we despise the precious blood, we shall be liable to a charge, and it shall be said against us: "Of what sort of worse punishment, does it seem, will he be worth who tramples the Son of God and has considered the blood of the covenant, with which he was sanctified, to be something base and has insulted the spirit of grace?"[37] For we insult the spirit of grace when we sin after redemption, but we even consider the pure and holy blood of the

33. Origen's dramatization of the biblical message by means of an invented dialogue is akin to Jewish hagaddah as well as to the dialogue hymns of Syriac Christianity (and the *kontakia* of Romanos that are inspired by them). See Kristi Upson-Saia, "Caught in a Compromising Position: The Biblical Exegesis and Characterization of Biblical Protagonists in the Syriac Dialogue Hymns," *Hugoye: Journal of Syriac Studies* 9.2 (July 2006).

34. 1 Pt 1.18.

35. 1 Cor 6.20.

36. See 1 Cor 1.30 and *Comm. Jo.* 1.22.140.

37. Heb 10.29.

covenant to be base and profane. But we also trample the Son of God whenever we sin against him, for we trample justice when we act unjustly; we trample truth when we lie; we trample logos when we act unreasonably; we trample the light when we do the deeds of darkness.[38] The Lord has therefore redeemed the rod of his inheritance, that is, the scepter of his own kingdom.

6. "*This Mount Zion, the one on which you set up a tent*";[39] Mount Zion has also come to be subject to enemies: for the oracle-place, the vision-place, and the viewing-place—it is translated various ways—have become subject to enemies. If you see a clear-sighted soul, if you see a soul that is perspicacious and intelligent, that has become captive to a spirit of fornication and to sins, do not hesitate to say that Zion, the viewing-place, has become subject to enemies. If, then, you see such a one turning around and adopting a different attitude and behaving as he should with clear-sightedness, do not hesitate to say that God has redeemed this Mount Zion, the one on which he set up a tent.

How has he set up a tent on it? The Jews look at Scripture from below and drag it to the earth, supposing that it is on this Zion that the God who created heaven and earth set up a tent. And now God has set up a tent on the mountain, according to them, where animals and gentiles have had tents set up for them.[40] But we say that Mount Zion, where God set up a tent, is the soul endowed with genius, the soul that thinks and sees clearly. How does God set up a tent in it? Fulfilling the promise that says: "I will make my home in them, and walk around in them, and I shall be their God, and they shall be my people."[41] And often also on this Mount Zion, in which God and his logos set up a tent, there are produced failings and sins. But God does not abandon the captive Mount Zion, but redeems it, so as to fulfill: "*I shall redeem a rod of your inheritance, this Mount Zion, the one on which you set up a tent. Raise your hands against their arro-*

38. See Rom 13.12 and Jn 3.19.

39. Ps 73.2c.

40. The Romans built temples on the Temple Mount during the reign of Hadrian. The reference to animals (*tetrapoda,* "quadrupeds") on the Temple Mount probably indicates that Origen himself saw a stable there.

41. Lv 26.12.

gances to the end, as many as the enemy did wickedly in the holy."[42] For all arrogance is a loathsome thing; it is found either in a human being or in an opposing power, and God truly sets himself against the arrogant, but he gives grace to the humble.[43]

But, remarkably, it is possible that this is somehow occurring bodily in the place due to the arrogance of those who surrounded the Jews, but somehow occurring mentally due to the opposing powers; in some manner they are arrogant and rise up against the just ones of God. These are—if they have actually been enabled to seduce someone and take him captive—such things as the arrogant Babylonians, when they defeated the people, likely said in a bodily place against the holy human being, such things as those surrounding the Jews likely said with freedom of speech.[44] Those things are bodily, but if your soul ever is defeated by an opposing power, so that it comes to be under the devil, you will see the manner in which the devil is arrogant against the holy human being.

But I say that the enemy also abused the Savior, when he humbled himself and became subject "even to death, death of a cross,"[45] not understanding the plan[46] of our Savior and his humility. He was arrogant over him, as if he had defeated him, as if he had prevailed over him. He did not know the wisdom of God; if he had known, he would not have crucified him, the Christ of God. Likewise, if he was arrogant over him, for how long was he arrogant? I am bold to say that it was for one moment: for just as the Savior departed, he took what had become bare of a soul, a body that was bare, seeking the devil and his angels, whom he did not have so accessible, when the body was burdened. See him with me getting in motion, see him with me descending into Hades and him having descended to Hades, see those whom he had to bind there, and after he was bound, see him in Hades as one free among the dead and ascending

---

42. Ps 73.2b–3.

43. Prv 3.34.

44. See Neh 4.1–3 (which Origen would have known as 2 Ezr 13.33–35). These counsels of despair, he believes, are like those that demons insinuate into the minds of the righteous.

45. Phil 2.8.

46. *Oikonomian,* God's plan of creation and redemption. See 1 Cor 2.8.

alone from there and saying: "I have become as a man without assistance, free among the dead."[47] For all of them were put in bondage by him, but he, free among the dead, ascended. I have said these things on *"Raise your hands against their arrogances to the end, as many as the enemy did wickedly in the holy."*[48]

7. Still, before moving on to the next passage, let us look at the extent to which the enemy did wickedly in the holy. I do not propose to speak about what is considered holy by the Jews. He did wickedly against the holy, the Savior, when he took him up onto the mountain. "Speak, so that these stones may become loaves,"[49] "throw yourself down from here,"[50] and "all this I shall give to you, if, falling, you prostrate yourself to me,"[51] was his act of wickedness. See to what extent the enemy did wickedly in the holy. After that, he again did wickedly against him, as it is written in Luke, "he left him until an opportune time."[52] Later he approached him again for testing, so that he might test him, so that he might kill him. When? When the devil inserted into the heart of Judas Iscariot the son of Simon to betray the Savior, and after the sop Satan entered into him.[53]

The devil did many other things wickedly against the holy. He did wickedly by inciting the high priests and the elders and the people to say, "Crucify, crucify him,"[54] "remove such a one from the earth."[55] He did wickedly inciting them to say, "His blood is on us and on our children."[56] He did wickedly making Herod become a friend to Pilate, when they had been enemies before.[57] He did wickedly making Pilate wash himself and foolishly forgo responsibility; he washed his hands after having the Savior

47. Ps 87.5.

48. Gregory of Nyssa has a similar account of deceiving the devil in *Great Catechetical Oration* 24.

49. Mt 4.3.

50. Mt 4.6.

51. Mt 4.9.

52. Lk 4.13.

53. Jn 13.27.

54. Lk 23.21, Jn 19.6, 19.15.

55. Acts 22.22, Lk 23.18.

56. Mt 27.25.

57. Lk 23.12.

flogged and said, "I am guiltless of the blood of this just man."[58] It is written that such things were said, but there are other such things that were not written that he had done wickedly to him, for I suppose that "the cosmos could not contain the books"[59] applies not only to the other activities of Jesus, but to the wicked deeds perpetrated by the devil, such things that the enemy did wickedly in the holy.

8. *"And those who hate you railed in the midst of your feast."*[60] According to the statement, come with me to the time of that feast, when my Jesus, when it was Passover, was betrayed to be crucified. The Jews railed, the enemies of Jesus, and the Jews were motivated in the midst of the feast, for it was a feast, when he was betrayed and instead of a sheep they killed the Savior, who as a sheep was led to the slaughter and as a lamb before his shearers was dumb.[61] I do not hear the prophet saying simply, "as a sheep he was led to the slaughter," for secretly the prophet said, knowing that the Passover was Christ, who was sacrificed for us,[62] that "as a sheep he was led." As in the Passover the sheep, so in the genuine Passover Christ is led. And *those who hate you railed in the midst of your feast.*" Therefore, they no longer celebrate with that feast, for they polluted the feast; they polluted the holy things. Should the Jews want to celebrate, they cannot.

For it is impossible to celebrate the Passover as prescribed in Scripture, except in the place considered holy, from which they were cast out. Thus they no longer celebrate it, or the Feast of Pentecost, or the Feast of Booths. But their feasts have been taken away from them and have been given to us, and it has been fulfilled in them what Amos said: "Your feasts will be turned to mourning, and your songs to dirges."[63] We, then, received the feasts differently from how they received them. For we received them figuratively, until the truth came, but when the truth

58. Mt 27.24.

59. Jn 21.25.

60. Ps 73.4a.

61. See Is 53.7.

62. 1 Cor 5.7. Isaiah, Origen claims, knew that this was not just any sheep, but the Passover lamb.

63. Am 8.10.

came, we say that we received the genuine Passover. For our genuine Passover, Christ, was sacrificed and we celebrate the feast, not with the old leaven, the leaven of malice and wickedness, but with the unleavened bread of sincerity and truth.[64] Thus we hold Pentecost, and yet from spiritual fruits, thus also we celebrate the Booths, not by making huts, for we do not dwell in huts, not in huts since we are aliens and sojourners[65] on the earth.

9. *"And those who hate me railed in the midst of our feast. They placed their signs for themselves, signs, and they did not know, as in the entrance up above."*[66] The adverse powers and those doing wickedness against the Savior placed for themselves signs; they placed them for themselves, and they laid down signs of their sin to this day, the overthrow of Israel. What are the signs of their sin? Christ's transition transferred from them; it went to us. They threw out Christ. He came to those who did not throw him out but received him, and they did know as in the entrance up above; we see some other logos in the statement, because often those doing wickedness against the truth place for themselves some signs such as *"in the entrance."* You may see such a thing among the heterodox: the promise of an entrance, false logoi, and the opposite of the truth, not leading to an entrance according to their promise. Whenever you see them promising lofty and heavenly explanation, say, *"They placed their signs for themselves,"* but *"signs as in the entrance up above."*

See with me that the adverse powers are doing what follows: *"as in a forest of wood they cut its roots with axes together; with an adze and a chisel they smashed it."*[67] When enemies plot against you, see them outside your doors, holding axes to rational doors and breaking them, so that they may come toward you and, by entering, despoil the strong man of his equipment. [68] As in the Gospel it is written in the form of a certain parable: "Whenever an armed strong man guards his own hall, his possessions

64. 1 Cor 5.7–8.
65. 1 Pt 2.11.
66. Ps 73.4–5.
67. Ps 73.6.
68. See Mk 3.27, Mt 12.29.

are in peace, but if a stronger man should enter, he takes away his armor, in which he trusted, and divides his spoils."[69] And as in war the enemies enter and take armor, so when the adverse powers are beating down your doors around the governing faculty, they take your armor, so that you may no longer have the breastplate of justice, so that you may no longer be girded with truth, so that you may no longer have the helmet of salvation, or the shoes of the preparation of the Gospel, or the sword of the Spirit, or the shield of faith.[70] If you do not want to admit this interpretation, who is the stronger one, who takes his armor, in which he trusted, and divides his spoils? What sort of armor does the enemy take, when he enters with axes shattering the doors of our soul, unless it is the one I have just mentioned: "*with an adze and a chisel they smashed it*"? They have the axes, they have the chisels, so that they may overturn every house that we have built.

10. "*They have burned your holy place with fire.*"[71] Each of us, to the extent possible, builds for himself a holy place to God and builds an altar within. Yet the adverse powers enter and burn it, as they burned the holy place of God with fire. Well, I shall demonstrate from the Scriptures how they burn with fire the holy place of God. Understand with me what was said in the Apostle: that you can "quench all the fiery arrows of the evil one."[72] For when he dispatches a fiery arrow, what else does it do? It burns the holiness, and the holiness turns into this—where I once prayed, where I once held Christ, where God once walked about—if I sin, and a fiery arrow comes into it, "*They have burned your holy place with fire.*"

Let us all beseech God together, that this holy place may never be struck by the fiery arrows of the evil one, either impure desires or desires for money or desires for approval or any other inflammation, nor that this may occur: "*They have burned your holy place with fire; they have defiled with fire the tents of God's name.*"[73]

69. Lk 11.21–22.
70. See Eph 6.14–17.
71. Ps 73.7.
72. Eph 6.16.
73. Ps 73.7.

When you see a soul already lifted up, already imagining heavenly things, that has been taken captive by sin and has fallen, do not hesitate to say that the adverse powers *"have defiled the tents of God's name"* in such a person.

And this is what occurred in the case of "He fell from heaven, the dawn-bearer, the one rising early";[74] he was crushed to the earth; he tumbled from heaven to earth, an ordinance for Israel.[75] But may we not suffer such a thing, every day bringing our enemies to naught with God's help; for us may those who have the holy place be upright, the temple not destroyed by Nebuchadnezzar, not overturned by a spirit of evil, but, rather, even being always built up by a spirit of power and holiness and moderation and made holy in Christ Jesus, to whom is the glory and the might now and always and to the ages of ages. Amen.

74. Is 14.12.
75. See Ps 80.5a.

HOMILY 2 ON PSALM 73

UST AS THERE are kinships of bodies and, among kinships, some are closely related, some a little more distant, and relatives may be either closely or very distantly related, so understand with me concerning the kinships of souls. For the kinship of souls is related to similar manners of life. If they are honorable,[1] they are related, having a beginning from God; but if they are mean and wicked, they have a beginning from the devil. And just as in kinships there are many fathers and many brothers, so it seems to me that, with regard to spiritual kinships, there would be fathers: God, of those who are excellent (those having the spirit of adoption);[2] the devil, of sinners. But there are fathers lower than these, some among human beings, but some among powers, either the adverse powers or the better ones.

Let this make plain what I am saying. For example, among human beings some are our fathers spiritually, those who have begotten us in Christ, as Paul, being a father, said: "You may have thousands of pedagogues in Christ, but not many fathers."[3] And analogous to these, the powers who work together with us for salvation are somehow our fathers. That is how I hear: "You will depart to your fathers in peace,"[4] since Abraham had fathers with God, all the holy angels of blessedness and salvation.

---

1. *Kalai kai agathai.* See PS36H1.3, n. 49 above.

2. Rom 8.15. At the end of the recapitulation that concludes and summarizes *Princ.*, Origen speaks of a kinship (*consanguinitas* in Rufinus's Latin translation) between human beings and God (*Princ.* 4.10.10) by virtue of the creation of human beings in the image of God. In Plato we read that, by love of wisdom, *philosophia,* the soul is akin, *suggenēs,* to the divine (*Resp.* 10.11, 611E). We find the same idea in Plotinus, *Enn.* 4.7.10.

3. See 1 Cor 4.15.

4. Gn 15.15.

But thus there is also kinship and there are many fathers among the adverse powers.

2. Whence *"their kinship"* (of the enemies of God's people) *"said together, 'Come, and let us cause them to cease,'"* from the mountains of God, *"'from off the earth.'"*[5] For our Savior and Lord was plotted against by the invisible powers and the Jews motivated by them according to: "The kings of the earth stood by, and the rulers are gathered together against the Lord, against his Christ,"[6] when all the Jews, being of the same mind, said, "Take away, take away such a one from the earth."[7] "Crucify, crucify him."[8] "His blood be upon us and upon our children."[9] At the time of the Savior's passion, all the adverse powers, scheming against the Savior, motivated those who were doing evil to him—and the evil kinships—said, *"Come, and let us cause all God's feasts to cease from the earth."*[10]

For because the Savior was plotted against on the feast of Passover, every feast has been abolished from the people, and their feasts have been turned to mourning, and their odes to lamentation.[11] *"Their kinship said together, 'Come, and let us cause all God's feasts to cease from the earth.'"*[12] They say such things, but what they had said was produced for the Jews. Therefore, the people said: *"We do not see our signs."*[13] When our Savior suffered, signs stopped for the people. There are no longer signs and wonders,[14] even though they had been produced then up to the Savior's birth itself, when such signs were produced, for example, such as the vision of an angel that appeared to Zachariah,[15] such as the signs that were at the Savior's passion.[16] After these

5. See Ps 73.8.

6. Ps 2.2.

7. Lk 23.18.

8. Jn 19.15.

9. Mt 27.25.

10. Ps 73.8b.

11. Am 8.10.

12. Ps 73.8.

13. Ps 73.9a.

14. See Mt 24.24, Mk 13.22, Jn 4.48.

15. Lk 1.11.

16. Presumably such events as described in Mt 27.45, Mk 15.33, Lk 23.44–45, Mt 27.51–53, and Mk 15.38, though these are not specifically designated "signs."

signs, signs were produced, but not to Jews or by Jews, but the signs went over from the people to the gentiles. Therefore, the people said: "*We do not see our signs; there is no longer a prophet.*"[17] For prophecy was stopped since "the law and the prophets" prophesied "until John."[18] And when prophecy was stopped, the Holy Spirit, as a consequence, stopped from them, and the benefit went over to the gentiles, unless we also run riot,[19] unless we also are watered down, unless we become coarse and destroy the grace poured out[20] on us by God, so that the people would once more be speaking in our dispensation the truth concerning it: "*We do not see our signs; there is no longer a prophet.*"[21]

If, indeed, you, Christian, called to such a grace, run backward again and abandon a people called by God's grace, so that you return to a people estranged from God's grace,[22] not having the Holy Spirit—"the daughter of Zion has been forsaken like a tent in a vineyard and like a watcher's hut in a cucumber field"[23]—why do you flee and take the side of those who are forsaken? You have arrived where God's Church is; you have arrived where the Holy Spirit is, where the power of Jesus is gathered according to "when you are gathered together and my spirit with the power of our Lord Jesus Christ."[24]

Still, after "*there is not to us a prophet,*" they also say, "*he will know us no longer*";[25] the forsaken Jews prophesy, so to speak, regarding themselves, saying not only does he not know us right now, but he will not know us anymore.[26] For until the completion he will no longer know this people, since his knowledge has gone over to a people from the gentiles.[27] This is according to one interpretation concerning that people.

17. Ps 73.9a–b.

18. Lk 16.16.

19. See Rv 18.7 and 18.9, 1 Tm 5.11.

20. See Ps 44.3.

21. Ps 73.9.

22. Apparently some in Origen's congregation had once belonged to the Jewish community.

23. Is 1.8.

24. 1 Cor 5.4.

25. Ps 73.9c.

26. See Is 29.15.

27. Acts 15.14. Israel's estrangement from God will end when God's plan

3. See to it that the kinship of the evil one never says about you: "*Come, and let us cause all God's feasts to cease from the earth.*"[28] For you also are called to holy feasts, as it has been said: "so let us celebrate the feast not with the old leaven, not the leaven of malice and evil, but with unleavened breads of sincerity and truth."[29] If you understand all the feasts and the unleavened bread, see to it that you also are never plotted against by the evil ones so as to make God's feasts cease from you. But when do God's feasts cease from you? If you do not have the unleavened bread of sincerity and truth—as, for example, if there were no grain there would be nothing then to leaven, there would be no matter for unleavened breads—so if your unleavened breads were without truth and honesty, if I may so term them, they will fall and thus they could not be kneaded; if you destroy the honesty and replace it with guile, if you destroy the truth and replace it with falsehood, you will be saying to the kinship of the evil one: "*Come, and let us cause God's feasts to cease from the earth,*"[30] to the extent that you make God's feasts cease.

No one having wickedness celebrates the feast of unleavened breads, of Christian unleavened breads. But those who want also divine learning with Christianity, must celebrate with the unleavened breads of sincerity and truth; they celebrate with the unleavened breads apart from grain, apart from sensible matters—which Christ has abolished by fulfilling the law in spiritual matters—but evidently, by falling away from God's grace, they celebrate neither the one feast nor the other. That other feast does not exist when Christ is not present in it; when the Holy Spirit is not present, there cannot be a feast. Please, if there are some silly women laden with sins, led by diverse desires,[31] desiring to walk on both feet at once, and to act as Jews and to act

------

is complete. The (temporary) estrangement of Israel from God is a warning that Christians should not presume on their status as God's people. See Rom 11.25–32.

28. Ps 73.8b.

29. 1 Cor 5.8. Paul's image implies that our sincerity and truth constitute the grain from which is prepared the unleavened bread that is offered in worship to God.

30. Ps 73.8b.

31. See 2 Tm 3.6.

as Christians, think it over, change, become either a Jew or a Christian. I say to you the logos of Elijah the prophet, who said once to those who were double-minded, "How long will you go limping on both of your two legs?"[32]

But the Christian people also has signs, making the demons disappear, driven out, not with amulets, not with drugs, not with the accustomed charms, not with Solomon's stones,[33] as if the name of Jesus had no power, but in the manner of the Gospel, and this is a sign with a greater power to make them disappear. Day by day signs occur among Christians: the blind see again, the lame walk, lepers are cleansed, the destitute are told good news.[34] For what sign occurs now and occurs as greater than how it occurred in sensible matters? Do I want the body's eye to see again, or the soul's? If you go ahead and do wrong, you will not say in a bodily way, as the Jews speak, but concerning spiritual signs: "*We do not see our signs.*"[35] And when you delete the prophets, or you acknowledge their statement, but do not fully receive their mind as you ought, there is no prophet for you; a prophet is for one who hears the prophetic logoi as the Holy Spirit wants.[36] And just as the Marcionites reading the prophets do not have the prophets (for they do not have the Creator God who has given the prophecies), so also you, if you malign the prophets—for the Apostle says, "Do not quench the Spirit, do not despise prophecies"[37]—you will say, "*There is no longer a prophet, and he will know us no longer.*"[38]

When you do anything unworthy of those who know God, so

32. 1 Kgs 18.21.

33. On ancient magic and Origen's other testimonies to it, see Naomi Janowitz, *Magic in the Roman World: Pagans, Jews and Christians* (London: Routledge, 2001).

34. Mt 11.5.

35. Ps 73.9a.

36. Those who follow God's teaching in the whole Bible see in their lives the "signs" of God, such things as cleansing from sin and deep insight. Marcionites, who "delete" the prophets, do not see those signs. Neither do simple Christians who retain the Old Testament and accept the obvious sense of its words, the "statement" (*rhēton*), but do not receive its "mind" (*nous*), the deeper sense. See introduction, pp. 31–32.

37. See 1 Thes 5.19–20.

38. Ps 73.9bc.

that he does not even know you and pay attention to you, you also will say, "*He knows us no longer.*" The Lord does not know everyone, but those who are his.[39] But does it seem that someone is not God's and someone else is God's? Everyone who sins is not from God, but from the devil.[40] Everyone conforming with justice both by logoi and by works, with Christ that is, becomes from God. Therefore, God knows those who are his, and it is evident that they are truly God's.

4. After this let us look at what those who are abandoned say in prayer: "*Until when will the enemy chide, God; the opponent provokes your name completely.*"[41] The unseen enemy chides, and that one is always doing so. And we say concerning sinners, if we actually win them over and want them to have a change of heart, may they say, "*Until when will the enemy chide, God; the opponent provokes your name completely. Why do you turn back your hand and your right hand from the middle of your breast completely?*"[42] When God oversees, his hand offers good things from the breast—this is said figuratively—and gives us from his breast, but when he does not oversee, he does not give Christ from the breast. For "he is God's only begotten, who is in the Father's breast, that one has been brought forth."[43] But if you do not know Christ and sense that you are empty of him, full of sins, go ahead and pray and say: "*Why do you turn back your hand and your right hand from the middle of your breast completely?*"[44]

"*But God is our king before the age; he has worked out salvation from the middle of the earth.*"[45] Happy is he who can say this with truth, because he is not reigned over by sin reigning in his mortal body,[46] but is reigned over by God alone ordering and ruling

39. Nm 16.5.
40. See 1 Jn 3.8.
41. Ps 73.10.
42. Ps 73.10–11.
43. Jn 1.18.
44. Ps 73.11. Origen considers these particular words to be helpful in the case of dereliction. This is an early example of using a Bible verse or a formulaic prayer to pull Christ towards oneself, the impulse that will later find expression in the Jesus Prayer.
45. Ps 73.12.
46. See Rom 6.9.

his soul when it is governed. That is, when God is our king. But this our God is our king: "*Our king has worked out salvation from the middle of the earth,*"[47] of our souls. And he is "*in the middle of the earth,*" not so that you would consider some place on the earth to belong to the God who works out salvation, but ["*the middle of the earth*" refers to] whenever he works out the salvation of souls. Concerning which salvation they have sought out, the prophets have sought out and examined. Well, then, when God works something out, he works out salvation not outside the earth, but "*in the middle of the earth.*" For this is the surprising thing: that, being on earth and in the body, we have God working out salvation "*in the middle of the earth.*"

5. "*You are the one who controlled the sea in your power.*"[48] According to a simpler interpretation the maker of the universe controlled the sea and gave a great power to the sea, in particular, saying to it, "You shall come just this far, and your waves shall be smashed in you."[49] But according to a spiritual interpretation the sea is the life of human beings even when it is full of many waves, since the rest of the wording shows that this fits better, that is, to be controlled by God. The sea is also a strong antagonist to the human race, and it is impossible while in this life not to be in the sea. The good steersman struggles with the opposing winds[50] and stands against the waves flying at him and does not give up the boat, but keeps at his task while devoting himself with prayer to God.

So, according to our logos, one who has mastered steering, having logos in him as steersman,[51] takes on all the winds, either bodily ones or anything outside that tests him; he bears

---

47. Ps 73.12b.

48. Ps 73.13a.

49. Jb 38.11.

50. *Pneumata,* here translated "winds," also means "spirits." We find a similar use of the sea as a metaphor for human life and the same use of *pneuma* in a double sense in the Desert Mother Amma Syncletica, recorded in the *Alphabetical and Systematic Apophthegmata.* See Tim Vivian, "'We Sail by Day': Metaphor and Exegesis in the Sayings of Amma Syncletica," *Cistercian Studies Quarterly* 54 (2019): 3–24.

51. Philo often identified logos, conceived as Origen conceived it, as an emanation of God by which the cosmos is created and as human reason, as a steersman (*kubernētēs*).

his own tiller and moves his hand, so that he gives way to nothing, but rather stands fast in the storms of life and appears to be in a calm and peaceful state, able to steer himself, whatever happens. But even in stormy weather and in battle, why, according to us, are the holy blessed? Because they have become good steersmen in the storms, in troubles extraordinarily, in beatings extraordinarily, in prisons exceedingly often, those, to be sure, those who have received from the Jews forty save one, because they have been beaten with rods three times, because they were stoned, because they were shipwrecked, because they endured danger in a desert.[52] Do you see their steering logos, how they had it? Because of it, in whatever storms occurred, they did not suffer shipwreck. But in all of these they sailed straight through; they reasoned well, until they reached the haven[53] of God's will. This is on account of, "*You are the one who controlled the sea in your power.*"[54]

6. That the sea is more in tune with the spiritual than the bodily is clear from what follows: "*You have smashed the heads of serpents on the water.*"[55] For are there, in fact, on this water of the sea and rivers, the many serpents, and is God smashing, in a sensible manner, the heads of the serpents; or has the life of human beings been filled with serpents? Is this the same great and wide sea, where ships travel, where there are small and large and living things, where there is that serpent that "you fashioned to play with him"?[56] For the same sea is completely full of serpents, and God's work is to smash the heads of the serpents on the water. Whenever you are plotted against by adverse powers, sense that an unseen serpent is scheming against you, and a snake[57] as well, about which the Savior said, "I give you authority to tread on snakes and scorpions and upon every power of the evil one."[58]

52. See 2 Cor 11.24–26.

53. See Ps 106.30.

54. Ps 73.13a. The image of the Christian life as a risky voyage through dangerous waters occurs frequently elsewhere in Origen's work, perhaps most tellingly in *Princ.* 3.1.19. See below PS76H4.5, PS77H3.1, and PS77H9.2.

55. Ps 73.13b.

56. See Ps 103.25–26.

57. See Rv 12.9, perhaps also Gn 3.

58. Lk 10.19.

So, whenever you are schemed against by an adverse power, pray, and, when you pray, you will be helped, becoming worthy of God's logos crushing the head of the serpent in you[59] whenever you have won and the serpent's head is crushed. At times some desire comes to you, and some thought has caused trouble about descending with you into an impure action. This desire: when it has been swept out, when it has been put to death, the logos has crushed the head of one serpent. But when evil rises up against the governing faculty—from within, for wicked calculations come out of the heart—it again summons God to send the logos to you. The logos, coming, smashes the heads of the dragon. And it is blessed for your soul to be filled with dead serpents that were once alive in you. "*For you have smashed the heads of serpents on the water*,"[60] that is, the unsteady affairs of life, upon things that are unfixed and unstable smashing the heads of the serpent.

There are many serpents, each of which has a head, and there is one many-headed serpent. If you want to hear more simply, even if more figuratively, evil is one many-headed serpent. Each form of sin and form of evil is a head of this one serpent. Thus thoughtlessness is a head of the serpent of evil, as are cowardice, irreverence, greed, and a list of the other heads of the serpent. If you want to learn in another way, know that the adversary, the old serpent, the devil, is written in John's Revelation as having many heads,[61] for it is not single-headed.

According to one logos I will say that all his rulers[62] are his

59. On the snake as a spiritual adversary in third-century Christianity, compare *The Passion of Perpetua and Felicitas* 4.

60. Ps 73.13b.

61. See Rv 12.9 and 20.2. This many-headed serpent resembles the Lernean hydra of Hesiod, *Theogony* 313–19.

62. *Archōn* (pl. *archontes*) means "ruler" or "magistrate." According to one logos, these are the demonic, spiritual rulers of Eph 2.2. (These spiritual rulers assume great importance in Valentinian Gnosticism.) According to another logos, that is, another way of understanding the words of the Bible, *archontes* refers to ordinary human beings, in this case, the "rulers" or "initiators," of heresies. *Archontes*, "rulers," is the participial form of a verb that originally meant "take the initiative" or "lead the way," but came to mean "begin" or "start." Origen interprets it in the latter sense in PS76H2.1, below. A noun with the same root, *archē*, means either "beginning" or "rule." In the Septuagint, *en archēi* translates the first word of the Bible, *beresit*, "in beginning," where the noun is closely related to the

heads, but, according to another, the rulers of the heresies; thus Basilides is a head of the devil, Valentinus is a head of the devil, Apelles another head, and, in general, all the rulers among the heresies are heads of the one serpent.[63]

"*You,* then, *have crushed the heads of serpents on the water*";[64] if you ascend by the logos, you will see a certain logos they have in the adverse powers, in the most highly placed and in those subordinate: some are heads of the serpent; others constitute the rest of his body. For Scripture knows a body of a serpent that has some extremities, some higher parts, so that "when a whole fleet gathers, it cannot lift one hide of its tail,"[65] because a whole fleet coming together in the body could not carry the extremities and the full limits of evil, unless God were to help. There are many heads of the serpent, which God crushes away for our sake, according to the Apostle saying the blessing: "May the God of peace, who has raised me up, crush Satan under your feet right soon."[66] I know, when I say this, that that one seeks to bite us back, especially those saying these things about him: "But the Lord is my helper and my shield and my Savior; whom shall I fear?"[67] Let us pray that all his threats may be thrown into confusion. For God says: "Be of good courage, I have overcome the cosmos."[68]

7. Next is a figurative expression; who cannot allegorize? Say, you who are stumbling and not reckoning that we should say these things forcefully, "*You have crushed the heads of the serpent. You have given him as food to the Ethiopians.*"[69] Do the Ethiopians, the people from the edges of the inhabited world, actually take the serpent's body from God and cut it into pieces, so that they may eat the flesh of the serpent? Is this notion worthy of the Holy Spirit? Is this worthy of prophetic grace? Why are they

---

ros, "head." The notions of "head" and "ruler" are thus related; see PS15H2.8, n. 92 above. In PS73H1.4 above Origen identifies the *archē* of Gn 1.1 with Christ.

63. On Basilides and Valentinus, see introduction, pp. 9–10. Apelles was a follower of Marcion.

64. Ps 73.13b.

65. Jb 40.31 (only in the Septuagint).

66. Rom 16.20.

67. Ps 27.7. See Ps 26.1.

68. Jn 16.33.

69. Ps 73.14.

stumbling at logoi that lift up our soul? But it is possible to set forth that, just as the holy ones eat the body of Christ and the Lord says: "My flesh is true food, and my blood is true drink,"[70] so sinners eat the serpent's body. Whenever the Valentinians and Basilideans and the others from the sects make thanksgiving, do they then actually eat the body of Christ, whom they blaspheme, whom they do not know? Perish the thought![71] But, on the one hand, if we also pray to eat Christ's body, they, on the other, pray to eat the body of the serpent, about whom it is written, "*You have given him as food to the Ethiopians*,"[72] those in ignorance, those in darkness,[73] those who have been led apart by ignorance and by sins.

8. "*You have soaked a spring and torrents*."[74] According to the narrative, the simpler person will say that he has broken forth a spring from rocks,[75] as, when the people came out of Egypt, he broke forth a spring, or as when, in Samson's case, out of the jaw of an ass came water and he drank;[76] and other such instances might be found in the divine Scriptures. But I am one who finds in each one of these a promise from my Lord Jesus that from his belly will flow a spring of water welling up into eternal life.[77] And I would say that "*You have soaked a spring and torrents*" fits better spiritually with this passage. Whenever you pray for us, God breaks forth a spring in us and makes torrents go out, and this spring never fails. Bodily springs fail, if they are not supplied with water from the sky. Pray for us, that spiritual rain may fill the spring, and a torrent, and that you may be refreshed drinking from the spiritual water. "*You have soaked a spring and torrents*" in our Lord Jesus Christ, to whom is the glory and the might to the age of ages. Amen.

70. Jn 6.55.

71. *Mē genoito.* This expression is characteristic of the Apostle Paul, who uses it fourteen times.

72. Ps 73.14b.

73. "Darkness" possibly indicates a negative symbolism associated with dark skin pigmentation. See the reproaches of Abba Moses, an Ethiopian, in *Alphabetical Apophthegmata Patrum*, Moses 3.

74. Ps 73.15a.

75. See Ps 77.15.

76. Jgs 15.19.

77. See Jn 4.14.

HOMILY 3 ON PSALM 73

N THE ONE hand, we, who do not know what we should pray for as we ought,[1] need help and provision by the Spirit[2] along with an appropriate time of prayer, so that we may pray with the Spirit, but also that we may pray with the mind;[3] but the holy prophets, on the other hand, had made strides and progressed in prayer to such an extent that they prophesied in it. And here, as a matter of fact, a hidden prophecy is found in the prayer that says, "*You broke forth a spring and torrents; you dried up rivers.*"[4] Through this it is disclosed how a spring came to those who were from the gentiles, but drought came upon Israel. But I suppose that the prophecy concerning both peoples is more clearly seen in Psalm 106. There it is written that "God turned a desert into shores of water and a waterless land and a dry land into rivulets of waters; he turned a fruitful land into salt marsh on account of the wickedness of those who dwelt in it."[5]

One must learn what the spring was that broke forth and what the torrents were that God gathered. My Lord Jesus Christ is the spring, from which we drink. And the torrents come in a deluge at this spring, because the holy and marvelous apostles are torrents that have come in a deluge, as they are also in Psalm 77, the waters flowing from the rock and many torrents coming in a

1. Rom 8.26. This passage echoes the opening of Origen's treatise *On Prayer* (*Or.* 1–2). Lorenzo Perrone subtitled his magisterial work on prayer in Origen, *The Impossibility Bestowed* (*La preghiera secondo Origene: L'impossibilità donata* [Brescia: Morcelliana, 2011]).

2. See Phil 1.19.

3. 1 Cor 14.15.

4. Ps 73.15a.

5. Ps 106.33–34. He makes the same point in *Comm. Jo.* 28.24.214.

deluge.[6] Christ, then, came from heaven as a spring and has given many torrents, the apostles. And up to the present he gives torrents; for should you find studious souls and apostolic life, through them torrents flow and rivers of water are welling up to eternal life.[7]

But it must be perceived more clearly about the things that happened in that people concerning whom it has been written, "*You dried up ētham rivers.*"[8] This does not occur in the copies of the Septuagint,[9] but we find the line in the Hebrew and in the other versions. And, not knowing what is "*You dried up ētham rivers,*" we read in one, "old rivers"; in others, the rivers running in the prophets[10] are "old," "stiff," "vigorous," and "powerful,"[11] not because the prophets themselves have been dried up—far be it from us to say something slanderous—but because the Jewish prophets have stopped and there are no longer prophets among them.

2. After the prophetic prayer, God is again proclaimed in a hymn in the prayer when the prophet says: "*Yours is the day, and yours also is the night.*"[12] And who would not say that this is clear? I also say that by the wording it is most clear: no one is the creator of day and night except the one who says, "Let there be light"[13] and calls the light "day."[14] And no one else is maker

6. Ps 77.15–16. See PS77H3.3 below.

7. See Jn 4.14 and Origen's commentary in *Comm. Jo.* 13.5.26–39.

8. Ps 73.15b. See n. 11 below.

9. The line is omitted in one of the oldest manuscripts of the Septuagint, the Codex Vaticanus Gr. 1209.

10. Asaph was praying "with the mind" in this prophetic Psalm; he himself must have intended his words to refer to prophetic inspiration.

11. Origen must have discovered this line in the *Hexapla*, in which he had two additional versions of the Psalms. One version, the Septuagint, omitted the verse. One version transliterated the Hebrew without translating it. The rest gave four different translations. Translators may have sought to avoid an apparent contradiction; Hebrew *eytan* (spelled with an "n") means "permanent" or "ever-flowing." According to Eusebius (*Commentary on the Psalms* 73.15), who had access to the *Hexapla*, "stiff" was Aquila's reading, and "old" was that of Symmachus.

12. Ps 73.16a.

13. Gn 1.3.

14. Gn 1.5.

of night except the one who says, "I am the one fabricating light and making darkness,"[15] and calling the name for the darkness "night."[16] According to the wording, then, *Yours is the day, and yours also is the night*" seems to be simple.

Although I could, by moving on, not make trouble for myself in interpreting things that have been written, let me try to examine them reasonably. It appears in the Scriptures that certain days are spoken of as "the Lord's," which called them "designated,"[17] as if not all days were "the Lord's," but only some. For such a statement makes a stumbling block,[18] even though we can cope with the stumbling block from the wording itself that I have cited just now and from the logos concerning a man. What I say will be clear in this way: who would not say to God, if he were simple, "Yours are human beings," and that they would be so whether they were sinners or just? But Scripture does not intend this: for God's knowledge knows only just human beings. Moses, in the end, was barely called "a human being of God,"[19] and Elijah said: "if I am a human being of God, let fire come down from heaven and consume you and your fifty,"[20] but he spoke to the commander of fifty sent by that lawless king. Therefore just as, according to the simpler, every day is God's and all human beings are God's, but, according to the truth, not all are rightfully God's, yet only the just are God's according to "The Lord knows those who are his."[21] So, if, according to the simpler, every day is God's and every night is God's, but, according to the accurate logos, I would say that only in the just is the day God's and only in the honorable[22] is the night God's; for days and nights, understanding the day according to the Scriptures, have the shadow, in festivals, of good things to come.[23]

15. Is 45.7.
16. Gn 1.5.
17. Lv 23.2.
18. See 2 Cor 6.3.
19. Dt 33.1.
20. 2 Kgs 1.10.
21. Nm 16.5.
22. *Kalōi kai agathōi.* See PS36H1.3, n. 49 above.
23. See Heb 10.1.

To the one, then, for whom the sun of justice[24] has arisen and has made for that person a "day of the Lord," the one to whom the unspeakable and hidden sayings of wisdom are present according to what has been said: "He made darkness his hiding place,"[25] to that one is present God's night. About that night and those who have it, it has been written: "In the nights lift up your hands to the holy ones and bless the Lord."[26] But also the statements saying, "For, see, a day is coming,"[27] and, "Woe to those desiring the Lord's day,"[28] make clear that not every day is the Lord's day, by a logos equivalent to that which applies to human beings. All human beings are beings fashioned by God, even when they are most irreverent, but because of sin they have renounced God and have joined[29] the devil.

Thus indeed among us also, if the sun of justice arises, it has made a day Christ's, but if it is not this, but Satan transforming himself into an angel of light,[30] he makes a day of which the light is quenched. Concerning both lights Solomon speaks in Proverbs: "The light of the just continues unquenched through everything, but the light of the irreverent is quenched."[31] The just man speaks well about himself and the day and night that are in him: "*Yours is the day, and yours is the night*," just as he does in the case of "*You shaped illumination and sun.*"[32] And God shaped these things, the illumination and the sun, but especially the sun that he calls "of justice."

3. The Father also shaped the illumination, naming it as something different, alongside the sun. God shaped—who could this be but the Holy Spirit?—so that "*you shaped illumination and sun*" is a reference to Christ and, in figurative speech, to the Holy Spirit. As far as the statement is concerned, someone may seek why the illumination and the sun are shaped by God

24. Mal 4.2.
25. 2 Sm 22.12, Ps 17.12.
26. Ps 133.2.
27. See, perhaps, Is 13.9.
28. Am 5.18.
29. See Acts 17.4.
30. 2 Cor 11.14.
31. Prv 13.9.
32. Ps 73.16.

and why the illumination is different from the sun. Then, when I seek the statement, I take it from Genesis, and I may explain another illumination, another sun: "In the beginning God made heaven and earth. The earth was invisible and unformed, and darkness was above the abyss, and God's spirit was borne above the water. And God said, 'Let light come to be,' and light was produced."[33] See, I have the illumination. Then, on the fourth day: "Let lights come into the structure of heaven,"[34] and a little farther on, "and he made the big light for the rule of days,"[35] so that according to this, as far as the statement goes, it is said, "*You shaped illumination and sun.*" There is, then, this light greater than the sun, the firstborn of this creation[36] and produced before the sun.

What, then, would this be, but the light that he made, which is a light for the cosmos? God saying, "I am the light of the cosmos."[37] And God has shaped this, but, just as, when there is light, the blind person does not benefit from it, nor does the person who is in darkness and in the shadow of death,[38] nor does the person with his eyes closed have the benefit of the light, so the illumination itself has come forth for the cosmos, which is greater than this sun, but the blind do not see it. But, "Who is blind except my children?"[39] Such ones do not see such a great light, but Jesus Christ escaped their notice, the visiting light of the cosmos. He did not, however, escape the notice of those from the gentiles: "For those sitting in a countryside and in the shadow of death, the light has risen upon them."[40] This light is indeed great, which God has shaped for us, concerning which also in the Gospel it is written: "In the beginning was the logos and the logos was near God, and the logos was a god. This one was in the beginning near God. All things came into being through him, and without him nothing came into

---

33. Gn 1.1–3.
34. Gn 1.14.
35. Gn 1.16.
36. See Col 1.15.
37. Jn 8.12.
38. See Is 9.2 and Mt 4.16.
39. Is 42.19.
40. Is 9.2 and Mt 4.16.

being that came into being. In him was life, and the life was the light of human beings."[41]

4. The next passage is, "*You have shaped all the boundaries of the earth.*"[42] In turn, as far as the statement is concerned, it is clear that "the Highest apportioned nations, the sons of Adam whom he scattered. He has set boundaries of nations according to the number of the angels of God. And Jacob has become the Lord's portion, the allotment of Israel, his inheritance."[43] For the earth was not divided for dwellings haphazardly by God, so that these portions of the earth belong to the Egyptians, and their boundaries belong to Pharaoh, but those portions belong to the Jews, and those are the boundaries of Israel. The same thing holds for the rest of the nations, because "the Highest apportioned nations, the sons of Adam whom he scattered. He has set boundaries of nations according to the number of the angels of God." And it is to these boundaries, insofar as the statement goes, that the prophet is referring in the logos that says, "*You have shaped all the boundaries of the earth.*"

If one must also step up into the logos, know that all are going to be restored in boundaries shaped to our actions in a proportionate relationship to our life, so that just as the law holds the shadow of good things to come,[44] so "when the Highest apportioned nations" would also hold a shadow of good things to come. For there is coming another allotment to be produced of a new covenant and earth; when it is produced, according to the prophet Isaiah, "heaven is new and earth is new."[45] And just as God has established boundaries of nations on this earth in a proportionate relationship to each one's life and to the number of God's angels, in the same way in the new creation God will place the boundaries of nations in a proportionate relation to each one's life. And there will be among those boundaries ones arranged in better places in different portions of this earth, ones in second and inferior places, ones in third, ones in the last.

---

41. Jn 1.1–4.

42. Ps 73.17a.

43. Dt 32.8–9.

44. See Heb 10.1.

45. Is 65.17. See also Rv 21.1.

Hence, then, it is written, "*You have shaped all the boundaries of the earth.*" But I am ascending in the logos, and I am bold and I say: "You have shaped all the boundaries of heaven." And just as, among the stars, he shaped the boundaries of heaven; just as, in the case of the stars, some are below the Bear, others below the Meridian, and others in the so-called Zodiac, and at the same time one star is in the Bear itself and another is slightly away from it, in the same way those who inherit the kingdom will receive boundaries in heaven that God has shaped.

So that you may still be persuaded by the Scriptures that, if you become worthy of the kingdom of heavens, you will receive certain boundaries in heaven from the principal stars that have been mentioned, move over to the logos of the resurrection likened to stars: "There is a glory of the sun, another glory of the moon, another glory of the stars, for as star differs from star in glory, so it is in the resurrection of the dead."[46] As, then, for these stars God has set boundaries in heaven, so that you become "the light of the cosmos,"[47] and you are truly "like the stars in heaven in multitude,"[48] God will set boundaries for you, not on the earth, but in heaven. And why am I saying "in heaven"? I am bold, and I say that above heaven among all of the heavens there will be boundaries of the just. "The heavens explain the glory of God,"[49] and into all of them can ascend the follower of Jesus, about whom it is said, "We have a high priest who has gone through the heavens, Jesus, the Son of God,"[50] who said to the disciple, "Where I am going, you cannot follow me now, but you will follow later."[51] For if you will follow later, but he has passed through the heavens, so Peter, evidently, against whom the gates of Hades do not prevail,[52] will follow him as he passes through the heavens.

---

46. 1 Cor 15.41–42.

47. Mt 5.14. See also Jn 8.12 and 9.5.

48. Ex 32.13.

49. Ps 18.2. Origen understood the successive heavens as schools for souls, who advanced in the knowledge of God. See *Princ.* 2.11.6–7.

50. Heb 4.14.

51. In Jn 13.36.

52. Mt 16.18.

5. After this is, *"Summer*[53] *and spring, you fashioned them."*[54] Again, as far as the statement goes, God did not make summer only, but the whole year, according to what has been written: "You will bless the crown of the year with your kindness."[55] But since the Scripture is silent here about two seasons, winter[56] and autumn or fall, and it has named summer and spring, one must hear when we were saying[57] that the person fleeing the winter of the soul and seeking to have spring in him as well as summer knows that God makes spring in the soul and makes summer in the soul. If you want to understand spring in the soul, move with me from the bodily Passover, since it would occur in the season of spring, and see with me the Passover about which the Apostle speaks: "Christ our Passover has been sacrificed for us."[58] We know, because this Passover occurs in spring, just as the bridegroom calls the soul his bride and says: "The winter has passed; it went away by itself; the flowers have appeared on the earth."[59] And he might as well have cried out, "You made spring."

I also want to persuade you from Scripture about summer, because there is a summer in the soul, having the same name as the harvesting that occurs in summer, which is produced by God in the just. For the one going out to sow cast the seed wherever he cast, and when it fell to the good and productive earth, it bore fruit that grew a hundredfold;[60] accordingly, it makes a hundredfold, and this harvest does not need to be reaped. This summer, then, is produced within, and there is produced, "going they shall come in gladness, carrying their sheaves."[61] And should it be spoken in the Gospel by the Savior with respect to the time of harvesting, one must see that, on the one hand, he knows a harvest and the completion of the age,[62] but, on the

---

53. The Greek word for the season of summer, *theros,* also means "harvest."

54. Ps 73.17b.

55. Ps 64.12.

56. *Cheimōn,* the word for winter, also means "storm" or "stormy weather."

57. Perhaps in a previous homily, now lost.

58. 1 Cor 5.7.

59. See Song 2.11–13.

60. Lk 8.8.

61. Ps 125.6.

62. Mt 13.39.

other hand, he knows some other harvest, since, in gathering the perfected sheaves, there is no longer a stalk,[63] but a seven-fold fruit[64] has been produced, so that I may make more with my directing faculty, so that I may cleanse the chaff from the grain and that I may fill the place of the storehouses of the blessed ones, concerning which the law in a blessing says, "Blessed be your storehouses and your provisions."[65]

6. "*Remember this.*"[66] This fashioning? This creation? This prayer that I prayed? He has written elliptically, not saying what "this" is, leaving us to supply with impunity what was left out in the sequence of the thought. "*An enemy has reproached the Lord.*"[67] Someone saying to a just person, "Where is your God?"[68] seems to reproach the just, but in truth he reproaches the Lord. Do not reckon that I am being bold beyond Scripture, for you feed the just, but in return the Savior says, "When I was hungry, you gave something to eat." You also give drink to the just, but in return the Savior says, "When I was thirsting, you gave me something to drink."[69] Someone clothes[70] the just, as each of us has determined to clothe him, but likewise the Savior says, "I was naked, and you clothed me." Thus, then, someone reproaching the just person reproaches the Lord. And were I to say that to the person reproaching, this will be said: "When you

63. See, possibly, Mk 4.28 and 1 Cor 3.12.

64. One of the harvests that the Savior knows is the harvest of souls at the end of the age. The second is obscure. It may be a harvest of the fruit of the spirit, which comes through the spiritual growth and inner cleansing that faithful Christians can experience in the course of their lives here, or it may be a "sevenfold" harvest in which this process occurs in each of the seven heavens.

65. Dt 28.5.

66. Ps 73.18a.

67. Ps 73.18b.

68. Ps 41.4.

69. Mt 25.35. See also PS15H1.3 above.

70. See Mt 25.36. Origen, perhaps because he was relying on memory, changes the word for "clothe." The original word for "clothe," *periballō,* can also be translated "throw around." Origen uses a different word that can also mean "get into," *enduō. Enduō* can mean "give someone clothes," but more commonly means, "get into clothes." "Clothe" Christ by clothing the just; this leads Origen to the rich Pauline theme of "putting on" Christ in Rom 13.14 and Gal 3.27, where Paul uses the word *enduein,* advising us to "get into" Christ by acting so that the world sees Christ rather than us. See also PS81H.3 below.

reproached that one, you reproached me," and, "When you reviled that one, you reviled me, an Israelite." Just as the murderer and adulterer will be stoned,[71] so according to the law any man who reviles is stoned; he is stoned as if he were an adulterer, as if he were a murderer. But the Lord appears to me and says: "You did not revile that one, but you reviled me, the Lord." Someone is abusing a true Israelite; the person abusing him speaks ill of God. "Therefore, do not err: neither a sexually immoral person, nor an adulterer, nor a soft person, nor one who lies with males, nor a thief, nor a drunkard, nor a reviler, nor a robber will inherit the kingdom of God."[72]

And so that you may be more persuaded that if you revile your neighbor, you have reviled Christ, I will also present this from the holy letters: if anyone abuses the wooden or waxen image of an emperor, he is condemned as if he had abused the emperor, since he commits an abuse against the image. And you, if you abuse or revile someone who has already restored the "in the image" of the Creator,[73] it is his image that you have abused and reviled. Therefore, one must beware of speaking ill and reviling one's neighbor or acting in any way wickedly. For Christ receives all that happens to himself, either good or bad, that you do to the neighbor. This will suffice for "*An enemy has reproached the Lord.*"

7. "*And a thoughtless people provokes your name.*"[74] When the devil as an enemy was reproaching my Lord, because he willingly had recourse to the plan of the cross on behalf of those for whom he suffered, the thoughtless people provoked the name of the Lord, saying, "Take, take such a one from the earth; crucify him."[75] Therefore, when a thoughtless people provoked the name of the Lord, "the daughter of Zion was abandoned like a booth in a vineyard and like a watcher's hut in a cucumber field, like a city under siege."[76] See to it, then, that not one of us ever

---

71. Dt 22.24.

72. 1 Cor 6.9–10. We also see this widening of the application of Mt 25.25 in PS36H3.12.

73. Gn 1.26–27 and Col 3.10. See PS15H1.3 above.

74. Ps 73.18c.

75. Lk 23.21.

76. Is 1.8.

becomes like the thoughtless people and provokes the name of the Lord.

Again he prays and then teaches us to pray, saying: "*Do not hand over to the beasts a soul that confesses to you.*"[77] Many of the martyrs, therefore, in martyrdom were handed over to beasts, and I know in my own time blessed and holy human beings who endured being eaten. Would that I had been among them! Why did this happen? Did, then, the prophet pray about sensible beasts when he said, "*Do not hand over to the beasts a soul that confesses to you*"? Evidently those who were confessing and giving thanks were thrown to the beasts for that very reason. But maybe there are some other beasts; for example, I say, the one of whom it is said, "Our adversary the devil walks around like a roaring lion, seeking someone to devour."[78] And a lion and a leopard kept watch for their sacrileges, it is said in Jeremiah.[79] For a lion and a leopard did not watch for the sacrileges of Israel; the lion, that is the sensible one, the quadruped, does not watch the sins of Israel; and the same goes for the leopard. For leopards do not occur at all in Judaea, but the prophet, who comprehended spiritually the species of adverse powers, said that "a lion and a leopard had been keeping watch for the sacrileges of Israel." And again, that he had spoken of a certain "wolf"[80] as an adverse power. But when the coronations of martyrs occur from the Gospels, I want to add how the Savior, in turn, spoke, not about visible, but about invisible, beasts.[81] He promised his disciples, saying, "See, I give you authority to tread upon snakes and scorpions and every power of the enemy, and nothing will harm you."[82]

---

77. Ps 73.19a.

78. 1 Pt 5.8.

79. Jer 5.6.

80. Ibid. In Canto 1 of the *Inferno* these three beasts obstruct Dante, compelling his journey through the realms of the dead.

81. Origen's wolf of Jer 5.6 recalls the wolves of Mt 10.16 and its parallel, Lk 10.3. In Mt 10.16–23 Jesus warns his disciples that he is sending them out as sheep in the midst of wolves and exhorts them to maintain their witness (*marturion*) even to death. Origen applies that passage and its parallels to Christian martyrdom in *Mart.* 34. His point is that none of these "wolves" is an actual, four-footed wolf.

82. Lk 10.19.

Now what kind of snakes would he have given them authority to tread on? Is someone illustrious and a believer? Let him go ahead and tread on the snakes we see, especially the viper and cobra or some other of the lethal beasts and scorpions.[83] Christ does give such favors to us, but if we see the serpent, the old snake, the so-called "devil" and "satan," in this way he will be crushed under the feet of God's chosen ones, and we see that in the passage just expounded in this Psalm: "*You crushed the heads of serpents on the water,*"[84] and we shall see how the prophet prays about invisible beasts, saying: "*Do not hand over to the beasts, Lord, a soul that confesses to you.*"[85] For he tears away the soul of sinners from beasts. But I want at the same time to persuade the listener from the wording itself that the clarification is not forced, but handed over according to the intention of the Scriptures. For it is not said, "Do not hand over to the beasts a flesh that confesses to you," but "a soul that confesses to you." But it is evident that these "beasts" do not eat "souls," but "flesh," so other beasts eat souls. How often has a lion gotten hold of your feet and dragged, wanting to pull you outside the Church? How often has a lion grabbed your earlobe, through some appetizing teaching and logoi foreign to the Church? But when the good shepherd comes, who lays down his soul for the sheep,[86] "as the shepherd tears out of the mouth of the lion two legs or the lobe of an ear,"[87] he pries your feet from the invisible beast and your earlobe from its mouth.

8. When the prophet says, "*Do not hand over to the beasts a soul that confesses to you,*"[88] he is praying for our souls. But if we confess when we sin, so as not to be handed over to wild beasts on account of our sins, but on account of confession—for if by sins we are worthy to be handed over to beasts—let us not ever be handed over to them. For why is it not said, "Do not hand over

---

83. Origen is making fun of those who do not allow for a deeper sense: "If you think that is what Jesus meant, just try walking on a cobra and see what happens!"

84. Ps 73.13b.

85. Ps 73.19a.

86. Jn 10.11.

87. Am 3.12.

88. Ps 73.19a.

to wild beasts a soul that acts temperately and justly," but "*a soul that confesses to you*"? The intention of the phrase is something like this: "Some have sinned who are worthy to be handed over to beasts. Do not, then, do to them according to their sins, since they confess to you." If someone among us confesses and does not want to be handed over to beasts, let that person confess: "Confess to the Lord because he is kind, because his mercy is for an age."[89] The person who confesses must confess particularly to God, but if he has not given up hope, there are also physicians in the Church; show yourself to them; the wounds will be treated; let him not hesitate to communicate to physicians concerning his sins and to uncover the shame his soul has suffered. But good bishops are physicians; good and choice presbyters are physicians, well able to treat[90] the one who confesses.

That I am not the person who teaches this, but Scripture wants this, listen to the one who says, "You have recognized my sin"—are these words said to anyone but God?—"and I did not hide my sin."[91] Is it possible to reveal to anyone without revealing to Christ? "I declare my sin to the Lord." For say your violations first, so that you may be justified; do not simply "say," but "say first." Do not wait for another accuser; get ahead of your accusers, not human beings only, but the great accuser, the devil. If you accuse yourself first, that accuser will be muzzled, and you will be justified by being your own accuser. Scripture, even if there should be unjust deeds about which someone accuses himself, already has made him just, and it has said that he will be just in the words, "The just person accuses himself as soon as he speaks."[92] And someone might seek to know if the one who is his own accuser—and he really sinned; it is clear that he would be a sinner—how then can one who is his own accuser be just? But it must be said that changing and, as it were, becoming a different person, he is the first accuser of his own sinful conduct.

89. Ps 105.1b.

90. *Therapeuein.* In *Or.* 28.9 Origen speaks of those who can administer "God's treatment," *therapeia,* of sins. This passage ascribes the ability to do this to those bishops and presbyters who are "good" physicians of souls.

91. Ps 31.5a.

92. Prv 18.17.

Along with the other marvels that I have seen in other churches, I have seen this one, which I present to you. Some of the sinners, not having a human accuser, nor being known for the sins they had committed, pray and present sins to the bishop; but he as a physician weeps and does not call out or bring into the midst [of the church] the sin of the person who has sinned, but as a good father lamenting what has been confessed, applies rational plasters, spiritual infusions. He treats and turns his own son back to God, so that he is cured at a definite time and the wounds are removed so that the people will not be destroyed because of hidden abscesses on account of not confessing sin. For an abscess remains inside; therefore, I beg you all who are hearing this, if you are aware of any sins in yourselves, especially sexual or other dangerous ones, do not be silent about it, and show yourself to be treated, for if there is an abscess, as I just said, it stays inside. But present yourselves to the scalpel-logos, so that the hidden things may be removed, which are stored within, and it will bring you treatment, and you may be enabled to have complete healing for your wound now, and, because you have received that complete healing, you will be made holy; truly confessing to God, you will be saved. These things are said not as a digression, but as a necessary extension. It was necessary to clarify *"Do not hand over to the beasts a soul that confesses to you."*[93]

9. *"Do not forget to an end the souls of the poor."*[94] Not all the poor are God's, but there are some who are God's poor, the ones dedicated to God; they are worthy of the Savior's blessedness when he says: "Blessed are the destitute, because yours is the kingdom of God."[95] He did not say "theirs" but "yours," demonstrating that there were destitute persons present.

"Have regard for your covenant."[96] In the covenant this is covenanted: that he will be compassionate to the sins of those who confess. Then, "have regard for that." It is laid down in the vows, "If I flog them and they remain in their sins," it is definite that

---

93. Ps 73.19a.
94. Ps 73.19b.
95. Lk 6.20.
96. Ps 73.20a.

"I will add seven strokes,"[97] but, if they do not remain in their sins, it is definite that the wounds will be treated. The leper is cleansed ten days outside the tents, and at the time established he is restored to his own tents,[98] *"because the darkened ones of the earth have been filled with houses of lawless deeds."*[99] Right away the wording is something unclear, so one must see who the *"darkened ones of the earth"* are and what the *"houses of lawless deeds"* are.

All who are separated from the one who said, "I am the light of the cosmos,"[100] are darkened. But among those who are darkened, some are human beings and are on earth; they are the *"darkened ones of the earth,"* but others, sinners outside of bodies—I speak of the demons and evil spirits and souls of the unjust and those underground—are "darkened ones," but not "of earth," but, if one must speak in a bold way, "of the underground." But perhaps there are darkened ones of the air, concerning whom the Apostle speaks, "in which you once walked about according to the age of this cosmos, according to the ruler of the authority of the air, the spirit now motivating the children of unbelief."[101] But grant that the darkened ones of the underground or the darkened ones of the air or the darkened ones of the spirits of evil fill those things that are filled. What we are now seeking, since the logos discusses human beings, is what to say about the darkened ones of the earth.

If someone does not have Christ, he is one of the darkened ones of the earth; the darkened ones are those of the earth who inhabit houses for their own lawless deeds; they stay in their houses. *"The darkened ones of the earth have been filled with houses of lawless deeds"*;[102] just as each of us by sinning builds for himself a house of lawless deeds, so there is a house of sexual immorality, a house of greed, and a house of vain teaching; and of each of the sins and follies there would be a house in us, built by the lawless deed. The darkened ones of the earth, then, do not have

97. Lv 26.21.
98. See Lv 14.8–9.
99. Ps 73.20b.
100. Jn 8.12.
101. Eph 2.2.
102. Ps 73.20b.

one house, but many. The prophecy says: "*The darkened ones of the earth have been filled with houses of lawless deeds.*" So, on the contrary, the enlightened of the earth are together full of houses of ordinances, commandments, and decrees. And it is blessed to build them in us, becoming the enlightened ones of the earth, houses of justice, when the houses of lawless deeds have been cleansed by the logos, who razes, destroys, and demolishes in order that he may build and plant,[103] in the place of the razed houses of violations, houses of law and justice.

10. "*Do not let the humbled and shamed be turned away.*"[104] Whom do I regard, says the Lord, but the gentle and meek, and the one wearing out my logoi? I know those who read it both in relation to the humble person and to "learn from me that I am gentle and humble at heart."[105] This, then, is the humble person, the one who humbles himself according to Christ's teaching: "*Do not let the shamed be turned away, but let him come forward in glory, for everyone who humbles himself will be uplifted.*"[106]

"*The destitute and poor praise your name.*"[107] This can be taken either to refer to bodily things—the destitute are those who count for nothing[108] in life, but the despised poor are just—or someone can want to hear it in regard to those who are spiritual; many destitute and poor were rich, and those who were once poor and destitute praised the Lord's name.

"*Rise up, God, judge your case.*"[109] To whom does he pray this? To the God of the Universe? No. But since the Savior accepted a death for my sake, therefore the prophet says to him, "*Rise up, God, judge your case.*" If he were not dying and rising, it would not be possible for him to judge the case of human beings, which the Apostle makes clear, saying: "Therefore, Christ died and rose, so that he might be lord of the dead and the living."[110]

---

103. See Jer 1.10.
104. Ps 73.21a.
105. Mt 11.29.
106. Lk 14.11, 18.14.
107. Ps 73.21b.
108. See 1 Cor 1.28.
109. Ps 73.22a.
110. Rom 14.9.

"Remember your reproaches by the thoughtless for the whole day."[111]
He did not say "the reproaches of those who reproach us," but
"your reproaches." For those who reproach us, reproach you.

"Do not forget the voice of your enemies."[112] Whatever the enemies
in their arrogance say, let it be in your memory, so that their
wickedness may be cleansed.

"The pride of those who hate you ascends through all."[113] The proud
are raised up; pride is never humbled, but ascends and always
gets higher. Since, then, pride gets higher and ascends through
all: you, God, throw down their pride to the end, in Christ Jesus,
to whom is the glory and the might to the ages. Amen.

111. Ps 73.22b.
112. Ps 73.23a.
113. Ps 73.23b.

HOMILY ON PSALM 74

HE ONE SEEING "in the end" says, by virtue of that very seeing, "*to the end may you not destroy.*"[1] For, doing things appropriate to indestructibility, he has cried out, "*may you not destroy,*" in place of which one of the translators[2]—instead of "*to the end may you not destroy*"[3]—has put "*about indestructibility.*" The things recorded here, understood and practiced, lead us to indestructibility. And the Psalm is by Asaph,[4] and performing by instrument and voice[5] indicates that we must hymn God with an instrument through bodily motion and by mental voice through offering the mind to the maker[6] and thus procure salvation. At the beginning, the Psalm is spoken in the plural, but the rest of it is in the singular, and, as plural and singular are not the same, one persona is not speaking through the whole Psalm. The speaker is plural from "*We shall confess to you, God, and shall call upon your name*"[7] to "*I shall recount your marvelous deeds, whenever I receive an occasion.*"[8] The Psalm continues to employ the singular to the end.

Understand, then, the plural subject to be the Church called from the gentiles and listening to the one who calls, saying, because of prior sinfulness, "*We shall confess to you, God.*" Next, since it is not possible "to call upon the name of the Lord," so

1. Ps 74.1a.
2. Most likely, the translator Symmachus.
3. Ps 74.1a.
4. Ps 74.1b.
5. "By instrument," since the word "Psalm" implies "plucking" an instrument; "by voice," because it is designated "of a song" in the inscription.
6. See PS67H2.3 above.
7. Ps 74.2.
8. Ps 74.3.

it comes about by chance that "everyone who calls upon the name of the Lord will be saved,"[9] unless someone, having first renounced sin, confesses prior sins; therefore it is written, "*We shall confess, and we shall call upon your name*"; not, "We shall call, and we shall confess to you," but, "*We shall confess to you, and we shall call upon your name.*" If, then, we also want to be found among those who shall call and to be saved along with them—for it is written, "Everyone who calls upon the name of the Lord shall be saved"—let us become accusers of our own sin, in the end abandoning it.

For the Church when it says, "*We shall confess to you, God, we shall confess to you,*" is persisting in confession; it will not confess just once, but often, which is evident through the confession, because a second time, "*we shall confess,*" and next, "*we shall call upon your name.*" My Lord responds, giving thanks for the Church, and says what it implies: "*I shall recount your marvelous deeds, whenever I receive an occasion.*" Now, insofar as they still require confession even as they approach, they promise that they will call upon you, God, not yet having capacity for the explanation of secrets; but they require an occasion for their change of heart, for completely turning around, for cleansing. And I promise that "*I shall recount your marvelous deeds, whenever I receive an occasion.*" Each of us, if he wants to hear Jesus recounting the marvelous deeds of the Father,[10] let him give him an occasion in himself. The person who lives well gives an occasion, just as, on the contrary, the person who tarries in sins does not give an occasion.

2. That the voices are those of our Savior and not of anyone else saying these things in relation to the Father, the wording that follows cries out: "*I shall judge straight judgments.*"[11] And is someone bold to say, "*I shall judge,*" having been entrusted with a basis for judgment issuing from a human being, or is only the Savior and Lord the one to say that? For he alone will judge straight judgments. Next, when the Church has heard and

9. Jl 2.32.

10. The Son, that is the divine logos, recounts the marvelous deeds that God has done in the righteous person who speaks his words in the Psalm.

11. Ps 74.3c.

promised confession, he says, testifying to the change of heart of those who have believed, "*the earth melted*";[12] all that is earthly has melted. And may Jesus testify about us, so that he may say about the earth and the earthly things in us, "*the earth melted.*" Inasmuch as we bore the image of the one made of clay,[13] it is necessary to take off the image of the one made of clay, not to set it aside while it still exists, but to act as if it would, in the end, disappear.

For if such a thing is produced and we put to death with the spirit the deeds of the body,[14] so that in all things we bear about the death of Jesus in the body,[15] the Savior will say about us, "*the earth melted, and all who dwell on it.*"[16] It was once plural, when we were dwelling on this earth, because "sin was reigning in our mortal body."[17] This, then, is our good deed, about which the Savior testifies to the Church, saying that not only "the earth and earthly things have melted," but "anyone who dwells on the earth." Any adverse powers that were dwelling in earthly things, ruling and motivating us to sinful acts, these have melted with the earth. Just as if you had in mind a wax seat and someone seated on the seat, then fire comes and melts it, so if your earthly things melt and the powers around the earthly things acting in you, your Savior will say about you, "*the earth melted, and all who dwell on it.*"

That these are the voices of our Savior, hear the one saying, "*I have strengthened her pillars.*"[18] For who has strengthened her pillars on earth other than our Savior and Lord? Do you want to hear the names of pillars? First, Simon called Peter and Andrew his brother, James the son of Zebedee and John his brother.[19] But the whole Church, if it is really the Church, is the pillar and support of truth.[20] But also in the Revelation to John this

12. Ps 74.4a.
13. See 1 Cor 15.49.
14. See Rom 8.13.
15. See 2 Cor 4.10.
16. Ps 74.4a–b.
17. Rom 6.12.
18. Ps 74.4c. See also Gal 2.9.
19. See Mt 4.18–21, Gal 2.9.
20. 1 Tm 3.15.

promise is given to those who overcome: "The one who overcomes, I will make him a pillar in the temple of God, and he shall no longer go forth outside."[21] I have strengthened the pillars of the earth, those still bearing a body and steadfast, bearing up the buildings just mentioned. I did not just place them or make them, but I made the pillars on earth steadfast.

Because he has taught us sinners from the gentiles to turn around towards God, he says this to God: "*I said to those who violate the law, 'Do not violate the law,' and to the sinners, 'Do not lift up a horn.'*"[22] "*To those who violate the law*" is to those from the people;[23] "*to sinners*" is to those from the gentiles. For we do not "*violate the law*"; we are without a law;[24] but they violate the law, those who hear the laws and do not keep them. Accordingly then, he said to those who violate the law, "*Do not violate the law*"; and to those who sin, "*I said to those who violate the law, 'Do not violate the law,' and to the sinners, 'Do not lift up your horn. Do not speak injury against God.'*" For they, the idol-worshipers, spoke "*injury against God.*"

3. Next, in what follows, all are hindered from God's grace, but some to a greater extent, "*because neither from the sunrises nor from settings nor from the desert mountains, because God is judge.*"[25] These things, it says, "*I said, to those who violate the law, 'Do not violate the law,' and to the sinners, 'Do not lift up a horn, do not raise up on high your horn, do not speak injury against God.'*" No one else is a judge except God, for neither "*from sunrises*" does any judge come, nor "*from settings*" does any judge come, nor "*from the desert mountains*" does any judge come, because "*God is judge.*" This God, the judge, what does he do? "*He humbles this one and raises up this one.*"[26] "*He humbles this one*" indicates the people from the circumcision, for they have been humbled. But "*he raises up this one*" indicates the people from the gentiles. He will raise him up, according to what is said in the prayers: that "the proselyte who is among you shall ascend up, and up, upon you," for this is the

---

21. Rv 3.12.
22. Ps 74.5.
23. That is, the people of God.
24. See 1 Cor 9.21.
25. Ps 74.7–8a.
26. Ps 74.8b.

one he raises. "But you shall descend down, down,"[27] for this is the one he humbles.

And in our argument, in keeping with "*the earth melted, and all who dwell on it,*" we have interpreted "*he humbles this one and raises up this one.*" He humbles this one, the thinking of the flesh and the flesh:[28] "I wear out the body and enslave it."[29] He raises this one: the soul and spirit. The opposite, the soul of sinners, has been humbled by sin, but the other is raised up, that of the just, who are fasting, laboring, staying awake, putting to death the [bodily] parts on earth. The body has been humbled, but the soul is always renewed according to the inner human being,[30] and the mind is raised "in the renewal of the mind."[31] The good[32] God, then, humbles this one and raises up this one.

4. Next, what does it teach us about judgment, as it proceeds: "*A cup in the Lord's hand full of unmixed wine of mixed,*[33] *and he moves it aside this way and that, except that its dregs have not been emptied out.*"[34] Most copies have it this way, but the most accurate is "*not been emptied out; all sinners of the earth will drink.*"[35] He terms the punishments "a drink," but the logos also knows "a cup of deliverance,"[36] and we have examples of both. In Jeremiah it is written with respect to punishments: "Take a drink of this unmixed wine, and you will make all the gentiles drink, against whom I shall send you, and they shall drink, and they shall vomit."[37] With respect to the drink's being mixed with blessedness for the just, it is written in a Psalm: "Your cup was as powerfully intoxicating as possible."[38]

27. Dt 38.43.

28. See Rom 8.6–7.

29. 1 Cor 9.27.

30. Rom 7.22.

31. Rom 12.2.

32. Origen probably identifies God as "good" here to show that he has answered possible Marcionite charges that the God of the Old Testament is arbitrary.

33. Origen will seek, with the help of Philo, to make sense of "unmixed wine of mixed." In the ancient world wine was ordinarily drunk mixed with water.

34. Ps 74.9a–d.

35. Ps 74.9d–e.

36. Ps 115.4.

37. Cf. Jer 32.14–15 (Jer 25.15–16 in modern versions).

38. Ps 22.5. This is the LXX interpretation of the words translated "my cup runneth over" in the King James Version.

Each of us, then, is going to drink of whatever he has cultivated. And just as in the case of those who possess estates, those who take care over a long period drink from their splendid produce, and those who are neglectful drink, if I may so term it, sour wine or something from their neglect, and, so that I may use terms according to Scripture and in another way, the just drink from the Sorech vine,[39] but the unjust drink from the vine of Sodomites, regarding which it is written: "Their vine is from the vines of the Sodomites, and their branches are from Gomorrah; their cluster is a cluster of gall,[40] a grape of bitterness for them, their wine is a wrath of serpents and an incurable wrath of cobras."[41]

Thus always, understand with me, there are two drinks in the Lord's hand for each of us; and whenever we sin, according to the degree of the sin, we insert our sinful deed into the cup of sinful deeds, but when we do well, into the cup of upright deeds. Next, each of us is going to drink; if he has both sinful and upright deeds, he will not drink the sin straight, but mixed according to the proportion of things that were produced before the sin. If you can understand a cup of gall and another cup of wine, if the cup of wine should have a small quantity of wine mixed with gall, that little is tempered by gall and by evil, but if it should be full of the mixed wine, it is more tempered; if indeed, the cup of gall is small, because the sin is small, while the cup of wine has much wine, and the small cup of gall should be inserted, the large quantity of wine will be tasted with the gall, but much less of the gall will be tasted.

Because of the quantity of wine, all of us then must drink, if we have sins, the cup of gall itself, a cup of wrath, but if we do not have sins, but have done everything well, a cup of the Lord as powerfully intoxicating as possible.[42] But if we are mixed,

---

39. See Is 5.2 in the Septuagint. The Septuagint translators apparently considered the Hebrew word *sorēq*, usually translated "choice," to be a proper name, so that, instead of "choice vine," they put "Sorech vine."

40. "Gall" or "bile," the bitter secretion of the liver stored in the gall bladder, can also mean "anger." In English we say, "That galls me."

41. Dt 32.32–33.

42. The superlative formula in Greek, *hōs kratiston*, "as strong as possible," implies that there are degrees of strength to the wine that we must drink when

we drink according to the degree of good things and their opposites. See, then, if the logos has not spoken clearly, so that it might not teach the one conscious of having sinned to lose heart, nor teach the one conscious of better things to think himself great, since, when the one who is conscious of better things thinks himself great, he also pours into the cup, if I may so term it, of gall.

5. "*A cup,*" then, "*is in the Lord's hand, full of unmixed wine, full of mixture, and he tips from one to the other.*" We must take not just from the one of evils, but it must be tipped from the one cup to the other cup, so that the sinners may drink "*full of mixture.*" Someone before me[43] has sought: "If it is 'of mixture,' how unmixed? If it is unmixed, how 'of mixture'?" See if what is said cannot be understood this way: we ourselves are accustomed to say about this sensible cup,[44] "You have mixed it more unmixed," or, "You have mixed it unmixed," because one has poured in little water, or a little more water, and it is possible to detect the unmixed wine mixed in.[45] Some drinkers mix more unmixed, but others do not do so. Insofar as they are sinners, when they have ever done something worthwhile, they drink not simply an unmixed, but an unmixed mixture, more mixed to the extent that they have done better things; when they drink from the cup of their sins, they do not drink the unmixed mixture, but, if I may so term it, a well-mixed or a slightly-mixed mixture. Except that the mixture arises from nothing but conduct. And just as drugs are mixed with each other, and according to the degree of quantity or quality of the drugs they all mingle into one, and the dose appears, composed of different quantities, so it is necessary in the cup that we are going to drink to bring up each form of our sins and even of each idle logos. For no doubt even the idle logos goes to judgment, along with blasphemy, slander, and everything that we do.

---

we are held accountable for our lives. Those who are conscious of sin should not be discouraged, but should make sure that they do good more zealously; small changes matter.

43. Origen is referring to Philo. See Philo, *Quod Deus immutabilis sit* 17.76–77.

44. Origen may have been using the cup employed in the Eucharist as a visual aid.

45. It was the normal custom in the ancient world to drink wine mixed with water.

For "*a cup is in the Lord's hand, full of unmixed wine, full of mixture, and he tips from one to the other, except that its dregs have not been emptied out.*" For wrath is not destined[46] to us; if we do not sin, it does not have dregs. "*All the sinners of the earth shall drink,*"[47] not some to the exclusion of others, but all the sinners. Why, then, does it say here "*of the earth*"? For it does not simply say, "all sinners drink," but sinners "*of the earth*"; maybe, then, the sinners of the earth will drink from "*the cup of unmixed wine, full of mixture,*" because no one on earth has it unmixed; it is not unmixed for anyone. But the adverse power no longer drinks "*unmixed wine, full of mixture,*" but it drinks from unmixed evil.

6. "*But I shall proclaim to the age, I shall make music to the God of Jacob.*"[48] Our teacher and lord has such lessons to proclaim not for ten years, as a grammarian proclaims before he runs out of things to teach, nor as a philosopher proclaims handing down what he knows until he has nothing new to say, but Christ's lessons are such that he proclaims for the entire age.[49] Hear in an ordinary way "*to the age*" and what follows: "*I shall make music to God*" to the age. What else shall I do? "*And all the horns of sinners I shall smash.*"[50] Therefore, then, "Do not raise up on high your horn";[51] "*all the horns of sinners*" our Lord Jesus Christ "*will smash,*" but "*the horns of*" his "*just ones shall be lifted up*" through the grace of almighty God in Jesus Christ, to whom is glory and might to the ages of ages. Amen.

---

46. Or "apportioned."

47. Ps 74.9e.

48. Ps 74.10.

49. Elsewhere Origen contrasts the believer's access to God as an inexhaustible source of wonder (see PS76H1.2 below) and new ideas (see PS67H1.3 above).

50. Ps 74.11a.

51. Ps 74.5.

HOMILY ON PSALM 75

HAT "*God is known in Judaea*"[1] has been written, indeed, is clear, and it is evident that Jews[2] explain the passage through their having been apportioned that country and suppose that reverence to God exists with them alone. But I want to say to those who hear "*God is known in Judaea*" in a simpler way: all right, is not God "known" in Egypt, because signs and wonders occurred there? Why is God not "known" in the desert, because God rained manna for the people and water flowed out of a solid rock[3]? Why, when they had gone out of the holy land[4] and, being in captivity, turned back to God, was not God "known" to them? How was God not "known" to Daniel, who was not in Judaea, but in Babylon? Why, then, when God is "known" in so many places, is it written, "*God is known in Judaea*"? Could it be, even if they were unwilling, that they were compelled to admit that these things were prophesied in regard to the Savior's time, because Christ Jesus visited in Judaea, being a god and the Son of God, so that it came about that "*God is known in Judaea*"? Of this God—I actually speak of our Lord Jesus Christ—the name is "*great in Israel.*"[5] One must hear "Israel" as the Scripture says: "Not all of those from Israel are

1. Ps 75.2a. In Hebrew "Judah" is a personal name; the name of one tribe; by extension the name of the territory the tribe occupied; and the name of the smaller, southern successor kingdom to the Kingdom of Saul, David, and Solomon. In this case, presumably because it is the name of a territory, the LXX, which normally transliterates the Hebrew "Yehuda" as "Judas," translates it instead as "Judaea."

2. I.e., "Judeans," persons from "Judaea."

3. See Dt 8.15.

4. Origen frequently uses this term.

5. Ps 75.2b.

themselves Israel";[6] not all who are said to be Israel are Israel. Just as, then, not all who are from Israel are themselves Israel, so not all who are from the gentiles are gentiles, but someone from Israel is received as a gentile through unbelief and a gentile becomes Israel through good faith. And just as uncircumcision is reckoned circumcision when someone fulfills the law,[7] in the same way the believing gentile is reckoned among those who have been given to Israel. But thus, also, Israel is reckoned as a gentile nation not believing in the visitation of Jesus Christ our Lord. When what has just been said about Israel has been understood, it can be evident how *"his name is great in Israel."* The name of Jesus Christ is great, since he is a god, in Christians among those everywhere; the name is great through [their] life, for we magnify our Lord through a life,[8] through a holy logos, through a flourishing condition.[9]

2. *"And his place was in peace and his abode in Zion."*[10] Let the Jews seek as God's place the Jerusalem below, fallen, about which it has been said: "See, your house I have left to you."[11] We, by contrast, seek, as the Lord's place, one worthy of the Lord, about which it is written: *"And his place was in peace."* Reading the Psalms, I find David praying with a vow: "If I give sleep to my eyes and slumber to my eyelids until I find a place for the Lord, a tent for Jacob's God."[12] And I say that the holy person does not rest, will not give sleep to his eyes, until he has found a place in the Lord himself. For just as the sinful person gives a place to the devil, so an honorable[13] person gives a place to God seeking to dwell in us and gives a place to Christ. For God

6. Rom 9.6.

7. See Rom 2.26.

8. *Or.* 12.2: "In this way only can we accept 'pray unceasingly' [1 Thes 5.17] in such a way as to put into practice what is said, if we should say that the entire life of a holy person is one big connected prayer, of which what is customarily termed 'prayer' is a part."

9. Origen argued repeatedly that the flourishing of Christianity throughout the world was, in itself, a witness to the presence of God's power. See, for example, *Princ.* 4.1.1 and *Cels.* 2.13.

10. Ps 75.3.

11. Mt 23.38, read in the light of Gal 4.25–26.

12. Ps 131.4–5. See PS67H2.6 above.

13. *Kalos kai agathos.* See PS36H1.3, n. 49 above.

promises this by saying: "I shall dwell in them and walk around in them, and I shall be their God, and they shall be my people."[14] And truly, according to prophecy cited, he indwelled and walked around in Isaiah, saying, "I have begotten sons, and I have reared them, but they set me at naught."[15] For if God had not been dwelling in him, how would God have spoken through Isaiah? You can say the same for the rest of the prophets. But our Lord Jesus Christ, even he himself, indwells the souls of the just; or do you not know that "one who does not have Christ's spirit is not his"?[16] And the Savior taught clearly saying, "If anyone will hear my logoi and keep them, I and the Father will come to him and make a dwelling with him."[17]

Do we not then seek a place for the Lord in our governing faculty? Concerning this place it is said: "*His place is in holy peace.*"[18] If this is so, God's place is produced in peace. What sort of peace? That about which it is written: "The peace of God that excels every mind will keep your hearts and your understandings in Christ Jesus."[19] The heart that has God's peace is not warred on by the passions, it is not moved by anger, it is not disturbed by sorrow, and does not suffer anything else contrary to peace; but it is possible to see peace and calm in the soul of the just person, just as he becomes a son of peace by having peace in him. Thus, God's "*place was in peace and his abode in Zion.*"

We have often said about Zion: this Zion is not the abode of God, but the soul that has become the contemplative place and oracular place of the logos of God is the abode of God.[20]

3. "*There they crushed the strengths of bows.*"[21] Where peace has been produced, there he has crushed the strengths of bows and "*armor, sword, and war.*"[22] How have the strengths of bows been

---

14. Lv 26.12.

15. Is 1.2. God, that is, is speaking in the first person in Isaiah.

16. Rom 8.9.

17. Jn 14.23.

18. Ps 75.3a.

19. Phil 4.7.

20. See above PS73H1.6.

21. Ps 75.4a.

22. Ps 75.4b.

crushed? "Our wrestling is against the rulers, against the authorities, against the cosmic dominators of this darkness, against the spiritual matters of wickedness in the heavenly places."[23] And we must take up "the whole armor of God, so that we can stand against the crafts of the devil"[24] and in the whole armor of God is the "shield of faith, in which we can quench all the fiery arrows of the evil one."[25] Thus the strengths of bows are destroyed in the souls of men, but when the strengths of bows will be crushed in the souls of men, the strengths of bows will be crushed in God's house, where peace has been produced. Thus it has been written, "*There he crushed the strengths of bows.*"[26] All right, who is this, who senses that all the strengths of bows are crushed in him and that there is not one part, not one has stayed sound, but all of them have been crushed, as well as "*armor, sword, and war,*"[27] and all that is associated with war, the armor of the enemy, his sword, all war has been eliminated? "*His place was in peace, and his abode in Zion.*"[28]

4. Accordingly, we thank God for these things and say: "*You are fearsome, and who will stand against you?*"[29] For if you have made such things possible in us—armor, sword, and war are eliminated—you have crushed the strengths of bows; you are fearsome, and who will stand against you? In case you supposed that God does not eliminate every war in Zion, "*All the witless of heart have been disturbed.*"[30] "*God's place was in peace.*"[31] And those who are undisturbed have a place in them given to God. But if someone has not given a place for God in his own heart, it is full of disturbance by his witlessness. Thus it is written: "*All the witless of heart have been disturbed.*"

For this reason our Savior and Lord commanded, speaking to his disciples: "Do not let your hearts be disturbed or be

23. Eph 6.12.
24. Eph 6.11.
25. Eph 6.16.
26. Ps 75.4a.
27. Ps 75.4b.
28. Ps 75.3.
29. Ps 75.8a.
30. Ps 75.6a.
31. Ps 75.3a.

afraid."[32] Since, then, he commanded and said, "Do not be disturbed": when we are disturbed, we transgress his obligatory command, in which he said, "Do not let your heart be afraid." But we, if we fear death, we fear the antagonists, we transgress his commandment; therefore we are liable to punishment, as is written in the Revelation of John, in this way, "For the cowards, for the unfaithful, the idolaters, the fornicators, the poisoners, their portion is in the lake of fire."[33]

5. The witless in heart "*slept away their sleep and found nothing.*"[34] And "*all the men of wealth with their hands*"[35] find nothing. If you have been able to understand the soul's sleep and the soul's awakening, it is something different from the natural sleep of the body; you will see many souls of men asleep and few indeed that are awake.[36] For the commandment has been given by the Spirit, "Do not give sleep to your eyes or slumber to your eyelids."[37] "Do not give sleep to your eyes," is said to the soul, "nor slumber to your eyelids, so that you may save yourself like a gazelle from nooses and like a bird from a trap."[38] And the Apostle tells you, "Awaken, sleeper, and rise up from the dead."[39] It is good to be awake at all times "so that you may be enabled to flee the offenses that are going to occur."[40] But "*the witless of heart*" are not such persons; "*they slept away their sleep and found nothing.*"[41] No one who is asleep finds anything. If you want to find, wake up, so that Jesus may not say to you: "Do you not have the strength to stay awake with me one hour? Stay awake and pay attention, so that you may not enter into the testing."[42]

The sinful "*slept away their sleep, and all the men of wealth found*

32. Jn 14.27.
33. Rv 21.8.
34. Ps 75.6b–c.
35. Ps 75.6c–d.
36. Henry David Thoreau in *Walden* went further in the same spirit: "I have never yet met a man who was quite awake."
37. Prv 6.4.
38. Prv 6.4–5.
39. Eph 5.14.
40. See Lk 21.36.
41. Ps 75.6b.
42. Mt 26.40–41.

nothing with their hands."[43] As Scripture terms some "men of blood"[44] and cites "men of lawlessness,"[45] so it understands some as "*men of wealth.*" Who are the men of wealth but those who rely on this wealth below? They who truly rely on a blind thing, and who want to gather it when they do not have it. All who are men of wealth "*slept away their sleep and found nothing.*" If we want to find and not to be counted among men of wealth who find nothing, let us not heap up wealth. Let us not spend our time on bodily wealth. But would that one could do what was said for perfection: "Get up, sell all your possessions, and give alms to the destitute, and you will have treasure in heaven; and come, follow me."[46]

If you cannot do such a thing, wish for nothing, for those who want to be wealthy fall into temptation and many harmful traps for the witless, which sink human beings in ruin and destruction. "For the root of all evil is love of money, and those who are aroused by it have been shipwrecked as far as faith is concerned. But you, a human being of God, flee this, pursue justice, reverence, faith, love, endurance, mildness."[47] Do not seek wealth, so that it may not come about that "*they slept away*" both wealth and "*their sleep,*" and "*all the men of wealth found nothing with their hands.*"[48]

6. "*At your rebuke, God of Jacob, those riding on horses were drowsy.*"[49] Often the Scripture's "horse" figuratively says "the body"; for example, "a horse is false in salvation."[50] The flesh does not help at all,[51] and "the flesh lusts against the spirit,"[52] and "those, in chariots, and those, in horses, but we shall be made great in the name of the Lord God."[53] For the gentiles and those who are foreign to

43. Ps 75.6b–c.
44. See Pss 5.7, 54.24, 138.19, and Prv 29.10.
45. See 1 Thes 2.3.
46. Mt 19.21.
47. See 1 Tm 6.10–11.
48. Ps 75.6bc. Wealth is, as it were, a soporific, making us insensible to the needs of others as well as to God.
49. Ps 75.7.
50. Ps 32.17.
51. See Jn 6.63.
52. Gal 5.17.
53. Ps 19.8.

reverence rely on bodily things, but the just does not multiply a horse for himself, that is, bodily things. "Horse," then, is said to be "the body."

"*At your rebuke, God of Jacob, those riding on horses were drowsy.*" Another before me observed, and well observed, that "riding a horse" is not the same as "being a horseman," and "mounted" is not the same thing as "being a horseman."[54] In the case of the Egyptian, since he was "mounted," but not a horseman, "horse and the one mounted fell into the sea."[55] He fell because he did not ride a horse with skill. But someone who is skillfully riding the body and ruling his pleasures and taking the body wherever he wants and keeping charge of the reins of his appetites, so as not to be borne into flesh-biting appetites, that one is not "mounted" like the Egyptians, but is a horseman like Elijah, as "the chariot of Israel and its horseman"[56] is said about Elijah. For he was not "one mounted," but a "horseman" skillfully riding the horse.

"*At your rebuke,*" then, "*God of Jacob, those riding on horses were drowsy.*"[57] Bodily things, when you rebuked, are weighed down, they are confounded, they fall asleep not accepting your censures. But we pray, when God rebukes us, that we may confess and receive the censures and say, "We have sinned, we have acted lawlessly, we have acted irreverently"; "*you are fearsome, and who can withstand your face?*"[58]

7. "*From then*"—from a mountain—"*is your wrath*";[59] from then, not from today, begins your wrath, but the wrath lasts from when we sin, and the so-called wrath of God is a rage[60] that

---

54. See Philo, *Laws of Allegory* 2.104: "The work of a horseman is to subdue the horse and to check it with the bit when it disregards the reins, but a rider goes wherever the animal leads." As Origen knew, Philo's interpretation of horsemanship as the control of the body and its desires goes back to Plato, *Phaedrus* 253–56.

55. Ex 15.21.

56. 2 Kgs 12.

57. Ps 75.7.

58. Ps 75.8a.

59. Ps 75.8b.

60. Origen commonly uses two Greek words for anger; the more common one, *thumos*, I translate "anger," and the other, *orgē*, connoting greater intensity, I translate "wrath." Most philosophers believed that *orgē* should be eliminated;

lasts for a season. Scripture says: "He will not be angry to the end, nor will he rage for an age."[61] For if there were no rage, how do we pay back today's sin after years, when judgment occurs, either in two hundred or in three hundred years? And how is it that what they sinned many generations ago, they will repay after a thousand years? There is something, then, analogous to the so-called "wrath of God" and analogous to the so-called "anger" and, clearly enough, to his "rage"; it is a good thing, to the extent possible, to quench it with good deeds and stop it with actions that come from a change of heart. Since sin gathers and sustains wrath, hear what Paul says: "Or do you despise the wealth of his kindness, forbearance, and long-suffering, not knowing that God's kindness leads you to a change of heart? In accord with your hardness and your stubborn heart, you hoard for yourself wrath on the day of judgment."[62]

Does not my sin hoard wrath for me? But the change of heart dissolves the hoard of wrath.

8. "*From heaven you have heard a verdict.*"[63] What concerns judgment is not earthly but heavenly. From heaven the teaching about judgment has become audible to us and in Deuteronomy it is written: "From heaven his voice has become audible."[64] "*The earth was afraid and was still, when God stood up in judgment.*"[65] And the earth is afraid when judgment is produced, and "*the earth was afraid and was still, when God stood up in judgment to save all the gentle of the earth.*"[66] This is the most surprising thing:[67] that we might carry out gentleness while we are still on the earth, while still in the body, and we shall make anger

---

some thought that *thumos* could have its uses (see Harris, *Eliminating Rage*, 88–128). A third word, *mēnis*, the first word in the *Iliad*, conveys, one might say, an anger of epic proportions; a closely related verb, *mainomai*, means "act crazy." I translate it "rage." Origen contends that God does not have irrational mental disturbances. Furthermore, a fair and benevolent God does not cause disproportional or purposeless suffering. See also PS77H7.7 and PS77H9.1 below.

61. Ps 102.9b. See also PS73H1.2 above.

62. Rom 2.4–5.

63. Ps 75.9a.

64. Dt 4.16.

65. Ps 75.9b–10a.

66. Ps 75.9b–10.

67. "Most surprising," *paradoxotaton*, because anger is pervasive.

halt, and we shall halt from wrath. Halt from wrath and abandon anger! It is necessary as far as possible not to be overcome in relation to this mental disturbance, the opposite of the gentleness that makes us blessed,[68] to stand against anger and not to allow it to stir us up and move us, so that there may not come about for us what is written in Proverbs: "Wrath destroys even the thoughtful."[69] The mental disturbance is so dangerous that the thoughtful person is destroyed by wrath. It is not said: Fornication "destroys the thoughtful," nor is it said: "Greed destroys the thoughtful," but wrath [does]. This mental disturbance has been set beyond all the rest, and I run the risk of saying too little when it comes to recommending the absence of wrath.

"*Because a human being's awareness will confess to you, and a remnant of awareness will celebrate your feasts.*"[70] There are some things that are our objects of awareness; there is awareness for sin, and there is awareness for justice. A human being's awareness will confess to God, then, either by giving thanks or when that person confesses for having sinned, the confession of the awareness: "*a remnant of awareness will celebrate your feasts.*"

"*Pray and pay back to the Lord our God.*"[71] Pray prayers to God and return to him ones that have become worthy of God. "*All those in his circle will bring gifts to the fearsome one.*"[72] The just are said to be in a circle of God spatially, but being always around God, they are, as it were, arranged as a dance troupe, all of them arranged around "*in*" your "*circle will bring gifts*" to you, "*the fearsome one.*" All those who are far from the Lord and God, they cannot bring gifts.

Bearing gifts to the fearsome one, they bring them to "*the one who takes away spirits of rulers.*"[73] Are not these the rulers spoken of in "The kings of the earth have approached, and the rulers have gathered together against the Lord and against his Christ"?[74] Concerning whom it is written: "We speak a wisdom

---

68. See Mt 5.5.
69. Prv 15.1. See PS36H2.3 above.
70. Ps 75.11.
71. Ps 75.12a.
72. Ps 75.12b–13a.
73. Ps 75.13b.
74. Ps 2.2.

among the perfect, a wisdom not of this age or of the rulers of this vanishing age, but we speak a wisdom of God in a hidden secret that none of the rulers of this age knew, for if they had known, they would not have crucified the Lord of glory."[75] How, then, does God take the spirits of the rulers unless, perhaps, these rulers, when they wound our souls, fill us with their own spirit, that of the rulers?[76]

Therefore, "*pray and pay back to the Lord God*," and, "*all in his circle will bear gifts to the fearsome one and the one who takes away the spirits of rulers.*" So may he take away from you the spirits of the rulers of this age, so that you may give a place to the spirit of God and to the spirit of Christ, to whom is the glory and the might to the ages of ages. Amen.

75. 1 Cor 2.6–8.

76. Given that the "rulers" (*archontes*) themselves are evil spirits, God must "take them away" from our souls, where they do not belong.

HOMILY 1 ON PSALM 76

HERE IS A long, dry list of the appointment of priestly functions for songs. If someone wants to learn about it, reading the early part of Supplements[1] he should take care that the list of names does not weigh him down, but pay attention, because the Holy Spirit wrote everything for the building up of those who pay attention. One, though, of the priestly functions, when the temple was opened, was taking charge of certain singers. And because they were different, since some, on the one hand, were enabled to be moved by the Holy Spirit to write Psalms, but some, on the other hand, did not have this grace, but were assigned to hymn God, to recite Psalms, and to praise; sometimes those who were able to compose psalms were offering them freely for hymning God in the worship service[2] [and recited and sang those psalms themselves], and sometimes those able to compose bestowed the psalms on those assigned to hymning God in the worship service, to recite and sing.[3]

I think, then, that this clarifies how it has thus in the inscription of the Psalm: *"to the end, for Jeduthun, a Psalm to Asaph."*[4] Asaph must have been the one writing the Psalm, since he was among the prophets, but the one to whom he gave it, after writing it, was Jeduthun, assigned to hymn God,[5] so that he, tak-

---

1. See esp. 1 Chr 15.16–24. *Paraleipomena,* "Supplements," is "Chronicles."

2. *Leitourgia,* "worship service," gives us our word "liturgy," but, in Origen's time, had the broader meaning "public service."

3. The text of this sentence as we have it in CMG 314 is not fully coherent. I have reversed the order of the "sometimes" clauses and added the words in brackets.

4. Ps 76.1.

5. See 1 Chr 16.41–42, 25.1; 2 Chr 5.12; Ps 38.1; Ps 61.1.

ing it from Asaph, might sing it as a hymn to God.[6] It is likely that, consequently, Asaph wrote the Psalm for Jeduthun in his persona, when he had given it to him: "A brother helped by a brother is like a strong and lofty city."[7] For example, if someone newly instituted as a bishop, from a bishop who has spent a long time in worship service and no longer composing a thanksgiving painstakingly, should receive the model of the thanksgiving, inasmuch as he still is not able to compose a thanksgiving except painstakingly;[8] such may have been the case with Asaph and Jeduthun, because Asaph wrote, but Jeduthun took up and spoke the Psalm. Jeduthun is also a just person, and we have learned this about him, not only from this book, but from the first book of Supplements, and, being just, he took as his persona that of this just person.

2. Let us see, then, something that a just person would say, and let us watch throughout the Psalm, so that we may become such persons and ourselves say: "*I cried out with my voice to the Lord, with my voice to God, and he attended to me.*"[9] The voice of the majority is not offered to the Lord, nor does such a voice proceed according to the Lord; but the voice of the just, not

6. As we have seen in PS67H2.1 above, Origen regarded singing as an activity for specialists.

7. Prv 18.19.

8. This fleeting mention of a new bishop learning from another bishop how to compose a prayer of thanksgiving (*eucharistia*) is among the earliest indications we have of Christian liturgical practice. Other sources, notably *First Apology* (65–66) of Justin Martyr, from the second century, and the *Apostolic Tradition* (4 and 9) from the third, indicate that when the bishop offered a prayer of thanksgiving consecrating bread and wine at the Eucharist, he would compose his own prayer. The contents of that prayer should meet expectations established by custom. The *Apostolic Tradition* indicates that the capacity to offer the prayer eloquently was desirable, although not necessary. A newly consecrated bishop might ask an experienced colleague to provide him a "model" (*tupos*) for his prayer. The *Apostolic Tradition* gives an example of such a prayer. This passage confirms insights expressed by Harald Buchinger, "Early Eucharist in Transition: A Fresh Look at Origen," in *Jewish and Christian Liturgy and Worship: New Insights into its History and Interaction,* ed. Albert Gerhards and Clemens Leonhard (Leiden: Brill, 2014), 207–27, and Allan Bouley, *From Freedom to Formula: The Evolution of the Eucharistic Prayer from Oral Improvisation to Written Texts* (Washington, DC: The Catholic University of America Press, 1981), 138–57.

9. Ps 76.2.

only the voice in prayer, but every voice has been hallowed to the Lord.[10] But what I say about every voice of the just person being hallowed to God you will understand from the narrative concerning Hannah and Samuel. Before giving birth, Hannah vowed to present to the Lord the one to whom she gave birth.[11] And just as, among the gentiles, they offer irrational animals or statuettes, images, or some sort of clothing to idols, so among the holy, the person making an offering to God offers a son, a rational animal.

Then let us Christians ourselves learn to make worthy offerings to God. What are we to offer him? He has made us rational beings, and the many do not devote themselves well to logos. Let us ourselves then offer to God the logos that he has given us, so that we may always discuss rationally[12] concerning God and the things of God, that we may always speak for the edification of and usefulness to the soul. We offer the voice to God so that the whole voice may be God's voice, or we offer—if one must say it—the eyes to God, so that we may see everything as God sees and be blind wherever we should not see.[13] One should not see impurities or spilling of blood or those things accomplished on earth to the harm of the many in cities.

One offering the eyes to God, then, does not go off to horse races and will not look at theaters or go off to the cruel hunting shows held in them;[14] but, offering sight to God, he will always[15]

10. We see the same argument in PS75H.1 above.

11. 1 Sm 1.11.

12. Or "we practice dialectic," *dialegometha*. The way to offer our intellect to God is by using it as rigorously as possible.

13. The consecration of the voice and the eye divinizes the human body. See PS80H2.1 below.

14. Christian worship is *leitourgia*, but the gladiatorial games and sexually provocative shows provided for civic entertainment were *leitourgiai* as well. Origen agrees with an older contemporary, Tertullian, the first major Christian author in Latin, in condemning them, although, unlike Tertullian, he would never have promised Christians who did not attend the games a ringside view after death of the greatest show of all, the tortures of the damned in hell. See Tertullian, *De spectaculis.*

15. By repeating *aei*, "always," Origen stresses that, as opposed to the degrading spectacles offered in the hippodrome and the theater, which happen only

look at the sky while considering the one who has made it, he will always look at the earth while marveling at the things that have come to be in it, he will always look at human beings along with seeking some whom he will benefit,[16] he will look at money along with seeking to give from what he has, and he will seek clothing, not as much in order to have it as to distribute it to those who do not have, so that he may hear: "I was naked, and you clothed me."[17] Let us, then, try to offer all things as good offerings to God, and accordingly let us offer the whole voice, so that, praying and crying to God, we may be enabled to say: "*I cried out with my voice to God, with my voice to God, and he attended to me.*"[18] For when we do not pray with the whole soul relying on him, but pray only for the moment,[19] we have cried with the voice to God, but, not praying with a pure voice, we shall not be heard. If we are hallowing it and purifying it beforehand, because we always say what we should, we shall send it up to God; we shall say: "*I cried out with my voice to God, with my voice to God, and he attended to me.*"[20]

3. If God attends to me, in my case, because of the mindlessness in me, I do not sense that God has attended to me.[21] But the one who is already on the march and progressing in the wisdom of God is not insensitive to God's attention or turning away, but just as someone having a seeing eye perceives an eye turning

---

at given times, God "always," at all times, offers the elevating spectacles of the cosmos and of humanity made in God's image.

16. *Euergetēsei,* "he will benefit." Offering entertainments at the theater was considered to be a "benefit" to the public. The believer who offers his eyes to God sees the needs of the poor as God sees them and therefore is moved to convey real benefits to them. Origen discusses offering the voice and eyes to God in PS80H2.1. On Origen's use of Mt 25, see introduction, p. 28.

17. Mt 25.36. All of these actions, starting with seeing heaven and earth from Gn 1, are things that Scripture says that God does and that we should do, down to the last one, where we see the logos in others, just as God does in us.

18. Ps 76.2.

19. Praying only for the moment (*kairos*), addressing our voice to God only on special occasions, is opposed to "always" saying what we should. See also PS77H8.2 below.

20. Ps 76.2. See PS80H2.1 below.

21. Origen puts himself in the position of someone who does not perceive God's care.

away from him and not looking at him, in the same way the eye of the just person, being sighted and pure, neither blinded nor blurred, senses when the mind of God attends to him and when it turns from him. If you ever sense God turning away from you, by testing or however, say: "Why is your face turned from me?"[22] Let us then become such persons that we sense on our own when God attends to us, and that, when we sense, we may not say just the first line, but also the second, saying, *"with my voice to God, and he attended to me. In the day of my affliction I sought out God, with my hands at night before him, and I was not led astray."*[23]

The many, when they come to be in affliction, are darkened by the afflictions, and, in their darkened state, they do not supplicate when it is especially needful at that moment to give oneself all the more to prayer; and you would find, at the death of family members, the funeral party hesitating to send up prayer to God as if it were not the moment for such prayer; you would find those suffering loss of goods and reduced by sorrow, but still hesitating to arrive at prayer. Not to pray in affliction, then, is the work of a sinful person, but it belongs to the just person to pray and extend prayer whenever there is affliction.

4. Therefore, the just person says: *"In a day of my affliction I sought out God."*[24] Perhaps, then, it is nothing outstanding, when you are in affliction, to seek God especially then. But how does it say, *"I sought out God on a day of affliction"?* *"With my hands"?* And when? *"At night."* And where? *"Before him."* And what came about? *"I was not led astray."*[25] So, how one seeks God with the hands is to be understood. I remember saying elsewhere that *"with the hands"* is the same as "with conduct."[26] For this is to seek God in your conduct, out of which God is found.

And just as a person seeking something that has fallen on the

22. Ps 43.25a.
23. Ps 76.3.
24. Ps 76.3a.
25. Ps 76.3b.
26. For example, *Dial.* 20, *Fr. Lam.* 61, and *Hom. Exod.* 10.4. A believer who prays to God in time of affliction may be acting better than the many, who do not pray even at such times, but it is "nothing outstanding," *andragathēma ... ou to tuchon,* unless that prayer is done by a person who is dedicating his or her life to God.

ground seeks to perceive, to touch, and to make things happen in order to find, in the same way God is sought not with pet phrases, as with the heretics among whom silly talk appears before doing the works required to seek what might be the nature of God. But if someone seeking wants to find and comprehend, let him seek rightly. For it is written, "Those seeking him rightly find peace."[27] He seeks rightly who does not do so in mere words,[28] but in deeds. For thus God is sought: through justice God is sought, so that he might be found by justice; through temperance he is sought, so that through temperance he is found; through courage and sound thinking God is sought, so that he may be comprehended; through wisdom God is sought, so that God may be found by the one seeking with wisdom.[29] Therefore, wishing to stand by with confidence, the prophet says how one must seek God: "*With my voice I cried out to the Lord, with my voice to God, and he attended to me. In the day of my affliction I sought out God, with my hands.*"[30]

I have a second account as well for "*I sought out God with my hands.*" "I want," says the Apostle, "men to make supplication in every place lifting up holy hands without wrath and argument."[31] When someone raises "consecrated hands" seeking God with consecrated hands, he will find him who is divine; as it has been said in the Scripture, Moses sought God with the hands, so that when Moses lifted hands, Israel won, but if he ever grew weary and lowered hands, Amalek won.[32]

The logos is about to say something, and I say that Christ sought God with the hands, on behalf of the whole cosmos,

27. Prv 16.8.

28. The contrast between the conduct of a virtuous life and relying on *lexeidia*, "mere words," is characteristic of Epictetus, whom Origen admired. See, for example, *Disc.* 2.1.31. *Lexeidion* is the diminutive of *lexis.* See introduction, pp. 31–32 above.

29. Justice, temperance, courage, and sound thinking (forethought) all deal with conduct and are the basis for obtaining wisdom. They are the four cardinal virtues, the essential habits of conduct, first identified by Plato, that, by common agreement of Platonists, Aristotelians, and Stoics, constitute good character.

30. Ps 76.2–3b.

31. 1 Tm 2.8.

32. See Ex 17.11.

stretching them on the wood and making them fast so that, at that time, he would pray to him with stretching of hands and when the whole body and soul were stretched together, not over the body, but over the whole cosmos, on behalf of the whole cosmos.[33] But you as well, if you take up the cross and have followed Jesus,[34] you likewise seek God with the hands, especially if you are enabled to say, "May I never boast except in the cross of our Lord Jesus Christ, through whom the cosmos has been crucified to me and I to the cosmos."[35] Stretching out the hands on the cross, so as to be crucified to the cosmos, you also seek in the cosmos to be made dead to the cosmos and crucified to it, and seeking him you will find.[36]

5. *"With my hands at night, and I was not led astray."*[37] The whole cosmos of this life here is a night of genuine life, as the Apostle, teaching about the life of the cosmos here below, says: "The night has progressed, the day has approached."[38] For the day has approached of the exodus and of the second eon, which is different from this one.

At night, then, I sought God with my hands in this eon, when it is night and when we wrestle "against the cosmic dominators of this darkness."[39] The present eon, then, is night according to one model, for according to another it will be said again that it is day. When I seek God in this night, I need a lamp, about which the Savior says: "Stand, letting your loins be girded, and let your lamps be burning."[40] So, as to those in the night of this

33. The ultimate case of praying "with the hands" is Christ's self-offering on the cross. Compare the Collect for Mission composed by Charles Brent in the *Book of Common Prayer:* "Lord Jesus Christ, you stretched out your arms of love on the hard wood of the cross that everyone might come within the reach of your saving embrace: So clothe us in your Spirit that we, reaching forth our hands in love, may bring those who do not know you to the knowledge and love of you; for the honor of your Name. Amen." Compare also the Epiclesis from Eucharistic Prayer for Reconciliation I (1975), given for the Holy Year 1975.

34. See Mk 8.34 and parallels.

35. Gal 6.14.

36. See Mt 7.7.

37. Ps 76.3b.

38. Rom 13.12.

39. Eph 6.12.

40. Lk 12.35.

life, he says: "Let your loins be girded, and let your lamps be burning." But the prophet, as in Psalm 118, wanting to demonstrate that things here are all darkness and the light of a lamp is required, said: "Your logos is a lamp to my feet and a light to my paths."[41] Thus I seek God at night. I know also another account to this topic; occasions of relaxation are days for us, but gloomier times of affliction are nights in comparison.

6. "*I sought God,*" not being far from God, "*before him, and I was not led astray.*"[42] Blessed is the person who can truly say: "*I sought God, and I was not led astray.*" For many who have sought God have been led astray, and those from the sects have sought, but since they have not sought rightly or sought "*with the hands,*" they have been led astray. They, of course, have false opinions about Jesus, but some among us are also talking nonsense, those who seek concerning God before correcting character, before putting life in order. And those seeking God go astray and have false opinions concerning him. Who is it who can say, "*I sought God with the hands, and I was not led astray,*" except the person who has known the truth, the person who does not have false opinions or never lost his way by believing something other than the truth about God or Christ?

"*My soul refused to be comforted; I remembered God, and I was glad.*"[43] Two passions occurring to a human being in difficult situations are discussed, so that we can get help by learning what we say at first, and how, when we are undergoing them, we may be cured from mental disturbance.[44] Whenever something is painful or when, at times, we come wholly under the domination of pain and affliction, we do not even listen to the one who comforts us, but say, "*My soul refused to be comforted.*" But if we want, after being dominated by mental disturbance and refusing to be comforted, to be comforted and to rejoice, it suffices to remember God. For he adds and says: "*I remembered God and rejoiced.*"

If ever something painful happens to you, as you pray to be a

---

41. Ps 118.105.
42. See Ps 76.3.
43. Ps 76.3c–4a.
44. See introduction, p. 32, on *pathos,* "mental disturbance."

man of the Church, and you see yourself darkened by pain and dominated by the pain itself, remember his logoi of hope, of the blessedness in Christ, and the pain will immediately fall away.

For just as "what participation does justice have in lawlessness, and what does light have in common with darkness, and what agreement does Christ have with Belial?"[45] similarly, "What agreement does remembering God have with mental disturbance?" Where there is remembering God, mental disturbance has been put to flight. Where there is mental disturbance, someone has not remembered God. Therefore, "the one remembering you is not in death; in hell who will confess you?"[46] To remember God is already a great good, and the holy ones have names, so that their names signify remembering God.

"Zachariah" is interpreted "memory of God," since "Zachar," according to the Hebrew language, is "memory."[47] When someone is remembering the Lord, the father prays for what he would possess by means of his son's name.[48] Just as some, in accord with prayers, give to sons the name of what they want, as when someone who loves money gives to his son the name "Philargyros"[49] (and we know some who have that name), but another gives to his son the name "Philotheos,"[50] praying to be loved by God or for his son to be a friend of God. In the same way saints bestowed this name on Zachariah, praying that they might always remember God. Accordingly, when in the Gospel they wanted him to call John "Zachariah," but the spirit in Elizabeth did not want him to be called that name, but "John," his father, when he, too, chose not to call him "Zachariah," but "John," got back his voice.[51]

Therefore, I want to say why John is not called Zachariah. Well then, someone is wanting to remember God when God is absent; by remembering him he makes clear that God is not present with him. But for one who is present, there is no need

---

45. 2 Cor 6.15.
46. Ps 6.6.
47. Origen's etymology is correct.
48. That is, by embodying his prayer in his son's name.
49. "Loving money" or "greedy."
50. "Loving God."
51. See Lk 1.63–64.

for memory about the one present. Thus, for instance, I have remembered an absent brother or I have remembered an absent friend, but I do not remember someone who is present, for I am looking at him. Since, then, John said, "Look at the lamb of God who takes away the sin of the world,"[52] and he was going to show forth the Son of God, God the logos, for this reason he is not called, as his predecessor was, "Zachariah" and "Remembering God," but "Showing."

And let us ourselves pray to move from "Remembering God" to "John," so that we may see him present, because we have no more use for the memory of God, but for the vision of God, because of his presence, since indeed, "Blessed are the pure in heart, since they shall see God."[53] For if the memory of God makes glad, his presence to someone who senses it does what? I am coining a term for that: "it overgladdens."

7. "*I prattled,*[54] *and my spirit was dejected.*"[55] Everything that a man says, even if he be just and blessed in life, is talkativeness in comparison with what he will say in the eon to come. Thus even Isaac went out into the plain to be talkative,[56] but when the complete comes and what is partial passes away.[57] Thus the prophet labels all conversation about divine things that occur now as talkativeness, as he said: "*I prattled, and my spirit was dejected.*" That is, "In afflictions, reckoning what was happening as chastisements, I became dejected and so reckoned them." He will say this: "*My eyes determine watches.*"[58] We have other eyes besides these, enlightened by the Lord's commandment, for

52. Jn 1.29.

53. Mt 5.8.

54. The Septuagint uses a Greek word that means "talk too much" to translate an obscure Hebrew word that may have meant "meditate." Origen recognized that the translation was inexact (see *Fr. Ps.* 118.15). *Adoleschia,* talking too much or prattling, was a recognized character flaw, the subject of one of Plutarch's moral treatises. (Plutarch thought that barbers were especially prone to it.) Origen recognized that this word did not necessarily mean something blameworthy in the Septuagint. Here he uses it as a term for human speech insofar as it—inevitably, in our present situation— is inadequate to the divine logos.

55. Ps 76.4b.

56. Gn 24.63.

57. See 1 Cor 13.10.

58. Ps 76.5a.

"the Lord's commandment is conspicuous, enlightening eyes."[59] Those eyes keep watches as if the goals determine the watch. You will understand what I have said from an example: as in the case of those who are at war or expecting war, they station watches around the walls and set there, for example, ten to guard that place so that the enemy do not encroach, but also the general visiting the watches determines watches and guards everything—something similar, as I understand, to the case of the eyes when a just person has learned from Scripture, "In every watch guard your heart."[60] For when there are many watches and cities from which the enemy plots, in which man must guard himself with the eyes, and in thought determining all the watches, he observes and makes predictions so that the enemy will never encroach through some kind of watch, seizing an unguarded place.

8. For this reason, it says, "*My eyes appoint watches. I was troubled and did not speak.*"[61] He also sensibly testifies to his personal experience and says, "When trouble had reached my governing faculty, I was not so far overcome as to put forth a logos of trouble." But you will understand "*I was troubled and did not speak*" from an example like this: often I am irritated by someone speaking ill of me or railing at me, when someone is doing this in order to induce me to respond in kind. Even as a human being[62] I am troubled and want, when I am reviled, to fend off the one who has been railing by the same kind of logoi. Accordingly, when I know from the logos[63] that one who has believed should not do this, trouble reaches only my governing faculty,

59. Ps 18.9.

60. Prv 4.23.

61. Ps 76.5.

62. That is, as a human being, *anthrōpos,* someone subject to human imperfections, as opposed to a god, *theos.* Origen discusses this distinction most fully in the *Homily on Psalm 81* below.

63. Here is an excellent example of the ambiguity of the word *logos.* As we see below, *logos* is the word Origen uses for an angry invective that tempts a response in kind. Here *logos* with a definite article would seem to be the divine *logos,* who was with God and incarnate in Jesus Christ. It may refer to a specific biblical passage through which the divine *logos* teaches us not to respond in kind to someone reviling us, perhaps this one or perhaps Prv 15.1, "A soft answer turns away wrath."

but I do not also speak. If, then, I have been enabled, when I am troubled, not to be overcome by the trouble, but to be silent, I can say on my own behalf, "*I was troubled and did not speak.*" Blessed, then, is anyone who, when he is troubled, does not speak.

Are you troubled by wrath? Nonetheless, see to it that you do not speak a logos of wrath, but as a good person holding the reins, you hold back the logos about to escape through your teeth. Are you troubled by some logos? See to it that you do not speak a logos of wrath, but as an honorable person,[64] as I said before, rein in your voice, so that you also may say: "*I cried out with my voice to God, with my voice to God, and he attended to me.*"[65] See to it that you do not put forth a logos of pain, for often out of pain some have even blasphemed against the divine and cast blame on Providence. But you, even if you are imperfect and still making progress, act so as to say, "*I was troubled and did not speak.*" For if, after having suffered further, after a struggle with trouble, you do not express the trouble in your speech, you will no longer be troubled, but you will have peace, according to: "The peace of God passing beyond all understanding will guard your hearts and your thoughts in Christ Jesus."[66]

9. "*I reviewed the ancient days, and I remembered the eonic[67] years, and I took care.*"[68] One who wants to be helped also considers the ancient days beginning from Adam. What occurred to Adam? What befell Cain? What did Enoch accomplish? What worked out right for Noah? And, so to speak, considering in detail all the days from the beginning, he stretches his mind over all the matters recorded to have occurred in the earliest days. "*I reviewed,*" then, "*ancient days.*" And then, having reviewed ancient days, he still refers them higher to things of eonic years. But, if

64. *Kalos kai agathos.* See PS36H1.3, n. 49 above.

65. Ps 76.2.

66. Phil 4.7.

67. Origen generally construes the Greek word *aiōnios* to mean "lasting for an eon." An eon is a very long, but limited, time, the length of an entire world. This world is often translated "eternal" or "everlasting," but Origen understands it, as we shall see, to refer to a fixed, temporal period. I have therefore coined the term "eonic" as a translation, since "eternal" would imply a lack of temporality altogether and "everlasting" would seem to imply an unlimited period of time.

68. Ps 76.6.

one must say so, since things that are seen are temporary and years among temporary things are temporary, the years before the cosmos are "eonic" in a different sense, perhaps also those after the cosmos, which years are encompassed in, "The law has the shadow of future good things,"[69] teaching about what one must do every seven years and what one must do every fifty years.[70] The one who understands the law in accord with its being spiritual refers these things to eonic years. The just person, then, ascends from considering "ancient days" to "eonic years."

These eonic years consist of eonic days, concerning which it is written in Deuteronomy this way: "Remember eonic days, be aware of years of generations of generations."[71] At any rate, let us pray to ascend from these days and these months and these years to "the days of the eon" and "the years of the eon," and, if I must be so bold as to say so, because the new moons are spiritual, also to the eternal months in which we have our citizenship, we who are not indicated by this sun, for the Lord will be your eternal light and God will be your glory.[72]

10. "*I then remembered the eonic years and took care. At night I prattled with my heart, and my spirit stirred.*"[73] Learn from the text; whenever sleep abandons you and you lie awake, do not waste the time of wakefulness in what is unnecessary, but, for as long as you are awake, while sleep has abandoned you, take considerations of reverence, taking such ones as this says: "*At night I prattled with my heart, and my spirit stirred,*"[74] and say, "*The Lord will not reject unto the eons or restrain his mercies in his wrath.*"[75] These things, it says, "*I*

---

69. Heb 10.1. Here Origen seems to imply that *aiōn* and *aiōnios* can have a second meaning when applied to the periods before the creation of the cosmos and after its end, "eternal" in the sense of non-temporal. This is a distinction we first find in Plato, who distinguishes between our world of becoming, characterized by change and subject to time, and a transcendent reality of "being," in which there is neither change nor time.

70. See Lv 25.10–12. Origen refers to the jubilee year, in which debts are canceled and slaves are freed, and suggests that it is the shadow of an eschatological reality. Origen makes this clear in *Or.* 28.14–16.

71. Dt 32.7

72. See Is 60.19–20, Rv 22.5.

73. Ps 76.6b–7.

74. Ps 76.7.

75. Ps 76.8a and 10b.

reviewed at night, and," by myself, "*I prattled with my heart, and my spirit stirred.*" Since the spirit is given by God to be as much help as possible to our soul, one who wishes to find what he seeks, let him not stir the soul, nor let him stir the body, but let him stir the spirit. And just as someone who wants to find something on the ground stirs the ground, so that he may find what he imagines in the earth, in the same way if you seek spiritual things, stir the spirit, and always seek from the spirit to find the fruits of the spirit.[76]

"*I roused my spirit.*" When you also "search all things, even the deep things of God,"[77] you stir your spirit, but I say that [you stir] also the spirit of God. Is it possible to reach this and search it: "*The Lord will not reject unto the eons*"?[78] While the spirit is stirring these things, I consider and say: Grant that God rejects someone for a year and abandons him to afflictions, grant that he abandons someone for two years, grant it for the whole time of this life—how many years is that?—fifty or sixty? Grant that God abandons someone for this entire age. Does God still abandon for the entirety of eons? "*The Lord will not reject unto the eons,*" so, may he not reject us for one eon! For there are some whom he rejects in another eon beyond this one eon, concerning whom the Savior says, when they sin against the Holy Spirit, that he will not be let off either in this eon or in the eon to come.[79] Woe to that person for whom sins are not let off either in this eon or in the eon to come! For example, someone has sinfulness in the times of Adam and is punished from then until the completion for that sinfulness; see how great the punishment is, and, if it is possible to add another, whether or not it lasts the length of this eon, for I do not know the magnitude of eons. Notice that someone punished even to this eon and see the magnitude of the punishment, and do not despise and do understand what is said here by the prophet, that "*the Lord will not reject unto the eons,*" about God's rejections.

But see that to be rejected by God for even one hour is a great loss, for whenever God rejects me, the devil takes me as

76. See Gal 5.22.

77. See 1 Cor 2.10.

78. Ps 76.8a.

79. Mt 12.42. This interpretation, that Jesus leaves open a possibility of eventual forgiveness after two ages have passed, occurs also in *Comm. Jo.* 19.14.88 and in *Or.* 27.15.

someone who has been rejected and handed over to him, as Paul rejected the sexually immoral person in Corinth. For this reason he rejected him from the Church: he gave him over to Satan "for the destruction of the flesh, so that the spirit might be saved."[80] And each of us, should he be rejected by God, none other than Satan and his angels take us over; it is fearful to be under him, and if any comes under him, there is some verdict by God that hands him over as one liable to be under him.

But do we say, "*The Lord will not reject unto the eons, and he will not add to be pleased any longer*"?[81] Even if God's judgments have been issued, we should do what the Ninevites did—they did not say, "The Lord will have a change of heart," but, "Let us pray and fast. Who knows if the Lord will have a change of heart and turn away his anger?"[82]

"*Shall he cut off his mercy to the end from generation to generation? And I reviewed this, and my spirit stirred.*"[83] When God is giving us over to punishments, does he cut off his mercy from us, so that he will never reverse himself and be merciful to us, but, cutting off his mercy, will abandon us from generation to generation? "*Or will God forget to have compassion?*"[84] Is he possibly going to forget us in travails and sufferings and never have compassion?

"*And I said, Now I have begun.*"[85] "When I have considered all these things, I said, Now I begin to understand." He himself understood, but, while he understood, he did not see fit to say what he understood, but, just as Paul heard "unspeakable utterances" and John heard "the seven thunders," and Paul did not write the unspeakable words nor John the words of the seven thunders, so also this man, as he was wailing and raising new doubts, saw the secret; but, seeing the secret, he hid it, since it was better to hide it than to say all these things that he had understood. So much is the multitude of your kindness, Lord, which you hid for those who fear you in Christ Jesus, to whom is the glory and the might to the ages of ages. Amen.

80. 1 Cor 5.5.
81. Ps 76.8.
82. Jon 3.9.
83. Ps 76.6a, 7b.
84. Ps 76.10a.
85. Ps 76.11a.

HOMILY 2 ON PSALM 76

FTEN SOMEONE living a godly life, in preliminary stages of that godly life, supposes that he has made the beginning of living as he ought to live, but when he has understood the difference between the preliminary to the godly life and that which occurs after the preliminary stage on the road of a godly life; recognizing that, at first, he seemed to be beginning when he was not actually beginning, but later, he knew what the beginning was; he says, "*Now I have begun.*"[1] But, if this should be made clearer by an example, let us pay attention to these things that will be said. Often someone who has dedicated himself to following the Christian religion[2]—who is at the beginnings of his self-dedication, either because he is, on his own, unaware of how one must follow Christ, or because he has fallen among teachers who do not have it straight—seems to be following Christ, but is not actually doing so as he should. But later that person, having sought, finds,[3] through God's aid. He is fortunate enough to get a teacher who provides good guidance; after having spent a long time seeming to follow the Christian religion, once he has truly come to that religion, he says, "*Now I have begun.*"

For example, someone wanted to be a Christian after life as a gentile, but falls in with an Ebionite[4] who teaches him to observe the wording of the law; that person has lived for a time in Ebionism, thinking that he is practicing Christianity when he is actually practicing Judaism. Later, by God's aid, he learned

---

1. Ps 76.11a.

2. *Theosebeia,* "religion," in the sense of "worshiping and serving God."

3. See Mt 7.7.

4. Ebionites recognized Jesus as the Messiah, but believed that the Torah remained binding on his followers in the same way that it was binding for Jews.

that the law has the shadow of coming good things[5] and that even they are not the genuine secrets.[6] Learning, after wearing himself out in Ebionism, the road that is not the figurative one, but the genuine one, and knowing that he does not have the genuine road, he would say—even if he had spent a long time in a spurious observance—because he began to live by the truth, "*Now I have begun.*"

From this example, also pass beyond it, seeing some comparable things that occur in many instances. For the beginnings, especially if they are not completely apparent because of darkness and ignorance in the soul, make it so that someone is living confusedly, and, after living confusedly for a long time, when clarity gradually appears, he comes to live in accord with the spirit of God; and, living in such a way, if it should be perceived what true religion is, he says, "Indeed, what I had been doing before was empty, for I came to know later what was true, and, '*Now I have begun.*'"

Thus someone who has grown old in Judaism—let it be granted that he has not understood Christianity and seems to have been practicing religion in a godly way—recognizing that this was not religion, but a figure of religion, grant that he say, when he has become a Christian, "*Now I have begun.*" Thus someone previously aimed at virtue and teaching and has imagined that he was worshiping God; let him approach the logos of truth and say, "*Now I have begun.*" Thus someone who has previously lived very stupidly because he did not at all understand the clarity of truth, when later he becomes aware of truth, grant that he has lived by it, and let him say, "*Now I have begun.*" Now, then, it is possible for a man who is progressing and understanding that certain things that he did earlier were not in accord with considered knowledge, being aware of this, to say, "*Now I have begun.*"

It is said that something comparable occurs with skills, that, after spending a long time, those being introduced to the skills, being confused because they do not understand the purpose

5. Heb 10.1.

6. The law is the body of Scripture; the coming good things, the lessons that inform Christians when it is interpreted figuratively, are its soul; the genuine secrets are its spirit.

of those skills, it is as if they have not even made a beginning at mastering the skills; but when they have become more familiar with those skills, spending a long time in the introductory phase, they begin to understand clearly, so that, often, after two or three years, when they seem to have been introduced to the skill, having become aware that they are just beginning to master the skill, they each say, "*Now I have begun.*" If such things occur in the case of ordinary skills and in the case of matters preoccupying the soul in ignorance prior to knowledge, is it not possible that the beginning of the call, in each of us, is somewhat confused, but later becomes clear, and, when the clarity is perceived, he says, "*Now I have begun*"?

I have often heard believers testifying that they have been deemed to be in the faith for a long time and to have been taught the secrets of the faith, at some point finding a teacher who makes it clear, saying, "'*Now I have begun*' to become a Christian, now I am learning for the first time what Christianity is." They say these things not to take away from their earlier practice, but seeing that earlier they did not get the point of the secrets, on the other hand they have a beginning of understanding when they have been formed by good teaching. So let us, then, make an effort to become such persons as to say, thanks to progress in our condition, "*Now I have begun.*"

2. But why, "*Now I have begun*"? Because "*this is the change of the right hand of the Most High*";[7] because of the change I understand "*Now I have begun.*" I do not think that "*the right hand of the Most High*" is anything other than my Lord and Savior Christ Jesus. He, Christ Jesus, is the right hand of God, who, when he was "in the form of God," was not changed, but was what he was, but when "he did not consider it something to be grabbed to be equal to God, he emptied himself."[8] He was changed, so that through this change of this right hand and—if I may use such terms—its transformation and humiliation, we human beings have been done a kindness, and we have been helped in our human affairs.[9]

---

7. Ps 76.11b.

8. Phil 2.6–7.

9. Note that Origen applies the process of divine humiliation to the presence of Christ in himself as an individual Christian.

To the extent, then, that I, in my religious observance, did not perceive "*the change of the right hand of the Most High*" because I was participating in it, I seemed to be religious, but I had not even started. But when "*the change of the right hand of the Most High*" occurred in me, "*Now I have begun.*" For example, someone brought up among the Jews, never knowing anything about my Lord Jesus Christ, thinks that he is conducting himself according to the law of Moses, and after wearing himself out for a long time in it, he has later understood that it consists of secrets concerning Christ Jesus, and finding that out, let him say, "Things that were going on before that one's appearance were not true, but figurative. But since he has appeared, being the right hand of God and having changed, I am also beginning to live according to his teaching, and therefore what I held earlier is a loss, but, '*Now I have begun*'; 'whatever was profit to me, that I consider a loss, but I also hold all these things as loss through the exceeding excellence of the knowledge of Jesus Christ our Lord,'[10] who is the changed '*right hand of the Most High.*'"[11]

3. But when is it "*I have begun*"? When the right hand of the Most High has been changed. But when? Just when "*I remembered the works of the Lord.*"[12] For if earlier, before the right hand of the Most High had been changed, I seemed to be wearing myself out in the works of the law, because I did not understand Israel, I did not remember the works of the Lord, but later, I remembered the works of the Lord; for example, I recognized that Moses's hand was stretched out and, while it was stretched out, Israel was prevailing, and when Moses's hand was lowered, Amalek was prevailing, but, recognizing this work, I was not understanding it. But later, knowing that the logos referred to the secret of Christ, "*I remembered the works of the Lord,*" and I see that "all these things took place figuratively, but they were written for our sake, on whom the ends of the eons have come."[13] And

10. Phil 3.7–8.

11. The Jew who becomes aware that the law is figurative is not a hypothetical figure, but the Apostle Paul, who also undergoes the change, within him, of the right hand of the Most High.

12. Ps 76.12a.

13. 1 Cor 10.11.

I see that "all the fathers were under the cloud, and all were baptized into Moses in the cloud and in the sea, and all ate the same spiritual food, and all drank the same spiritual drink, but they drank of the spiritual rock that was following, but the rock was Christ."[14]

And seeing such things, why they took place then, and of what they were tokens, "*I remembered the works of the Lord,*" and in each case I examine how it took place, and I say that "*I will remember your marvels from the beginning.*"[15] I roll out[16] and examine all the Scriptures from the beginning of making the cosmos and see all the secrets of Christ: "Because of this a man abandons his father and his mother and cleaves to his wife, and the two will be one flesh."[17] These things were not about Adam and Eve, but this is a great secret, as one wiser than I am has said: "But I speak concerning Christ and concerning the Church."[18] I recognize Abraham and two women, Sarah, barren, and handmaiden Hagar, and that a child first came from the handmaiden,[19] after that from the free woman as a result of God's promise.[20] When, recognizing the logos, I do not know anything beyond the narrative, I do not "*remember the works of the Lord*" God, but when I understand that "these things are said allegorically, for they are two covenants, one from Mount Sinai born into slavery, which is Hagar," and what follows,[21] then I say: "*I will remember your marvels from the beginning, and I will study all*"[22] the works of the Lord.

4. Insofar as things turn out well, they are from God, just as good logoi are from God, for one is not speaking these things

14. 1 Cor 10.1–4.

15. Ps 76.12b.

16. Origen alludes to *1 Clement* 31.1: "I roll out the things that have happened from the beginning." He uses *anatulissō*, "roll out," metaphorically; his Scriptures were not on scrolls, but on codices, leaves written front and back and bound together, resembling our books.

17. Gn 2.24.

18. Eph 5.32.

19. See Gn 16.15.

20. See Gn 21.2.

21. See Gal 4.24.

22. Ps 76.12b–13a.

well on his own, but he speaks them from God. But just as, when the logoi proceed from my mouth, those that are unassailable and divine are not mine but God's, so that I say confidently: "or do you seek proof of Christ who speaks in me?"[23] To the extent that I act well, so as to choose all the works of God's logos, ones that are to be completed according to God's commandment, it is God's doing. But chastity is also God's doing, for it is a gift of grace, so that accomplishing chastity is not my doing. Listen to "I want all human beings to be as I am; each individually has a gift of grace from God, one this way and one this way."[24] If it is God's gift of grace, chastity is not my doing. But these also are oracles of God; if someone is speaking oracles of God, it is not so much his doing if he acts well, "sharing in simplicity, leading in zeal, showing mercy in cheerfulness."[25] The Apostle accounts all these as gifts of grace, but if they are gifts of grace, they are God's works.

Why, then, is it said: "*I will study your works*,"[26] or is it clear that, doing them, I study your works? And this study is blessed, when one studies, not catchphrases or verbal formulas, but "*all God's works, and in your pursuits I shall be talkative.*"[27] Whenever someone reading the divine Scriptures comes across "these things says the Lord, ruler of all," or that he has made these things, or that God killed these persons, or that God threw stones of hail, as God did to some in Joshua,[28] he is talkative, inquiring into [God's] pursuits.[29] If, then, you want to be talkative, be talkative, yet seek God's pursuits and be talkative in them, keeping the law that says, "speaking about them seated in a house, walking on a road, lying down, arising."[30] Do not let your

---

23. 2 Cor 13.3.

24. 1 Cor 7.7.

25. Rom 12.8.

26. Ps 76.13a.

27. Ps 76.13.

28. See Jos 10.11.

29. Origen encourages inquiry into such passages, confident that such inquiry will vindicate the goodness of God, demonstrating that the simple reading of such passages, in which God seems to be acting unfairly, cruelly, and vindictively, is false.

30. Dt 6.7.

conversation be worldly, not about how the horses have done, not what the driver did or performed, not what occurred in the theater, not what the gentile governor decided. All these things are alien to the command that says: "Let your mouth open with a logos of God,"[31] but when your mouth is opening with a logos of God, be bold and say: "*In all your pursuits I am talkative; God, your road is in the holy.*"[32]

5. What is God's road, leading to God, but the one who says: "I am the road and the truth and the life"?[33] Where is God's road? In the holy one, if you are holy, keeping the command, "You shall be holy, because I the Lord your God am holy."[34] In a most surprising matter, his road is in you just as God's kingdom is not outside us—for I am persuaded by my Savior's saying, "God's kingdom is within you"[35]—so is the road. If we travel on it, it is within us. Grant that it concerns the soul, for the road must not be outside us, the life must not be outside us, the resurrection, the genuine light, but may all other things that Christ is be in me,[36] so that the words may be true: "*His road is in the holy. What god is great as our God is? You are our God who performs marvels.*"[37]

With whom does one contrast and compare him, saying, "*What god is great as our God is?*" If he is speaking about idols, the idols are presumably blessed ones, among which God—even if they are excelled by him—is compared, but let it be far from us to say this: that "*What god is like our God?*" can be said to be comparing idols with God. One of our predecessors found fault with this,[38] and it is well that he did this, in regard to Jethro saying, "Now I know that the Lord is great beyond all gods,"[39] because

31. Prv 31.8.

32. Ps 76.13b–14a.

33. Jn 14.6.

34. Lv 11.45.

35. Lk 17.21.

36. All, that is, of the *epinoiai,* the "aspects" or "devices" of Christ. See PS36H2.1 and introduction, p. 18.

37. Ps 76.14–15a.

38. "Someone before us" is Origen's way of citing Philo. See Philo, *On Drunkenness* 41–45.

39. Ex 18.11.

he seemed to say something about God, comparing him to idols, not understanding other gods than these. If, then, Scripture says, "*What god is great as our God is?*" one must give an accounting concerning the subject of the logos, and concerning with what and about what it is speaking when God is compared in "*What god is great as our God is?*"

First one must keep in mind the Apostle's words, how he did indeed say somewhere, "There are so-called gods either in heaven or on earth, just as there are many gods."[40] But, look, catechumen, do not be perplexed and run back to idols because Christians say that there are many gods. For listen to God's Scripture saying: "All of the gods of the gentiles are demons."[41] But just because he does not begrudge his beneficence, God says: "For I said, 'You are all gods and sons of the highest.'"[42] The Scripture says that if someone has received God's logos, he becomes a god,[43] but also, "God stood in the gathering of the gods, but in the midst he distinguishes gods,"[44] and if you are gathered as human beings, God is not in the gathering. If the gathering itself is of gods, gods are being called such because the logos of God is among them and they do not walk as human beings do; God is in such a gathering, and there is where "God stood in the gathering of gods; in the midst he distinguishes gods."

In a way, something analogous holds concerning the glory of these gods and the glory that the sun has; something similar holds concerning the glory that the moon has; something similar holds concerning the glory of stars. "For the glory of the sun is one thing, the glory of the moon another thing, and the glory of the stars yet another, for star differs from star in glory, so also in the resurrection of the dead."[45] These are to demonstrate that "God stood in the gathering of gods," and, "I have said, 'You are gods,'" so that from here I can move to "*What god is great as our God is?*"

---

40. 1 Cor 8.5.
41. Ps 95.5.
42. Ps 81.6.
43. See Jn 10.34–35.
44. Ps 81.1. See PS81H.1–2 below.
45. 1 Cor 15.41–42.

For a great god—if it is fitting for me to speak boldly—is Abraham; Isaac is a great god; Jacob is a great god; and because they were divinized, since indeed God linked his own name, "God," to their names, saying: "I am the god of Abraham and the god of Isaac and the god of Jacob."[46] But saying this once, "I am the god of Abraham and the god of Isaac and the god of Jacob," graciously allowed even Abraham to be a god, since indeed there was a participation by him in the divinity of God. And when you come to the Savior, you say something similar about this "god"—for he is god, since, "In beginning was the logos, and a god was near God and the logos was a god."[47] Do not shrink from saying that many just persons are gods, but if the just will become equal to angels,[48] the angels are much more numerous; I am not speaking about demons, I am not speaking about idols. I am careful to be respectful of God's logos, but our Savior and Lord incomparably exceeds all of these.

6. Because the one who makes holy and those who are being made holy are all from one: *"What god is great as our God is? You are the God who does marvels."*[49] Either you may take this in reference to the Father, I see that he is a god doing marvelous things—the whole creation, the wonderful things among the people, and surprising things generation by generation—or to the Savior, you, Jesus Christ are the god who does marvelous things—raising the dead, making the blind to see again, the lame to walk—and you are not idle when it comes to doing wonders today. Let it be seen where each of us comes from to God's Church, who on what logoi; perhaps some of us were among idols not many days ago, not many months ago, [but are] now in God's Church. Is this not marvelous, since once an idolater, hating Christianity, rejecting God's logos, now you follow after

---

46. Ex 3.6. The Septuagint reproduces in Greek the form of the Hebrew construct state, so that Origen's text could also be translated "god Abraham," "god Isaac," and "god Jacob."

47. Jn 1.1. Origen substitutes "a god" for the "the logos" in the second phrase. He must have expected his students, at least, to catch the substitution and to understand why he made it and why he would consider it a legitimate modification. See n. 71 on PS67H1.4 above.

48. Mt 22.30, Lk 20.36.

49. Ps 76.14b–15a.

Christ, already bound by bonds of love, fulfilling the Scripture that says: "They shall follow behind you, bound in handcuffs, and they shall worship you, and in you they shall pray."[50]

If you understand that you the fornicator, you the adulterer, not just an idolater, you the thief, you the one who robbed others, you now have arrived at learning that cleanses you and changes you and transforms you from such wickedness, and because you have already sensed the change, because you are going to become temperate and just, prudent and courageous, you are bold to say that Christ Jesus, who did these things and is now doing them, has done marvels in you. And if your ailing body has been cured by Jesus, you marvel that, being blind, you see again, or lame, you walk, when that is because, having been paralyzed in soul and lamed in the ability to choose, having been blinded in calculations, now you have thrown all that off and have received back the health of your ability to choose, you say: *"You are the God who does marvels."*

7. In addition, I say to God: *"You have made known your power among the peoples."*[51] What sort of power has he made known among the peoples? Christ, for Christ is "the power of God and the wisdom of God."[52] But if Christ has made his power known to us, how is it that "when you are gathered together and my spirit is with the power of the Lord Jesus Christ"?[53] The power of Jesus is here, and when the power is present, you are all gathered, and we are united every day by his power, for "he who is joined to the Lord is one spirit."[54]

"You redeemed your people in your arm."[55] The Savior stretching out his own arm has redeemed his people from the hand of the enemies; he gathered them from the countries; he redeemed the *"children of Jacob,"*[56] but by *"children of Jacob"* we must not un-

---

50. Is 45.15.

51. Ps 76.15b.

52. 1 Cor 1.24.

53. 1 Cor 5.4.

54. 1 Cor 6.17. Repeatedly in his works, Origen appeals to the spread of Christianity and the transformed lives of Christians as evidence for the truth of Christian teaching.

55. Ps 76.16b.

56. Ibid.

derstand the Jews. You are more a child of Jacob than they are. It is said to those who boast that they are children of Abraham: "If you are children of Abraham, do the works that Abraham did,"[57] because they denied both through their works and through their unbelief in my god Jesus Christ that they were children of Abraham, and so of Isaac, and so of Jacob. But you by faith, in which you have imitated Abraham—for Abraham believed God, and it was reckoned to him for justice[58]—have become children of Abraham, and so of Isaac, and so of Jacob.

And God redeemed *"the children of Jacob and of Joseph,"*[59] for we pray to become imitators, understanding the lives of the fathers, of Jacob, of Joseph, and of other just persons, their children, so that, by becoming their imitators, we may become their children. Still with one voice I shall proclaim the Gospel so that I shall demonstrate to the faithful that not they, but we, are children of Jacob and of Abraham and of Isaac: "For God from these stones can awaken children for Abraham."[60] What sort of stones? He indicates you the gentile, the silly, the senseless, and truly prophesies concerning you that you are the stone that will become a child of Abraham and of Isaac and of Jacob and of the rest of the chosen, just patriarchs in Christ Jesus, to whom is the glory and the might to the ages. Amen.

57. Jn 8.39.
58. Gn 15.12.
59. Ps 76.16b.
60. Mt 3.9 and parallels.

HOMILY 3 ON PSALM 76

HAT SORT OF things, would you say, are these waters that see God,[1] when human beings require great effort to achieve this goal according to the Scripture that says, "Blessed are the pure in heart, because they shall see God"?[2] It would seem that these waters are equivalent to the pure in heart who are going to see God or perhaps greater than human beings who are pure in heart, since, if they are blessed and divine powers seeing God, they must necessarily be greater than human beings. And at all events it would seem to be implied in the 148th Psalm, where every Israel is ordered to hymn God. For it says: "Praise God, heaven of heavens, and let the water above the heavens praise the name of the Lord."[3]

How much I would have to labor in order to ascend into the first heaven; how much more difficult it would be for me to be worthy of the second! I would need to become an equal to Paul in order to ascend into the third;[4] even if I were to become like Paul, I would hardly get to the sixth heaven, but these waters, the ones praising God, are, according to the prophet, "above the heavens";[5] so, then, would they actually be said—because they are above all the heavens—to see continually, not the persona[6] of the Father in the heavens, but God—"for the angels," on the one hand, "continually see the persona of the Father in the heav-

1. See Ps 76.17.
2. Mt 5.8.
3. Ps 148.4–5. For "every Israel," see n. 15 below.
4. See 2 Cor 12.2.
5. Ps 148.4.
6. *Prosōpon,* normally translated "face" but understood by Origen in the technical sense of a "mask" or "persona" distinct from God. See intro, pp. 13–14.

ens"[7]—but do not these waters—the ones concerning whom the logos says, "*The waters saw you, God*"[8]—continually contemplate God himself? But at the same time let someone[9] explain this who is able to compare spiritual things with spiritual things;[10] for has the logos spoken by chance about the angels yoked with human beings:[11] that they see, not God, but "the persona of the Father who is in the heavens," but about these waters, "they saw you," not "the waters saw your persona, God"?

"*The waters saw you and were afraid.*"[12] I myself—seeing in the beginning of the making of the cosmos both a "spirit of God," as the prophet says, borne, in the arrangement of the universe, "above the water," and a "darkness" not "above the water" (for the spirit of God was there), but "above the abyss," where darkness was, and water where the spirit of God was[13]—beseeching God, after much prayer, was moved to seek concerning these references to positions—since also the firmament is produced on account of waters, so that some may stay above and some may stay below[14]—maybe "Israel"[15] is not about sensible waters but about

7. See Mt 18.10. This passage provides a scriptural warrant for the belief that each human being is yoked with a "guardian angel," one that Origen shared (see *Or.* 11.5) with Jews and Platonists. Here he makes a distinction between what the angels of the little ones do, seeing "the face/persona (*prosōpon*) of the Father in the heavens," and the waters that "saw God." Origen distinguishes these angels, who see the persona of the Father "in the heavens," from waters "above the heavens" that praise the name of the Lord. It is these waters "above the heavens" that would see God. Clement of Alexandria (*Paed.* 1.57.2) identified "the face/persona of God" as the logos.

8. Ps 76.17a.

9. This hypothetical "someone" is Origen himself.

10. See 1 Cor 2.13.

11. "Yoked" can refer to marriage. Origen taught that the requirement for a bishop to be "once married" in Ti 1.6 referred, not to marriage between two human beings (since a bishop might not be married at all in that way), but to the bishop's "marriage" to an angel. A bishop who had fallen into sin would have been divorced from his angel and married to an angel of lower rank. See *Comm. Matt.* 14.21–22.

12. Ps 76.17b.

13. See Gn 1.2 (LXX): "The earth was invisible and unorganized, and a darkness [was] above the abyss, and a spirit of God [was] borne over the waters."

14. See Gn 1.6.

15. Retaining "Israel" in CMG 314. "Israel" = "[he] sees God." See p. 420, n. 69

powers more divine than those that stay below the firmament, those that were the abyss above which was the darkness (for we even fight against "cosmic dominators of this darkness"),[16] but the waters above which the spirit of God was were better powers. Right when the cosmos was created, it was one; these things, in some manner I do not know, were not at all distinguished; the making of the cosmos distinguished the better and those to whom the spirit of God was fitting from the worse ones, and the worse ones and those to whom they are yoked[17] are the darkness that is mentioned in reference to "the persona of the abyss."[18]

That these things are not in Genesis by coincidence, the wording here makes clear, saying: "*The waters saw you, God, the waters saw you and were afraid,*" no longer simply "*waters*" but "*abysses, multiple reverberation of waters.*"[19] Do you see there the difference between water and abyss? The spirit of God is on the waters; darkness is on the abyss. Here the waters see God and

---

below. Origen has already referred to the "waters above the firmament" and other natural phenomena in Psalm 148 as "every Israel" commanded to praise God. He thus introduces the notion, soon to be discussed in detail, that spiritual powers have the same names as the natural phenomena they manage.

16. See Eph 6.12. In *Comm. Jo.* 32.24.313 Origen identifies the "darkness above the abyss" as Satan.

17. The waters/worse powers beneath the firmament are demons yoked to human beings in a similar way to the angels who see the face of God, now identified as the waters/better powers above the firmament. The identification of the human souls to whom they are yoked as "darkness" recalls Eph 5.8: "You were once darkness ..."

18. This reference to the "persona" or "face" of the abyss occurs in Jb 38.30, where that phrase is used, but is more likely an indication that Origen checked out Gn 1.2 in the *Hexapla*, where the Hebrew text has "face [*prosōpon* in translation] of the abyss." Origen's interpretation of the "firmament" of Gn 1.6 is similar to that in Philo, *De opificio mundi* 9. Origen shared with contemporary Platonists like Plotinus the belief that the creation of the cosmos involves the differentiation between good and evil that ultimately proceed from an original unity, the One. As he does also in *Hom. Gen.* 1.2, Origen here summarizes conclusions that would have been set forth in detail in one of his earliest works, a commentary on the opening chapters of Genesis. Unfortunately, that work has largely disappeared. Among the supposed errors of Origen that Jerome lists in *Letter* 51 is the accusation that he taught the interpretation of the waters above and below the firmament that we see here. Most of Origen's congregation probably got little from this discussion.

19. Ps 76.17. The "waters" become discordant "abysses" once they are afraid.

are not disturbed; the abyss does not see God but is disturbed; the abyss, above which is darkness, is always in disarray and in turmoil. That is why the party of demons both "beg the Lord, that he may not order them to go out into the abyss"[20] and say to him: "What are we to you, son of God? Why have you come ahead of time to torture us?"[21] But these things are in the more divine concept,[22] that concerning the waters of the abyss.

2. Let us not pass over the statement even on its own, but let us see if it is possible that the wording that says, "*The waters saw you and were afraid, the abysses were disturbed, multiple reverberation of waters,*"[23] holds something to understand. It comes to me that it says that everything is animate and nothing in the cosmos is empty of soul, but everything is animate in various bodies.[24] The heaven is animate, because to it, as to a living being, Scripture says: "Give ear, earth, and I shall speak," and, "Hear, heaven."[25] The earth is animate: "utterances from my mouth and give ear, earth."[26] If indeed the heaven is animate and the earth also is animate, could the sea and rivers be inanimate? Or are they also animate? And we see, to be sure, that "the sea saw and fled, Jordan was turned backward."[27] And that the logos is conversing as with animate beings, I am now advocating by the wording. I am proving this by the statement alone, wishing to show that we often fail to notice that even the wording, according to its statement, holds divine secrets and things not knowable by casual readers.[28]

20. Lk 8.31.

21. Mt 8.29.

22. The explanation that follows may be the "more divine concept" (*theioteran ennoian*), or he may be hinting to those familiar with his teachings that the demons eventually will themselves be saved. (See *Princ.* 2.9 and 3.5.)

23. Ps 76.17. It takes a soul to see, be afraid, or be disturbed.

24. Philosophically, Origen holds the position that no body can initiate movement unless it has a soul. See especially *Or.* 1.7.3 and *Princ.* 3.1.2.

25. Is 1.2 and Dt 32.1.

26. Is 1.2.

27. Ps 113.3.

28. "Wording" (*lexis*), "statement" (*rhēton*), and "understanding" (*nous*) designate three stages in the processing of knowledge. *Lexis* is the words themselves. *Rhēton* is what those words say. *Nous* is mental reception of those words. The *lexis* is thus the embodiment of *logos*, rational discourse. When he dealt

I seek, then, whether some power is clothed in the body of the sea and another power is clothed in a river, the Jordan, and another power in another river, the Gihon, for example, and so forth in every case. And perhaps those among the Greeks are imagining such things when they superstitiously sacrifice to rivers as to gods, not having entirely fallen away from the truth, but having fallen away partially. For if they sacrifice to them as to gods, they are sinning, but if they imagine there to be some power in them, they are not sinning.[29] For there are powers that they call "nymphs," and they say that they are over springs, and they maintain that a power superintends every place.

But someone might say that, if the sea and each of the rivers were animate, it would entail a long logos to seek how it is that they are animate; nonetheless, all have been assigned to a holy power. And there are angels put in charge of managing marine affairs and other angels to manage the affairs of this or that river, so there are angels to manage the air, and when more divine angels manage the affairs of the air, then the air does not sicken or become noxious. But because another power has been associated with managing the air entirely through the sins of human beings, because a worse power is associated with the air,[30] the air is changed and noxious weather is produced, so that a person breathing the air corrupted by the plague-making power languishes and is ill. If then, when all of the powers are assigned and all the affairs in the cosmos that are to be managed have been divided up, why is it out of place for the managers to have

---

with the words "the waters saw you and were afraid, the abysses were disturbed, multitude reverberation of waters," he showed, as he often does, that the immediate sense of the words is unacceptable; they imply that "waters" that see and fear God are the equivalent of the "pure in heart" who see God. Origen therefore suggests an interpretation, based on comparison with other scriptural passages, in which "waters" signify spiritual powers. Here, though, he argues that the *rhēton* on its own, arising directly from the *lexis,* "water" in the normal sense of the word, reveals a secret about the cosmos to the careful reader. In this passage Origen himself is doing the same thing when he preaches; only attentive students could fully comprehend what he is saying.

29. The word translated "sin" (*hamartanein*) can also mean "make a mistake." It is a sin (idolatry) to sacrifice to rivers, but recognizing that a river has a soul is not a mistake.

30. See Eph 2.2.

the same names as what they manage, for those powers over the waters to be called "waters," those over the sea to be called "seas," and so the powers over the abyss to be called "abysses"?

That those dwelling in places are called by the same names as the places and regions, the spirit speaking in Isaiah attests to me: "Hades below was embittered on meeting you."[31] Do you see that Hades is the place of souls, concerning which it is written, "Let sinners be turned away to Hades," and that there is a living being by the same name as that place, who is named "Hades"? If, then, it were to be said concerning the sea that "it saw and fled,"[32] the power directing marine affairs and making a road for the people of God is named by the same name. When, then, it is said, "Jordan turned backwards," the power undertaking the direction of the river Jordan is named with the same name as the Jordan River.

Often I sought, reading the Psalm that says, "Praise God in the heavens, praise him in the highest, praise him all his angels, praise him all his powers."[33] Then it adds, "Praise the Lord from the earth, serpents and all abysses, fire, hail, snow, ice, spirit of a whirlwind, things doing his logos, mountains and all hills, fruit-bearing trees and all cedars."[34] Reading, then, I sought whether it intended these things, and right away I took refuge in figurative language, seeing the incongruity of the wording; but later I considered, on my own, if perhaps the managing powers are called by the same name as the things that they manage—those put in charge of serpents, "serpents"—because some managing power is put in charge of each kind of living thing. On account of logoi that God knows, because this one has become worthy, not to be the one entrusted with greater things, but to manage serpents, but that power has become worthy to cultivate along with human beings, since it manages cultivated trees, in terms of what is said, it is under every human farmer, but in terms of what is understood, it is under one or more angels managing these things. Maybe there, then, "Praise the Lord

31. Is 14.9.
32. Ps 113.3.
33. Ps 148.1–2.
34. Ps 148.7–9.

from the earth, serpents and all abysses, fire, hail, snow, ice, spirit of a whirlwind, the things doing his logos" shows the one put in charge of fire, the one put in charge of hail.

But that the sea is rebuked as a living being by the Lord, either because it is a living being itself or because a power is put in charge, is evident from "He rebuked the sea, and Jesus rebuked the winds."[35] No one rebukes something inanimate, but it is evident that he did rebuke and said, as Lord of the whole creation: "Silence, be still."[36] And the sea fell silent and became calm. If I also were to become an actual human being of God, I could, by Christ Jesus speaking in me,[37] rebuke the creation, so that I would say to the sun, "Stand still at Gibeon."[38] For truly, "What sort of precious seed? The seed of a human being."[39] The seed of a human being is precious, when it has received great power from God—as long as he pays attention, he is a god[40]—but if not, it is all the more worthless, treated with contempt by himself and written off[41] by God.

3. There are several ways to understand "*The waters saw you, God, the waters saw you and were afraid.*" Everything is in fear of God; if God were not to sustain us so that we flourish, we are destroyed. For "when you turn away your face, they are disturbed."[42] Therefore, it is not only when we sin that we need God's aid, but I am bold and I say, "When we are perfected, we shall need more aid." Why? Because when we are perfected, we are plotted against by more adverse powers. The existence of many powers requires us to have a greater ally, so that we may not fail on account of our perfection, so that "how he fell from

35. Mt 8.26.

36. Mk 4.39.

37. See 2 Cor 13.3.

38. Jos 10.12.

39. Sir 10.19. The context of this citation in Sirach is a rebuke of pride.

40. Origen's claim that attention is key to divinization recalls the role of attention in Stoicism and Neoplatonism. See Pierre Hadot, *What is Ancient Philosophy?* (Cambridge, MA: Harvard University Press, 2002) and *Plotinus and the Simplicity of Vision* (Chicago: University of Chicago Press, 1993), both trans. Michael Chase.

41. See Ps 68.28, Ex 32.33, Phil 4.3, and numerous other references to names "written" in heaven or in a book of life.

42. Ps 103.29.

heaven, the morning star rising before morning"[43] not happen to us. Many holy ones have fallen, for the secrets of Scripture disclose such things, such as, "You have walked about blameless in all the roads, until injustice was found in you."[44] All of us, then, fear God, both the imperfect and those who have been perfected.

But someone hearing will say: "Perfect love casts out fear."[45] The subject of fear is difficult to explain, especially when the logos has already established that it is necessary to be in fear of God, for maybe should it cast out fear, it does not cast it out completely, but only a certain kind of it. For I know also that fear is termed in various ways in Scripture. "The one who fears is not perfected,"[46] but when the use of the same word in different ways is understood, it will make us see how "fear," I might say, is equivocal. For there is a fear that must always be in fear, and there is a fear about which John says: "The one who fears is not perfected." This fear holds a chastisement, which someone who is perfected by love no longer fears.

"The waters saw you, God, the waters saw you and were afraid; the abysses were disturbed, multiple reverberation of waters."[47] "Narrow and difficult is the road leading to life, and there are few who find it."[48] And the people of God is the smallest "beside all the nations"[49] on the earth. And in Noah's ark, the higher things were, the more narrow and small a space they occupied,[50] but as concerned the things that were disturbed in the abyss, there it was termed "multiple": *"the abysses were disturbed, multiple reverberation of waters."* And in the case of those waters that see God,

---

43. Is 14.12.

44. Ezek 28.15. The reference is to Ezekiel's prophecy against the prince of Tyre, whom Origen took to be Satan.

45. 1 Jn 4.18. Clement of Alexandria contrasts fear and love as motivations in *Strom.* 7.11.67.2.

46. 1 Jn 4.18.

47. Ps 76.17.

48. Mt 7.14.

49. Dt 7.7.

50. See Gn 6.14–16. Like a ship's hull, the width of the ark would narrow toward the top, since the deck of an ancient ship was normally a bit narrower than the greatest width of the hull.

there is no reverberation, there is no meaningless sound, but there are a certain stillness and calm, when the only waters being afraid are those observing him, but concerning the abyss, *"the abysses were disturbed, multiple reverberation of waters."* You see that there is a reverberation among those things that are disturbed, not a clear, meaningful, and articulate sound.

"The clouds have given voice, for your arrows also spread abroad."[51] If we want figurative language again, we have often spoken, especially about "the clouds I have commanded not to shower rain on it, but what is 'the vineyard' but the house of Israel?"[52] and about "the truth of God that reaches as far as the clouds"[53] (and not, certainly, as far as bodily clouds, but there are certain just persons exalted from the earth in bodies, who have become clouds). Such a person was Moses,[54] who said, "Pay attention, heaven, and I shall speak, and let the earth hear the words from my mouth; let my sayings be awaited as rain."[55] Does this cloud act as if it were speaking of bodily, inanimate rain when it says, "and let my logos be awaited as rain"? So, because Moses was a cloud, he said, "let my sayings be awaited as rain and my utterances as dew."[56] And because he was a cloud, he said, "as a downpour on wiregrass and as a snowstorm on grass, because I called the name of the Lord."[57]

4. Such were all the chosen prophets, the marvelous apostles. And because there were certain rivers of living water coming out of their bellies,[58] they spoke as rivers, and they gladdened the city of God, for "the streams of a river gladden the city of God."[59] Since the logos says here, "the clouds have given voice,"[60] it is not

51. Ps 76.18.

52. Is 5.6–7.

53. Ps 35.6.

54. Origen transmitted traditions that Moses did not die a normal death; some implied that he may have been taken up directly to God in a cloud. See James L. Kugel, *Traditions of the Bible*, 862–63. See Origen, *Homilies on Joshua* 2.1.

55. Dt 32.1–2. Moses's sayings are like rain; by implication, he is a cloud.

56. Dt 32.2.

57. Dt 32.2–3.

58. See Jn 4.14.

59. Ps 45.5.

60. Ps 76.18a.

hard to speak figuratively; similarly, one will seek to see those who are accounted for in "the waters saw you and were afraid" and what follows, so that nothing about clouds may be missed.

Perhaps, then, just as there are powers over seas, over rivers, over earth, over plants, over the birth of living things, so there are also powers over the clouds, so that some are assigned to thunders, some to lightning bolts, some to rains, and when God orders and commands rain to come on this city and not to come on another city according to what is said in the prophet or the statement: "And I will shower on one city, but I will not shower on another city."[61] "*The clouds have given voice*":[62] thunders are nothing but the voices of clouds, as are observed in storms. Never when the sky is clear has anyone heard thunder or seen lightning. "*The clouds have given voice*," at the discretion of the angels managing and entrusted with them.

But perhaps, even if it is unspeakable, a certain helpfulness is produced in events through the voice of the thunder of the clouds, a helpfulness sensible, on the one hand, because the thunders generate certain things that are sustaining to human beings, so that as often as the thunders occur, certain plants are produced on the earth and are found. It is also sensible, on the other hand, because the majority of human beings obtain reverence toward the divine from the voice of thunders.[63] In fact, are demons, then, not sometimes turned away or deterred from bad activities by reverberating thunders? But why should not angels of the devil be deterred sometimes by thunders, when the very voice associated with thunders interferes with bad activities?

All of us, as human beings, do not know what is occurring nor what is the logos of each thing that comes about, but it is the wisdom of God that searches out and tracks down; for will someone track down an abyss and wisdom?[64] Therefore, I beg

61. Am 4.7.

62. Ps 76.18a.

63. Origen may have in mind the thunder, the inarticulate but sensible voice of the Lord, at which everyone in the temple says "glory" (Ps 28.9). Compare Giambattista Vico, *Scienza nuova*, book 2, chapter 1, section 1, published in English translation as *The First New Science*, ed. and trans. Leon Pompa (Cambridge: Cambridge University Press, 2002), on the role of thunder in the origin of piety.

64. See Wis 9.16.

that I myself and you hearers not be precipitous out of ignorance in such a way as to stumble, when you do not see a reason
for famines, for a plague, for a war, for any of the haphazard
events that occur, for untimely deaths, for illnesses and bad ac-
cidents from the beginning of life to its end. The holy say that
all these things are in all cases judgments of God, even if they
do not understand the logos for judgments of God that are not
justified.[65]

5. "*The clouds have given voice, for your arrows also spread
abroad.*"[66] That Christ is an arrow of God, he himself teaches
us in the prophet's saying, "He has made me a chosen arrow,
and he has hidden me in his quiver,"[67] and, "He said to me,
This is a great thing for you, for you to be called my servant,"[68]
and what follows. It is evident that it is likely, on the analogy of
Christ's being an arrow of God, a chosen arrow, that there are
also other arrows. An arrow cannot be understood to be chosen
if it is the only arrow, but if Christ is the chosen arrow of God,
therefore there are other arrows, for this arrow is the one chosen as opposed to those arrows. What, then, would be another arrow? Perhaps the holy powers, which God showers from a
bow next to him on the earth, but perhaps some human beings
are holy arrows, such as the prophets, and the logoi of the just
wound and, as it were, strike those who hear them because they
have some power of arrows.

The "*arrows,*" therefore, of God, akin to Christ, "*spread
abroad.*"[69] But do you want to see how sometimes, apart from
any human being, someone is wounded by a spiritual arrow, a
chosen arrow, an arrow from God? It seems to me that those cat-
echumens who, in some way, sometimes come to the logos, without any human being's having taught them to be Christians, just
as if they were goaded in soul and wounded in their governing
faculty by some arrow, show what it is to be Christians and make
a vow and learn things pertaining to the logoi. For these arrows

65. See Ps 17.23, Ps 35.7.
66. Ps 76.18.
67. Is 49.2
68. Is 49.6.
69. Ps 76.18b.

of God are spread abroad, and we pray that arrows might thus be spread abroad, so that we might have many brothers and the Church of God might grow!

I suppose that there is also another sort of arrow called "hand," as in, "Send out your hand and touch all that he has, if he will bless you to your face,"[70] and what Job himself said, "For it is the Lord's hand that is touching me,"[71] and whenever these things are said to him, it may be that some of his arrows are upon those who are unworthy of blessedness, imposing chastisement and redeeming those who have fallen into sins. I take it that the same things are evident in "the arrows of a strong one are sharpened with desert coals,"[72] for there the arrows cannot be doing anything but chastising those worthy of chastisement. And such arrows enter into the soul; sometimes they penetrate only as far as the body;[73] sometimes they disturb the soul itself and derange it: "For I will strike you with apoplexy, loss of sight, being out of your mind, and you will be groping about at noon as one gropes on a wall."[74]

Many arrows of God, then, are spread abroad; some wound us for the better—as I would want to be wounded, so that I might say, "I am wounded by love"[75]—but others wound for chastisement. Therefore, let us beg the God of the Universe that we may be worthy to be wounded by his marvelous arrows, even the choice ones, and especially by our Lord and Savior, Christ Jesus, to whom is the glory and the might to the ages of ages. Amen.

70. Jb 1.11.
71. Jb 19.21.
72. Ps 119.4.
73. See Heb 4.12.
74. Dt 28.28–29.
75. Song 2.5. Origen discusses this verse in *Comm. Cant.* 3.8. See Catherine Osborne's examination of Origen's image in *Eros Unveiled: Plato and the God of Love* (Oxford: Oxford University Press, 1994), 71–85.

HOMILY 4 ON PSALM 76

N DIVERSE ways God intends to arouse and to waken,[1] as if from sleep, a lazy human nature, so that through the eyes it may see the cosmos, and, seeing the cosmos and the composition of elements[2] on the earth, it will, from the order of the universe, marvel at the one who has made it.[3] But through hearing he has found just the art by which he may awaken the one who is made to the one who has made him. What sort of thing has God found and made? He has fashioned thunder, so that through thunder he may awaken the sleeper and arouse the soul, so that it might seek who it was who made the thunder and contrives such great sounds in the universe.[4] But we, wretched as we are, having abandoned looking at the cosmos and what is in it, are interested instead in human arts,[5] and the more those arts lead us astray, the fonder we are of looking at them rather than the cosmos. We receive music and literary works[6] so well that they

1. This metaphor does not just echo Scripture, especially Eph 5.14, but also the Platonic tradition, where wonder leads to philosophy and "waking" signifies coming to a new and more profound awareness of reality. See Plato, *Theaetetus* 155d; Plotinus, *Enn.* 1.6.8.28.

2. The ideas and the vocabulary of this passage echo Plato's *Timaeus*, especially 52d–53c and 69bc. Both the order of the cosmos, exhibited in the heavenly bodies, and the composition of the four elements on the earth testify to the marvelous order of the whole.

3. According to a student of Origen, he was taught to appreciate the arrangement of the universe in such a way that a rational replaced an irrational wonder (*Address of Thanksgiving* 8.111). See also the divinization of the eye in PS8oH2.1 below.

4. See above PS36H3.4.

5. *Technai*, "arts," "skills," or "crafts." The relatively critical attitude of the arts echoes sentiments in Plato's works, especially *Republic*, Book 3.

6. *Mousikai*, works associated with the muses, not just "music" in the narrow sense.

tug on the soul and carry it toward idolatry; when we use our eyesight and examine God's work, we should marvel at the one who made it, and we should recall through hearing, whenever we hear thunder, the heavenly sound[7] of God again reminding us from heaven above to listen to a sound that is a greater and better voice than every sound made by those on earth.

I say that also through the other senses, inferior to sight and hearing, God's art exhorts[8] us to look at the creator. He has made things tasty, of themselves, as it were, and on their own, without needing human arts, so that the sense, drawn to them, will seek the very sweetness of this plant or the tartness of that or whatever quality it is of another; and human nature, as it seeks, will marvel at one who brings us into such an intricate banquet.[9] It is also possible to see, concerning smell, that God has made certain natural things to attract, on their own, the sense of smell, which we can observe in plants and flowers. And he stimulates us through the sense of touch, at one time making the air warm, at another time cold.

We need, if God finds the same arts in the senses so as to exhort us to reverence, to seek whether maybe in the greater thing—I say, a different thing from the senses—he has made a power, so that it might judge the things of the senses, apprehending both in sensible things and in things apart from the cosmos the one who has made the cosmos. For "no human being has seen God, nor can see,"[10] while at the same time, that in us which is above the human—the mind, that is—sees God, if it is pure, for "blessed are the pure in heart, because they shall see God."[11]

7. The Greek word *phōnē*, like the Hebrew word *qōl* that it translates, can refer either to sound in general or to an articulate voice.

8. *Protrepei*, "exhorts," recalls the *Protrepticus* of Clement of Alexandria, with which this passage shares many features. "Exhortation" was an established literary genre among philosophers as well, although few of their works have survived. Augustine testified to the power of such a work, the lost *Hortensius* of Cicero, in *Confessions* 3.4.7–8.

9. *Sumposion*, "banquet." Origen's use of this particular word may have been intended as a hint that his argument continues to echo Plato, though not so much the dialogue of that name as the discussion of the senses in *Timaeus* 65b–69a.

10. 1 Tm 6.16.

11. Mt 5.8.

And this is why the majority of human beings do not perceive God, because they have an unpurified eye of the soul. And the majority of us,[12] to the extent that we purify the eye of the soul, the mind, and withdraw from things that disturb us, to that extent we perceive God more clearly, but to the extent that our mind is thwarted by vice, by love of daily life, by the cares and preoccupations, and the eye is filled with evils of daily living, to that extent it is thwarted from perceiving God purely. And God so loved, because of his love of humanity, that he graciously bestows on the one who does not perceive these activities the ability to be saved by believing.[13] These things, if I were to digress, are abundant, but the logos was having its beginning on account of "*a voice of your thunder in the wheel*,"[14] for a few preliminary things needed to be said about the thunder we perceive with the senses.

2. But how shall we give an account of the sensible thunder produced "*in the wheel*"? Someone will say that it is impossible and we cannot stand by the wording that says: "*a voice of your thunder in the wheel.*"[15] But as far as possible, where it is allowed, intending to stand by the wording for the sake of a step up,[16] we understand something like this about the passage. If we consider the nature of thunder, how it is produced—a continuous reverberation arises from the activity of clouds beating against each other—we can say that the image of "*a voice of your thunder in the wheel*" is not absurd to accept. But, because of the thunder, we might seek a wheel in something sensible, not something

12. "Us Christians," that is, who have the benefit of being saved by faith even if we do not study the cosmos.

13. In refuting the philosopher Celsus, who contrasted the intellectual sophistication of Plato with the appeal of Christians to faith, Origen had recently argued in *Contra Celsum* that the ability to speak to ordinary people who could not follow a philosophical argument was a major advantage to Christianity. See especially *Cels.* 6.10.

14. Ps 76.19a.

15. Ibid. "Someone" (a student of Origen?) will say that the received wording must be emended in order for it to make sense.

16. *Pro tēs anagogēs:* "for the sake of a step up" (to a more spiritual interpretation) makes more sense than a possible alternative translation, "before a step up." If the *lexis,* the wording as it is, is disallowed, there can be no higher sense on its basis.

bodily or in outward appearance, but in activity, as it were, understanding something wheel-like[17] and produced in relation to the sound of thunder, at the moment of the thunder. But if, before I step up to the things that are understood, you want a different approach to grasp the sensible thing, come up with me to Ezekiel and see there the God of the Universe holding the reins and seated upon the so-called "Cherubim," which are four-faced; there are the forms of a lion, a calf, an eagle, and a human being among the Cherubim.[18] And the Cherubim were winged, and they were covered all over with eyes, for "they are full of eyes within and without."[19] And concerning the Cherubim there will be an occasion, should God give it, for it to be explained in the treatise on the Cherubim.[20]

And concerning wheels, why is it said, when also a wheel is in a wheel? And God was, as it were, driving a chariot among the Cherubim, in which chariot there are living creatures and wheels. I seek, then, these wheels and especially because they are wheels, according to what is written: "as a wheel in a wheel."[21] Seeking, I find[22] that the motion of all things is borne in a circular fashion, as Solomon also says in Ecclesiastes: "Circles of circles, the spirit goes about, and the spirit rotates in its circle."[23]

---

17. *Trochasmon tina*, "something round," i.e., "wheel-like"; it is absurd to think that thunder is a *trochos*, a "wheel," if that is understood as a body, a solid object. That absurdity would be reasonable grounds for supposing that the *lexis*, the received biblical text, is corrupt and for seeking to correct it, but Origen, who criticizes those who rush to alter a text (as in PS77H1.1 below), always seeks a way for it to make sense. Here he argues that *trochos* is not a round object, but something "wheel-like" related to thunder. An extended sense of *trochos* is a "circuit" such as the course for a race or the orbit of a heavenly body.

18. See Ezek 10.10–12.

19. Rv 4.8.

20. Origen speaks about his intention to write about the Cherubim in *Contra Celsum* (7.11), written around 248 and considered his last datable work before these homilies were discovered. Celsus, an anti-Christian writer, criticized the prophets for making absurd statements, the charge Origen is dealing with here in relation to the Psalm. On the Jewish sources of Origen's understanding of the vision of Ezekiel, see David J. Halperin, *The Faces of the Chariot: Early Jewish Responses to Ezekiel's Vision* (Tübingen: J. C. B. Mohr [Paul Siebeck], 1986), 332–56.

21. Ezek 1.16.

22. See Mt 7.7–8.

23. Eccl 1.6. Origen considered Ecclesiastes to be Solomon's inspired treatise

The freight of all things is borne circularly, as is clear to those who take notice of what appears to the senses. There is in all things a twofold principal motion, the one from sunrise to sunset, the other from sunset to sunrise. And the motion of everything is from sunrise to sunset, but there is a motion from sunset to sunrise in each of the so-called "seven planets," among which are the sun and moon. And according to this it might say in Ezekiel, "a wheel in a wheel," that is, in the one containing what is a perceived sphere within, the second wheel according to the movement of the planetary spheres, so called by the Greeks.[24]

"*A voice,*" then, "*of thunder in the wheel*" occurs according to the circular motion of all things and the movement of the cosmos: whenever the sun comes among these twelve divisions and has affinity toward some of the stars and toward the heavens, it continually makes thunder on the earth. Just as an eclipse of the sun and an eclipse of the moon are predicted, so also are rains and weather change, and thunders and similar things; thus a voice of sensible thunder is produced "in the wheel," as Ezekiel said,[25] in accord with the movement and conveyance of all.[26]

3. But nonetheless let us not stay there, but let us also step up in the logos to another thunder. I know that John the Apostle and his brother James were the "sons," not of a sensible "thun-

---

on "physics," the philosophical discipline we would call "science" (see *Comm. Cant.* Prol. 3) and implies that Solomon anticipated Hellenistic astronomy.

24. In the Ptolemaic cosmology the earth is thought to be at the center of the cosmos, which moves in a circle around it in the same direction as the sun. The planets, however, occasionally move in a contrary direction. From this they derive their name: "planet" means "wanderer." It was not fully understood until the seventeenth century that the apparent motion of the planets can be explained by their elliptical orbit around the sun. The Ptolemaic system accounts for these movements by positing so-called "epicycles," circular motions that move with the circular motion of the whole but account for occasional retrograde motion. Origen identified these epicycles with Ezekiel's "wheel in a wheel."

25. See Ezek 1.24–25.

26. In his discussion of the movement of the cosmos and of the soul, Origen echoes two passages in Plato that deal with circular motion, *Politicus* 269E and *Laws* 10.893CD. Plato, like Aristotle after him, considered circular movement the closest approximation that bodily activity in the realm of becoming can make to the immobile activity of the divine realm of being. Origen's reference to "movement," *kinesis,* and "conveyance," *phora,* echoes Plato's words "as many things as move by conveyance" in *Laws* 10.293D.

der," but of some intelligible thunder, and that, knowing this thunder, the one who applied names to them called them "Boanerges," that is, "sons of thunder."[27] Because John was a son of thunder, he wrote in his Revelation that he had heard seven thunders of one thunder and of other brothers of his own thunder and such things as, it says, "the seven thunders spoke, I was going to write, and a voice came to me, 'Do not write them.'"[28]

Accordingly, there are certain powers that teach the saints the eloquence of God. And perhaps, if one diligently examines the seven thunders that John heard, one would not be mistaken in saying that the seven thunders that he heard are wisdom and understanding, counsel and might, knowledge and reverence and fear.[29] These are the seven thunders that the blessed John heard. If, indeed, these are the thunders, the voice of wisdom would be a voice of thunder, for wisdom is one of the thunders.

How is it "*in a wheel*"? Hear, the holy person does not have corners,[30] nor does he have any crooked places[31] in him, but he has been made to imitate heaven, seeing that he has "the image of the heavenly,"[32] and just as heaven does not have corners, but is curved and spherical, and the spirit does not have corners—"Circle of circles, the spirit goes about, and the spirit rotates in its circle"[33]—so also the saint, imitating the spirit, going about circling circles, but also imitating the heaven that has "the image of the heavenly" in it, is not angular, but is a wheel; and the voice in such a person as has nothing crooked in him, but imitates heaven, belongs to wisdom; so, on this account, it is said, "*a voice of your thunder in the wheel.*"[34]

27. Mk 3.17.

28. Rv 10.4.

29. See Is 11.2.

30. According to George Prochnik, "... Native Americans believed that devils lurk in corners. (Zen gardens also incorporate the idea that devils can only travel in straight lines.)" See *In Pursuit of Silence: Listening for Meaning in a World of Noise* (New York: Anchor, 2010), 263.

31. A possible allusion to Is 40.4.

32. 1 Cor 15.49.

33. Eccl 1.6.

34. Plotinus also teaches that the natural movement of a soul is not straight, but circular. See *Enn.* 6.9.8.

For more evidence that the holy person does not have corners, I shall make use of the statement of the Gospel, where the Savior, intending to reprove the prayer of hypocrites, said that they stood on the corners of the streets making supplication. For when any sinner prays, he prays on lines enclosed by corners and not on a road carrying his soul in a straight line; but the holy person is not so, but he has a prayer moving as the heaven, arising and always moving circularly, as the heaven is moved.[35] These things, as far as I am concerned, are to be said about "*a voice of your thunder in the wheel.*"

If someone is able to see more powerful things than these, because the Holy Spirit is rich for revealing deep things and great things and things not tracked down, let those things be heard rather than these, if they are found to be more excellent than these.

Yet I shall add that God, who is also the father of the universe, when he was witnessing to the Lord Jesus Christ, also said, "I have also glorified and will glorify again."[36] Those standing around heard the voice in different ways, some as thunder, but some as an angel speaking; for some said that thunder had been produced, but others that an angel had spoken.[37] Accordingly, the voice of God is heard by some as thunder, but by others it is heard not as God's voice, but that of an angel.

4. But thus also "*your lightning bolts appeared in the inhabited world,*"[38] and sensible lightning bolts turn us back towards the God who thunders and makes lightning. And they have some-

---

35. See Plato, *Timaeus* 34A4. According to Plotinus, the soul "is running around and lovingly embraces God, so that it is around him as much as possible, for all things depend on him. Because it cannot be next to him, it moves around him" (*Enn.* 2.2.2). The tenth of fifteen alleged teachings of Origen anathematized by the Second Council of Constantinople in 553 was that he taught that the resurrected body of the Lord was spherical and that the same would be true of the resurrected bodies of believers. There is no evidence in his surviving works that Origen taught this, but this passage may be hinting at it, even though he is here discussing the motion of the soul, not its shape. Neoplatonists after Plotinus taught that the soul could assume a spherical, "astral body." See Christoph Markschiess, *Gottes Körper* (Munich: C. H. Beck, 2016), 159–62.

36. Jn 12.28.

37. Jn 12.29.

38. Ps 76.19b.

thing marvelous about them: that their flashes, appearing, suddenly reveal the inhabited world, so that the darkness of night is dissipated. It is not only the sun that dissipates darkness; lightning does so as well. If it is necessary to ascend again in the logos, in a manner akin to what has been said about thunder, I do not hesitate to affirm a logos about lightning: just as, in accordance with some pattern, being wheels, the blessed and grandiloquent apostles and teachers of the logos according to the Gospel receive the voice of thunder, so they also flash lightning. And their light shines before human beings,[39] and it is possible to see lightning bolts of their ideas and lightning bolts of their works. But why is something marvelous if they are the just? The Savior likened himself to a lightning bolt, saying, "For just as a lightning bolt comes down from under heaven and lights up what is under heaven, so will be the coming of the Son of the human being."[40]

But once my enemy was a bolt of lightning also, just as, once, he was a morning star.[41] That he also was once a morning star is shown from: "How did the morning star fall out of heaven, the one who rises at dawn?"[42] That he was also a bolt of lightning, Jesus himself taught us, saying: "I observed Satan falling as a lightning bolt from heaven."[43] He had fallen, then, the same one who once was a lightning bolt. But one who learns these things will turn himself around so as to pay attention to himself, so that he may never fall from heaven, but may be enabled, grasping those places of moderation, of hymning God, of having respect, so that he always maintains a need for God and abides in God. For when someone imagines that he does not have a need for God, whatever his situation may be, if he should ever become such a person, it shall be demonstrated to him by God that he does have a need for God, and by suffering he shall learn that he is not on his own, in those situations that seem to be good, but is such a one to the extent that God assists him.

39. Mt 5.16.
40. Lk 17.24.
41. *Heōsphoros,* "dawn-bearer," the morning star.
42. Is 14.12.
43. Lk 10.18.

5. "*It was shaken, and the earth came to be trembling.*"[44] The earth was shaken. The earth came to be trembling. It was not something else shaking it when the earth came to be trembling, but it came about when there was thunder in the wheel. When lightning bolts appear to the inhabited world, the earth shakes and comes to be trembling. This occurred at the coming of our Savior. For both through his amazing voice and through the lightning bolt of his works, "*it was shaken, and the earth came to be trembling.*" But it always comes about, whenever a lightning bolt of genuine light is produced from the intelligible and a thunder clap is produced by eloquence in logos, our earth is shaken; that is, what is earthy and bodily goes away, and it enters, as it were, a more divine character, so that when the trembling of the earth occurs to each one of us, the parts of the body that are on earth are put to death; as we bear about everywhere in the body the death of the cross, all of us are already enabled to receive the life of Jesus to be revealed in our body.[45]

"*Your road is in the sea.*"[46] What is the road of God in the sea? The road of God in the sea is the one who says: "I am the road."[47] The road of God is God's logos. It is amazing that the same thing is said above in reference to the holy—"*For your road is in the holy*"[48]—but here it is in the sea, both in the holy and in the sea. If you are a holy one, Christ is in you, the road is in you. And since John says, "He was in the cosmos,"[49] he must have been "in the great sea, the wide one, where there are great and small animals, where there is the serpent whom you fashioned to play with it";[50] also in that sea there is a road, who is the Son of God. For if there were not a road of God in the sea, you could not travel and be saved because you would be separated from God's logos, the genuine road; nor would Peter, doing something secret by walking on the waves of the aforesaid sea, have had the capacity

44. Ps 76.19c.
45. See 2 Cor 4.10.
46. Ps 76.20a.
47. Jn 14.6.
48. Ps 76.14a.
49. Jn 1.10.
50. Ps 103.25.

to walk when he stepped onto the sea.[51] But since there is a road in the sea and Christ is the road in the sea, therefore also there was a rock[52] on the road that was in the sea. "*In the sea*," then, "*is your road*"; then it is blessed to seek the road that is still in the sea.

"*And your paths are in many waters*";[53] even if many waters overflow, the paths of reverence are not dissolved. For much water cannot quench love and rivers do not overflow it.[54] But if you want, we shall compare the two inexpressible things, "*your road is in the sea*," and, "*your paths are in many waters.*" If you will, let us refer first to the narrative about the Red Sea, when it became a road for the people of God in the sea. Hear also this: "You have given a road in the sea and a path in the waves."[55] But, second, we see the Jordan River also somehow thus traveled by the people by means of Joshua, and it was traveled also by Elijah and Elisha.[56] The "*paths*" of God "*are in many waters.*" If you want to see another way in which the paths of God are in the waters, look with me at the just person, from whom rivers of water flow from the belly, springing up into eternal life, and you will see in those many waters and in the spring and in the river the path of God's salvation.[57]

There is, as it were, a path, a path in these things that have been said—his "*paths are in many waters*"—but on all of these, "*your tracks*," it says, "*are not to be known.*"[58] This is why, I suppose, the Apostle, having understood, had said, "How unsearchable are his judgments, and how his roads are not to be tracked."[59] As much as a human being wants to find out how to grasp the tracks of God, he is not enabled to track down everything; for example, what does God intend in the limitless age, or what did he intend from the limitless age? The head, that is, the beginning of God's plans, is hidden by the Seraphim as well as

51. See Mt 14.29.
52. *Petra*, "rock," is a play on the name of Peter.
53. Ps 76.20b.
54. Song 8.7.
55. Wis 14.3.
56. See Jos 3.14–17, 1 Kgs 2.8.
57. See Jn 4.14.
58. Ps 76.20b–c.
59. Rom 11.33.

the feet, the completion of things that are going to be.[60] Just as there was a certain announcement from him: "Say certain first things, and we shall know that you are gods; announce the last things, and we shall know where you are from."[61] We do not know, then, when the last things are or when the first things were, but, being precipitous, we want to track down what cannot be tracked and to comprehend the ancient things, to comprehend the final things. I know only this: that, as a human being, I have hope of blessed life, just as the just did before me, and it is possible to learn, if I am enabled to hear the Scripture, from the holy letters, except that the tracks of God have not been known. Even if the tracks of God cannot be known, nonetheless God shows the holy ones his roads, even when they do not understand his tracks, and he himself is leading his holy ones by unknown tracks, as it is written, *"You lead your people like sheep in the hand of Moses and Aaron."*[62]

Then he led his people like sheep, without tracks by an untrodden road, as it says, "You led them through that large desert, great and fearsome."[63] Now God leads us, not by Moses, nor by Aaron, but by a better road than that through which he led the people then. For our Lord is better than Moses and differs from Aaron, insofar as the son is better than the attendant, insofar as the genuine high priest is greater than the figurative high priest. If, then, we ourselves, traveling towards a god,[64] want somehow to understand his own roads to grasp the road and travel towards a god, let us beseech the God of the Universe to send us this holy logos leading us on the road perfected by him, to whom is the glory and the might to the ages of ages. Amen.

---

60. See Is 6.2. In Origen's interpretation of Isaiah's throne vision, the wings of the fiery beings cover, not their own feet and heads, but God's. See *Princ.* 4.3.14.

61. Is 41.22–23.

62. Ps 76.20.

63. Dt 2.7.

64. On the logos.

HOMILY 1 ON PSALM 77

FTEN WE SAY that the Psalms inscribed "*of sagacity*"[1] alert the hearer, in the inscription, to seek for what is said in the Psalm as something requiring interpretation and explanation because dark logoi, riddles, and parables are included in every Psalm "*of sagacity.*" This is what has occurred here, for it is inscribed "*of sagacity by Asaph,*" and in it he immediately says the following: "*I will open my mouth in parables; I will proclaim problems from a beginning.*"[2] This should also be known: that Matthew mentioned the statement. For concerning the Savior, writing about how he spoke in parables, he said, "in order to fulfill 'I will open my mouth in parables; I will proclaim problems from a beginning,'" or actually, "'from the sowing of the cosmos.'"[3] When the statement was paraphrased by such wording as said here by Matthew, there occurred a scribal error with regard to the copies of the Gospel: "So that what was said by Isaiah might be fulfilled, 'I will open my mouth in parables.'"[4] Apparently, finding the words, "so that what was said by Asaph," one of the earliest copyists, unaware that Asaph was a prophet, assumed that there had been an error, and was emboldened by

1. *Sunesis,* translated here as "sagacity," is quick and intuitive comprehension, "getting it."

2. Ps 77.2.

3. Mt 13.35. New Testament translators normally translate *katabolē* according to its extended meaning, "foundation," and some, following a different manuscript tradition, omit "of the cosmos." Origen understood the use of *katabolē*, as opposed to the ordinary word meaning "creation" (*ktisis*), as an indication that the cosmos exists as the result of a descent from an original unity in God. See *Princ.* 3.5.4 and *Comm. Jo.* 19.22.149–150.

4. Mt 13.35.

the strangeness of the prophet's name[5] to substitute Isaiah for Asaph.[6]

In general, it must be said that the devil plots against the living and wants to scatter the churches, but daily contrives to generate heresies and schisms, and yet still to set a thousand more traps for human beings. It is no marvel if he even plots against the Scriptures. Because our salvation is through them, he contrives contradiction among the Scriptures, so that by means of the contradiction there might arise a stumbling block to those who read: which account is to be accepted, this or that? And as much as we labored through God and his grace, examining together both the Hebrew and the versions[7] in order to see to the correction of errors, God knows. What we intend to do about the rest he will guide.[8]

So this is something you must know. If something out of Scripture is held up as a contradiction, we must not assume a contradiction, knowing that either we do not understand or that a scribal mistake[9] has occurred. For example, we find an outright contradiction in the third book of the Kingdoms. It is written there that "Rehoboam became king when he was sixteen years old and reigned over Jerusalem twelve years,"[10] and again, "he became king when he was forty-one years old and reigned over Jerusalem seventeen years."[11] But there is no way of explaining that he became king when he was sixteen years old and reigned seventeen years.[12] And if much scrutiny had

---

5. "Asaph" not only is an obscure figure, but his name sounds like *asaphēs*, "obscure," in Greek.

6. Origen counts the substitution of "from the sowing of the cosmos" as a paraphrase on Matthew's part not unlike his own occasional paraphrases to clarify the meaning of the text. The ascription to Isaiah, on the other hand, is simply wrong.

7. Origen is referring to his *Hexapla*, which contained a column in Hebrew and at least four Greek translations, his "versions," side by side.

8. In this, his last known work, Origen indicates that the *Hexapla* is a continuing project.

9. *Hamartēma*, the word normally translated as "sin."

10. 3 Kingdoms 12.24a, found only in the LXX.

11. 1 Kgs 14.21, which is 3 Kingdoms 14.21a in the LXX.

12. Emendation is necessary to reconcile two inconsistent statements of fact. The Hebrew text that we have received states only that Rehoboam became king

not taken place, as we examine together these readings in the
other versions, we might have supposed that there is a conflict
in what has been written, because we find that one or the other
has been interpolated.

Thus the devil plots even in the Scripture, but we must not on
that account be bold and move precipitously to emendation.[13]
That is the sort of thing that happened to Marcion; assuming
that the Scriptures had been tampered with and had come to be
interpolated by the devil, he undertook to emend the Scripture.
In this project, he took away some of the foundations of the Gospels—among many others, the birth of the Savior—and he took
away apparitions and prophecies even when they were essential
to the Apostle.[14] Therefore, having faith is a reasonable thing,
not so much on account of the Scriptures as on account of the
cosmos and the order that is in it, in the one who made sky and
earth and the things in them. And it is reasonable to believe in
Christ Jesus, not so much from what is read as from the resplen-
dent power of the churches and from his superlative strength,
which has overcome the inhabited world, and then to move to
the letters after having again asked grace from God, that we may
not misconstrue what is written.[15]

---

at forty-one and reigned in Jerusalem seventeen years. Origen may have thought
that Rehoboam, whose conduct he recounted in PS77H2.1 below, acted more
like a teenager than a forty-one-year-old man.

13. Marguerite Harl, *Le déchiffrement du sens: Études sur l'herméneutique chrétienne d'Origène à Grégoire de Nysse* (Paris: Études Augustiniennes, 1993), 115: "The
fault of the heretics is a wish to understand too fast. It is a fault of 'precipitousness,' *propeteia,* lack of patience and excess of boldness at the same time. They
push the questioning of texts too far and imagine that they can grasp all the
mysteries without divine aid." See *Philoc.* 1.29.

14. Marcion's Scriptures were an expurgated Gospel of Luke, leaving out
the birth narrative among other things, and expurgated Epistles of Paul, leaving
out the citations—visions and prophecies—of the Old Testament. Origen argues
that by doing so, he removed elements essential to the whole, with the result
that Marcion's scriptures were incoherent as well as misleading without them.
"Apparitions," *optasias,* deleted from Paul's epistles would have included 2 Cor
3.7, Paul's allusion to the glory that made Moses's face unbearably bright when
he brought down the tables containing the Ten Commandments (Ex 34.29–35).

15. Origen summarizes here an argument more fully elaborated in *Princ.*
4.1.1–2. See also *Cels.* 1.29 on the power of Jesus. The "letters" are not epistles,
but the words of scripture (see PS80H2.5 below). Origen normally refers to

The letters provide a pretext for much death to make its way into souls.[16] Every sect takes impious notions from the letters and they suppose that they are proving them from the Gospels, from the apostles, or, in the case of some sects, from the law or from the prophets. I do not say this to criticize the Scriptures, but in the wish that the faith I was talking about should come to rely not so much on Scripture as on a demonstration more splendid than the Scriptures: heaven, earth, and the things in them. In a discussion with the adherents of Marcion,[17] I remember saying: "You have two options—to rely on Scripture, as you say, about the Father, or to rely on the cosmos and by its order about their creator[18]—which should you do? For even if Scripture did not encompass all these things,[19] would it not be reasonable, for one going to the cosmos and seeing its order, to have relied on its creator, rather than making such assumptions about God as you do?" And it is truly possible to say, it seems to me, that it must impress the seeker as a more splendid demonstration compared to an inferior one. It is a more splendid demonstration to see the sky, stars, sun, moon, fixed stars, earth and the animals on earth, the human being their king, endowed with such skills, and to be amazed at the one who has made these and to accept the herald of such teaching, Jesus Christ our Lord.[20] And this will suffice as a defense for what was written in

---

them as *lexis* (plural, *lexeis*), but uses the biblical term here, since he is about to cite Paul.

16. See 2 Cor 3.6b: "The letter [*gramma*] kills, but the spirit gives life." Origen elaborates this argument in *Princ.* 4.2.1–2.

17. Marcion, like Valentinus, denied the identity of the god of the Old Testament, whom both of them identified as the creator of the cosmos, with the God and Father of Jesus Christ. The beauty and order of the cosmos are, in Origen's view, proof that it is not the production of an inferior and incompetent god.

18. "Creator" here is *dēmiourgos*. See PS77H2.6, nn. 57 and 58 above. Origen also likens Scripture to the cosmos itself in one of his earliest works, written as much as thirty years before he delivered the homilies. This is a fragment from an early Commentary on the Psalms preserved in *Philoc.* 2. See Trigg, *Origen*, 69–72.

19. Scripture itself testifies to the beauty and order of the cosmos. In these homilies Origen cites Gn 1.31 (PS80H2.1 below) and Ps 18.2 (PS67H2.3 above) to this effect.

20. The Marcionites have it wrong both about Scripture and about cosmology. In the homily he preached after this one, PS77H2.4–5 below, Origen laid out other issues in contention with the Marcionites.

Matthew: "So that what was uttered by Isaiah the prophet might be fulfilled, saying, 'I will open my mouth in parables.'"[21]

2. As it is our custom, in the Psalms and in the prophets, to see who is the persona speaking, so also here, who is speaking must be sought. If, then, "so that the prophecy might be fulfilled, saying, 'I will open my mouth in parables,'"[22] did not come in Matthew, I would be inclined to doubt if I ought to take "*I will open my mouth in parables; I will proclaim problems from a beginning*"[23] in the persona of the Savior. I would have hesitated to refer the ascription to the Savior on account of what follows: "*as many of these things as we have heard and known and our fathers have reported to us, I have not hidden from their children, proclaiming the praises of the Lord to another generation,*" and so on.[24] For it seems that these things cannot rightfully be about the Savior: "*I will proclaim problems from a beginning,*" and, "*as many of these things as we have heard and known.*"

For the Savior neither knows from hearing nor, for that matter, has he learned from the fathers. No one among those begotten is a teacher of the teacher of all, concerning whom it has been written: "Do not call anyone an instructor on earth, because Christ is the one instructor."[25] If the Savior were to make use of a teacher (as he actually does), he will not make use of human beings, or angels, or archangels, or even of the Holy Spirit. For he has a teacher of everything who is peculiar to him, the Father, concerning whom he says: "As I hear, I judge, and my judgment is not mine, but belongs to the Father who sent me."[26] Our Savior and Lord has, then, the Father and God of the Universe as a teacher.

If Matthew had not said that the Psalm is in the persona of the Savior, I would not then have been so bold as to refer to what is written subsequently: "*as many of these things as we have*

21. Mt 13.35. The ascription of the persona to Christ in Scripture is definitive, but creates its own problem to be solved: how to account for the same persona in subsequent verses. See a similar dynamic in PS15H1.2 above.

22. Mt 13.35.

23. Ps 77.2.

24. Ps 77.3–4.

25. Mt 23.10.

26. Jn 5.30.

heard and known and our fathers have reported to us."[27] Nonetheless, when Matthew says this, what am I to do? Do I say that the whole Psalm is in the persona of the Savior, or that these words are the Savior's but in what follows the persona changes? For often in one or another Psalm many personae are speaking.

And as an example it suffices, regarding the Savior, to take the 31st Psalm: "Blessed are those whose lawless deeds have been put away and whose sins have been covered. Blessed is the man to whom the Lord will not reckon sin nor is there guile in his mouth."[28] The persona saying this, "Blessed are those whose lawless deeds have been put away," is more of a teacher, and it could be said by the persona of the prophet, or of the Holy Spirit, or of Christ. But admittedly we see in what follows a change in persona: "I recognized my sin, and I did not hide my lawlessness. I said, 'I will acknowledge concerning myself my lawlessness to the Lord.'[29] Concerning this, every holy one will pray in an appropriate time: so that a flood of many waters may not approach him. You are my refuge from a tribulation that encompasses me, my rejoicing; ransom me from those who encircle me. I will make you understand and instruct you in this road, in which you walk."[30] But, in contrast, the one saying, "I will make you understand and instruct you in this road, in which you walk," is God. But the one saying, "I recognized my lawlessness and did not hide my sin," is a human being confessing his own failings. But observe, where in the Psalm it says, "I will strengthen her pillars,"[31] in what way the entire Psalm cannot be either in the persona of God or in the persona of Christ. This, then, is the custom in one Psalm; it is possible that there is not one persona speaking, but many. If this occurs in some Psalms, it should be sought if the equivalent is to be understood here.

"Pay attention, my people, to my law."[32] By virtue of the authority of the one who says, "my people," it would not be the proph-

27. Ps 77.3.
28. Ps 31.1–2.
29. Ps 31.5.
30. Ps 31.6–8.
31. Ps 74.4b.
32. Ps 77.1b.

et who says, "*Pay attention, my people, to my law.*" It is the Lord's voice saying, "*my law. Bend your ear to the utterances of my mouth. I will open my mouth in parables; I will proclaim problems from a beginning.*"[33] If all these things are not spoken in the plural—for "*I will open my mouth*" and "*my law*" and "*I will proclaim*" are spoken in the singular—but the following are spoken no longer in the singular but in the plural, accordingly the persona has changed. "*As many of these things as we have heard and known and our fathers have reported to us, I have not hidden from their children to another generation.*"[34] Evidently a speaker began in the singular, but the rest is no longer singular, but the speakers are plural. Keep in mind, then, that the Savior is the speaker, as Matthew recorded, and that the Savior does not speak throughout the whole Psalm, but the prophetic persona speaks some things concerning him and those from the people or simply the majority, and the Church speaks the rest. This will serve to clear up the persona speaking.

3. According to the wording we might hear, "*Pay attention, my people, to my law.*" "I shall establish a lawgiver for them, so that the gentiles may know that they are human beings"; does not the spirit pray in the prophet in the Ninth Psalm, while there is a law according to Moses, that you may raise up a lawgiver for the gentiles?[35] For our Savior was not going to visit us in order to subject us to the attendant's law. If the law of the attendant had been saving[36] and if that law, concerning which it is written, "Remember a law of Moses, my servant,"[37] were sufficient on its own, would Christ's visit still be necessary? I have legislation, I conduct myself according to it; I do not need another legislation. But right now, the God and Father of the Universe, seeing that the needs of the times demand changes of legislation and practice, began, on the one hand, with the legislation through Moses, but, on the other hand, he indicated in Moses

33. Ps 77.1–2.

34. Ps 77.4a.

35. Ps 9.21 (LXX): "Establish a lawgiver for them, Lord, so that the gentiles may know that they are human beings." Origen rephrases this as a first-person statement by God.

36. Following the CMG 314 reading, *esōzen*, "was saving," rather than Perrone's emendation, *esōthēn*, "I was saved."

37. Mal 4.6 (3.24 in LXX).

the visitation of Christ[38] and established other, more beneficial, laws for those from the gentiles, having done this earlier.[39]

Those before Moses were saved without reading Moses's law, for they were not circumcised on the eighth day. And should the Jews press their point, Enoch and Abel did not comply with the letters of the law, as they were recorded in Leviticus, but there were in each generation things that were fitting for the times, saving those who wanted to be saved. God did not allow the gentiles to be given the law that was given to the children of Israel who were conducting their affairs according to it. When the children of Israel want to conduct themselves according to the law of Moses in all that they do, they cannot. Let them make the Passover in the place the Lord chose, but that is not possible for them. Let them stone an adulterer, but, when it comes to stoning, the emperors are in charge. One thing and another are written concerning purifications—if those things actually purify—but it does not happen; those under Moses's law are not purified, but are under a curse.

Thus it is evident, according to what is said by the prophets, that my Lord came as a lawgiver to the gentiles, and, according to what Jeremiah said, "See, days are coming, says the Lord, and I will finish for the house of Israel and for the house of Judah a new covenant, not according to the covenant that I established with their fathers."[40] And elsewhere it is said, "I will give them another heart to fear me and another road."[41] So, has he given them another road, and has he not given them another heart? But the ingenious Jews say that these things are said about the age to come. But we shall say to them, "As for 'to fear me,' are we going to refer this to the age to come; because now is the time to fear, the time for fearing is not when we shall have been

38. An allusion to Dt 18.15.

39. Origen claims that "my people" in, "Pay attention, my people, to my law," refers to the gentiles and that "my law" does not refer to the law delivered to the Jewish people through Moses, but to a law for the gentiles. He will go on to show how, as the (putative) author of both Deuteronomy and Genesis, Moses not only announces a new, saving legislation for the gentiles but recounts a precedent for it.

40. Jer 38.31–32 LXX.

41. Jer 39.39 LXX.

perfected, 'for perfect love throws out fear'?"[42] If the one who fears has chastisement, are we also going to be chastised there, for is it possible for us, after blessedness, to fall into chastisement? There, it is not possible for fear to be educational or useful; love is perpetual.[43] Because fear cannot be useful then, hear Paul saying, "Give back to all what is due, tribute to whom tribute is due, fear to whom fear, tax to whom tax, honor to whom honor."[44] But it is due, then, to be given back; this is what he tells us to owe, saying, "Owe no one anything, except to love one another."[45]

4. But I am reminded that these things were said to Christians; nonetheless, they were said to them earlier, for we have not gone crazy; why would we quote the epistles of Paul to them to trouble them? If, then, my Savior should say, "*Pay attention, my people, to my law*," he speaks to Christians, for Christians are the people of Christ. And he says, "Pay attention, my people, to my law, no longer to that of Moses, no longer to be circumcised, no longer to keep sabbath, no longer to walk according to the first and according to the old"; see, new things have come about; the old things have passed away.[46] But you also hear, "the silly women, laden with sins"[47] and you see why the Savior says, "*Pay attention, my people, to my law.*"

If, then, you would pay attention to the law as the people of Christ, you would not make unleavened bread again whenever the days of unleavened bread come around, but you will make the unleavened bread of sincerity, the unleavened bread of truth.[48] If you pay attention to the law, you will not again make the Jewish fast, on account of which those who do not understand the Day of Atonement are rightly expelled from the Church. For once there was a Day of Atonement, when they fasted, but the Day of Atonement was figurative. The genuine one

42. 1 Jn 4.18.
43. See 1 Cor 13.8.
44. Rom 13.7.
45. Rom 13.8.
46. See 2 Cor 5.17.
47. 2 Tm 3.6. The Apostle testifies that believers must still need to be told to attend to the law.
48. See 1 Cor 5.8.

was when my Lord Christ Jesus was crucified for the cosmos, the lamb of God who takes away the sin of the cosmos.[49] The Day of Atonement, then, has occurred in me, so that I no longer have need of fasting: the sons of the bridal chamber do not have to fast, as long as the bridegroom is with them.[50] If you want to fast in the Jewish manner, the bridegroom will be taken away from you according to what is said: "When the bridegroom is taken away from them, then they will fast in those days."[51] If you want to fast, perform a Christian fast. The lawgiver of the gentiles taught, saying, "When you fast, anoint your head and wash your face and petition your father in the hidden place, so that you may not appear to be fasting to human beings."[52]

There is, then, a legislation of Christ, concerning which Christ says, "*Pay attention, my people, to my law*," namely the law according to the Gospel. Figuring this out and knowing the difference between old and new observances, the sacred apostle of Christ Jesus says, "I have become to the lawless as a lawless person, but not being lawless with respect to God, but lawful with respect to Christ, so that I might gain the lawless."[53] For if someone becomes lawful with respect to Christ, that person has not become lawless with respect to God, but lawful with respect to Christ, since God established this: the lawgiver is lawful with respect to God. For as one in the law of Moses, before Christ's visit would come, was not lawless with respect to God, even if he seemed to be relying on Moses's law—for the law of Moses was a law of God—so, by the same token, the law in which one is classified "lawful with respect to Christ" has been given by the Father to the gentiles: "in manifold and versatile ways God once spoke to the fathers in the prophets; in the last of these days he has spoken to us in a son."[54]

49. See Jn 1.29.

50. Mk 2.19.

51. Mk 2.20.

52. See Mt 6.6 and 6.17–18.

53. 1 Cor 9.21.

54. Heb 1.1–2. Christ is the giver of the new law, just as Moses was the giver of the old law, and the laws both of them gave may be considered laws of God. Origen cites Hebrews, in which the same God speaks in the Old Testament and the New, to demonstrate that Scripture itself makes this point.

5. Following "*Pay attention, my people, to my law*" is "*Bend your ear to the utterances of my mouth.*"[55] But this very simple distinction in it must be apprehended, if we are enabled to grasp it by your prayers. We shall speak in the plainest and clearest way as we interpret Scripture: the perfect person pays attention both to the law and to the logos, for neither is one perfected by the law without involving the logos of wisdom and of knowledge,[56] nor is it possible for a logos of wisdom to be produced within someone who is not corrected first by the law. Therefore, also in Isaiah, first, "From Zion comes forth the law," then, second, "and the logos of the Lord from Jerusalem."[57] And in one of the Twelve[58] we are enjoined to do both things in order to be perfected: both to live well and to see the logos. The wording goes like this: "Sow for yourselves in justice. Gather in the fruit of life," and following this, "Enlighten yourselves with the light of knowledge."[59]

Thus indeed our Savior and Lord, when he created the sequence for teaching, did not begin with parables or secrets, but, as it were, with lawgiving and teaching. On the hill, opening his mouth, he taught them, saying, "Blessed are the destitute in spirit, because the kingdom of the heavens is theirs,"[60] and what follows. This entire discourse was not parable, but logos, and it could seemingly be said about it, "*Pay attention, my people, to my law.*" Subsequently, after a short interval, Matthew recorded the parables, so that there might be fulfilled, on the one hand, "*Pay attention, my people, to my law,*" referring to the lawgiving of an ethical passage, but "*Bend your ears to the utterances of my mouth*" in relation to their teaching through parables, which, plainly interpreted, says, "*I will open my mouth in a parable; I will proclaim problems from a beginning.*"

Marvel at the sequence, because he did not first say, "*Bend your ear to the utterances of my mouth.*" For the first thing to learn is the law of Christ Jesus: we see how one must behave accord-

55. Ps 77.1.
56. See 1 Cor 12.8.
57. Is 2.3.
58. The short books of "Twelve [Prophets]," sometimes referred to, misleadingly, as "Minor Prophets," were treated as a single book in the Septuagint.
59. Hos 10.12.
60. See Mt 5.1–3.

ing to it. The second thing to learn: if you have the law, if you behave according to it, if you are seeking logos and wisdom, you progress in them. And elsewhere it has been marvelously written, "Do you desire wisdom? Thoroughly keep the commandments, and the Lord will supply you with it."[61] If, then, before observing the commandments we go in search of secrets, not traveling on the road, we go astray.[62]

This is responsible for the existence of heresies. For they have sought—and I will confirm that they have worn themselves out seeking—but they did not seek by a road,[63] and they did not seek purely. If they had sought rightly, first they would have corrected their conduct; first they would have been confirmed in the faith; then, after correcting their conduct, and thus making progress, they would have arrived at discourse about God and the seeking of things that are deeper and more secret. But now, without having laid a foundation in behavior, going into deeper seeking, they have given a place to the evil one to sow in their souls false logoi.

Let us not pass over "*Bend your ear to the utterances of my mouth.*"[64] We cannot bend this ear to the utterances of Christ's mouth. For Christ is not sensibly present speaking utterances, so that bending this ear,[65] we might fulfill the command spoken here, "*Bend your ear to the utterances of my mouth.*" But there is another ear in us, concerning which the Savior said, "Let the one who has ears to hear, hear."[66] We must not allow that ear to be too distant from Christ, but bend to him and offer the ear to the logos. This is the ear that the apostles bent to the utterances of Christ's mouth. Therefore, he says to them, "What you have heard in the ear, proclaim on the houses."[67]

Yet let us not pass over this: "*Pay attention, my people, to my law.*" He did not say, "the laws," but "*my law,*" so that he might say

61. Sir 1.26.

62. See PS80H2.5 below for a similar critique of those who seek secrets too soon.

63. Or "by a method." See introduction, p. 32, on the translation of *hodos.*

64. Ps 77.1b.

65. As he spoke, Origen would have touched or pointed to one of his ears. See PS77H8.4, n. 32 below.

66. Mt 11.15.

67. Mt 10.27.

that all the legislation is one and all is one law, and that it is not possible to separate law from law, for they are not plural, but the customary law is singular, just as one administers the law of Christ.

"*I will open my mouth in parables.*"[68] Opening the mouth there, he taught them before speaking parables. What he taught them was ethical conduct, so that he might fulfill "*Pay attention, my people, to my law,*" then, later, so that "*I will open my mouth in a parable*" might be fulfilled. What is said to us about the law fits also with the parable; he did not say, "*I will open my mouth in parables,*" as some of the copies of Matthew have, but, "*I will open my mouth in a parable.*"[69] For all concur on one thing; the parable is one, even as all law is one.

6. "*I will proclaim problems from a beginning.*"[70] Just as, among those who engage in Greek philosophy, there are certain problems that are proposed to those who are going to study, so that they may ponder them—either those teaching or those making trial of those who demonstrate those teachings—so there are also certain problems of Scripture. What are these? How could there have occurred three days, when neither sun, moon, nor stars had been created? For it is on the fourth day that it is recorded by Moses that the lights and the stars came into being. Again, among the "*problems from a beginning*" is how the darkness was above the abyss, but the spirit of God was above the water,[71] and why was not the spirit of God above the abyss and darkness above the water? When, then, the Savior should say, "I will proclaim problems from a beginning," hear him saying, "I will make plain problems from a beginning," for, individually, with his individual disciples he explained all the problems and spoke to them the logos concerning God.[72] Those were the problems concerning which he taught, making them plain to the disci-

68. Ps 77.2a.

69. Mt 13.35. Unlike the ascription of the passage to Isaiah rather than Asaph, small discrepancies between the Gospel and the LXX are of little concern to Origen.

70. Ps 77.2b.

71. See Gn 1.2.

72. See Mk 4.34. Note that Origen effectively defines Jesus's parables as "problems" and puts his listeners in the same position as the apostles, listening as the divine logos, now speaking through Origen, explains them.

ples, which John riddled about, saying, "I do not think that the whole cosmos could hold the books written."[73]

Take it, for the sake of argument, that as many things as the Savior said about God to the disciples had come to be recorded; if so, the cosmos would not have borne them, but it would have undergone some earthquake and disturbance. For it is said by the divine logoi that earth was shaken and heaven was altered.[74] And if we must state the cause of the earthquake that came about in the suffering of the Savior and the cause of the solar eclipse, we shall say that it was because the magnitude of the prayer to the Father was extraordinary: it even moved the elements of the cosmos.[75] Such things were truly said by the Savior that, on account of their disturbing the cosmos, often remained unspoken. And in fact the holy ones intercede with God with unspeakable groans,[76] perhaps unspeakable so that they may not move the cosmos. For even Paul, when he was going to hear unspeakable utterances, did not hear them upon earth, for the earth was going to tremble and be startled. But I very boldly say he did not hear them on the earth; he did not hear them in the first heaven; he did not hear them in the second heaven. For all these created things would have been upset if there had been said to him the unspeakable utterances while he was among these created things. I say that in relation to "*I will proclaim problems from a beginning,*" because he proclaimed the problems and

---

73. Jn 21.25. Origen expands on this idea in *Comm. Matt.* 14.12 in relation to the parable of the unforgiving servant, Mt 18.23–35: "In general, it must be borne in mind concerning every parable of which the explanation is not registered by the evangelists, that Jesus, 'apart with his own disciples, solved everything,' [Mk 4.34] so that those who were writing the Gospels concealed the clear meaning of the parables, because what was disclosed by them was greater than the nature of things written, and, in fact, each solution and the clarification of such parables was such a thing that 'the cosmos' itself 'could not contain the books written' [Jn 21.25] on such parables. But it could be searched out by a suitable heart and one containing, on account of purity, the things written about the clarification of the parables, so that, in it, they would be written 'in the spirit of the living God' [see 2 Cor 3.3]."

74. See Is 13.13.

75. See Mt 27.50–51, Lk 23.44–45. This is the power of the divine logos to make things happen as it did in the beginning of creation.

76. See Rom 8.26.

solved them for his students, but they were not recorded, for the writing of them would not be expedient for the cosmos.

7. And these things were said by the Savior, but the apostles next to him and all his students replied. And in their personae these things are said: "*As many of these things as we have heard and known*"; that is, "we know other teachings, as many as we have heard; '*as we have heard, we have known, our fathers explained*' them to us, before you came and announced them to us." "*And our fathers explained to us, it was not hidden from their children in another generation.*"[77] For they taught those after them, and they were "*proclaiming the praises of the Lord.*"[78]

What follows amounts to this: "*And our fathers explained to us, it was not hidden from their children in another generation, proclaiming the praises of the Lord and his acts of power and his marvels, that he did.*"[79] And they proclaimed to us the praises of the Lord, and they proclaimed "*his acts of power and his marvels, that he did, so that God raised up a testimony in Jacob and established a law before 'your law might come.*'"[80]

The one says: "*Pay attention, my people, to my law,*" but we hear an earlier law: and "*he set a law in Israel, as many as he commanded to our fathers.*"[81] But if indeed he commanded a law to them, but you say, "*Pay attention, my people, to my law,*" we proclaim that we distinguish two laws, "*to make them known to our children.*"[82] For this purpose he commanded the fathers to make known to their children, "*so that another generation, sons who will be given*

77. Ps 77.3b–4a.

78. Ps 77.4b.

79. Ps 77.3b and 4b.

80. "Our fathers" are the people of Israel, the "our fathers" of Heb 1.1 alluded to earlier. Since they are "our fathers," we are the "generation yet unborn." Origen sees the Psalmist as speaking in the persona of Christ, who is speaking to his disciples. They respond that "their fathers," the people of Israel, or perhaps more specifically the inspired prophets who wrote the Old Testament, proclaimed the praises of the Lord. "Your law" is the law of Christ.

81. Ps 77.5b.

82. Ps 77.5 begins with "the law" in the singular and ends with pronouns in the plural. Origen takes this to mean that God established one law for Israel, but that the prophet announced two laws, the law of Moses and "your law that should come," that of Christ.

birth."[83] Thus to a people that will be given birth, that the Lord made, Christ proclaims the great deeds of the Father.

"*And they will rise up, and they will proclaim to their sons to be born.*"[84] The people to be born are raised up from the dead and say, "We have been buried with Christ through baptism,"[85] and we will rise together with him. And that one, the one risen up, is not walking around.[86] Each, then, proclaims to children, "*so that their hope may be set on God and they may not forget God's works,*"[87] both the ones before and those at the visitation of Christ.[88]

"*And they seek out his commandments*"[89]—to "seek out" a commandment involves both understanding it and doing it—"*so that they may not become like their fathers.*"[90] And those fathers before us were not taken unawares, for our fathers were all under the cloud and all were baptized into Moses,[91] but God was not well pleased with most of them.[92] I want to learn, so that I may not become like our fathers. That was "*a crooked generation,*"[93] especially on account of the plot against the Savior, and embittered and having signs of having been embittered, "*a generation that did not straighten out its heart.*"[94] Let us learn about them and their faults, so that by learning about them we may straighten our hearts and not become like them, concerning whom it is written, "*their spirit was not set after God.*"[95] For the spirit of that generation was not set after God; they did not keep the covenant with God. But let us pray, having received the spirit of peace, to be set after God, in Christ Jesus, to whom is the glory and the might to the ages of ages. Amen.

---

83. Ps 77.6a.

84. Ps 77.6b.

85. Rom 6.4.

86. I.e., not yet alive (walking around) at the time that the prophecy was made.

87. Ps 77.7a–b.

88. While the prophecy was given before the visitation (*epidēmia*) of Christ, the command still applies.

89. Ps77.7c.

90. Ps 77.8a.

91. 1 Cor 10.1–2.

92. 1 Cor 10.5.

93. Ps 77.8b.

94. Ps 77.8c.

95. Ps 77.8d.

HOMILY 2 ON PSALM 77

T IS WORTHWHILE to establish why at this time the Scripture makes a list of sinful actions, referring the sinful activity not to the whole people, but to the sons of Ephraim alone. For it says, "*Sons of Ephraim stretching with bows turned back in the day of war; they did not keep God's covenant,*"[1] the one with David. Rehoboam, the son of Solomon, ruled them harshly, so that the sons of Israel sent to him asking for relief, but, after putting off giving an answer, he first took advice from the older counselors, who were familiar to him. And the older counselors advised him to relieve the harsh treatment of the people, so that they might willingly remain Rehoboam's subjects. But the younger ones advised the opposite, saying what gratified the king, and he took their counsel.[2] He responded this way to those who had been sent to him: "My smallness is thicker than my father's thigh. My father disciplined you with whips, but I will discipline you with scorpions."[3] And on account of that harshness ten tribes departed, with Jeroboam son of Nabat, he who caused Israel to sin, leading them.[4]

And they said as they departed, "There is for us no portion in David, nor inheritance in the son of Jesse."[5] They acted wickedly, then, because they were responsible for splitting in two the unity of the people, coming to be in schism and departing from Jerusalem. Rehoboam became responsible for this evil by ruling the people wickedly, but those also acted blessedly who, when Rehoboam was harsh, bore up and remained on account of

---

1. Ps 77.9–10a.
2. See 1 Kgs 12.4–14, 2 Chr 10.4–11.
3. See 1 Kgs 12.10–11, 2 Chr 10.10–11.
4. See 1 Kgs 22.52, 2 Kgs 1.18.
5. 1 Kgs 12.16.

God's covenant with David. For they did not say, "There is for us no portion in David, nor inheritance in the son of Jesse." Therefore, they had the temple and the altar of sacrifice, and also the Levites who had been scattered among the rest of the tribes, who did not remain in schism, came to the two remaining tribes in unity of mind, that is, with the harsh Rehoboam.

2. These narratives and these logoi, when we read them, can also help our character, but if we are enabled to go higher, it is possible that they will teach us divine secrets. First, then, we see how the narrative itself helps character. Let us say that a certain human bishop[6] is very harsh, as has occurred in former times and in other places, when a father is in charge of subordinates. If, then, such a thing should happen, troublemakers imitate the ten tribes and choose Jeroboam, son of Nabat, who caused Israel to sin, but the peaceable stay put and tolerate the harshness of Rehoboam, remaining where they are on account of David, on account of the tribe, on account of the succession, until God's foresight should either cure him or arrange what it intends.

You see, then, that the narrative is useful according to the statement. And if there have ever occurred schisms in the churches, some have come about entirely on the pretext of the sins of Rehoboam. For those who break away are imagining that they broke away because of the harshness, but those who depart from the Church, as they depart, have imitated that man, Jeroboam. Sinful actions such as this are the beginning, not just of schisms, but also of heresies.[7] But we, as the tribe of Judah, as the tribe of Benjamin, let us not depart from the Church, so that we may not turn out to be outside the people, but let us imitate their patience, seeing that if we turn back faintheartedly, we may as well say what was said then by them: "There is for us no portion in David, nor inheritance in the son of Jesse." For the one saying, "There is for us no portion in David," seemed then to be speaking about David, about that son of Jesse, but now he speaks about Christ, about whom is written, "I shall raise up for them David my

6. Origen believed that angels had the oversight of churches in addition to human bishops. See esp. *Comm. Matt.* 14.21.

7. Jeroboam's schism continues in Samaritanism. In Acts 8.5–25, Simon Magus, the archetypal Christian heretic, is from Samaria.

servant who will shepherd them."[8] And he is the one about whom it is written, about whom the prophecy says, "A rod shall come out of the root of Jesse, and a flower shall rise up out of the root, and a spirit of God will rest upon him, a spirit of wisdom and of comprehension,"[9] and so on.

And just as we are taught not to commit sexual immorality or adultery or theft, and as many other things as we always learn in the churches to depart from, so we learn never to say, "There is for us no portion in David"; we learn never to come to be in schism. For when two leaders are proposed—one who seems more sinful but does not make a schism and one who does not appear to be sinful but makes a schism—it is highly preferable to accept the more sinful rather than one whom we imagine to be just when he separates and divides God's people. Do you see, then, that the Scripture ascribes the whole sinfulness of the people to Ephraim on account of Jeroboam and it says that all these sinners are sons of Ephraim on account of Jeroboam? And just as the sons who are corrected are called "of Abraham"—for the Savior taught this[10]—so all who are involved in schisms, all who are sinning, all who have forgotten the commandments of God and his mighty acts are, we say, Jeroboam and the sons of Ephraim.

3. In many places, then, we might find in prophecies something said about Ephraim, particularly in the prophet Hosea, about the rest of whose oracles it is said, because they are difficult to grasp and not easy to grasp for anyone: "Who is wise and understands these things, or understanding and apprehends them?"[11] And I can recall just a few prophecies where Hosea

8. Ezek 34.23.

9. Is 11.1–2.

10. See Jn 8.39.

11. In *Fr. Ps.* 4.7 Origen refers to Hos 14.10 to illustrate that when we see "Who is …?" the implied answer is "Scarcely anyone." Hosea is notoriously difficult in Hebrew, and translating it into Greek did not make it easier. Only here in these homilies does Origen provide an extended, phrase-by-phrase interpretation of a passage other than the assigned Psalm. He probably had the text of Hosea in his hands as he went through it. Conceivably the phrases about "grasping" Hosea were a spontaneous response to some awkwardness handling the codex; more likely Origen is referring to an earlier discussion with one or more

names Ephraim, so that we see there, in particular, how they grasped the name of Ephraim. The Lord says there: "When I turned the captivity of my people, when I healed Israel, both the injustice of Ephraim and the evil of Samaria were revealed, because they carried out lies, and a thief shall enter him, a bandit shall rob on his road, whenever they are singing together as singers in their hearts."[12] What, then, do these things in Hosea intend concerning Ephraim, so that we may understand in a loftier way the saying, "*sons of Ephraim stretching with bows and shooting arrows*"?[13] From the tribe of Ephraim, when the ten tribes separated from Jeroboam, he did not just make a separation, but, making sure that they not have the temple and its association with Rehoboam as a motive to return, he made up out of his heart feasts that differed from the feasts of God and also made two golden calves and placed them in the allotment of the ten tribes.[14]

What, then, does Scripture want to say in this? That, as a general principle, those who make a schism from love of rule undergo this thing: they are not satisfied with having made a schism, but they want to introduce some novelty in teaching, so that, through the novelty, scouring away things associated with the Church, they lord it over those who have been led astray by an imagined truth.[15] A token of the novelty is the feast made up out of Jeroboam's heart, for, as if they were fabricating for themselves celebrations and feasts, those innovators introduce a different teaching apart from that of the Church. And, just so, they make golden calves, a farm animal, working the earth (while gold is a token of the mind).[16] Out of their own mind

---

persons reading Hosea who found it difficult. The seemingly tautologous "hard to grasp"/"not easy to grasp" paraphrases the parallel clauses of Hos 14.10. See n. 67 below.

12. Hos 6.11–7.2.

13. Ps 77.9a.

14. See 1 Kgs 12.28.

15. In keeping with a tradition that identified a Samaritan, Simon Magus of Acts 8.9–25, as the first heretic, Origen associates Samaria with heresy elsewhere in his writings, notably in *Hom. Ezech.* 9.1 and *Comm. Jo.* 3.6.39.

16. Origen understands gold as a "token," *sumbolon,* of the mind because smelting metal is a common biblical image for the process of separating the

they make up fables, ages, and yokefellows, or different gods—
one god of the law, another god of the Gospel—and untimely births, soul transfers, various denials, and whatever else they
make up.[17]

Those who separated then from the people and were attending feasts made up by Jeroboam are a token of the heretics who
separate from the Church. Attend to the statement, because the
prophecy refers to such people: "When I turned the captivity of
my people, when I healed Israel. And the injustice of Ephraim
will be revealed." I am speaking of the heresies when they bring
in and hide their teaching by a fantasy of secrets. But this es-
capes notice as long as the genuine Israel has not been con-
verted, as long as the souls of those who read or hear are not
healed; but should they be healed and learn genuine things,
then the secrets of the heretics will appear to be made-up things
that have nothing to do with salvation.[18]

4. And we know this from personal experience, for when we
were young the heresies were flourishing, and there seemed to
be many gathered in them. So many were starving for Christ's
lessons, not being supplied with enough teachers in the Church,
that on account of the famine they imitated those who eat human flesh during a famine;[19] separating from the sound logos,
they paid attention to any logoi whatsoever, and their teaching
was cobbled together. But when the grace of God brought to
light more teaching, the heresies were daily demolished, and
things they considered unspeakable were made into an example and shown to be blasphemies and irreverent and godless
logoi.[20] Therefore, it is said in the prophecy, "When I turned

---

mind from worthless, earthly things. See esp. 1 Cor 3.12–13. Heresies pervert
the mind, concerning it solely with earthly things. See Col 3.1–3.

17. In the preceding homily, Origen discussed the Marcionites; the description here is more appropriate to Valentinians.

18. Origen paraphrases the text he has quoted from Hosea in such a way as
to apply it to heretics with whom he is familiar.

19. Cannibalism during times of famine was notorious. Origen uses this image to speak of those who substitute a fleshly logos for the divine logos that
Christians feed on when they come together. Origen already has in mind the
discussion of feeding on the logos that he will give shortly in PS77H4 below.

20. Irenaeus's *Against Heresies*, written shortly before Origen was born, refuted

the captivity of my people, when I healed Israel. And the injustice of Ephraim was revealed and the injustice of Samaria."

Samaria is figuratively the mother city of the heresies,[21] the mother city where Jeroboam son of Nabat, who "caused Israel to sin,"[22] made his home. But, to be sure that the logos is about heresies, pay attention to "that they performed falsehoods."[23] But also what follows is even plainer in referring to heresies: "and the thief came into it."[24] You have it on John's part, in the Gospel, that those not receiving the divine oracles lawfully, but exploiting them wickedly, are thieves and robbers: "For, as many as came before me," it says, "all were thieves and robbers, and the sheep did not hear them."[25] And "a thief," then, "will come in to him." If you were to hear what the Apostle has said, what the Gospel has said, know that those statements they are using are like stolen goods.[26] And just as when you recognize what is yours being used by a thief, you know that a thief has what belongs to you—for you have them legally—so if you see them being used by the heretics, by comparing the wording, hear them as if they were goods being used by thieves.

A thief, then, comes in to Ephraim according to the saying: "A thief will come in to him," and "a robbing bandit" does not "come in," but "a robbing bandit" does come in to the heresies, for a robbing bandit comes in to masquerade as the Lord Jesus

---

those he considered heretics by exposing their secret teachings in detail. Though written in Gaul, Origen could have known and used it since it quickly reached Egypt; see Colin H. Roberts, *Manuscript, Society and Belief in Early Christian Egypt* (London: The British Academy, 1979), 23 and 53–54. Eusebius tells how Origen became familiar with heretical ideas as a young man in Alexandria (*Hist. eccl.* 6.2.14); dedicated himself to teaching (*Hist. eccl.* 6.8.6); convinced his patron, Ambrosius, to abandon Valentinianism; and gained, as a teacher, the respect of heretics (*Hist. eccl.* 6.18.1–2).

21. See especially *Comm. Jo.* 13.13.82.

22. 1 Kgs 22.52.

23. Hos 7.1.

24. Ibid.

25. Jn 10.8.

26. The Church owns the Gospels and Epistles, so, when heretics cite them, they are, in legal terms, stealing. Origen's older contemporary, Tertullian, in *On the Prescription of Heretics,* argued in similarly legal terms that heretics have no right to Scripture.

Christ. By this imagined Christ they rob Christ, but it is not really Christ, for they offer an Antichrist, robbing Christ from you. Is it not an Antichrist, being called by Christ's name, but without the truth about Christ? But the truth is about Christ: he was born of a virgin. Antichrist: he was not born at all. The truth is about Christ: he had a body just like ours, so that he might save us. Antichrist: his body was spiritual. Christ was prophesied by the prophets. Antichrist, never. Furthermore, our Lord Jesus, proclaimed ahead of time by the prophets, is the Christ Jesus of the Creator of heaven and earth, but not of some higher and good god. A thief then accosts him, a robbing bandit. Therefore, pay attention, so that a thief may not rob you. If you want not to be robbed by the thief, do not go down from Jerusalem to Jericho. If you go down, leaving Jerusalem, for Jericho, the thief finds you and robs you.[27]

"A thief," then, "will come in to him, and a bandit robbing on his road."[28] Do not be in the bandit's road! There is no bandit on your road: "I am the road and the truth and the life."[29] Travel on this, and no bandit molests you. "Three things are impossible for me to perceive,[30] the roads of a snake on a rock."[31] The road of a snake on a rock cannot be perceived: the road of the snake who is an adverse power on Christ, the rock, "For the rock was Christ,"[32] for it is the road of a snake on a rock that cannot be perceived. "A robbing bandit," then, "is in his road;

27. The reference is to Lk 10.30, the parable of the Good Samaritan as Origen interpreted it. See PS73H1.2 above.

28. Hos 7.1.

29. Jn 14.6.

30. Origen has given his congregation tools for detecting the road of an Antichrist, "a snake" on Christ, "a rock." *Noēsai* is a form of the verb *noeō*, closely related to the noun *nous*, "mind" or "intelligence." Often, when Origen uses it, *noeō* is best translated "understand" (put one's mind to), but it can simply mean "mind" in the sense of "perceive" or "be aware of," much as we say, "Mind your manners" or "Mind the step." One does not "perceive" the road of a snake on a rock because it does not leave a track. Similarly, most Christians cannot perceive heresy because the heretics quote Scripture and appear to honor Christ (compare Augustine, *Confessions* 3.6). The *Dialogue with Heraclides* shows that Origen was a recognized heresy detective.

31. Prv 30.18–19.

32. 1 Cor 10.4.

nonetheless, they sing together as ones singing together in their heart."[33] How hard to perceive they are before they have been detected! But pray that we may perceive such things! This is how they rob; this is how a thief accosts him: "nonetheless, they sing together as singers." They do not actually sing, but they imitate singers. They imitate those who hymn God, not hymning him but "speaking injustice in a high place."[34]

5. But let us postulate, as someone hearing interpretations like this might suspect, that we are forcing the statement and manipulating it to refer to heretics. Show us next what to do with: "In their hearts they made kings glad and, with their falsehoods, rulers."[35] The children of Ephraim "in their hearts made kings glad." Which ones? Must it not have been those about whom it is written, "The kings of the earth stood by, and the rulers gathered in the same place against the Lord and against his Christ"?[36] And "rulers with their falsehoods." In the earlier statement they performed falsehoods, but here they made rulers glad with their falsehoods. For they make glad with their falsehoods the rulers of this age, whose wisdom is being brought to naught.[37] And just as, when we honor the truth, we distress the rulers of this age, so, when we tell lies in our hearts, with their own falsehoods we make emperors and magistrates glad.[38]

Postulate that we have forced the second statement by referring it to those who adhere to the heresies. And what about the third? Hear it: "Ephraim has become a loaf baked in ashes left unturned."[39] Hear the heretics: "The adherents of the Church are children, fools, and irreverent; these are the ones about whom it is written: 'I gave you milk to drink, not solid

33. Hos 7.1–2.

34. Ps 72.8b. "Singing" is a sacred activity; see PS67H2.2 above. The heretics only imitate singers, "singing *as* singers."

35. Hos 7.3.

36. Ps 2.2.

37. See 1 Cor 2.6.

38. For "rulers of this age" see 1 Cor 2.8. *Basileus,* "king," is also the term for the Roman emperor, and *archōn,* "ruler," the term for a Roman governor, the chief magistrate and judge of a province. Origen applies the words of the Psalm to witnessing the truth before Roman magistrates who would demand that Christians "perform falsehood" by offering incense to the emperor as a false god.

39. Hos 7.8.

food.'[40] But with us are the unwritten and hidden things of God, as many things as Jesus taught his students individually." That is why, then, it is said, "Ephraim has become a loaf baked in ashes left unturned"; so the "loaf baked in ashes" emphasizes the promise of hidden things on their part, but "left unturned" is the equivalent of "not having a change of heart."

"Aliens have devoured his strength, but he himself did not know."[41] No alien eats what belongs to Ephraim, but the aliens to the truth make use of that bread.[42] But let us pray—hearing the one who says, "I am the living bread who came down from heaven; the one who eats this bread will live to the age"[43]— not to eat other bread than the bread of truth belonging to the Church, which God gave to the holy ones, about whom it is possible to say, "My God, the one nourishing me from my youth."[44]

And in fact, when we pray, we say, "If the Lord God be with me and give me the bread to eat,"[45] for Jacob did not say, "Give me bread to eat" that all men eat, but "the" bread that God gives. For God gives Christ, real bread, nourishment for the worthy, just as to that man, Jacob.

6. Let us also see another statement concerning Ephraim: "And Ephraim was a mindless dove, not having a heart; he summoned Egypt and went forth to Assyria."[46] The Holy Spirit is a dove that has a mind, but, by analogy to the Antichrist, the unholy spirit, nonetheless posing as holy, is a mindless dove not having a heart. And just as Antichrist calls himself by the name of Christ, not having Christ, so one who does not have the Holy Spirit says, "The Lord says these things," by an evil spirit. He

40. 1 Cor 3.2.

41. Hos 7.9.

42. I.e., the loaf baked in ashes.

43. Jn 6.51.

44. Gn 48.15. Origen does not mention that the citation comes from Jacob's blessing of Ephraim. When Joseph's two sons kneel before Jacob, he crosses his hands to give Ephraim a greater blessing than Joseph's firstborn son, Manasseh. Origen probably saw this blessing as somehow foreshadowing the defection of the tribe of Ephraim.

45. See Gn 28.20, Jacob's prayer after the vision of the ladder. This is the first time, according to Origen, that the Bible speaks of prayer. See *Or.* 3.1. The Greek version of the Lord's Prayer also speaks of "the" bread. See *Or.* 27.1–6.

46. Hos 7.11.

[Hosea] says, then, about the spirit among them, "And Ephraim was a mindless dove, not having a heart."

But what does it summon? A dove summons Jerusalem to us,[47] but the mindless dove, Ephraim, summoned Egypt, the nation that is hostile to the people of God. But God threatens them, "As they go forth, I will cast my net over them, and I will bring them down like the birds of heaven."[48] When they are elevated and say, "Fly!"[49] you need to know that, just as according to the law of Moses, it is possible for one bird to be clean and another unclean,[50] so according to the secret logos,[51] the dove of the Church is clean, as is any other elevated thing in the Church,[52] but carrion-eating vultures[53] and whatever is equivalent to them is unclean, lofty things lifted up against the knowledge of God.[54] So God pulls down the unclean things: "I will bring them down like the birds of heaven; I will educate them in the hearing of their affliction."[55] God is a lover of humanity and intends to cleanse and educate the adherents of heresies. How many do

47. Reading *peristera* instead of *peristeran*. A dove perching on Noah's ark is the common North African visual image of the Church.

48. Hos 7.12.

49. "*Petason*," "spread [your wings]" sounds like the word that means "bird" in the Septuagint, *peteinos*. Perhaps the heretics say, "Spread your wings and fly!" as a motivational speaker might do today. Plotinus similarly criticized overweening "gnostics" in *Enn.* 2.9.9: "Then the respectable person must go up in a measured way without boorishness, only so far as our nature is able, and consider that there is space for others alongside God and not placing oneself alone with God, as if one were flying in dreams, in that way keeping oneself from becoming as much like God as is possible for a human soul." In relation to this passage from Plotinus, Pierre Hadot cites Pascal's *Pensée* 358, "Qui veut faire l'ange fait la bête" ("he who wants to make angel, makes beast"), in *Plotinus and the Simplicity of Vision,* trans. Arnold L. Davidson (Chicago: University of Chicago Press, 1993), 21. Hadot's translator, Arnold Davidson, points out that "flying in dreams" comes from Plato, *Theaetetus* 158b. Origen may also have been alluding to such high-flyers who "think they are gods."

50. See Lv 11, Dt 14.19–20.

51. The "secret logos" is the law spiritually understood.

52. Origen's own elevated teachings fit this classification.

53. Origen thought that the prohibition against eating a vulture, something no one would think of doing, was a hint Moses wove into the law to encourage close readers to look beyond the literal sense. See *Princ.* 4.3.2.

54. See 2 Cor 10.5.

55. Hos 7.12.

we have here who have been pulled down from the heresies, caught in Christ's nets![56] "As they go forth, I will cast my net over them, and I will bring them down like the birds of heaven; I will educate them in the hearing of their affliction."

Next the logos threatens those who are being educated: "Woe to them, because they wandered from me"—they wandered from the Church and from the truth—"They are wretched because they spoke irreverently about me. I ransomed them, but they spoke falsehoods against me."[57] Are you still in doubt that the sons of Ephraim are speaking to the heterodox? "They spoke falsehoods against me." All right, look at what they say: "The creator[58] is savage, the creator is inhumane, there is another, higher, good god."[59] They speak ill, then, and say a multitude of such things: "They spoke falsehoods against me." Hear more about the sons of Ephraim from Hosea: "They have considered evil things towards me, they have turned around towards nothing."[60] They have abandoned things that are and have departed for nothing.[61] A god above the creator is nothing; a Christ who was not born of a virgin by a visitation in this life is nothing. They have turned around toward this "nothing."

Next see what sorts of things he [Hosea] threatens against their bishops and those who expound heresies: "and their rul-

---

56. Origen implies that he, like the apostles, is a fisher of human beings, but this time he casts nets in the sky.

57. Hos 7.13.

58. *Dēmiourgos.* Plato (*Timaeus* 37b) wrote of a *dēmiourgos,* "demiurge" or "maker," who brings time and space into order as the moving image of eternity. Valentinus and others adopted the term, without the positive evaluation of the cosmos that Plato and his followers shared with Origen, to distinguish the God of the Hebrew Scriptures, maker of a flawed cosmos, from the God of the New Testament, whom Jesus proclaimed.

59. In *Hom. Jer.* 1.16, Origen also says that heretics call the god who gave the Mosaic law "savage" and "inhumane" (*agrios* and *apanthrōpos*). They do so because they fail to recognize that Scripture has a deeper sense. Simpler Christians are guilty of the same fault. In *Princ.* 4.2.1 Origen commends simpler Christians for understanding that there is no higher God than the creator (*dēmiourgos*), but accuses them of believing worse things about God than one would believe about the most bloodthirsty and unjust of human beings.

60. Hos 7.15–16.

61. By seeking precipitously after divine mysteries, the heretics end up with nothing. See PS80H2.5 below.

ers[62] will fall on a blade on account of the lack of education of their tongues."[63] What sort of blade? "For God's logos is living and active and sharper than any two-edged sword."[64] He goes on to say about them: they have been made "like an eagle upon the house of the Lord."[65] Just as rapacious eagles come upon flocks, so that they may snatch the kids or lambs, in the same way the heretics come upon the house of the Lord, the Church, like eagles intending to snatch someone. Concerning them, then, he says: "and they have transgressed my covenant and have dishonored my law."[66] You will find that nearly all the heretics are of the same mind, dishonoring the law of Moses and the god who gave the law. We have other things to present as evidence, but, from these things you have grasped while reading Hosea, you will find thousands of things about Ephraim; however, these things have been grasped[67] sufficiently as concerns "*Sons of Ephraim stretching with bows and shooting arrows turned back in a day of war.*"[68]

7. The narrative[69] does not include a mention that those sons of Ephraim, those under Jeroboam, came to be tightening and shooting with arrows. But if you see in what way the utterances of the heterodox are a wounding dart,[70] you will understand also what is said in the Psalms. You will see that they have become sons of Ephraim, tightening and shooting arrows. "See, the sinners have tightened a bow and have readied arrows in a quiver so as to shoot down in the dark of the moon," because

62. *Archontes.* See n. 38 above.

63. Hos 7.16. Origen unexpectedly omits the phrase "they became like a stretched bow," a verbal link between Hosea 7 and Psalm 77.

64. Heb 4.12.

65. Hos 8.1.

66. Ibid.

67. Origen signals the end of his lengthy excursus on Hosea 7 by again repeatedly using forms of *lambanō: elabete,* "you have grasped," and *elēphthē,* "have been grasped." See n. 11 above. Here he indicates that this remarkable excursus has been sufficient to help those who do further reading in the prophet. In Origen's usage the verb *lambanō,* which can be translated, "take," "receive," or "grasp," when used, as here, with forms of the verb *heuriskō,* "find," recalls Jesus's promise, "Everyone who asks, receives; the one who seeks, finds ..." (Mt 7.8).

68. Ps 77.9.

69. I.e., the passage in Hosea just discussed.

70. See Jer 9.8.

they cannot shoot "the upright in heart"[71] in the light.

But when did they turn back? "*In a day of war.*"[72] The whole day of this age is then a "*day of war,*" for war does not merely happen in life, but, certainly, in the day of war peace ceases in their souls. For then they turn and tighten and shoot arrows.

And "*they did not keep God's covenant*";[73] the sons of Ephraim alone failed to do this—for all who pay attention to logoi outside the Church are sons of Ephraim—and these did not keep his covenant, but stepped outside the old covenant, by which our Lord Jesus Christ is prophesied, as he himself teaches, saying, "If you believed in Moses, you would have believed in me, for he wrote about me."[74] He himself teaches, saying, in the parable of the Gospel, "They have Moses and the prophets, let them hear them."[75] And the Gospel was produced, according to the saying, "from the mouth of the holy ones from an age, God's prophets."[76]

The sons of Ephraim, those in schism, those in heresy, "*did not keep God's covenant, and in his law they did not intend to walk.*"[77] We make steps in the law of God, in the genuine one, not in the figurative one.[78] Then let the Jews have the figurative law, even though they cannot keep it either. Where is service[79] to God? But we have that service—because we know that the law is spiritual[80]—and in God's law we walk, "for the Jew is not the one in appearance, and circumcision is of the heart in spirit, not letter, whose praise is not from human beings but from God."[81]

"*And they have disregarded his good works.*"[82] Look at the heretics; see if "they have disregarded his good works" does not fit exactly what is said about them by the prophet: enjoying heaven

71. Ps 10.2.

72. Ps 77.9

73. Ps 77.10.

74. Jn 5.46.

75. The parable of the rich man and Lazarus, Lk 16.29.

76. Lk 1.70.

77. Ps 77.10.

78. I.e., in the Gospel, not in the Law of Moses.

79. That is, divine service in the Temple.

80. Rom 7.14.

81. Rom 2.28–29.

82. Ps 77.11a.

and earth, seeing such great spectacles, they say, "Let us malign the creator[83] and the cosmos, and let us turn back to nothing"[84]— when they ought, as they see what are observed to be things understood by means of the things made from the creation of the cosmos,[85] to ascend from these and say, "If these things are so great in what is temporary and of short duration, how great must be those things that God has prepared for those who love him,[86] the age-long things?"—"*They have disregarded his good works and his marvels, which he demonstrated to them.*"[87] The marvelous things of God are not only those in the Scriptures, but these as well; we are no longer marveling on account of familiarity, since all the marvelous things are present to the logos of the one who chooses to observe them.

Or is it not marvelous that every day the sun rises from the place of rising and, in twelve hours, revolving around such a great heaven, goes into the place of setting? Why is it not marvelous that the moon, in its motion, sometimes flees from the sun and sometimes approaches the sun, for it must have a purpose in conjunction with the sun, although the beginning is to be standing away from the sun, so that the two lights, dividing and uniting, nourish plants and animals upon the earth? But why is it not marvelous that the sun has charge of the magnitude of days and nights, and sometimes it expands the days, sometimes reduces them, the reduction at the time when we require more nightly restoration, the expansion at the time when we can have the use of more light (for the light is greater at the time of a harvest day)? I have not yet said what can be said about the Bear that stands still in the sky,[88] so that pilots who travel through the sea, which does not have a path, nor a track nor road, when they look with comprehension at the sky and the stars, see where they are and where they are going, and how the stars always show them. And, observing, they can see more

---

83. *Dēmiourgon.* See n. 58 above.
84. That is, in Hos 7.16.
85. Rom 1.20.
86. 1 Cor 2.9.
87. Ps 77.11.
88. I. e., the North Star in Ursa Minor.

than just the positions of the stars; those who are clever about these things are enabled, as they handle them well, to see that all things are God's marvels.[89]

I have not yet descended in the logos to the earth, so that I might explain the marvels there as well. A grain of wheat is sown and a sprout appears within so many months, and the same thing happens in the case of many other seeds. Or is this not marvelous? For if we had never observed it—but someone told us, while showing us a grain of wheat, "Look at this, this is going to rise up and increase a hundredfold, to increase sixtyfold, or to increase thirtyfold"[90]—we would not have believed that this one grain could make so much wheat. But in this way God always demonstrates his marvels to us, so that we may believe even about the resurrection and not draw the conclusion that we are believing in impossible things. If someone says: "How are corpses raised, in what sort of body will they come?" the Apostle answers him and says: "Thoughtless person, in your case, what you sow, it will not be made alive if it does not die, and what you sow, it is not the body that it will become, but you sow a bare seed, which might happen to be of wheat or something else, but God gives it a body as he has willed, and to each of the seeds its own particular body."[91]

But the sons of Ephraim did not cherish "*the marvels that he performed before their fathers.*"[92] For you will find them saying about the law and the covenant, "'The old things have passed away; see, the new things have come to be';[93] what is Moses any more to me?" I myself once heard, when Deuteronomy was being read in the church, some hearers saying, "This is a gathering[94] of

---

89. This whole discussion is a commentary on Gn 1.14–19. Implicitly appealing to discoveries of Hellenistic astronomy, Origen argues that the stars work in complex and wonderful ways to help us. They are not demonic powers hindering our release from a hostile cosmos, as some whom he considered heretics taught. See, for example, *Apocryphon of John* 10.27–11.33.

90. See Mt 13.8 and 13.23.

91. See 1 Cor 15.35–38.

92. Ps 77.12a.

93. 2 Cor 5.17.

94. Or "synagogue," *sunagōgē*. This is both the word that Origen uses for Christian gatherings and the ordinary word for a Jewish synagogue.

Jews. It is being read as if there were no Gospels to read!"[95] But did not that person see that our Savior and Lord put great reliance on Deuteronomy, because, from Deuteronomy, when he was wrestling[96] with the devil, did he not say these things: "You shall prostrate yourself before the Lord your God, and him only you shall serve,"[97] and, "A human being shall not live on bread alone, but by every utterance proceeding from the mouth of God a human being shall live"?[98] And he took, "You shall not put the Lord your God to the test,"[99] from Deuteronomy. So, when the Savior was relying on ancient things and the Apostle was teaching that when the veil is taken away, we shall read them with unveiled face,[100] am I about to take away the ancient things?

I, then, do recall *"the marvels"* he performed *"before the fathers in the land of Egypt, in the plain of Zoan,"*[101] and I seek to understand Egypt, so that I may see the signs that always do come about in Egypt. For when does God not deliver the people from the land of Egypt? When does he not say, "I am the one who led you out of the land of Egypt, out of the house of slavery"?[102] When does he not deliver souls from the furnace of iron,[103] from the furnace of sin, so that he might lead them out through many struggles, through many marvels, through heavenly bread,[104] through water from the rock—the rock was Christ[105]—to the holy promise, in Christ Jesus, to whom is the glory and the might to the ages of ages. Amen.

95. Origen defends Deuteronomy as he is wrapping up his homily. This suggests that he is recounting an incident that recently happened in his own congregation. We do not know how common it was to read and expound the Old Testament during Christian assemblies.

96. Origen assimilates Jesus's temptations to our "wrestling" in Eph 6.12.

97. Mt 4.10, Dt 6.13.

98. Mt 4.4, Dt 8.3.

99. Mt 4.7, Dt 6.16.

100. See 2 Cor 3.18. The heretics appeal to Paul. Origen does not bother explaining that Paul actually valued the Old Testament.

101. Ps 77.12.

102. Ex 20.2. The heretics do not realize that the deeds described in Exodus, like those described in Hosea, are ever-present realities.

103. Dt 4.20, Jer 11.4.

104. See Ps 77.24.

105. 1 Cor 10.4.

HOMILY 3 ON PSALM 77

HE SIMPLE, hearing these things and learning how, in the case of the people long ago, *"breaking apart a sea,"* God *"led them,"* and how *"the waters stood apart like a wineskin,"* and that *"he guided them in a cloud by day and for the whole night by an illumination of fire,"*[1] consider blessed those who have seen such signs and portents, but they suppose that they have obtained less than those people did, because they have not observed such things. We have all been taught that there are different kinds of signs and portents; some are bodily signs and portents, but others are spiritual signs and portents. And to the extent that spirit differs from body, so much more effective and helpful are spiritual signs in comparison with bodily signs. Therefore, if, hypothetically, God himself should propose a bargain and give someone the choice to take the one he wants, as he once gave to David,[2] and, in bargaining with us, he should say, "I will do you one of two favors, either spiritual signs concerning something or bodily ones," the unsophisticated and faithless, who would not believe without signs and portents, would choose the bodily ones, but the experienced person who does not believe in God because of these things would without doubt choose the spiritual signs.

In what we have now, it says, *"He broke apart the sea and led them through."* Why is it a big thing, that God should break apart a bodily sea and guide me through? But if you understand the sea of life and the waves in life, and the bitterness and brine of the business of life, you will be enabled, having been benefited by God to understand in what way it is not a bodily Pharaoh who

1. Ps 77.13–14.
2. See 2 Sm 24.12.

pursues me, nor bodily Egyptians, and, when you understand that, you will be enabled to flee Pharaoh. What else should I pray for than that God may break apart the sea of the business of life and make the waves stand like a wineskin, and that I may pass through all things that have become walls on my right and on my left?[3] And I would want to see the Egyptians pursuing me, the spiritual Egyptians, thrown into the sea, so that, as I go through the Red Sea when God has opened it for me, I may be enabled to say, "Let us sing to the Lord, he has been glorified gloriously, the horse and rider"—not the bodily things but spiritual things of wickedness[4]—"he has thrown into the sea,"[5] so that I may be enabled to say: "he has become for me a helper and protector for salvation."[6]

If you ever read about signs and portents, either in matters that occurred according to the old covenant or those that occurred in Christ's presence, see that you do not become like that hard-hearted and bodily people seeking signs and portents,[7] preferring material and bodily ones to better, spiritual ones. Bodily signs are nothing compared to these. The ones will make the faithless faithful, but the others will help the faithful and experienced as much as is possible. Therefore, if we ever see ourselves beside the sea in persecutions, in afflictions, in dangers, in tight circumstances,[8] let us pray as well that God may break apart the sea of such situations and lead us through without suffering any harm and make those waters stand aside, restrained as in a wineskin, and guide us in a cloud by day and for the whole night by an illumination of fire.

2. For it is possible to speak in two ways about these things; it says in a bodily way to be guided by a bodily cloud by day, but the soul is not helped, for it does not see a genuine light. But if you

3. See Ex 14.22.

4. See Eph 6.12.

5. Ex 15.1.

6. Ex 15.2. If Christians in Origen's congregation sang the Song of Moses, he is showing them the disposition they should have.

7. This echoes various gospel criticisms of those who seek signs in wonders, especially Jn 4.48, which links such a desire to lack of faith.

8. See 2 Cor 6.4.

understand a spiritual cloud, a better one, the translucent[9] one, seated on which the Savior is prophesied to visit Egypt,[10] you will see that it secures to us a great help and salvation that such a cloud is sent from God to guide us. And the cloud is present now and guides us, if, in fact, we are in the light of the day, and this cloud oversees us, so that there may be applied to us the blessing that says, "The sun shall not burn you by day, nor the moon by night."[11] It leads us, and whenever there are dark and distressing things, it covers us in an illumination of fire. For an intelligible fire appears, the one about which the Savior said, "I have come to throw a fire upon the earth, and would that it were already kindled."[12] And when this fire appears, we are led, since we are not in darkness, even though the surroundings are darkness as far as others are concerned, but we see daylight.

For this reason the intelligible fire, the one that was even in Egypt, this also is produced when the people of God are being led. Why was it in Egypt? Palpable darkness constrained all the Egyptians, and no one even saw his neighbor, but there was light for them alone among all those who were dwelling there.[13] Something like this occurs also when we walk the road; the cosmos has been darkened and all things are full of ignorance, but we alone, wrestling "against the spiritual matters of wickedness" and "the cosmic dominators of this darkness,"[14] we are not in the darkness, but in a light, on account of the genuine light, even our Lord Christ Jesus.

3. But even as he "*broke apart a rock in a wilderness and gave them drink in a great abyss*,"[15] God breaks open rocks now in the des-

---

9. *Kouphos* ordinarily means "light" as opposed to "heavy," but Origen takes it in the extended sense of "insubstantial." The "light" or insubstantial cloud is sufficiently transparent for the logos, the genuine light, to shine through it.

10. See Is 19.1. A prophecy of judgment is transformed into an assurance of God's presence in hard situations, lightening our darkness.

11. Ps 120.6.

12. Lk 12.49.

13. See Ex 10.21–23.

14. Eph 6.12. Origen preached these homilies on the eve of the attempt by the Emperor Decius to compel all Romans to sacrifice to the emperor. He was preparing his congregation for trouble.

15. Ps 77.15.

ert of the cosmos and gives us waters in a waterless place. Who, reading these Scriptures,[16] especially the more difficult passages, will not say that these things are dry, without resources as to water, without resources for finding something to drink? But, even so, if God should grant, the rock, the hardness of the Scriptures, is struck and waters come out and rivulets flow down. For God "*broke apart a rock in a wilderness and gave*" us "*drink as in a great abyss and brought forth water from a rock.*"[17] Who, on seeing Christ Jesus, about whom it has been written, "We saw him, and he did not have either form or beauty, but his form was dishonorable, abandoned by the sons of human beings, a human being in a calamity and in trouble and knowing how to bear infirmity,"[18] would not say, "This is a rock. What can this do?" But, even so, from that one see how great rivers come out and stream down through all the inhabited world, so that, for instance, today, the churches under heaven are drinking, in remembrance[19] of the resurrection of Christ Jesus, from the water that came out of that rock, about which some said, "We saw him, and he did not have either form or beauty." He then is the rock, as it says, "but the rock was Christ."[20]

God "*has brought down waters like rivers*";[21] if, then, he should wish also now to bring down from the heavens above "*waters like rivers,*" he brings them down. When all these things have happened, we are sinners again, and they are crossed out. For it is written, not in order that we should see that the people sinned, but so that we will also see to it that we do not do so ourselves, "*and they continued to sin against him, they embittered the Highest in a waterless place.*"[22] If, after this gathering, after this teaching, after this exhortation, after logoi of warning, we sin again as soon as we leave, willfully forgetting the logoi nurturing us and the

16. Perhaps Origen held up the codex he had in his hand to make this point.

17. Ps 77.15–16a.

18. Is 53.2–3.

19. See Lk 22.19, 1 Cor 11.24–25. This indicates that Origen is preaching on Sunday, when churches throughout the *oikoumenē* were celebrating the Eucharist. Origen regularly associates the Eucharist with teaching from Scripture.

20. 1 Cor 10.4.

21. Ps 77.16b.

22. Ps 77.17.

water from the rock, are we not also embittering the Highest in a waterless place, and are we not "tempting God in our hearts," and are we not saying these things, just as it is recorded that they were said then, "*when they asked for food for their souls*"?[23]

4. Therefore, we often do not believe that God would give us food in this desert. And being without resources and despairing of nourishment, since we do not see sensible nourishment, do we rail against God and say, "*Can God not prepare a table in the desert? Since he struck the rock and waters flowed and rivulets gushed down*"?[24] If we have even been given drink, should we not, it would seem, be enabled to share nourishment? "*Can he not*" also "*give bread, or prepare a table for his people?*"[25] But hear, just because we despair of his being able to prepare a table in the desert, he does not take us to task for our sins, but, having made a table full of spiritual foods, he sets it before us.

About this table we have learned such things as this: "When you sit to dine at a table of nobles, understand carefully what is set before you, and put out your hand, knowing that such things ought to be set before you."[26] We say, then, "*or can he prepare a table in the desert?*" And we say in addition, "*Because of this the Lord heard and was put off, and fire was kindled in Jacob.*"[27] If there is unbelief anywhere, fire is there, for the fiery darts of the evil one[28] come upon the unbelieving. If fire was kindled in Jacob then, it is all the more so now. Whenever we sin, fire will be kindled. And that fire was sensible; it did not harm the soul. But the fire now, when it is kindled, procures death for us, not such a death as they[29] died, according to what happened in token to them, but an age-long death. Therefore, let us not lack faith in God, so

23. Ps 77.18.

24. Ps 77.19–20a.

25. Ps 77.20b.

26. Prv 23.1–2. Origen does not say why he here cites another text that speaks of sitting at table for a meal. Probably his students would be familiar with an exposition of this verse that he had given elsewhere. A comment on these verses by Evagrius Ponticus is suggestive: "For not all can accommodate the more secret meaning of the Scripture" (*Scholion* 250 in SC 340, p. 346).

27. Ps 77.21a.

28. Eph 6.16.

29. "They," that is, the people of Israel who perished in the wilderness.

that fire may not be kindled in us and "*wrath arise upon Israel.*"[30] Let not, then, wrath arise upon us; let the Holy Spirit arise! For when it finds us more humble, wrath arises upon us; but when it should arise, why does wrath arise? If a fire is kindled. But why fire is kindled must be learned.

5. Because it says, "*They did not have faith in God, nor did they hope in his salvation.*"[31] It is well to believe, not just "God," but "in God." For I know that there is a distinction between believing God and believing in God: "Abraham believed God, and it was reckoned to him for justice."[32] But those whom the logos finds fault with "did not believe in God." How, then, shall we understand both to believe "God" and to believe "in God"? I call to mind the gospel statement that I have explained, in regard to which it becomes needful for me to say how believing "God" differs from believing "in God." The statement holds, "Whoever will confess in me before human beings, I also will confess in him before my Father in heavens, but whoever will deny me— not 'in me,' for the one who denies is not 'in' Christ, but whoever will deny 'me'—I also will deny—he does not say 'in him' but I will deny—him."[33] In the logos, then, if the confession occurs "in" the Savior, the Savior also confesses in the one confessing; but if denial occurs, it is not "in" the Savior, but the one denying is not in him; he denies him. And the Savior, not being "in" the one denying, denies him. According to this logos it is a better thing to believe "in God" than to believe "God." The beginning of progress is to believe God, so that after that, coming to be in God and standing,[34] we shall believe God himself through Jesus Christ our Savior, to whom is the glory and the might to the ages of ages. Amen.

30. Ps 77.21b.

31. Ps 77.22.

32. Gn 15.6, Rom 4.3.

33. Mt 10.32–33.

34. A possible allusion to Eph 6.13. Compare the idea of identification with God to Plotinus, *Enn.* 5.8.10: "Everything that someone sees as a spectacle, he sees outside. But one must actually transfer into oneself and see as one, and see as oneself, just as one escorted by a god, taken by Phoebus or by some Muse, could make the vision of the god in himself, if he should have power in himself to see a god."

HOMILY 4 ON PSALM 77

"MERCIFUL man is a grcat and honorable human being,"[1] and it is possible to find many signs and tokens of the greatness of the human soul, but perhaps better than these—I speak of those found in a human being—are those produced by God through the human being. For God, making a great provision for him, also opens heaven to him and gives him heavenly nourishment. And he leads him, as he himself becomes a light to those who travel and guides them on roads that human nature, by itself, does not apprehend. On the one hand, all Scripture—including the Psalms that are being read—as "god-inspired and helpful,"[2] teaches the one who can hear it the extent of greatness possible for the human soul and the extent of the forethought God takes for it.

2. But since the reading is now assigned to be interpreted, should God grant, come, let us see what great things God has done on behalf of the human being: "*For he commanded clouds from above and opened the doors of heaven and showered manna upon them to eat.*"[3] These, then, are unusual[4] clouds, the ones that God ordered to rain manna, unusual compared to those in Isaiah, concerning which it is written, "I shall command the clouds not to shower rain on it."[5] And perhaps, just as among clouds perceived by the senses, some are very high and elevated, but some are very low, so also among spiritual clouds, there are different ones, either those that rain upon the vineyard or those that rain manna upon the people of God, and the higher ones, so

---

1. Prv 20.6.
2. 2 Tm 3.16.
3. Ps 77.23–24a.
4. *Kainai,* "new," in the sense of "unusual" or "strange"; they rain bread.
5. Is 5.6.

to speak, are the ones raining manna; but there are lower ones higher than the many,[6] but lower than those that rain manna. And in fact we shall say that the prophets are the inferior ones—to these clouds it was ordered not to shower rain any more upon that people—therefore, "there is no longer a prophet,"[7] and they say, "we do not see our signs"[8]—but the angels of God are the better and more distinguished clouds, serving the heavenly bread, then in token and now in truth. According to me and those greater than I,[9] the heavens are always opened and their gates are spread apart,[10] and those taken as clouds rain upon those traveling and leaving the land of Egypt and leaving for the holy land.

3. "*And he gave them bread of heaven; a human being ate bread of angels,*"[11] and I do not suppose that they can thus be serving to men a bread of angels to eat as angels do and to share through their own common property the bread which they eat with the nature of men. For as those who are very rich share their own bread with the destitute, so the angels, who are loftier and better than we, who, being men, are destitute on account of the body of abasement,[12] they, being richer than we, share their own nourishment with us.

And the logoi that we eat, "the living bread that came down from heaven,"[13] is sometimes given by God, but sometimes by the angels. That when this bread is given by God, it is possible to hear when the Savior says, "I am the living bread who came down from heaven," which the Father, he says, gave to the cosmos.[14] But when it is also given from angels, you will find

6. "The many" are not spiritual clouds, but ordinary human beings.

7. Ps 73.9b.

8. Ps 73.9a.

9. Those greater than he are Paul, who wrote that all followers of Christ have eaten the same spiritual food that the Israelites ate (1 Cor 10.3), and Jesus himself, who identifies himself as the bread that came down from heaven (Jn 6.33–35).

10. See Ps 77.23.

11. Ps 77.24b–25a.

12. See Phil 3.21.

13. See Jn 6.51.

14. See ibid. See also Jn 6.33.

angels speaking in the prophets.[15] Thus all share with us the bread from their surplus, accommodating it a little to us, for we cannot have an angelic habit of mind and accommodate as much learning as the angels accommodate, but, if one must use that term, the inwards of our soul accommodate little and have small space. Even if you were to mention Paul, or if you were to name Moses, he eats little nourishment in comparison with an angel. For each of these was a human being, even if the one was a human being of God,[16] and the other a human being in Christ.[17]

4. But let us be downcast when we hear these things, and let us see what great effort we make for the sake of the body, taking precautions about being hungry. And often, having bread, we want to have more and to exchange it for whiter bread, and to have not only what is needful but also what serves luxury and pleasure. If most of us are such people, I might say against myself and against those who have this experience, that we are not ashamed of putting such forethought as we do concerning bodily food and intend in its preference to eat the purest food and to eat most healthy for the occasion, but taking no thought at all that our wretched soul may be nourished; but it is destroyed by famine, and we have not given it any thought. Or is not the soul destroyed by want of living bread, so falling into sins? And just as, if the athlete stops eating an athletic diet, he falls defeated by the antagonist because he has become weaker, in the same way the human soul, whenever it abandons eating nourishment suitable in preparation, nourishment that makes it stronger, necessarily becomes weaker and, when it becomes weaker, it is worsted in the wrestling match.[18]

Have you deliberately forgotten that your "wrestling is not against blood and flesh," but against such, so many, and such great antagonists? "Against the rulers," not against some subordinates, but against the rulers; "against the authorities," not

---

15. See Hermas, *Mandates* 11.9.

16. For Moses, see Dt 33.1, Jos 14.6, Ps 89.1, Ezra (2 Esdras in LXX) 3.2, 1 Chr 23.14.

17. For Paul, see 2 Cor 12.2.

18. Wrestling (see Eph 6.12) is the primary metaphor for human struggle.

against some inadequate antagonist, but an authoritative one; "against the cosmic dominators," dominating not parts of the cosmos, but the cosmos, "the cosmic dominators of this darkness."[19] Should you not still make provision to hear, so that you may learn to be nourished with athletic nourishments, because your wrestling is even against the "spiritual matters of wickedness in the heavenly places."[20] By all means, struggle! No one is crowned if he does not train according to the rules; as part of training according to the rules after the games, adopt the athletic diet.

Or do you not see what is recounted about those contests called the Great Games? In them are present, sent by the chief judges of the games, those who keep watch over the athlete, how he eats; and, just as they show up for the games, and they keep watch to assure that the games occur according to rule and according to logos, so they show up also for the athletes when they are being nourished. And they shout out to those being nourished, as if they were competing, and at the time when they are being nourished, they say, "You are eating well, you are eating nobly, you have good hopes," and shout out in regard to the nourishment itself. Next, so that they may receive a perishable crown, they accept workouts: workouts in diet, in games, in being displaced for a variety of reasons, and in making trips. And often human beings among them, going down on their knees, are struck and put up with being struck by their trainers and taking blows on the back and on the belly.

But when you are training, you do not want to endure the blows that God applies to you, intending to make you an athlete by whippings. You do not want to give yourself an athletic diet, but often you let one day go by while your soul lacks nourishment. And why did I say one? For you also let the second, and the third, and the fourth go by, and that is not enough, but often six or seven days go by, so that you nourish yourself on one. After all, if you could, you would come on the Lord's day, take your spiritual nourishment, and thus be nourished for salvation in a way that would last, not just six or seven days, but

19. Eph 6.12.
20. Ibid.

many Lord's days! Already some are disdainful and stay without nourishment for a whole year, but they come on the few days of the so-called "Passover," so that they are nourished on those. Do you suppose that those people could compete as athletes, that they could struggle against the spiritual things of wickedness, after neglecting their own diet? They cannot be strong without following a strength-building diet.

5. Here is what needs to be said about the heavenly manna, so that you may not consider blessed those then, picturing for yourself manna, a food that goes into the mouth of human beings, as food chewed by angels. Even if these things did somehow come to pass according to God's plan then, nonetheless they also had come to pass for our sake, to whom the completion of the ages have come.[21]

So, as to the manna produced according to the narrative, should you actually be bold to say, in interpretation of "*a human being ate the bread of angels,*"[22] that those men were eating, chewing with their teeth, just as the angels of God in the heavens were eating, and that the angels had also, as it were, a sacrifice so that they would grind the manna as the Israelites did, and they had an earthenware pot so that they might boil the manna?[23] And was the consistency of the manna, even for the heavenly powers, like a honey cake, and was the appearance of the manna, even among the heavenly powers, as of a thin coriander seed for them, like frost, and was it white on the ground?[24]

Or do you not know that the Holy Spirit was folding into the narrative nakedly figurative speech, so that he might alert the hearer who is about to lapse entirely into bodily and entirely into sensible things, so that he might alert him to spiritual things and to better things?[25] And angels, then, are nourished spiritually, and thrones, and lordships and rulers and authorities also do not remain unnourished. Why do I say angels, thrones,

---

21. By the logic of 1 Cor 10.11, Israelites ate the manna then in order to instruct us now.

22. Ps 77.25a.

23. See Nm 11.8. See PS80H1.5 below for a similar argument.

24. See Ex 16.31.

25. Origen continues the cooking metaphor; only now it is the Holy Spirit doing the cooking. Origen discusses this process in detail in *Princ.* 4.2.9.

lordships, rulers, authorities? My Lord Jesus Christ himself is nourished. He confesses as much and teaches it, saying, "My food is that I do the will of the Father who sent me."[26]

6. And the logos[27] is being somewhat bold to speak because of the nourishments, if, in fact, it will be bold to speak such things seasonably before this audience; but let the logos be bold and not be bold, and let it speak and let it judge. God's logos knows that what is nourished has its life supplied, so that if, for the sake of argument, it were not nourished, it would be deprived of life. A human being, then, confesses, when it comes to what is related to the body, that also he furnishes life from nourishment and that, if he were to neglect nourishment and completely stop furnishing it, he would die of starvation. Let the naïve suppose that that starvation will not occur in the case of a just person, since it is written, "The Lord will not starve a just soul."[28] But the person who perceives divine things knows that there is another nourishment of the soul and it is possible for the soul by its own logos to be mortal in terms of another death, not this one.[29] Some who misconstrue "The soul that sins, it will die"[30] have supposed that the human soul perishes entirely, so that it does not exist, not grasping that every soul has its own ordinary life; whether it wants to or not, being rational, it always lives, but there is, nonetheless, another life by which each soul lives. For many souls have died, "for the soul that sins, it will die." The soul, accordingly, as I said, being mortal by logos, receives nourishment so as not to die; when nourishment is

26. Jn 4.34. "... His refreshment comes from another source. In the soul of the woman and in the influence that she has gone to exert, a work of God is manifest; the doing of that is His refreshment." William Temple, *Readings in St. John's Gospel* (Wilton, CT: Morehouse Barlow, 1956), 69.

27. The logos—that is, discourse—is about to be bold, risking misunderstanding and rejection, as it addresses the divine logos's need for nourishment. It is unclear whether "the logos" here is the divine logos, the logos (discourse, in this case a homily) Origen himself is giving, or both at the same time. Origen believed that the divine logos, nourished by God, could speak through him.

28. Prv 10.3.

29. Someone who perceives divine things knows that the soul's true mortality is its death to God. "Its own logos" may be Mt 10.28, which distinguishes between killing the body and killing the soul.

30. Ezek 18.4.

kept away, a death inimical to life lords it over the soul. And to the extent that you are nourished, death cannot lord it over you, but whenever you lack nourishment, then you will die. Lacking nourishment you sin, but sinning you die according to what is said, because "the soul that sins, it will die."

Someone hearing these logoi will then ask, "Do the angels, indeed, since they are maintained, have nourishment furnished, so that if they were not nourished, they would die?" Let the logos be manifested, and let it show and let it say that if indeed God has kept for the judgment of the great day, in eternal chains under gloom,[31] the angels who did not preserve their own rulership but abandoned their own proper dwelling, it is evident that these are the ones who received a death sentence because of sinning. But before they sinned, even in the case of those who would neglect nourishment, each one's nourishment is God's logos, the living one, who says, "I am the living bread who came down from heaven."[32] In just this way, say that every power has a life furnished.

7. Having gotten as far as these things, it suffices for me to leave to the hearer, if he should be intelligent, a logos something like this: the Apostle says somewhere, always marvelously speaking about God, "the only one having immortality,"[33] making this evident, that only the life of the God of the Universe is not furnished, nor is such a thing produced when it comes to God's life, as becomes the case concerning the life of those who have it furnished. If, accordingly, only God has immortality, let all beings think ahead to furnish their own life, persuaded that if they neglect nourishment, they also neglect life and will die. And such is the case in, "For I have been young, and I am old, and I did not see a just person who had been abandoned or his seed seeking bread; all day he is merciful and lends, and his seed will be for a blessing."[34] The same thing holds for, "The

---

31. Jude 6, referring to the "sons of God," understood as fallen angels, in Gn 6.2–4.

32. Jn 6.51. If Christ was the living bread who came down from heaven, he is bread in heaven sustaining the angels.

33. 1 Tm 6.16.

34. Ps 36.25–26. See Ps36H4 above.

Lord will not starve a just soul,"[35] and, "When the just eats, he fills his soul, but the souls of the irreverent are needy."[36]

The just person, then, always eats, and it is not possible that he neglects delight. For he keeps the commandment saying, "Take delight in the Lord,"[37] and eats, for sure, to delight. For the person who has tasted spiritual nourishment knows what the delight of the soul is. Look with me at legal exposition. Thoroughly understand prophetic clarity. Look at the gospel logos as it is unrolled. Thoroughly understand an Apostle enlightening you with the clear knowledge of Scripture, if you do not sense that such delight is a delight opposite to the delight of the body, the delight in which God intends us to delight.[38] Therefore, in creating man, he placed him in the paradise of delight.[39] But the man who sins does not eat nourishment from heaven, but from earth. For it is written, "Cursed is the earth in your works; in sorrows you shall eat of it all the days of your life. Thorns and thistles it will bring forth for you, and you shall eat the grass of the field. In sweat of your face you shall eat your bread until you return to the earth from which you were taken."[40]

8. But the one who is not sinning down in the desert, having left Egypt, no longer eats bread from earth, he no longer receives nourishment from the cursed earth, but see from where he is nourished, for it says, "*He commanded to the clouds from above.*"[41] If you live well, it says that the Lord will open to you the good, heavenly treasury. Let those hearing such logoi take wing, let them be uplifted, let them be no longer in the flesh, let them be in the spirit! Those who are in the flesh cannot please God.[42] Let them accomplish such things, that it may be said to them by the Spirit, "You are no longer in the flesh, but in spirit, if indeed God's spirit dwells in you."[43]

35. Prv 10.3.
36. Prv 13.25. See PS15H1.9 above.
37. Ps 36.4. See PS36H1.4 above.
38. See PS34H1.4 above.
39. See Gn 2.8, 3.23–24.
40. Gn 3.17–19.
41. Ps 77.23a.
42. Rom 8.8.
43. Rom 8.9.

"And he opened the doors of heaven."[44] I am confident that this is impossible according to the statement. For in creating this heaven God did not make doors in it, so that, from time to time, heaven might be opened and closed. But this is true according to figurative speech. Seeking doors of heaven, I do find some things that are doors of heaven. I have one, the one who said, "I am the door."[45] Similarly I find another one because the Holy Spirit is another door.[46] These doors of heaven are opened. But one can see the doors of heaven in another way. The virtues are doors of heaven, but the vices are doors of death. "The one who lifts me up," it says, "from the gates of death, so that I may announce to all your praises in the gates of the daughter of Zion."[47] One cannot come to be at the gates of the daughter of Zion and proclaim all the praises of God, unless one has been lifted up by God from the gates of death.

What, then, are the initial gates of death and doors beside the gates? Fornication, idolatry, faithlessness, greed, vanity, and, in a word, the works of the flesh, about which the Apostle says, "fornication, impurity, insolence, idolatry, poisoning, enmities, strife, jealousy, angers, intrigues, divisions, heresies, envies, drunkennesses, riotings."[48] All these are gates and doors of death. They are also gates of hell, the ones that could not overpower Peter and those who are equivalent to him according to what was said, "You are Peter, and upon this rock I shall build my Church, and gates of hell shall not overpower it."[49] These gates are animate, for the adverse powers overpower some, but they do not overpower Peter.

If you have seen the gates of death and gates and doors of hell described by the logos, ascend to the opposite ones and you will see that the gates of heaven are the virtues themselves, the gates of the daughter of Zion, the doors of life, the doors of justice, as it says, "Open for me the gates of justice; entering into

---

44. Ps 77.23b.
45. Jn 10.9.
46. See *Princ.* 1.3.7.
47. Ps 9.14–15.
48. Gal 5.19–21.
49. Mt 16.18.

them I shall give my testimony to the Lord."[50] Either according to the initial, or according to the next interpretation, or according to another, deeper one, it can be said also in the Psalm, "Lift gates, those who are ruling you, and be lifted up, age-long gates, and the king of glory will enter."[51]

This will do for "*He opened the doors of heaven and rained down manna on them to eat.*"[52]

9. But let us not pass over unexamined the singular noun "heaven." God opened the doors of "heaven" to those departing Egypt. Because they knew in part and they prophesied in part,[53] the other doors of the rest of the heavens were not opened to them at all, but the person who ascends through the doors of the first heaven and is educated in the first heaven will need to ascend also to the gates of those higher than the first, even in this way following Jesus, who passed through all the heavens,[54] so that he came to be next to the God and Father of the universe, so that one could grow to be beside God by following Christ.[55]

"*He rained down manna on them to eat.*"[56] God has given without stinting a bread from heaven to his people that is appropriate for activating every pleasure and fitting every taste. For whatever someone has wanted, the nature of the logos nourishing the soul has been mixed, adjusted to the strength of the one being nourished.[57] If the logos is nourishing an infant, it becomes milk;[58] if a weak soul is being nourished, since those who are

50. Ps 117.19.

51. Ps 23.7. See PS15H2.8 above. Both passages concern the divinization of the body.

52. Ps 77.23b–24a.

53. See 1 Cor 13.9.

54. Heb 4.14. See *Princ.* 2.11.6.

55. By following Christ, we become more and more like God.

56. Ps 77.24a.

57. See Wis 16.20–21. There is an apparent discrepancy between Ex 16.31, cited above, and Nm 11.8 concerning the taste of the manna. Early Jewish traditions, including the one cited here, resolved this discrepancy by arguing that the manna suited every possible taste. See James L. Kugel, *Traditions of the Bible: A Guide to the Bible as it Was at the Start of the Common Era* (Cambridge, MA: Harvard University Press, 1998), 618–19.

58. See 1 Cor 3.2.

weak eat vegetables,[59] the logos becomes vegetables; if someone is mature, about whom it is written, "solid nourishment is for the mature,"[60] the logos becomes solid nourishment. The manna that God rained down is all this.[61]

10. The manna does not come to us when we stay where we are, but when we go outside the tents, so that when we are outside, then we will gather the manna. What, then, is the intent of this? Let us see. If our body, in which our soul is confined, is the tents, the soul must no longer be in the flesh but in the spirit and go out of the tents. I am talking about the tents of the body.[62] It shall seek and it shall find[63] manna coming out of heaven. For he showered on them manna to eat, the thing that, whenever you find it, you say, struck with amazement, "Manna? What is this?"[64] Therefore, it is named "manna"—"What?"—for that was the exclamation said in amazement by those who did not know what to think at the surprise of finding bread below.[65] This came to be the name for the bread, it is called "manna," and he gave them bread from heaven.

The one being of the earth is from the earth and speaks from the earth, since it appears from the earth. The one who comes from heaven,[66] that one bears the bread from heaven and puts the image of the heavenly[67] on those who are going to eat the bread of angels. But no one bearing the image of the one made of earth can eat the bread of heaven. Therefore, the soulish[68] human being does not receive the things of the spirit of

59. See Rm 14.2.

60. Heb 5.14.

61. Origen extends the manna's versatility to nutritional needs. In *Comm. Jo.* 1.20.119–124 Origen explains that, while the logos is one, it becomes multiple to meet the various needs of souls. This explains why the logos takes so many titles such as "light," "resurrection," "shepherd," and "king" in *Comm. Jo.* 1.20.119–24.

62. See introduction, p. 20 on "tent."

63. See Mt 7.7.

64. Ex 16.15.

65. "What?" One obtains spiritual nourishment by grappling with "problems" or *aporiai*. See PS77H1.1 above.

66. See Jn 3.31.

67. See 1 Cor 15.49.

68. See PS67H1.5, n. 80 above.

God, for they are foolishness to him.[69] Do not think, then, that anyone can eat heavenly bread while bearing the image of the one made of earth.

"*He gave them bread from heaven; a human being ate the bread of angels.*"[70] Do you suppose that the angels are blessed, because they have the life, the one who said, "I am the life"?[71] The angels are blessed, because they are nourished by a nourishment that is not fleshly, not by the one disposed of in the toilet,[72] not the nourishment excreted by the body, but they are nourished by a heavenly nourishment, delivered for the subsistence of their being.[73] For which nourishment you also have been taught to pray, if you have in mind to obey Jesus who said, "Give us today bread for existence,"[74] "this bread for existence, the one that is not digested, the one that is not excreted, the one delivered for the being of the soul, give us this." Blessed are the angels who eat this bread, the one that did not come down from heaven, but stayed with them. But we, when we eat, eat what came down. For it is written, "I am the living bread, who came down from heaven."[75] Towards them it did not come down, unless, in fact, a deeper and more secret logos is demonstrated, that even to them the living bread came down and came down from the Father.

69. See 1 Cor 2.14.

70. Ps 77.24b–25a.

71. Jn 11.25, 14.6.

72. Mt 15.17, Mk 7.19.

73. *Ousia,* "being." Origen's use of this term is a major legacy of the Greek philosophical tradition, which distinguishes "being" from its attributes. Origen, for example, in *Comm. Jo.* 1.28.200, wants to make sure that his hearers do not misconstrue his distinction between the *epinoiai,* "aspects" or "devices" of the divine logos, which are many, from his *ousia,* "being," which remains one and the same. See Christoph Markschiess, "Was bedeutet οὐσία?" in *Origenes und sein Erbe: Gesammelte Studien* (Berlin: Walter de Gruyter, 2007), 173–93. In *Comm. Jo.* 13.33.214 and *Or.* 27.10 Origen identifies this "bread of angels" as the wisdom of God and states that, when Abraham fed angels (Gn 18.2–6), he was nourishing them with heavenly teaching. In the latter passage he identifies this teaching with what we share with Christ should we open the door to him and invite him to sup with us (Rv 3.20).

74. Mt 6.11. Origen interprets *Arton epiousion,* the obscure phrase usually translated as "daily bread," as "bread for [sustaining our] existence." See *Or.* 27.9.

75. Jn 6.51.

If you understand the magnitude and loftiness of the Father and understand, "Thus says the Lord, the loftiest, the one dwelling in lofty places, the holy one resting on the holy ones,"[76] you will see that all things, in relation to God, are below. For even the angels are below in relation to the loftiness of God, as well as thrones, lordships, rulers, and authorities. Even concerning the Savior when he says, "The Father is greater than I,"[77] I would say that, as regards the Father, he is below. For he is also above, near the Father, since "In a beginning was the logos, and the logos was near God, and the logos was a god,"[78] but if the logos had remained in a beginning near God, he would not have benefited what is below.

Then let the sole bread descend next to all those below—but every generated nature is lower than God—and when the bread descends, let it nourish all! But when this bread descends, look how far it descends, not just to earth, but to those farthest below earth. For the one who descended is also the one who ascended far above the heavens.[79] Accordingly, this bread descends to all those below, and among those below there exist differences, so that those who are below in relation to God are above in relation to others, as, for example, the holy angels are below in relation to God, above in relation to other beings such as us, in relation to whom they are above. But among us human beings ourselves, Moses, as he is above in relation to us, is below in relation to Jesus Christ. Perhaps in the case of every human being among those below, someone might find one even lower.

For who would be lower than all? The human being of sin, the son of perdition,[80] the adversary who is lifted up over every so-called god or object of worship.[81] Because, then, we human beings are relatively below, therefore the logos exhorts us to ascend and says, "Ascend upon a lofty mountain, the one announcing good news to Zion."[82]

76. Is 57.15.
77. Jn 14.28.
78. Jn 1.1.
79. Eph 4.9–10.
80. Jn 17.12.
81. 2 Thes 2.4.
82. Is 40.9.

"*A human being ate the bread of angels.*"[83] Blessed are the angels who partake of truth and are nourished by the wisdom of God and by the logos through which all things were made.[84] The aforementioned contemplation is the amusement of angels, but the imperative practice among us. For whenever those who are ministering spirits, for the sake of those who are going to inherit salvation,[85] are sent out and they are coming together, surrounding those who fear God,[86] they do something practical and imperative. The work set before them is to contemplate reality and to enjoy the wisdom of God and to see the logos of the ordering of the universe. A human being has also received a bread of angels, which nourishes angels, for whenever I gain understanding about God, about the cosmos, about Christ, about his divinity, and about his inhabiting a human body and soul, I eat a bread of angels. When I explain the logoi of the Holy Spirit, I eat a bread of angels. "*A human being ate the bread of angels. He sent them provision in abundance.*"[87] You pray that God may send us provision in abundance, so that we may not just taste, but may be surfeited with the logoi of life and be made strong in them; only the preceding nourishment is that very thing![88]

11. After this is: "*He sent out a south wind from heaven and led in his power a southwest wind and rained on them flesh as dust and winged birds like the sand of the seas, and they fell in the middle of the tents around their tents, and they ate and were extremely satiated, and he brought their desire to them; they were not separated from their desire.*"[89] When they ate the manna then, the sons of Israel were saying, "Our eyes are on nothing except this manna, for we remember that once we were sitting at the pots of meats in Egypt."[90] When we are hearing these things, we say that they were wretched, those who were eating the bread of heaven;

---

83. Ps 77.25a.

84. See Jn 1.3.

85. Heb 1.14.

86. See Ps 33.8.

87. Ps 77.25.

88. Origen's congregation is praying for the bread of heaven when they say the Psalm and they have just received that bread in the homily.

89. Ps 77.26–30a.

90. Ex 16.3.

they desired onions, and garlic, and leeks, and cucumbers, and gourds, and completely preferred this nourishment to that.

And we say these things as we read and consider them wretched for having sinned then, not seeing that such sins also arise among us. Or whenever we despise the spiritual nourishment and divine nourishment available to us, we scurry after wealth and want luxury. Do we not lust to eat stinking leeks; and onions that sting the eyes of the soul; and garlic, putrid sins; and do we not acquire for ourselves the stench of pleasures? Thus also, desiring the hollowness of the cosmos and the nature of bodies, we desire gourds, and, taking away what has been imparted for the being[91] of the soul, we want to substitute cucumbers.

If, then, we ever do such things, so that even when we have one who furnishes provision in abundance and gives bread of angels, we want worldly things and lust for things of the cosmos, God will send us meat like dust—for we do not want the bread of heaven—and, when he sends out such meat he keeps giving it, until it comes out of our nostrils and until it fills us with sickness and infirmity. So that one could say against us, "Such is the spiritual wealth I intended you to seek and the heavenly glory that is with me alone and to desire what is eternal, but since you do not wish to do this to find refreshment, you are ill. For you intend to have these wounds from the cosmos; see all those enjoying worldly affairs and making the soul ill on account of them, that they are in bitter things and illness and in every bad thing because of their doublemindedness. On account of this, understanding and comprehending the assessment of the Scriptures, be satisfied with the heavenly manna, the bread of angels, so that foods associated with earthly bread may not come back up and their taste may not still be in your mouths."

And "*the wrath of God arose upon them, and he killed among their fat ones*,"[92] those who had become well-fed, whose flesh was like the flesh of donkeys from their fleshy and material diet. Abstaining from that diet, may it come about that we fast the acceptable fast that the Lord accepts.[93] For when we do not nourish the

---

91. *Ousia,* "being," or "existence." See nn. 73 and 74 above.

92. Ps 77.31ab.

93. See Is 58.5.

mindset of the flesh,[94] we fast a good fast, a fast in which it is appropriate to anoint the head with oil,[95] not that of a sinner (for there is a certain oil of a sinner, about which the just person says, "Let me not anoint my head with the oil of a sinner").[96] In this fast, when I abstain from nourishing the mindset of the flesh with material and bodily nourishments, I wash my face and do not look glum, but I am cheerful. This fasting has become for me a prologue[97] to the spiritual things and the holy things in Christ Jesus, to whom is the glory and the might to the ages. Amen.

94. See Rom 8.6–7.
95. Mt 6.17.
96. See Ps 140.5.
97. Cheerful, shining faces make Christians look like angels.

HOMILY 5 ON PSALM 77

HEN THE people "desired a desire" in the desert and spoke wickedly about God's heavenly bread, but praised the foods of the Egyptians and said about the manna that it was empty bread.[1] God sent to them a corncrake,[2] threatening them then that they would eat it, not for one, or for two, or for five days, but they would eat it until they were glutted and the meat that they ate would come out of their nostrils.[3] For the God who loves humanity wanted to cleanse their soul from the desire. But a desire is cleansed and expelled not when there is a lack of the thing that is desired, but whenever someone replaces what is desired with something else, so that the desire is rejected.[4] And some such things befall us. For while we are still thoughtless, we desire some foods because they are sweet, because they are very expensive; then, when we have experienced those foods that we desired, we lose desire for them. For there is satiety of all things, not sleep alone,[5] but there is also satiety of foods.

1. See Nm 21.5. For "desired a desire," see Nm 11.4.

2. The corncrake (*ortugomētra*), a species of bird, was probably as obscure to Origen as it is to most of us. See Ex 16.13, Nm 11.31.

3. See Nm 11.20.

4. Those familiar with Origen's thought would recognize here a case study in the human condition. Just as the Israelites in the wilderness became dissatisfied with manna because of a voracious desire for flesh, but God made satisfaction of that desire the means of their cure, so all human beings have made their own misery, a misery that, paradoxically, evidences God's love of humanity. This is not only a recurring pattern in human experience, but, as those familiar with Origen's thought would know, it explains and justifies our condition as souls joined to a body, capable of either good or evil and eventually learning through our choices. See especially *Princ.* 1.6.2 and 2.7–9.

5. This is an allusion to Homer, *Iliad* 13.636–37 ("There is satiety [*koros*] of

See, then, God's plan, seeing a people that long for their desires; wanting to cleanse them from desire—having seen that
it is not cleansed by a teaching logos, but that it is cleansed by
the desire itself when it becomes surfeited—he sent the thing
desired. He knew that they would still desire one day after they
had obtained what they had desired, and not only that, but they
would hold out for two days, but after more days they would
make a change in what they desired so that they would turn
back, abstaining from what they desire. For thirty days he gave
them an abundance of what they desired; they ate as they desired, they ate to satiety. Because of the voraciousness of their
desire, they ate so much that it nauseated them. When this had
occurred to them, they put an end to the desire, and their soul
came out clean from it, because God was accomplishing this by
the effective means of cleansing.

2. But when I came to be comparing spiritual things with
spiritual things[6] in regard to this passage, I was finding that
the people were eating corncrake twice: once right after they
came out of the land of Egypt, the second time—as recorded in
Numbers—when they spoke wickedly of God's bread and called
it empty. Why is it, then, that when they first ate the corncrake,
no wrath at all arose upon them, but that did occur the second
time? Seeking, in fact, on my own and wanting to find and to receive[7] from God, I came to understand something like this.[8]

----

all things, both sleep and love, sweet song and blameless dance"): one becomes
sated with anything, even good things. Here Origen alludes to the *Iliad* in the
way he often does to Scripture, using a few words to recall a larger context in the
minds of those who are familiar with it. In Greek classical tradition after Homer,
koros is the precursor to *hubris,* the outrageous behavior that provokes *nemesis,*
retribution. Those familiar with Origen's thought would be reminded by this allusion that *koros* plays an important role in his thought. "There is satiety of all
things," not just food; since manna is a token of the sustaining teaching of the
logos, the implication is that the people of God reject it because they are sated
with it. Such satiety, it would seem, accounts for the fall of souls before their embodiment as human beings. See Marguerite Harl, "La satiété de la contemplation," in *Le déchiffrement du sens* (Paris: Études Augustiniennes, 1993), 191–223.
Origen's argument here is reminiscent of Plato's treatment of desire (*epithumia*)
in *Symposium* 200.

6. See 1 Cor 2.13.

7. See Ex 16.13 and Nm 11.31–32 and 21.5.

8. The main verbs are in the imperfect, indicating a continuing action. By

Every human being makes use of certain bodily things, sometimes necessarily, sometimes unnecessarily: necessarily when they are directed toward better things, but unnecessarily when the better things are rejected and that person becomes entirely attached to bodily things.[9] It would seem then that these things can be presented through both passages about the interpretation of the corncrake. In the first instance they ate corncrake without disparaging God's bread, but they ate corncrake while they were having manna without making light of it, because they were eating fleshly things. And we have a similar experience involved in bodily things after doing spiritual things, for in the same way we eat manna and also, by necessity, the corncrake given by God, and not as a result of desires. For whenever, entirely consumed by a desire for wicked things, we do not achieve spiritual things, making light of manna and rejecting divine things, then desire has occurred on our part. Thus what has been written, "*While the food was still in their mouth, God's wrath also ascended over them,*"[10] does not pertain to those in the first situation, but to those in the second.

3. At the same time I seek also concerning "*the wrath of God ascended over them,*" for there is no secret about what is indicated. To the extent that a human being vowing to be a human being of God does not sin, the wrath is lying below, but, should he sin, he himself comes to be below, but the wrath ascends over him. "*And the wrath of God ascended over them*": it "*ascended,*" since it was somewhere below.

Let someone who is capable of it scrutinize together what is written about the wrath of God in the first book of Supplements and in the second book of Kingdoms, so that he may find what is the wrath of God, which was also recorded in Exodus, that God sent out.[11] No one "sends out" a mental disturbance in

---

using the verbs "seek," "find," and "receive," Origen grounds his investigation in Jesus's promise (Mt 7.7–8). The discussion of desire (*epithumia*), followed by a discussion of mediation between the divine and the human, parallels Plato, *Symposium* 200–202d.

9. Compare Augustine on "use," *uti,* and "enjoy," *frui,* in *De doctrina Christiana* 1.22.20.

10. Ps 77.30b–31a.

11. See 1 Chr 13.10 and 27.24, 2 Sm 24.1, Ex 15.7. In the Septuagint,

his own soul. But if there is any "sent out wrath" it is something of God's that is not a mental disturbance but, by contrast, something that can be sent out. And you will seek what this wrath is, "sent out wrath," concerning which it is said by the Apostle to those able to understand: "we are by nature children of wrath like the rest."[12] Accordingly, this wrath, ascending over them, "*killed among their fat ones.*"[13] It did not say that it killed the people or killed many of the people, as some suppose who do not understand "fat ones" and have turned it into "he killed among their multitudes," but "*he killed among their fat ones.*"

First, I want to persuade the hearer that the copy that says: "killed among their multitudes" is mistaken. First, because the rest of the editions have no word equivalent to "multitudes," but have instead, "their sleek ones," and the Hebrew itself has it so. Moreover, if it had been written "among their multitudes," it would not be possible for it to be understood with the text "six hundred thousand" went out of the land of Egypt and "three thousand fifty."[14] Clearly, then, if he had killed "among their multitudes," fewer would have been left. Accordingly, it is not "among their multitudes," but "*among their fat ones,*" and he necessarily added "*among their fat ones.*" Perhaps the people did not sin this sin, "they desired a desire in the desert,"[15] but some sinned, either the majority or a minority, while some, perhaps, did not sin. As many, then, as sinned, became fat from the flesh by taking part in the sin. Therefore, it is written, "he killed," not "among their slender ones," not "among their thin ones," but "*among their fat ones,*" namely those who bore the traces of what they desired in the flesh.[16]

Chronicles is "Supplements," and 1–2 Samuel and 1–2 Kings are the four books of "Kingdoms."

12. Eph 2.3.

13. Ps 77.31b.

14. Nm 1.46. Such a large number of Israelites could not have been counted in the census at Sinai, had the widespread slaughter implied in the alternative reading, "multitudes," actually taken place.

15. See Nm 11.4.

16. "*Leptos,*" "thin," also means "subtle." Origen prefers being thin or subtle to being fat or, as we might say, "dense." See *Comm. Jo.* 13.21.129, *Hom. Lev.* 9.8, *Hom. Jer.* 18.10, and *Hom. Isa.* 6.5. Origen is using the *Hexapla* to adjudicate among competing texts.

4. "*He killed,*" then, "*among their fat ones,*" but he did not kill "*the chosen of Israel,*" but "*he fettered*" them,[17] so that he turned them around and hindered their march toward evil. "*In all these things they still sinned, and they did not believe in his marvels, and their days disappeared in emptiness, and their years with haste.*"[18] The sins of those traveling, then, are the sins of those traveling at all times, for just as those who were traveling after leaving Egypt for the holy land became involved in sins, so the majority of us, leaving bodily concerns and promising to follow the logos of God, traveling on the basis of the promises, commit sins in the meantime.

"*And in all these things they still sinned, and they did not believe in his marvels.*"[19] This also happens in our case, and we still sin: after leaving Egypt, after being assisted often by God, we do not believe in his marvels. So let each of us, in self-awareness, examine his own thinking, [examine] whether faithlessness never entered into him, whether doubt about the teachings never entered, whether or not he stays faithful, conformed to God's logos without quibbling. But if, then, unfaithfulness occurs, that is what is recorded in "*and they did not believe in his marvels.*" What, precisely, has been said? For it has not been said: "they did not believe in all his marvels," but, "*they did not believe in his marvels.*" Even when you may say that someone is faithful, you will find that he is faithful in some things, but not faithful in others.

5. "*And they did not believe in his marvels, and their days disappeared in emptiness.*"[20] Come, let us take that seriously. A human being gets up at dawn after the body has been refreshed by sleep and spends the whole day either in divine works, logoi, and thoughts, or in ordinary bodily ones. You will find most spending time in bodily, rather than spiritual, and spending the whole day in ordinary affairs. When someone spends the day on bodily affairs, he spends it in emptiness, even when, at intervals, it is not just spent in emptiness but in something good. And may it

17. Ps. 77.31b–c.
18. Ps 77.32–33.
19. Ps 77.32. GCSO13 retains the reading of CMG 314, "in all his marvels," but this is not attested as a variant text in the LXX and contradicts Origen's interpretation.
20. Ps 77.32b–33a.

be that most of us may not pass the whole day in emptiness, but the lesser part in emptiness, the greater part not in emptiness!

Times of gathering[21] are not in emptiness, times of prayer are not in emptiness, times of looking after one's neighbor are not in emptiness. It is not in emptiness when, in haste and without shirking, we are zealous for our neighbor. But it is in emptiness when I take down storehouses and build bigger ones and I say to my soul, "Soul, you have goods laid up for many years; relax, eat, drink, enjoy."[22] It is in emptiness when our soul is moved by commonplace worries and concerns as if it were among thorns[23] and were wounded, as the Apostle says thus about such people in one of the Epistles, "in emptiness of mind, being darkened in understanding."[24]

It is not, then, also to be "in emptiness of mind" when the mind is engaged in understanding God; preparing itself to understand the things of God and seeking skill in understanding,[25] it will seek things connected to salvation. But when it seeks how it may most skillfully apply itself to increasing wealth and how it may make its possessions greater, it is a mind of emptiness. When someone calculates, not how he may understand Scripture, not how he may do a good work, not how he may find a disputed wording from the divine Scriptures, he does such things in emptiness. Learning, then, that "their days disappeared in emptiness" applies, not just to those people then, but also to those people at

21. "Gathering" (*sunaxis,* from the same root as *sunagōgē*) for worship. See PS15H1.7 and PS67H1.4–6 above.

22. See Lk 12.18–19.

23. See Mt 13.22, Mk 4.19.

24. Eph 4.17–18.

25. Origen's wording implies that the studies of ethics, physics, and logic are not at all a waste of time. Compare PS80H2.1 below, where study of the cosmos is a divinization of the body. Compare also Plato, *Timaeus* 90BC: "For the person busied, then, with desires and contentions and who has put too much effort into these things, it must be that all beliefs turn out to be mortal and, altogether, to the extent possible for a mortal, not to fall the least short of this, having augmented what is mortal in him. But for the person who has devoted himself to the love of learning and to true states of mind, and has exercised these aspects of himself to the greatest extent, it must absolutely be the case to think deathless and divine things, should he catch hold of truth, nor must he in part be lacking, to the extent that it is possible for human nature to partake of immortality ..."

any time whose days are disappearing in emptiness and wasting time. Let us try to make our days pass no longer in emptiness, but to make our days pass filled with good works, with divine logoi, with saving thoughts. In this way what follows will not apply to us: "*and with haste their years disappeared.*"[26]

6. The years of a sinner hurry by, but the years of a just person do not hurry nor are they pursued, for an angel of the Lord is recorded as pursuing sinners.[27] The just person does not hurry, because an angel of wickedness does not loom over him and hurry him.[28] But so that you may perceive more accurately "*and with haste their years,*" look with me at the foremen in Egypt, in what manner they forced the Hebrews to hasten and to pass the day in mud, in masonry, and in straw.[29] Their years passed in haste, in haste dealing with the works of Pharaoh. We undergo something similar whenever our days disappear in emptiness. Since the year consists of days, our years also disappear as days of emptiness passing with haste. For the whole year disappears from us with a haste of days of works of emptiness.[30]

If such things did not happen just for those who traveled then, but still happen now, when we sin, but, after hearing divine logoi, we make our way back to justice, such a thing is recorded to have occurred to the people after sin. For after "*in all these things they still sinned, and they did not believe in his marvels, and their days disappeared in emptiness, and with haste their years,*" it is written, "*when he killed them, then they sought him out and turned back and woke early for God, and they remembered that God is their helper and God the highest is the redeemer of their souls.*"[31]

26. See Ps 77.33b.

27. See Ps 34.6b.

28. Origen does not find it problematic that an "angel of the Lord" should be "an angel of wickedness"; since "pursuing" is not something a good angel would do, Origen seems to identify this "angel of the Lord" of Ps 34.6 as an "evil angel" in *Princ.* 3.2.1. Origen believed that sinners put themselves under the control of evil powers. A wicked angel can still be "of the Lord" since harassment by evil angels serves God's purpose of inducing sinners to repent.

29. See Ex 1.14 and 5.7–18.

30. On making use of time, see also PS36H2.5, PS36H4.4, PS73H3.2–3 and 5 above.

31. Ps. 77.34–35.

7. It is necessary to understand thoroughly what has been said, disposing us to a turn-around: "*when he killed them, then they sought him out.*" For the one who is being eliminated seeks out God, for God says, "I will kill and I will make alive."[32] God's work is to kill me, insofar as I am a sinner, so that when he kills me, insofar as I am a sinner, he may make me alive. And I will seek God after dying to sin.[33] Therefore, it is written: "*when he killed them, then they sought him out.*" For example, God, if he kills each one insofar as he is an adulterer, a fornicator, an idolater, or a faithless person, then, when death is produced, that person is able to seek God. Insofar as it is not being eliminated, but he lives to sin, he cannot both live to sin and live to God. Therefore, let us pray that the Lord may also kill us and that we may say: "If we die together, we shall also live together."[34]

We, those of us who claim to belong to the Church, understand these things reverently concerning the Holy Scriptures, and we do not say anything bitter or make a case against God concerning, "I will kill and I will make alive, I will strike and I will heal."[35] But we say about God that, being good, he kills to sin, he makes alive to virtue. "For the one whom he loves the Lord disciplines, but he whips every son whom he accepts."[36] But those from the heresies, specifically those who seek to make a case against God and want to share with the devil the lot of one who wants to accuse[37] God, hear "I will kill" without also hearing "and I will make alive," and they hear "I will strike" without also

32. Dt 32.39. Origen cites this passage frequently in his writings, using it, as he does here, to argue that God's punishments are for a salvific purpose: he kills in order to bring new life. Examples are *Comm. Matt.* 15.11, *Comm. Rom.* 6.5, *Cels.* 2.24, and *Hom. Jer.* 1.16.

33. See Rom 6.11.

34. 2 Tm 2.11. Origen distinguished three kinds of death: what we commonly call death, the morally neutral death of the body; a good death to sin; and a soul's bad death to God (see PS81H.7 below). See especially the discussion of immortality in *Dial.* 167–74. Like the body, the soul needs constant nourishment from God to stay alive; see PS15H1.9, PS36H3.10, PS77H4.3–6 above and PS80H2.7 below. Through the power of Christ, the soul can experience resurrection; see PS67H1.1 and 5 above.

35. Dt 32.39.

36. Prv 3.12, Heb 12.6.

37. "Accuse" is *diaballein;* the "devil" is the "accuser," *diabolos.*

hearing "and I will heal," and they connive in catching simple souls for heretical godlessness. Thus the Marcionites, thus the Valentinians, thus the Basilideans and any others who introduce a God separate from the God of the law, by misconstruing, lead astray the hearts of the innocent.[38] But as for us, as the logos intends, let us hear in "I will kill and I will make alive": "for whom will I kill but the one I would make alive, or whom would I strike but the one I would heal?" For the same one "makes to grieve and again restores, disciplines, and his hands heal."[39] For he was killing them when they were seeking him. What a good thing it is that God kills me, so I may seek him out!

8. "*And they turned back and woke early for God*";[40] they did not put off coming near to God but woke early, so that they say, "By night my spirit woke early for you, God."[41] For just as the sun of justice rose for me[42] and that was a spiritual sun for me, I wake early for God. And you will find many such things in the prophets, such as, "I sent out my prophets at dawn."[43] "At dawn" was not put there by chance, but because at the same time as the logos of God or the oversight of God dawns in their souls, the prophets are sent out to the people, proclaiming a logos of the light of truth. "*And they woke early for God*"; and so, in fact, that you also may wake early for God, hear the Apostle teaching you and saying: "The night has progressed, the day is near. Let us walk about suitably for the day, not in reveling and drunkenness, not in sexual license and insolent behavior."[44] And again, "We are neither of the night nor of darkness, but we are sons of the day and sons of light."[45] Let us, then, pray that the light may rise upon us, so that we may wake early for God.

"*And they remembered that God is their helper*"; after having, be-

---

38. See Rom 16.18. The fundamental issue Origen has with these second-century figures, whom he often names together, is their denial that the God of the New Testament is the same as the God of the Old Testament.

39. Jb 5.18.

40. Ps 77.34b.

41. Is 26.9.

42. Mal 4.2.

43. Jer 25.4.

44. Rom 13.12–13.

45. 1 Thes 5.5.

cause of their sin, forgotten that God was their helper, they later recalled, "*God, the highest, is their redeemer.*"[46] He was redeeming them by killing them, and after that he made alive, "*and they loved him in their mouths.*"[47] See the phases in those who are neither entirely sinful nor entirely corrected; sometimes they sin, sometimes they turn around, and then again become involved in sin. For hear how it talks about sin, then about turning around; then again it speaks about sin. It describes our life in its inconsistency. After saying, "*and they returned and woke early for God,*" and, "*they remembered that God is their helper, and that God, the highest, is their redeemer,*" it accuses them again and says, "*they loved*[48] *him in their mouth, and with their tongue they lied to him, while their heart was not straight with him, nor were they faithful in his covenant.*"[49]

And these things speak to us, so that we might be educated to love God, not with the lips, not with the tongue, but with the heart, as it is written. For it is not written, "You shall love the Lord God from your whole mouth and from your whole lips," but, "You shall love your Lord God from your whole heart."

For see that he wants the depth and root of love to be in the heart, but also "from your whole soul and from your whole power."[50] He does not want us to have a cheap love, as is the love of ordinary people, concerning which it is written, "*They loved him in their mouth, and with their tongue they lied to him.*" For the consequence of the love with the mouth is to lie to God himself with the tongue.

"*Their heart was not straight with him*"; the heart must be

46. Ps 77.35. Recalling these words of the Psalm brings them to a better mind.

47. Ps 77.36a.

48. Origen has "they loved" (*ēgapēsan*) where the Septuagint has "they deceived" (*ēpatēsan*). Unlike PS36H3.9 above, where Origen builds his interpretation on a text corrected by the Hebrew without mentioning his departure from the LXX, in this instance the LXX agrees with the Hebrew. Perhaps the appointed reader confused one word for a similar one that makes sense in the context, and Origen followed him without noticing, or, copying this homily, a scribe did the same thing.

49. Ps 77.36–37.

50. Dt 6.5.

straight and not crooked. What makes the heart crooked but wickedness, the serpent, the snake, the fugitive from God? The one about whom it is written, "He will apply the holy sword to the serpent, the crooked snake,"[51] God, then, straightens the heart, and his logos next to the Father makes our soul straight, but the adverse power makes the heart crooked and turns us away from straightness.

Therefore, if we sin, we are not faithful to his covenant, just as, again, if our heart be straight, we are faithful to God's covenant and we meet with the heavenly spiritual blessings in the covenant in Christ Jesus, to whom is the glory and the might to the ages of ages. Amen.

51. Is 27.1.

HOMILY 6 ON PSALM 77

OD SHOWS that he is the merciful one[1] by works rather than by logoi. For who, perceiving the cosmos and especially actions on earth and such great sins among human beings, does not marvel at God's long-suffering and kindness,[2] putting up with so many and such great offenses and not making full use of authority against human beings? For "judging them little by little, he gives a place for change of heart."[3] But who, perceiving the things arranged[4] in each generation, does not see God's mercies, since he was sending prophets to the sinners, and by sending them he turned offenders around? But who, seeing that, on occasions of what is considered wrath and chastisement, he summons to change of heart, does not marvel at the mercifulness of God? For he never employs unmixed[5] anger against human beings. For example, when he intended to make a deluge, since "all flesh corrupted God's road on the earth,"[6] nonetheless, once he intended to make a deluge, in the five hundredth year[7] he began to proclaim that there would be a deluge, and he taught Noah and made him take one hundred years to prepare the ark. What, then, did he intend, through

1. See Ps 77.38a.
2. See Col 3.12.
3. See Wis 12.10.
4. That is, arranged or planned (*oikonomēthenta*) by God.
5. On mixture, see *Hom. Jer.* 12.2, where the degree of chastisement is calibrated to each person's requirements. See also PS74H.4–5 above and PS77H6.2 below.
6. Gn 6.12.
7. Origen probably relied for his chronology on the Book of Enoch (Enoch 60.1), a Jewish apocalyptic work of the Second Temple period respected by early Christians. Genesis does not say that Noah took an especially long time to build the ark or that he tried to warn his contemporaries to repent before it was too late.

the hundred years of the preparation of the ark, other than that human beings should turn back, so that there would be no need for the ark?[8]

But why also, when he was going to overturn Sodom and Gomorrah, the impious cities, did he send angels to Lot who said things such as, "If you have sons inside, in-laws or daughters there, so that you might take them along"?[9] And love of humanity was expressed through the angels, so that human beings might again be saved. But he also wanted to save completely all those leaving Sodom. Therefore, he said: "Do not look around backward or stand in the vicinity. Save yourself in the mountain, so that you will not be caught up with them."[10] And if some did not believe Lot as he proclaimed, they were destroyed by themselves. If the wife turned around, transgressing the command, she had done this herself.

He once intended also to lead a people out of the land of Egypt when they were being punished by the Egyptians, and God, lover of humanity, since he is merciful, even spared the Egyptians, "for his almighty hand, which created the cosmos out of formless matter, did not lack means to dispatch a crowd of bears or fierce lions or newly created unknown beasts full of fury or breathing fiery breath or exhaling a pall of smoke, but, carrying out judgment little by little, he gave them a place for change of heart."[11] And with grasshoppers and flies and gnats, and by death of birds, he punished the Egyptians,[12] with no other intention than to turn them back and go with the people.[13]

Come on, see, that when they remained in the sin, he made the death of the firstborn son the very last scourge;[14] but also when the Egyptians pursued the people and he gave the people the opportunity to travel through the Red Sea, what else did he

8. The Qur'an also maintains the tradition that Noah preached repentance. See James L. Kugel, *Traditions of the Bible*, 183–86.

9. Gn 19.12.

10. Gn 19.17.

11. Wis 11.17–18 and 12.10.

12. See Ps 104.31 and 104.35 and Ps 77.45.

13. See PS77H7.2, below, on God's intention to give the Egyptians the opportunity to join the people of Israel.

14. See Ex 11.

intend than to save the Egyptians who were not pursuing but fleeing and going with them? But since they did not want to do this, but they wanted to pursue, after all these things had occurred, they were destroyed by themselves. And why do I need to speak about each generation? It would take a long time for someone who was going to recount how God always, being merciful in keeping with his love of humanity, did what he did with kindness.

But I shall still add one thing: he decided to make a famine for the Egyptians. Go ahead, God, make the famine. The Egyptians deserve being destroyed by famine. "But I do not intend," it says, "to punish them utterly. What then shall I do? I shall arrange for Joseph to go down from the holy land and make use of the sin of his brothers, and by means of dreams I will make him to be known in the prison. I shall show Pharaoh, the king of the Egyptians, what is going to occur. But since this will come to be said, but not understood—understood, that is, by a wise and holy person—it will be no help to Egypt. What do I do? I will arrange for Joseph to judge the dreams, to believe that the famine will come, and to gather the food of abundance, so that the Egyptians may not utterly be destroyed by famine."[15] Why, indeed, have not all turned away, have they not become useless and have not all come short of God's glory,[16] even in the times of the Savior's presence? But even so, the merciful God did not abandon the race of human beings. But what did he do? From the heavens he sent his holy servant.[17] And in order to suffer what? Not in order to die for just persons, for scarcely among us would someone die for a just person,[18] but for sinners; he was to die for the cosmos, so that he might take away the sin of the cosmos.[19]

See how great is God's mercy, or rather, the multitude of God's mercies,[20] that he not only did not spare the only-begotten

15. See Gn 41. Here, as in the account of the plagues of Egypt in PS77H7.2 below, Origen stresses that God is consistently benevolent, doing the best for the Egyptians as well as for the children of Israel.

16. See Rom 3.23.

17. A reference to the servant of the Lord in Is 52.13–53.9.

18. Rom 5.7. Paul makes this observation after Christ had come.

19. Jn 1.29.

20. See Ps 50.3 and 68.17.

Son,[21] the only son he had, his image,[22] but gave him up[23] for all of us, and gave him up so that those from the gentiles might be saved and might be called. And after all these things we sin again, and God is the merciful one. But heresies have even come about, and they slander the Creator, and, nonetheless, God is merciful. He does not yet punish their blasphemy, for he says, "Some of them will have a change of heart; they will escape from the devil's snare, having been held captive by him for God's own purposes."[24] And for the sake of the change of heart of those turning away from the heresies, God holds back and is long-suffering when reviled and even slandered, but we, wretched as we are, we lash out if ever any human being should slander us, not seeing that God, when reviled,[25] does not punish. If he does not punish when he is reviled, we also ought not to revile in return and slander and avenge ourselves on one who reviles us. Otherwise, we do not become children of the long-suffering God.[26]

The mercies of God and his long-suffering have a limit, and I am being rather bold to say so, but it is true. It is not suitable for his mercy to last forever. For if his mercy remains forever and he does not destroy the cosmos, and heaven and earth should not pass away,[27] the kingdom of the heavens will not be established. It is necessary for the cosmos to be destroyed, so that the just may receive the promises. And I will say something actually surprising, that the destruction of the cosmos comes about according to God's mercy, and his wrath also comes according to God's mercy, and even his fury appears according to his mercy. If his wrath did not begin, how would those requiring his disciplining wrath be disciplined? If his fury did not appear, how would those be rebuked who need his rebuking fury? Understanding just these secrets, the prophet said, "Lord, do not rebuke me in your fury nor discipline me in your wrath."[28] And I reckon that,

21. See Jn 3.16.
22. See Col 1.15.
23. See Rom 8.32.
24. See 2 Tm 2.26.
25. See 1 Pt 2.23.
26. See Mt 6.9.
27. See Mt 24.35.
28. Ps 6.2 and 37.2.

just as a physician is being merciful when he cuts, merciful when he doses with hellebore,[29] merciful when he cauterizes, so wrath, so fury, so the punishments are fitting for the God who does these things. But I do not want to require a sensible physician cutting me, nor do I want to need him cauterizing me, but I do everything so as not to require cauterization and cutting nor to require hellebore for a cure.

But if, in bodily affairs, I flee from the application of unpleasant cures that are painful to my body, what shall I do concerning the wrath of God and his marvelous deeds? Let us, then, not despise the mercies, so that it may never be said with reference to us: "Do you despise the wealth of his kindness and forbearance and long-suffering, not knowing that God's kindness leads you to a change of heart? Because of your very hard and unchangeable heart you treasure wrath for yourself on the day of wrath and of the revelation of God's just sentence."[30] For someone treasures wrath for himself by doing the works of wrath; and someone treasures for himself wood by constructing sins resembling woodwork; one treasures for himself hay; and another treasures stubble[31] by such things, by sins. And he is going to say to those who treasure such things, "Walk in the light of your fire and in the flame that you kindled."[32]

2. Since, then, "*He is the merciful one, he will propitiate their sins, and may he not destroy.*"[33] How will he propitiate their sins? Creating the things that are, and being about to make the universe, he made the "firstborn of all creation" the propitiation through faith in his own blood.[34] For just as he is justice,[35] just as he is truth,[36] just as he is wisdom,[37] just as he is sanctification,[38] just as

---

29. A drug with unpleasant and potentially lethal side effects. Origen discusses ancient medical practices as an image of God more fully in *Hom. Jer.* 20.

30. Rom 2.4–5.

31. See 1 Cor 3.12.

32. Is 50.11.

33. Ps 77.38a.

34. Col 1.15 and see Rom 3.25.

35. 1 Cor 1.30.

36. Jn 14.6.

37. 1 Cor 1.24 and 30.

38. 1 Cor 1.30.

he is light of the cosmos,[39] just as he is light of human beings,[40] just as he is physician of souls, so our Savior is also propitiation.[41] He will then propitiate our sins. Therefore, this one is the Lamb of God as propitiation, taking away the sins of the cosmos.[42] But, "if anyone sins," it says, "we have an advocate next to the Father, Jesus Christ the just, and he is the propitiation concerning our sins, and not concerning ours only, but also concerning the whole cosmos."[43]

"*And he will multiply to turn away his fury*."[44] What does he multiply in "*to turn away his fury*"? For it is silent about what is multiplied and says that, through this, "*he will multiply*" what it is silent about in order "*to turn away his fury*." For whenever I, on my part, will do the works of God's fury, I will require works that avert God's fury from me. A few lucky works cannot avert God's fury, but many strong ones can, and I need for a multitude of works to occur so that I may avert from myself the fury of God that looms over me because of sin. In order to do the works, I require God empowering me in Christ Jesus, so that "*he will multiply to turn away his fury*" may occur.[45] He will multiply good works for me. He will multiply the best conduct for me. He will multiply for me the flourishing life that turns away his fury. And if he does not multiply good things beforehand, it is impossible, unless good things are multiplied for me, to turn his fury from me. "*And he will not actually kindle his entire wrath*"[46] on the part of those for whom he multiplies the turning away of his fury, from those for whom he avoids kindling his entire wrath.

For his entire wrath is great and fearful; therefore, it is written, "*He will not kindle his entire wrath*." It could have been written, "One will not kindle his wrath," but, as it is, it is written, "*He will not kindle his entire wrath*." For every person wrath is kindled just as much as is required to be kindled for the wood hold-

39. Jn 8.12.
40. Jn 1.4.
41. Rom 3.25.
42. See Jn 1.29 and 36.
43. 1 Jn 2.1–2.
44. Ps 77.38b.
45. See Phil 4.13, 1 Tm 1.12.
46. Ps 77.38c.

ing one's sinful deeds, and wrath is kindled proportional to my wood, proportional to my hay, proportional to my stubble. Only "*he will not kindle his entire wrath*" on us, but perhaps he will kindle his entire wrath on one alone among those who exist; for on the devil he will kindle his entire wrath.[47]

And "*he remembered that they are flesh, a spirit that goes out and does not return.*"[48] We are a composite of spirit, soul, and body,[49] and, being composite, we should be controlled by the better spirit; but we are, for the most part, controlled by the flesh: the soul is saved if it is controlled by the spirit, but it is destroyed if it is controlled by the flesh. Since we are composite, then, and controlled by the flesh, God remembers "*that they are flesh,*" but he does not remember concerning them, that they are spirit. For the spiritual examine everything, but they are examined by no one.[50] Let us, accordingly, become such persons, so that he may not remember that we are flesh.

I am often reminded of, "Let not spirit continue in these men to the age because they are flesh."[51] "*He remembered that they are flesh*" is akin to this text. The whole sinner becomes flesh, for his soul becomes flesh. In the doubtful matter of the spirit I do not know what to say, except that the whole sinner becomes flesh and the whole just person becomes spirit.[52] Therefore, if the resurrection should occur of those to whom it occurs, his flesh is no longer flesh, for it changes and becomes spirit; thus "flesh and blood cannot inherit the kingdom of God."[53] When the holy person inherits the kingdom of God, he is no longer

47. See n. 5 above.

48. Ps 77.39a.

49. See 1 Thes 5.23.

50. See 1 Cor 2.15.

51. Gn 6.3.

52. Origen believed that the full human person is constituted by the Pauline formula "body, soul, and spirit" (as in 1 Thes 5.23). The spirit is best understood, not as one of three constituent parts, but as the relationship of the whole person to God. Either the flesh, the body and the urges that spring from it, or the spirit comes to be predominant. The soul, the governing faculty and principle of life, can become subordinate to the flesh, but the spirit cannot. See esp. *Comm. Rom.* 1.21 and *Or.* 26.6. Divinization is the process whereby the entire righteous person becomes spirit.

53. 1 Cor 15.50.

flesh, he is no longer blood, since "it is sown a soulish[54] body, but it is raised a spiritual body."[55]

For it says in the logos that the entire just person is spirit; the entire sinner becomes flesh; his soul becomes flesh. By being stuck to the flesh and abandoning the spirit, it becomes equivalent to flesh and flesh. I just said that I was in doubt; that what I do not know is what to say about the spirit. The prophet taught me what I must say about the spirit: "*He remembered that they are flesh, a spirit that goes out and does not return.*" And so that you may not reckon that the spirit becomes flesh, it says, "*a spirit that goes out and does not return.*"[56] The spirit abandons the flesh and the soul and "returns to God who gave it," as it is written in Ecclesiastes.[57] Therefore, if we are punished, the spirit is not punished along with us, for "fear, rather, the one who is able to destroy both body and soul in Gehenna";[58] the spirit, then, is not destroyed.

3. But even if you are reading "*How often they embittered him in the desert and angered him in a waterless land,*"[59] just as often as you abandon God in God's desert and go after sin, arriving in the desert, you embitter God. As often as there is present a spring of water gushing up to life lasting for an age[60] for you in the Church, are you lazy concerning gatherings[61] and do you neglect being given drink, so that you arrive at a waterless place, and you embitter God when you turn out to be in the desert?

So, when you are embittering God in the desert, seek a spring, so that it may not be said about you, "They have abandoned me, a spring of living water."[62]

And those who are embittering God in the desert and angering him in a waterless land, turn back and test God. For be-

---

54. See PS67H1.5, n. 80 above.

55. 1 Cor 15.44.

56. Ps 77.39a.

57. Eccl 12.7.

58. Mt 10.28.

59. Ps 77.40.

60. See Jn 4.14.

61. See Heb 10.25. On "gatherings," *sunaxeis,* that is, regular meetings for worship, see PS67H1.4 above.

62. See Jer 2.13.

ing in sin, when they were in Egypt, they were treading mud in bodily evils; leaving Egypt, they were brought out and sinned again. Therefore, it is well said that they "turned back." For they turned back to the sin that they had left behind, just as occurs if you see a believer from the gentiles today, after seeming to believe and hearing God's logoi, turning back again to his own sin. What do you say about that person: that he is a dog turning back to his own vomit and a hog washing itself by rolling in mire?[63]

"*They turned back,*" then, "*and they tested God and provoked the holy one of Israel.*"[64] But always we also, if we sin, test God, for we are not content with the signs of salvation that we see, nor are we content with the logoi exhorting us to virtue, but we are again testing God, wanting new signs, and we provoke the Holy One of Israel, not remembering his hand directing us and the days in which he redeemed us from the hand of the oppressor. Who was that oppressor then but Pharaoh? And who is the oppressor now but the spiritual Pharaoh, the devil? For the adversary that is truly oppressing us is the devil. And we do not remember what God's signs were in Egypt. For among us in this Egypt he has made signs. For example, for me, each of God's benefits is a sign.

If I ever understood the relief of an illness because God was patient, so that I was enabled to live well after recovering from the illness, this has occurred to me as a sign from God. If I have ever been delivered, after coming into any sort of danger, I have received a sign from God so that I may speak about it. If I have ever seen sights truly indicating to me future things that turned out in keeping with what had been seen, this is a sign to me; this is something amazing for me. Or, since we do not see the one present, we therefore say that there are signs among us. How many times have we prayed, and we received just what we prayed for! But is this not a sign, to be successful in prayer? But, being faithless, "*we do not remember his signs for our benefit in Egypt*"—the cosmos—"*and his portents in the plain of Zoan.*"[65] Zoan is mentioned. It is a city of Egypt, a city where they espe-

63. Prv 26.11 and 2 Pt 2.22.
64. Ps 77.41.
65. Ps 77.42–43.

cially hate the head and throw this away from bodies. Thus, being in Egypt they hate the head, but the head of human beings is Christ, and the head of Christ is God.[66] The Egyptians are, then, such, in the metropolis of Egypt, who hate the head by whom they were made, because they do not control the head from whom every body, having been fitted and framed together, grows the growth of Christ.[67] Therefore, we treat well and revere such a great head, because the head of a man is Jesus Christ,[68] to whom is the glory and the might to the ages of ages. Amen.

66. See 1 Cor 11.3.
67. See Eph 4.16.
68. See 1 Cor 11.3.

HOMILY 7 ON PSALM 77

HE APPOINTED Scripture appears to abridge the logos about the scourges in Egypt in two Psalms, in the Seventy-seventh Psalm—the wordings we still have in our hands—and in the One-hundred-fourth. It is to be observed that Scripture does not name the ten scourges in either this one or that one, but in this one it was silent about the third, the sixth, and the ninth, and in that one it was silent about the fifth.[1] And this is to be observed, that the prophet did not set out the list in order either in this one or in that one.

For "*and he turned,*" it says, "*their rivers into blood*"; this first scourge among the Egyptians is the same in all accounts. Then, "*and their cisterns, so that they might not drink. He sent to them the dog-fly; they consumed them*" (but the dog-fly is the fourth scourge); "*and the frog, and it destroyed them.*"[2] The frog is the second scourge; it is silent about the gnats.[3] "*And he gave their fruit to the red blight and their labors to the grasshopper*";[4] the grasshopper is the eighth scourge. It is silent about the ninth, which was the palpable darkness.[5] "*And he gave their livestock to the hail and their substance to the fire*";[6] this is the seventh scourge.[7] "*And*

---

1. Compare Ps 77.44–51 with Ps 104.28–36.

2. Ps 77.44–45a. Compare Ex 7.14–25. Origen gives the list in Exodus priority. In his homily on Exodus that deals with the plagues of Egypt (*Hom. Exod.* 4), at least as we have it in Rufinus's translation, Origen did not mention the alternative accounts in the Psalms. Compare this to the list of Psalms that are referred to as "monument writing" in PS15H1.1.

3. See Ex 8.1–15.

4. Ps 77.46.

5. See Ex 10.1–29.

6. Ps 77.48.

7. See Ex 9.13–35.

he closed up their livestock in death";[8] this is the fifth scourge. It is silent about the sixth, which was sores and boils erupting.[9] "*And he struck down every firstborn in the land of Egypt*";[10] the last scourge it names last.[11]

But if you want, by the comparison of what is in each, to hear how the matter of the scourges is set out both in this Psalm and in the One-hundred-fourth, hear. The turning water into blood in the One-hundred-fourth is written, "He turned their waters into blood and killed their fish."[12] But in the case of the frogs, "Their land brought forth frogs in the chambers of their kings."[13] In the case of the gnats the logos here is silent; there it is written, "and gnats in all their borders."[14] And about the dog-fly it said: "He spoke, and the dog-fly came," to which it added, "and gnats in all their borders."[15] Although the gnats preceded the dog-fly, but the death of livestock is left in silence there, in this [Psalm] and in that one, silence is kept about both the sores and the boils erupting. And the hail that came upon the live-stock is described this way in the One-hundred-fourth Psalm: "He made their rains hail, a consuming fire in their land, and he struck down their vines and their sycamores, and he smashed every tree of their border."[16] The account of the grasshopper is in that one spoken of thus: "He spoke, and the grasshopper and the cricket came, which were without number, and they con-sumed all the grass in their land and consumed the fruit of their land."[17] Silence is maintained in this one about the palpabili-ty of the darkness, but in that one, it is recounted in this way: "He sent forth darkness and darkened."[18] But the account of the firstborn in that one is recounted thus: "And he struck down

---

8. Ps 77.50b.
9. See Ex 9.9.
10. Ps 77.51a.
11. See Ex 12.29.
12. Ps 104.29.
13. Ps 104.30.
14. Ps 104.31b.
15. Ps 104.31. Cf. Ex 8.17–24.
16. Ps 104.32–33. Cf. Ex 10.13.
17. Ps 104.34–35. Cf. Ex 10.15.
18. Ps 104.28a. Cf. Ex 10.21–23.

every firstborn in their land, the first-fruits of their labors in the tents of Ham."[19]

2. But come, let us see whether God grants us to speak about these scourges of the Egyptians, and first, let us say, about the one referred to as coming about *"to change their rivers into blood and their cisterns so that they might not drink."*[20] Compare the scourges of the Egyptians to acts of kindness to the Hebrews and marvel at the comparison, that the Egyptians were thirsty next to the river, but the Hebrews had a water supply in the desert, "for they drank from the spiritual rock that followed them."[21] On the one hand, the Egyptians were consumed by a dog-fly and destroyed by frogs, the puniest animals; on the other hand, the fangs of poisonous snakes could not overcome the children of God with their bites.[22] One must know that those who are estranged from God are in trouble in ordinary circumstances and are devastated by random events. But if someone is a holy person, even in troubles he prospers, and he is not harmed by difficulties, for this is what Jesus tells me in, "I give you authority to tread upon serpents and scorpions and upon every power of the evil one."[23] These things, because there is one God both of the Gospel and of the Law, also came about then. And snakes that arose against the people, when they had sinned, were not able to hurt them when, after having sinned, they had a change of heart.

We also want to present evidence of God's goodness in distressing situations and in what are considered scourges, because, even when God might scourge, he would scourge as one who is good. And these things are particularly effective against the godless heresies. Those are the ones who want to divide their own one God from a logos, and when the logos forbids making divisions of the Church,[24] they make division of the one God him-

19. Origen appears to conflate a version of Ps 104.36 with Ps 77.51b. Compare Ex 12.29. He probably cited the verse from memory, not having it "in his hands" like Ps 77.

20. Ps 77.44.

21. 1 Cor 10.4.

22. See Wis 16.10.

23. Lk 10.19.

24. Origen identifies the divine logos with "a logos," Hebrew Scripture,

self. Therefore, the logos forbids his children to drink the water of Egypt and to walk on an Egyptian road. Thus it is written in Jeremiah, "What do you have to do with the road of Egypt and drinking the water of Gihon?"[25] There is, then, an Egyptian road, on which we must not travel, and there is an Egyptian river, from which we must not drink. For the Lord God gives water from the rain of heaven, but for the Egyptians there is water, not from above, but from below; thus the Egyptian river irrigates the land of the Egyptians like an herb garden.[26]

So that you may understand what the logos concerning these things intends, I shall put forward first the scriptural references to rivers, showing that the holy ones also have rivers, and we must drink from the rivers of the holy ones, but not drink from those of their opposites. Hear, then, Jesus promising to his own disciples and saying, "Rivers shall flow out of his belly"—whose belly is "his," but "my disciple's"?—"a spring of water gushing up to age-long life,"[27] not only one river, but many rivers. By means of each observation and by means of each teaching, a river goes forth. But also a river goes forth from Paul, a river goes forth from Peter, but a river proceeds from Eden, that in Paul, and from Eden, that in Peter, to irrigate the enclosed garden, the Church; and from there it goes in four beginnings.[28] There are many beginnings of teachings. A beginning is that concerning the Father, a beginning is that concerning the Son, that concerning the Holy Spirit, that concerning the Church, that concerning the holy powers.[29] And why must I list the be-

---

which the heterodox who divide the Church reject, and with the logos of the New Testament [1 Cor 1.10], which forbids dividing the Church.

25. Jer 2.18.

26. See Dt 11.10. This clarifies an enigmatic warning against drinking the "water of Egypt" in Evagrius Ponticus, *To Monks* 128–30.

27. Jn 4.14.

28. Gn 2.10. The LXX translates the Hebrew *rō'shim*, "heads," into Greek as *archas*, the word that occurs here. In doing so it treats it as if it were a plural of the related word, *rē'shīth*, "beginning," the word (with its attached preposition) that begins the Hebrew Bible. *Archē* has a core meaning of "start" or "initiative." The earliest Greek philosophers, Thales, Anaximander, and Anaximenes, posited respectively "water," "the unbounded," and "air" as the *archē*, the "start" or "first principle" of the cosmos.

29. This sentence almost reads as if it were a list of the contents of Origen's

ginnings, which go out from one spring proceeding from Eden, the one river?[30]

But also "the surges of the river make glad the city of God."[31] And it is evident that it does not speak of a sensible river, for we are neighbors to what was once Jerusalem, and we know that it does not have a river.[32] But it is written, "the surges of the river make glad the city of God," but if you see Christ, the genuine river, and the genuine city of God, the Church of God, you will see how "the surges of the river make glad the city of God." Just as, then, Christ, a river, makes glad, and rivers come out from his disciples, a spring of water gushing to age-long life,[33] so logoi adverse to the truth are themselves rivers, but rivers inimical to the city of God. And I would say that the teachings are false, and, in particular, if I see someone flowing with a great flow of logoi, I would say that the speaker is a river of Egypt, and that is the one to be avoided, according to the prophet when he says: "What do you have to do with the road of Egypt and drinking from the water of Gihon?"[34] And again, if I see another flowing with much logos, but that logos is false, I will say that he is another Egyptian river.

Peri archōn, or, as it often has been translated, *On First Principles,* and gives us a clue to a puzzle in that work's title. Marguerite Harl explained how Origen took a title that already existed for a philosophical genre, but she considered it anomalous that Origen would use the word in the plural when he only acknowledged one ultimate first principle, God the Father. Here Origen explains how the word can also be used to describe the various "heads," as we might call them, of Christian thought. See Marguerite Harl, *Origène: Traité des principes (Peri Archôn)* (Paris: Études Augustiniennes, 1976), 8, and «Structure et cohérence du *Peri archôn*» in *Le déchiffrement du sens: Études sur l'herméneutique d'Origène à Grégoire de Nysse* (Paris: Études Augustiniennes, 1993), 225–46. On Origen's understanding of *archē* see also Franz Heinrich Kettler, *Der Ursprüngliche Sinn der Dogmatik des Origenes* (Berlin: Töpelmann, 1966), 25 n. 110. We see Origen's fascination with the corresponding verb, *archō,* "take the initiative" in the sense of "begin," in PS76H2.1–3 above, and with its participle (used as a substantive), *archōn,* "ruling one" or "ruler," in PS73H1.6 above.

30. See Rv 22.1.

31. Ps 45.5.

32. The argument works the other way in *Comm. Jo.* 6.42.219, where Origen takes the lack of a river as proof that the earthly Jerusalem cannot be the city of God.

33. Jn 4.14.

34. Jer 2.18.

Scripture speaks of many rivers of Egypt besides the one that is apparent and perceptible. For hear how it says, "*He changed their rivers into blood,*"[35] from which you will persuade even those who do not want to speak figuratively, by saying that the Egyptians do not have "rivers." For there is one "river," the one referred to by Scripture as "Gihon," by some as "Egypt," and by the majority as "Nile." How, then, does Scripture say, "*He changed their rivers into blood*"? Might not the passage be figurative? Because rivers of Egypt are all the streams alien to salvation that God, whenever he wants to convert—not just his own people, but also the Egyptians, so when they go out they may drink from the rock ("the rock was Christ")[36]—has turned into blood. For whenever I recognize water as alien, because God has given me evidence that it is blood, I no longer drink, so that I may not partake of blood. And let us, for sure, pray that, if any river draws us apart as a river, God may change it for us into blood and we will not dare to drink from it. Whenever he turns it into blood for us, we will be among those going out of Egypt, for a mixed multitude went out.[37]

Since not all of the heterodox are ready to give heterodox logoi, but there are some who say things that are short but destructive, therefore God not only turned the rivers of the Egyptians into blood, but even "their cisterns."[38] You will understand this from its opposite in the case of the holy. Some have rivers, those who are eloquent concerning the logos of truth, but some have cisterns, such ones that are small, but sweet and drinkable, and able to turn around the hearer. For instance, it was about cisterns, not a river, when it is said, "In a church I wish to speak five logoi with my understanding, so that others may be instructed."[39] But it was a river when Paul argued from dawn to the middle of the night.[40] And the logos gives a cause, why God turned the Egyptians' rivers and their streams into blood. What was the cause, but so that they might not drink? For this was indicated

35. Ps 77.44a.
36. 1 Cor 10.4.
37. Ex 12.38.
38. Ps 77.44b.
39. 1 Cor 14.19.
40. Acts 20.7.

by it: to prevent them from drinking the stream of the Egyptians.

3. We see another, the second scourge spoken of here, but the fourth written of in Exodus: "*He sent out to them a dog-fly, and it devoured them.*"[41] Reading the Wisdom of Solomon, as it is entitled, I learn from where it was taken by the one who wrote this book: "the bites of grasshoppers and flies killed them."[42] And I was seeking to determine if it was stated there first, but when God gave the ability to keep and to pay attention to the reading,[43] I found that it was taken from here. For in Exodus we do not have a plain statement that the Egyptians were destroyed by frogs and dog-flies and gnats, but here it is clearly stated that "*he sent to them a dog-fly, and it devoured them, and a frog, and it destroyed them,*" as, when they died, they were being bitten by the puny dog-flies and frogs in such a way as to destroy them, so that they might be released from the Egyptian life.

There was no need for many enemies or for a great power to destroy them. A dog-fly was enough. A gnat was enough. A frog was enough. Puny and trifling things turned out to be enough, when he rebuked, for the destruction of Egyptian life. "But those who are not admonished by trifling rebukes, will be tried by God's rightful judgment."[44] Certainly the logos appropriately calls them trifling rebukes, "for the hand of the Almighty, who created the cosmos from formless matter," it says, "did not lack means to impede them with a multitude of bears or fierce lions or hitherto unknown new creatures full of wrath, snorting fiery breath or belching a fog of smoke, which not only could injure them, but the sight of which would destroy them by fear."[45]

Why, then, did the Egyptians run afoul of such scourges? Hear: "Judging them little by little, he gave them a place for change of heart."[46] Perhaps the logos, disparaging the Egyptians,

41. Ps 77.45a. See Ex 8.20.

42. Wis 16.9. Origen makes use of an argument from the Wisdom of Solomon in PS77H6.1 above. Here he indicates that he examined it to determine if it should be regarded as an independent source of information about the Exodus, but, by God's help, found that it must depend on Ps 77.

43. Origen finds divine enablement even for his source criticism.

44. Wis 12.26.

45. Wis 11.17–19.

46. Wis 12.10.

did not judge them to be human; therefore, he did not simply send flies to them, but a dog-fly, as if to dogs. "He sent out to them a dog-fly," from which is taken the statement in the secret scripture,[47] that a certain fly is around dogs, "for he sent to them a dog-fly."[48] Others[49] have interpreted it thus: because the animal sent to the Egyptians was entirely shameless, putting together two shameless animals he demonstrated by the word that he was describing their outrageous shamelessness. For the fly is a very shameless animal and lands where it is warded off, and why do I need to say about dogs that they are shameless? So that the logos might establish the utter shamelessness of the scourge by means of the dog-fly, he says, it uses the term "dog-fly."

And from every direction the Egyptians are attacked. They are attacked by changing water into blood, when God plans what is spoken about. They are attacked by the air, for the flying dog-fly is a creature of air. They are attacked again by animals in waters, for he sent frogs to destroy them. But someone said that this particular frog is a toad.[50] For the story concerning this animal is handed down, that it is a frog that lives on dry land out of water that develops a poison, so that being bitten by it is the equivalent of a viper, an asp, and other animals that are poisonous. Separated from water and a place to swim in the water, it gathers poison from its food, and the frog makes a poison equivalent to them in power, so that the frog is food for asps and venomous animals, and the animals also take poison from this food.

4. "*And he gave their fruit to the red blight and their labors to the grasshopper.*"[51] The Egyptians' fruit is not good, and the Egyptians' labor is not good, for they labor for what they should not, and they wear themselves out for what is not needful. And it is evident that the fruit of the Egyptians is not good, for the deeds of the flesh[52] are their fruit, and sins are their fruit, as it says in

47. *Rhēton en tēi graphēi mustikēi.* Origen is not appealing to a secret book of Scripture, but to a secret that can be inferred from what Scripture openly states. See PS76H3.2 above, where a secret is in plain sight.

48. Ps 77.45a.

49. Philo, in *Life of Moses* 1.130.

50. See Philumenus Medicus, *On Poisonous Animals* 36.1–3.

51. Ps 77.46.

52. See Gal 5.19.

the Proverbs of Solomon: "Sins are the fruit of the irreverent."[53] The work of the good God was to give to the blight the fruit of the Egyptians, so that the fruit of the Egyptians might be destroyed. But God did not give the fruit of the Hebrews to the blight, but when they sin and produce bad fruit, "what was left by the caterpillar the grasshopper ate, and what was left by the grasshopper the wingless locust ate, what was left by the wingless locust the blight consumed."[54] The good fruit, which was not handed over to the blight, which we ourselves pray to bear, hear what it is: The fruit of the spirit is love—God does not hand over love to the blight—joy, peace. God does not hand over joy or peace to the blight, but he hands over the Egyptian fruit, sexual immorality, uncleanness, insolence, idolatry, whatever works are of the flesh and Egyptian practices.[55]

While speaking of different fruits, we have something small to add, so that it might be clearer who the good fruit is and who its opposite is, and the same applies to various labors. Hear, then, what we shall add to the logos about fruits: "Every tree not bearing good fruit is cut down and thrown into the fire,"[56] on the grounds that it is bearing fruit, but not good fruit. I know that in copies of the Gospels the passage is, "Every tree not bearing fruit is cut down and thrown into the fire," and in some, "Every tree not bearing good fruit is cut down"; the difference lies not in copies but in the different Gospels.[57]

Let us look also at "of labors." The just person labors for the provision of good things and has a promise like this: "You shall eat the labors of your fruits."[58] For it is not, as some assume, "You shall eat the fruits of your labors," but it goes precisely like this: "You shall eat the labors of your fruits." For each, when he comes to relax, eats the labors of his own fruits and hands, since

53. Prv 10.16.
54. Jl 1.4.
55. See Gal 5.19–22.
56. Mt 3.10 and 7.19, Lk 3.9.
57. Origen seems to suggest that this saying in some manuscripts may omit the word "good" on all three occasions when it appears, but others have each version, in different passages, including "good," say, in Luke, but omitting it in Matthew.
58. Ps 127.2.

the other versions have "you shall eat the labors of your hands." Thus the just labor for the provision of more divine works and good practices, but sinners labor in such a way that their labors may rightfully be handed over to the grasshopper. For example, if you see heretics toiling and laboring zealously night and day, so that they might plot to invent fabrications and to speak godless teaching, so that you would say about them and those like them, "They have abandoned searching out a search,"[59] you would also see in the case of such people that they labor and they are engrossed in labors; but in labors that are rightfully handed over to the grasshopper, do not hesitate to say about them just what was written about the Egyptians: "*and their labors to the grasshopper.*"

5. We do not think of vines as animals,[60] but Scripture—even when it principally indicates a vine otherwise—says, "*he killed their vine with hail.*"[61] What can be killed is an animal; therefore, it says, "*and he killed their vine with hail.*"[62] Not just the vine was killed by God, but also the mulberry of the Egyptians. For it is written, "*and their mulberries with hoarfrost.*"[63] To understand how the vines of the Egyptians are animals, one must understand their opposite. Look deeply at what is said: "A vine was planted by my beloved on a hill in a rich place, and a paling was put around it, and he fenced it and planted a vine of Sorech,"[64] and, "Vine of the Lord of Sabaoth is the house of Israel."[65] And each vine is of genuine Israelites; in the same manner there is an Egyptian vine.[66]

So that you may understand the Egyptian vine and the just judgment of God, removing the vine of the Egyptians by means of hail, pay attention to what is said in Deuteronomy concerning condemned vines: "for their vine is a vine of Sodom, and their tendril is of Gomorrah; their bunch of grapes is a bunch

59. Ps 63.7.
60. *Zōa.* "Plant" is *botanē.*
61. Ps 77.47a.
62. Origen does not explain why it is anomalous to speak of killing a plant.
63. Ps 77.47b.
64. Is 5.1–2.
65. Is 5.7.
66. Origen is not denying that plants are alive, but points out that, in his view, Scripture ordinarily speaks of vines symbolically.

of wrath, their cluster is a cluster of wrath; their juice is bitter for them, their wine is anger of snakes and incurable poison of asps."[67] And our Savior and Lord is himself a vine, but a beautiful and genuine vine, and his disciples are tendrils growing on this genuine vine.[68]

See, then, the tendrils of the holy and blessed vines and the tendrils of the opposite vines. And just as God is a farmer of the genuine vine according to what is said by the Savior, "I am the genuine vine, you are the tendrils, my Father is the farmer,"[69] so, who would be a farmer of the vine of Egypt, except the devil himself? Cain was a figure of him, working the ground and offering from the fruits of the ground but producing what God would not receive from the fruit of the ground that he worked.[70] There is, then, a farmer of Egypt, and it is God's task to form the genuine vine and the tendrils on it, but to kill the Egyptian vine and its tendrils, and he does this as one who is good. If the bunch of grapes belonging to the wicked vine is a bunch of wrath, and the cluster is one of bitterness for them, and the anger of snakes and their wine is incurable poison of asps, what do we say about the one who kills the vine that bears them, except that he is good and is sparing those who would be about to eat the bunch of wrath and those who want to drink the incurable poison of asps?

He killed that vine with hail, just as he did also to their mulberries with hoarfrost. There is a good mulberry. There is an opposite mulberry. The mulberry is the sycamore. They are the same thing except for the name. If, then, Zacchaeus in the Gospel climbed onto a sycamore because he was short, so that, when he climbed up, he could see my Lord Jesus Christ, you can see that that was a mulberry not to be removed, since it held the one who was to see Jesus. But if it should be a mulberry of the Egyptians, you will seek also what is said by the prophet, "I was a goatherd trimming mulberries."[71]

67. Dt 32.32–33.
68. See Jn 15.1–5.
69. Jn 15.1.
70. See Gn 4.2–5.
71. Am 7.14. Various trees are called "sycamore." In the eastern Mediterranean a sycamore is a mulberry tree.

6. And God destroyed their mulberries with hoarfrost, and "*he gave their livestock over to hail and their substance to fire.*"[72] There is a certain livestock of Christ and a certain livestock not of Christ, and the Scriptures are full of examples. When the Savior says, "My sheep hear my voice,"[73] and for this reason you do not hear, "because you are not of my sheep,"[74] he knows some sheep that are his, and he knows some sheep other than his. It is still possible, though, for the different sheep to become his possession. For as Laban's sheep became Jacob's,[75] so those of the enemy can become subject to Christ, and, by the same token, Christ's sheep can become the sheep of the enemy. Accordingly the sheep, those he rejected as unworthy, he bestowed on Esau.[76] See to it, then, that you never be found outside of Jesus's flock; when he is sending gifts to Esau—selected as one to be rejected and unworthy of the spiritual Jacob—you might be sent out in the direction of Esau. This is in regard to the removal of the Egyptian livestock, which God gave to the hail.

But so that you may understand more, I would say that Christ's livestock are those who are more simple and more naïve among believers. God saves livestock, since it is written, "Lord, you save human beings and livestock"[77]—but the livestock are not Christ's if they are entering heretical gatherings in logos.[78] Far be it from me to enter thus among them, if not in order

72. Ps 77.48.

73. Jn 10.27. Although all Christians constitute the "flock" of Christ (see PS77H8.4 below), "sheep" or "livestock" refers specifically to those of low intellectual endowment. See *Comm. Jo.* 1.20.122, 1.28.198, and 13.6.39.

74. Jn 10.26.

75. See Gn 30.39–43.

76. See Gn 32.14–16. The original passage does not suggest that Jacob saw the gift to appease Esau as an opportunity to cull his livestock.

77. Ps 35.7.

78. "Entering heretical gatherings in logos" could involve hearing heretical discourses (logoi) or reading them, but Christians cannot avoid heretical teaching unless they recognize it for what it is. Origen states that he has made himself familiar with heretical ideas only in order to refute them (see also *Comm. Jo.* 5.8). One of his tasks as a preacher is to inform his congregation so that they can detect heretical doctrine for themselves; see especially PS77H2.4 above. Irenaeus (*Haer.* Prol. 1) also notes that heretics pose a special threat to those who lack learning and intellectual gifts, the simple, *akeraioi.*

that I might capture captivity[79] for Christ! If then, entering, I see naïve souls who are not learned, but are utterly simple, who have been brought under the rule of godless teaching and are irrationally subjected to it, I would say that these are the livestock of the Egyptians and that, because of Marcion, these are the sheep of Egypt.[80] But he similarly also handed over the rest of the livestock of the Egyptians to hail and their substance to fire. For whatever Egyptians have is given over to fire; whatever are Jesus's substantial things are not given over to fire. Abraham had substantial things; he gave the substantial things to Isaac, his son according to the promise. He gave, not substantial things, but payments to the sons of his concubines.[81]

7. "*He sent out to them wrath of his anger, anger and wrath and affliction, a dispatch by means of evil angels.*"[82] Against those supposing that the so-called "wrath" in the Scripture is an inner disturbance[83] of God and who on that basis are slandering the God of the law and the prophets, it is possible to say that they do not understand what they are saying. If it is an inner disturbance and remains in the soul, how can it be sent out? For what is sent out, is sent out only if it is different from the one sending it out, and the wrath is different from the one whose wrath it is, and if, then, the sent-out wrath is a living thing, let it

79. See Eph 4.8.

80. God saves livestock by delivering them from Egypt, the place of those who are earthly minded and subject to Satan, and forming them into a flock (see below). Heretics, such as Marcionites, remain in Egypt, where they are handed over to the hail and enclosed in death.

81. See Gn 25.5–6.

82. Ps 77.49.

83. No English word fully conveys the sense of *pathos*, here translated "inner disturbance," an internal change with a cause external to the one experiencing it. We might call it an "emotional reaction." *Orgē*, "wrath," is a particularly problematic *pathos* for Origen, not only because it is indiscriminate and destructive, but because it is the most difficult of all the *pathē* to overcome. See PS75H.8 above and PS77H9.1 below. To ascribe the wrath as a *pathos* to God is a slander, not only because it implies that God is subject to irrational and indiscriminate destructiveness, but because it implies that God, who is identified with changeless being rather than with becoming, is subject to change. See Max Pohlenz, *Vom Zorne Gottes: Eine Studie über den Einfluß der griechischen Philosophie auf das alte Christentum* (Göttingen: Vandenhoeck und Ruprecht, 1909).

keep away from all of us! For there is a wrath, whose children we were, according to the Apostle: "by nature we were children of wrath, just as the rest,"[84] and the wrath has reached them in the end. God, then, sends that wrath along with anger, wrath, and affliction, and sends a dispatch for the sake of those who merit such things, through evil angels, like the wrath sent out on the fornicator at Corinth. And do you want to see that there was a wrath sent out on the part of the Apostle as the sender? Hear: "I have judged that when you and my spirit are gathered, with the power of the Lord Jesus, to hand over such a person."[85] The one that has been given over to Satan has been given over to wrath; the wrath, then, is sent out.[86]

Since we have spoken about a good God and we have intended to rectify things, we also intend to demonstrate that "*He sent out to them wrath of his anger, anger and wrath and affliction, a dispatch by means of evil angels*"[87] is consistent with those things that we have been promised. Often calls come about even through evil angels, for many who are not willing to attend to the logos, when bad spirits come, when unclean spirits come, are compelled to turn around and seek God again.[88]

"*He constructed a path for his wrath.*"[89] He is not without method of wrath. If it were an inner disturbance, it would be without method, it would not be ordered.[90] For example, we, if we are wrathful, we do not construct a road for the wrath, for we become wrathful without method; but when the one who employs

84. Eph 2.3.

85. 1 Cor 5.4–5.

86. Satan is the wrath of God.

87. Ps 77.49.

88. The experience of evil may compel us to change our outlook on life and so may have a beneficial effect when nothing else would.

89. Ps 77.50a.

90. *Anodia orgēs,* "methodlessness," rather than "roadlessness," "of wrath." See introduction, p. 32, on the translation of *hodos.* Just as God's wrath is not an inner disturbance such as human beings experience, it is consistently purposeful, the means for achieving God's ultimately beneficent intention, not, like our wrath, indiscriminately destructive. See PS77H6.1 above, where Origen seeks to show how, from God's perspective, the flood story, the famine in Egypt, and the plagues of Egypt are patient and deliberate strategies of bringing all concerned to repentance.

wrath against sinners does so, he employs it with method and order and does not leave the effects of wrath to chance. Intending to establish this point, the prophet said: "*He constructed a path for his wrath, and does not spare their souls from death.*"[91] Not sparing from death sinful souls, he destroys the sinful souls, saying, "I will kill," so that he might also say, "I will make alive."[92]

"*And he enclosed their livestock in death, and he struck down every firstborn in the land of Egypt.*"[93] Perhaps it is possible that, just as, on the analogy of bodily birth, the firstborn inherits twice as much as, and more than, the other heirs and has greater honor in comparison with the other offspring, so among souls there is a certain firstborn of God, and there is a certain firstborn of Egypt. But he, I say, he is such a one referred to in "Sanctify to me every firstborn, the first birth opening the womb."[94] When God says these things, if indeed "the law has a shadow of the good things to come,"[95] he speaks concerning certain other firstborn, not bodily ones. And if you wish to see them with exactitude, hear Paul saying, "But you have arrived at Mount Zion and the city of the living God, the heavenly Jerusalem, and tens of thousands of angels, in a festival and the church of the firstborn recorded in heaven."[96]

Just as, then, the firstborn inherit a double portion and take a greater part, and as Joseph received an inheritance for Ephraim and for Manasseh, in the same manner also the firstborn of the Egyptians inherit a double punishment. Would God be the judge as to who is the firstborn on the side of the adverse power? Perhaps, should God give me the ability, I will find it possible to say who is the firstborn of the adverse power.

The first brought to birth in a teaching alien to salvation is the firstborn of that teaching, having been given birth by the devil. For example, not all the Marcionites are firstborn, but among them Marcion is the firstborn. And not all the Valentin-

---

91. Ps 77.50ab.
92. Dt 32.39.
93. Ps 77.50c–51a.
94. Ex 13.2.
95. Heb 10.1.
96. Heb 12.22–23.

ians are firstborn, but Valentinus, the father of that disgusting knowledge,[97] was the firstborn. Thus in each case the one who was first given birth in a teaching, to whom the evil one gave birth, is found to be analogous to a firstborn of the Egyptians.

"*He struck down,*" then, "*every firstborn in the land of Egypt, the first-fruit of their labors in the tents of Ham.*"[98] As there is a first-fruit of the holy ones, so there is a first-fruit of the Egyptians, and just as the first-fruits of the holy ones are put aside for God, so the first-fruits of the Egyptians are put aside for taking blows, so that the first-fruit may be punished, and after the first-fruit is punished, then the rest are punished. But would that we were those perceiving the two deeds: the Lord's legacy and the legacy of the scapegoat,[99] so that we might expel the scapegoat into the desert from our souls, that we might belong to the legacy of God the ruler of all, through Jesus Christ, to whom is the glory and the might to the ages of ages. Amen.

97. This "disgusting knowledge" is *gnōsis,* the term from which "Gnostic" comes.

98. Ps 77.51.

99. See Lv 6.6–11.

HOMILY 8 ON PSALM 77

SINCE IT HAS been written, "When the Most High divided up the nations, so that the sons of Adam might scatter, he established boundaries of nations according to the number of the sons of Israel, or angels of God, and his people Jacob became the Lord's portion, Israel the allotment of his inheritance,"[1] I sought, on my part, when it was that the Most High divided up nations and dispersed the sons of Adam, when it was that his people Jacob became the Lord's portion and Israel the allotment of his inheritance. And once I assumed that this happened at the confusion that is recorded as having occurred at the construction of the tower.[2] But looking again later, I found that "his people Jacob became the Lord's portion" could not have been a reference to that time before the birth of Jacob, and "Israel the allotment of his inheritance" could not have occurred before Jacob's name was changed to Israel. Examining painstakingly, I would say that "the Most High divided up nations" occurred when the people left the land of Egypt. For then the people of God first entitled themselves "Jacob," and "Israel the allotment of his inheritance"; and the distribution of allotments probably occurred then, and the boundaries of the land were laid out, so that each of the angels might have a boundary.

2. So it is, then, that the Lord "*took away his people like sheep and led them up as a flock in the desert and guided them in hope, and they were not afraid, and the sea covered their enemies.*"[3] But the pro-

---

1. Dt 32.8–9.

2. The confusion of tongues at the tower of Babel; see Gn 11.1–9. The spiritual interpretation of the various nations was a major concern to Origen. See especially *Princ.* 2.11.5, also *Princ.* 4.3.8 and 4.3.10. On the significance of this statement for dating the homilies, see introduction, pp. 4–5.

3. Ps 77.52–53.

phetic logos in Isaiah persuaded me about this, saying: "I"—
God—"have given for your"—the people's—"exchange Egypt
and Ethiopia and Syene,"[4] when "*he sent to them a dog-fly, and it
devoured them, and a frog, and it destroyed them, and he gave over their
fruit to the blight, and their labors to the grasshopper,*" when "*he killed
their vine with hail, and their mulberries with hoarfrost,*" when "*he
gave over their livestock to hail and their substance to fire,*" when "*he
sent out to them the wrath of his anger, anger and wrath and affliction
through evil angels,*" when "*he struck down every firstborn in the land
of Egypt, the first-fruit of their labors in the tents of Ham.*"[5]

For which reason, after the scourges of the Egyptians, it is
said, "*He brought out his people like sheep.*"[6] And, to the extent
possible for me, searching the Scripture and wanting to be faithful to my Lord, who said, "Search the Scriptures,"[7] I was seeking on my own if it is just by chance that the people of God are
referred to first as "sheep brought out" by God, but later they
are no longer "sheep" but, by then, a "flock"; and, on the one
hand, they are referred to as "sheep," when God "*brought out his
people like sheep,*" but, on the other hand, as a "flock," when "*he
led them up as a flock in the desert.*"[8] And seeking, I found[9] that
it is consistent for him first to take away his flock like "sheep,"
but later to lead them up as a "flock" in the desert; thus also
when they are guided, they are guided in hope, and because of
this they were not frightened of their enemies, who had been
covered by the sea.

Have in mind with me that the people were first in the land
of Egypt and see what was going on then, when they were in the
land of Egypt, especially when they were scattered about in it to
gather chaff.[10] They were not a flock, they were not a herd, but
they were scattered in the land of Egypt. When, then, God has

---

4. Is 43.3. In *Mart.* 13 Origen argues that a full understanding of this enigmatic statement will come as a reward for martyrdom.

5. Ps 77.45–49, 77.51.

6. Ps 77.52a.

7. Jn 5.39.

8. Ps 77.52b.

9. See Mt 7.7–8.

10. Ex 5.7–18. "Chaff," *achura*, stands for anything worthless and fit for destruction, as in Jb 21.18, Mt 3.12, and Lk 3.17.

gathered them by his own plan,[11] then, he brings his own people out from the Egyptians like sheep. Next, when he gathers them and makes them one, they are no longer just "sheep," but they are called a "flock." For he leads them, his people, united as a flock. Thus "*he led them up as a flock in the desert,*" but first he takes them away; then, after that, he leads them. For to be borne upward and to travel towards higher things was not an inner experience possible for them when they were still in the land of Egypt. Therefore, first he takes them away from the land of Egypt, and after that they are led up.

And do not consider this something that occurred to the people then but does not occur always.[12] For God brings out his people from the land of Egypt, from the whole cosmos, as sheep. Then he leads them up, the people that understands and comprehends the things spoken, through conduct that carries them upward, through the knowledge of lofty matters. And by bringing out and leading up, God makes a flock, so that, as there is one shepherd, all Christ's sheep might become one flock.[13] And insofar as we are gathered together, we keep the secret[14] of the flock; but when we neglect gathering,[15] we imitate the sheep that wander and are snatched from the flock. And see what a good thing it is for the believers to be one flock—not neglecting their gathering, as is the custom for some[16]—so as to be borne up, and "*he guided them in hope, and they did not fear.*"[17]

Whenever they are a flock, they do not fear; even though they are sheep, they are guided by God. But when someone abandons the flock and is isolated, then the enemies snatch, the warriors

11. *Oikonomiāi tēi heautou,* "by his own plan."

12. Taking his cue from the Apostle Paul (see especially 1 Cor 10.11), Origen taught that all events that are recounted in Scripture are not simply accounts of what happened "then" in the time of Moses, but of continuing spiritual realities that "always" occur. We see a similar use of "always" in PS76H1.2 above.

13. See Jn 10.16.

14. Origen alerts his students that the Church's unity is an earthly prefiguration of the "secret" of eschatological unity with God.

15. See PS67H1.4 above.

16. See Heb 10.25.

17. Ps 77.53a.

seize, then the wild beasts are lying in wait, powerful against those who are scattered. Therefore, if anyone should want us, on any pretext whatsoever, to be separated from the flock, we will still stay together: "For a brother is assisted by a brother, as a strong and lofty city, and is strong like a well-constructed castle."[18] And like these, the stones of a building come to be together and, set in place, make a building, but if the stones are scattered, they are scattered about; in the same manner we are a house of God; when we are like-minded and gathering together, we are together a spiritual house, a holy temple, offering acceptable spiritual sacrifices to God.[19]

3. I want to persuade you by the Scripture what a good thing like-mindedness is, how important it is for us to be a flock and not to be scattered. To the extent that the people was one and not scattered, the Assyrian could not take it, nor did they go away as captives to Babylon. Thus the adversary, wanting to scatter the people and make them susceptible to captivity among the Assyrians and vulnerable to exile in Babylon, first contrives a division to occur; and, when he has done so, when the like-mindedness of the people is scattered, the enemies are enabled to take them, no longer united. If we ourselves do not want to be plotted against by the adverse powers, let us not abandon the gathering.[20]

And remember these things, especially those of you who do not gather on any other occasion, but abandon the shepherd and separate yourselves from the little flock. It is possible, because I know some who lament, and lament appropriately, when separated for one Sunday, but they grieve even more over two Sundays, while you, in your neglect, separate yourselves for a whole year. What great sin must have occurred, so that you are separated from the Church for a whole year! As it is said, "I will judge you out of your mouth, faithless servant,"[21] now it will be said to those neglecting gatherings. It will be said thus: "Out of what you have done, I will judge you; you have expelled yourself from the Church, scarcely showing up for a year; be expelled

---

18. Prv 18.19.

19. See 1 Pt 2.5 and *Shepherd of Hermas,* Vision 3.2.3–9.

20. On gathering and scattering see also PS67H1.4–6 above.

21. See Lk 19.22.

by your own judgment. For when you judge another, you judge yourself unworthy to belong to the Church by being lazy and neglectful. The Jews have been manipulated by God on the pre-text[22] of the Sabbath and on the pretext of rest, to gather continually, so that they might hear God's logoi, so that they might be reminded and not use work as an excuse; but you, since the heavy yoke has not been placed on you but you are allowed to exercise discretion, are contemptuous on that account. And you do not even come together honoring the day of our Lord's resurrection, so that bone to bone of Christ and suture to suture, along with Christ's skin, and veins and nerves, even his individual hairs might be gathered? Or do you not know that you are the body of Christ?[23] And it is necessary for this body of Christ to be gathered, so that Christ may not say concerning us, "All of my bones have been scattered."[24] He did not say this concerning his bodily bones—for they were not scattered—but concerning those neglecting gathering, because body parts of Christ are scattered.

This will do for the assigned reading and on account of the neglectful, because "*he led them up like a little flock in the desert, and he guided them in hope.*"[25]

4. When you become a little flock, God guides you in hope. God does not guide one by one, but God guides the little flock together, and God "*guided them in hope, and they did not fear.*"[26] I do not say that God never guides just one person, for when the entire people sins, one just person is left, and God guides this one instead of the little flock. Such a one was Elijah, who said: "The children of Israel have abandoned you, they have killed your prophets, they have defiled your altars, and I alone am left."[27] And because he alone was left and remained in reverence, therefore the one who guides the whole people guid-

---

22. The Jews were "manipulated" (*ōikonomēthēsan*) by God on the "pretext" (*prophasei*) of rest to gather weekly to hear Scripture. Origen did not believe that God was punitive, but he did believe that God could be sneaky.

23. See 1 Cor 12.27.

24. Ps 21.15.

25. Ps 77.52b–53a.

26. Ps 77.53a.

27. 1 Kgs 19.10.

ed the one, counting him to be a little flock. Even you, then, should you be a little flock, you will not fear, "*for he guided them in hope, and they did not fear.*"

The wolves, as we learn from shepherds and those who have become acquainted with these things, if they ever attack a flock, cannot attack it when it is gathered, but they attend to where a sheep strays aside and where it leaves the flock, and they scheme against it. Thus, just as those sheep that are more prudent do not stray from one another, but make shelters and a plan[28] for grazing with each other so that they may not be schemed against, in the same manner, as for you, always be with the Church and do not depart from the shepherd, so that the shepherd may be with you, so that you "may come to be," it says, "one flock, one shepherd."[29] And if you were to be such, and you were not to be one who strays from the little flock, "*the sea covers your enemies.*"[30] For then the bodily sea covered up bodily enemies, but the intelligible sea covers up your invisible enemies, so that they cannot do anything to you, having been cast into the sea, for the genuine Jacob will drown our lawless deeds, and he will throw them into the depths of the sea.[31]

The enemies working to take captives by means of sins have been covered up by the intelligible sea, so that after this you may receive these promises that say, "*And he led them into the mountain of his holiness*":[32] and he led that people then into a mountain— since they were doing figurative deeds—to a mountain of bodily holiness, but he led you into a mountain of holiness about which the Apostle says, "But you have arrived at Mount Zion and the city of the living God, heavenly Jerusalem, and to myriads of angels in festal gathering";[33] that is truly the mountain of God's holiness, "*this mountain that his right hand acquired.*"[34] "This" one,

---

28. *Oikonomia,* "plan," is the word used for God's saving plan for humanity; see n. 11 above. Unlike the Jews, who are the passive objects of God's *oikonomia* in prescribing the Sabbath rest, Christ's flock can participate actively.

29. Jn 10.16.

30. Ps 77.53b.

31. See Mi 7.19–20. The genuine Jacob is Christ. See also Ex 15.1.

32. Ps 77.54a.

33. Heb 12.22.

34. Ps 77.54b.

it seems, was bodily pointed out by the prophet in Zion and now "this" mountain is pointed out to the mind seeing an intelligible mountain.[35] Just as the demonstration of a body occurs to eyes of a body, so the intelligible demonstration occurs to the eyes of the soul, so that "this" is not said in the manner of an illusory disturbance[36] to a mind seeing a being and substance of something intelligible.[37]

35. Origen believed that Asaph pointed with his finger to Mount Zion as he said the words, an indication that he himself pointed to "this" ear or "this" shoulder (see PS77H1.5 and PS36H3.7 above). Origen does the same thing intelligibly to his congregation.

36. *En kenopatheiāi*, "illusory" or "empty disturbance." Origen may have found the word *kenopatheia* in *Against the Learned* by the second-century physician and philosophical Pyrrhonist or Skeptic, Sextus Empiricus, where it refers to a sensory illusion such as a mirage (*Math.* 8.184), or in some other work from the Old Academy. See also n. 64 below.

37. *Ousian kai hupostasin noētou*, "being and substance of an intelligible thing." Compare Plotinus, "In the intelligible cosmos [*tōi kosmōi noētōi*] is genuine being [*ousia*]" (*Enn.* 4.1.1). "This" intelligible "being" is real and distinct, a "substance." Origen would have recalled the logical implications of the demonstrative pronoun from Aristotle, *Categories*, 3b10: "All being [*ousia*] appears to signify a 'this' [*tode ti*]." "This mountain" is thus as meaningful from the perspective of the inner eye of the mind, which distinguishes one substance from another, as it is from the perspective of Asaph's bodily eye, which distinguished "this mountain," Mount Zion, from the rest of the landscape. Mark James explains: "The intellect has the capacity to 'see' entities that are not empty affections of the subject but real external realities with qualities ('being') and a substrate of which one may predicate those qualities ('substance'). Intellectual deixis is the linguistic mechanism by which a speaker may point a hearer to this intellectual object as it appears to the mind, just as she may direct him to an object of the senses. By drawing this parallel between the deictic mechanisms of sense and intellect, moreover, Origen makes especially clear that he has in view concrete spiritual existences analogous to the concrete particulars apprehended by our senses, rather than mere abstractions. The notion that Forms are subsistent individuals rather than mere abstractions is the Platonic view, and as David Dawson has rightly emphasized, for Origen too 'spiritual' reality is not abstract but concrete [David Dawson, *Christian Figural Reading and the Fashioning of Identity* (Berkeley: University of California Press, 2002), 50]. However, populated as it is by analogues of physical realities—such as spiritual mountains, angels, and liturgies—Origen's spiritual realm is clearly far less abstract than Plato's. And as this example shows, one mechanism by which scriptural language can be used to refer to such things is spiritual deixis of place." Mark Randall James, *Learning the Language of Scripture: Origen, Wisdom, and the Logic of Interpretation* (Leiden: Brill, forthcoming, 2021).

5. "*And he threw out nations before their face and allotted them in allotments by a cord.*"[38] Then he threw out the nations—Canaanites, Hittites, Amorites, and so on[39]—before the face of that people, but now he throws out nations—not bodily Canaanites or some material and visible Hittites and so on—before the face. But if you understand "the spiritual matters of wickedness in the heavenly places,"[40] he throws these out of the heavenly places, so that you may inherit the kingdom of heavens as a distribution, when the heavenly nations have been thrown out before your face, and you receive a land distribution inside a cord such as the Savior has prepared, for by making a whip of cords he expelled them all from the Temple.[41] He braids this whip of cords and first cleanses you, throwing out of you those things that make the house of the Father a marketplace, those things making the house of prayer a den of robbers.[42] Next after this he employs the cord of land distribution, and each of us is given a proportional distribution. What was read in Joshua concerning the distributions of the tribes is a token.[43]

6. "*And he set up tents for the tribes of Israel in tents of Canaanites and Hittites.*"[44] Thus in the tents of those thrown out from the heavenly places, God would set up tents for the tribes of the genuine, well-born, and spiritual Israel. The next passage recounts the misdeeds of those who have been benefited, which often occur also among us: "*They tested and embittered God the Most High, and they did not keep his testimonies.*"[45] Which of us is pure from testing the Lord and from failing to keep his testimonies?

"*And they turned away and violated the covenant just as their fathers did, and they changed into a bent bow.*"[46] Whenever we sin, we turn away from God and do not keep covenants, which he set for us, and we imitate our fathers and we ourselves become as

38. Ps 77.55a–b.
39. See Jude 3.5.
40. Eph 6.12.
41. Jn 2.15.
42. See Mt 21.13, Mk 11.17, Lk 19.45–48, Is 56.7, Jer 7.11.
43. Jos 13–21.
44. Ps 77.55c.
45. Ps 77.56
46. Ps 77.57.

our fathers were. "*And they changed*," it says, "*into a bent bow*." Just as, in its nature, a bent bow is no longer straight, in the same manner, when we sin, we become bent like a bow. Whenever we become bent like a bow, the devil uses us and shoots arrows by means of us.[47] When you see a minister who has become sinful, so that someone else sins, imagine nothing else about him than that he has been changed and has become like a bent bow and has come into the hands of the adversary. And through that bent bow the devil, who has been summoned, discharges arrows, ignites fire, shoots and wounds by sin whomever he finds vulnerable.

But you will understand what is said by this example: in this way Marcion tested God the Most High; he did not keep his testimonies, he turned away from God, he deleted his covenants,[48] he changed into a bent bow. Then the devil used him as his own bow and discharged arrows through his mouth, and injured all those receiving the arrows and not beating them away with the shield of the straight faith.[49] Thus Basilides is another bow. Valentinus is another bow. And may you not think that they and their equivalents are the only bent bows, but if you see something spoken of as a stumbling block in the Church, that thing being one of the brothers, so that through him souls are hurt, through him they fall from the faith, know that such a person is serving the devil as a bent bow. He is using him as a bow, and an intelligible string stretches this bow, I say stretching the stumbling block, and he discharges the fiery arrows.

So also an eye of a prostitute is a trap for a sinner. And the prostitute becomes a bent bow, "when honey drips from a prostituting woman's lips and for a time it soothes your palate,"[50] and a burning arrow is released through that bent bow—the prostitute, I say—and the one who commits sexual immorality is wounded. And another provokes me to anger; that person is

47. The bow would not ordinarily be "bent" by being strung. That would make it a lethal weapon ready to use.

48. Marcion "deletes" the covenants by removing from the New Testament passages that treat the Old Testament positively.

49. See Eph 6.16.

50. See Prv 5.3.

a bow that has become a bent bow by the devil, so that it may wound through the arrow of anger. And another sins a sin provoking sadness; that minister of sadness to me is a bent bow. The Scripture does not vainly compare sinners to a bent bow. Therefore, let us attend to ourselves, so that the devil may not make use of us, intending to wound others, as by a bent bow, ready to come into his hand, "for look, the sinners have bent back a bow, they have prepared arrows in a quiver."[51]

7. And the human beings and the adverse powers "prepared arrows in a quiver," and those who had been changed into a bent bow "*incited God's wrath with their mounds.*"[52] This again fits the heresies, for "*they incited God's wrath with their mounds*"; for example, by gathering together some exaltations and imagination of lofty logoi promising secrets of worship, they incite the wrath of the true God with their mounds, and "*with their carvings they make him jealous.*"[53] It is possible that, just as there are sensible carvings, there are also intelligible ones, for thought, when it is sitting still, fashions images and, as it were, makes imaginary things for itself out of things that do not exist; what else must be reckoned than that such a soul is cursed for making something contrary to what is written and saying, "'Cursed is whoever will make a work carved or shaped by the hands of an artisan, and will set it in a hidden place,' and all the people said, 'Let it be so.'"[54] All, then, who fashion for themselves things that do not exist, and, for example, are carving for themselves useless figurines[55] and applying colors to the things that they fashioned, make God jealous with their carvings.

I am convinced that there are two kinds of idolatry: the one is something that happens sensibly with a visible idol, concerning which I consider that any faithful person is devoted to the commandment that one should not worship idols. For once we have rejected and recognized such idols, we will not fall for them, so as to consider that they are gods. But there is another kind

51. Ps 10.2.
52. Ps 77.58a.
53. Ps 77.58b.
54. See Dt 27.15.
55. See Is 44.10.

of idolatry, when the soul makes idols and drafts things that do not exist, and a mental draft adorned by a beautiful logos, as if by gold and silver. "For I gave them," it says, "silver and gold, but they made silver and gold things for Baal."[56] "*But God heard and overlooked them.*"[57] If he hears such things occurring, he does not supervise one who does them, but overlooks him.[58]

"*And he will set Israel at naught exceedingly*";[59] he will set at naught the one doing these things and fallen away after being called to the Israelite hearth. "*And he rejected the tent of Shiloh,*"[60] either, that is, the one in which he first set up a tent[61] bodily among human beings, the tent of Shiloh,[62] he rejected that one, or as he later rejected the one at Jerusalem. But even now, if we are leaving the genuine tent, which God, not a human being, staked out,[63] we will make some other tent and, as it were, artificialities;[64] the Lord rejects "*the tent of Shiloh, the tent in which he*

56. Hos 2.8.

57. Ps 77.59a.

58. God overlooks idolatry rather than supervising it, allowing idolaters to face the consequences of their bad behavior and learn by doing so to desist from it.

59. Ps 77.59b.

60. Ps 77.60.

61. *Kateskēnōsen,* "set up a tent." This is reminiscent of Jn 1.14a, "and the logos became flesh and tented [*eskēnōsen*] among us."

62. See Jos 18.1. Shiloh was the first place that the tent or tabernacle, the place of God's presence on earth, was set up. Solomon's temple would later become that place.

63. The genuine tent is the human body of the divine logos: Jesus himself and, in part, the Church (see PS15H1.3 above). See also introduction, p. 20.

64. *Anaplasmata,* "representations" or "artificialities," a word derived from *plassō,* "mold" (the root from which we get "plastic"). *Plassō* occurs in the description of the making of a golden calf (Ex 32.4), Aaron's false and illusory representation of God. Origen called *anaplasmata* (*Letter to Gregory* 3.3) the golden calves set up by Jeroboam in the alternative sanctuaries to the Temple in Jerusalem that Jeroboam set up at Bethel and Dan (1 Kgs 12.28–29). Thus the passage refers to leaving the Church for a heretical gathering. The philosophical concerns that surface at the end of section 4 above (see especially notes 36 and 37) come to the surface again. See Sextus Empiricus, *Math.* 8.354: "For if all existing things are, in fact, sensible or intelligible, the premises of the proof are, to be sure, obliged to be sensible or intelligible, but if they are actually sensible and if they are actually intelligible has been investigated, for the sensible things are such things as appear to have a substantial basis or they are illusions and

set up a tent among human beings, and he gave over their strength to captivity."[65]

8. If we sin, we hand our strength over to captivity and come to be subordinate to those who take us captive, not to human beings; would that it were human beings who took us into captivity and not adverse powers! What can human beings who take me into captivity do to me? Can they enslave me? Even as a slave I can be a Christian and keep God's laws, but if the devil takes me as a captive, he enslaves me to a fearsome slavery. What sort of slavery is it the Savior spoke of: "Everyone doing sin is a slave of sin"?[66] That is the fearsome slavery, and it fits that slavery to say, "For you have not received a spirit of slavery back into fear, but you have received a spirit of adoption, in which we cry, 'Abba, Father.'"[67] But do not be unaware that "you have not received a spirit of slavery" has another interpretation, which we have discussed.[68] He gave over, then, their strength to captivity. If you want not to become a captive or to have your strength

---

artificialities [*kenopathēmata kai anaplasmata*] of thought; indeed some of them also exist as well as seem, but some only seem, and, to be sure, have no underlying basis."

65. Ps 77.6ob–61a.

66. Jn 8.34.

67. Rom 8.15. For example, in *Comm. Jo.* 32.13.148, speaking of Judas at the Last Supper as a slave of sin after the devil had put it in his heart to betray Jesus. This is the "fearsome" form of slavery.

68. The "other interpretation" identifies "a spirit of slavery to fear" as the first stage of a process of assimilation to God. Thus Origen states in *Comm Jo.* 1.29.201: "But it is utterly plain, even to the random person, how our Lord is teacher and explainer for those who are straining toward religion and the lord of slaves who 'have received a spirit of slavery to fear.' But when they are advancing and hastening to wisdom and are deemed worthy, because 'the slave does not know what his lord intends' he does not remain a lord but becomes their 'friend'" (Jn 15.15). Prior to Origen, Clement of Alexandria also emphasized a positive role of fear as the preliminary stage of Christian life: "The human being progressing from faith and fear to knowledge knows to say, 'lord, lord,' but not as a slave; he has learned to say 'our Father,' because he has liberated 'the spirit of slavery' that is 'to fear' and, having progressed through love to 'adoption,' is already revering through love the one whom he earlier feared; he does not refrain by fear from what is to be avoided, but he keeps the commandments by love. 'The same spirit,' it says, 'testifies' whenever we say, 'Abba, Father'" (*Prophetic Eclogues* 19).

given over to captivity, do not separate from the Church, but be together, bringing yourselves into rhythm[69] with the prayer.

9. "*And their beauteousness into hands of enemies.*"[70] The human soul has great beauty, and if you want to see its beauty, see the beginning, how it was created: "Let us make a human being according to our image."[71] You see the beauty: the human soul is spoken of as "according to the image" and "according to the likeness" of God, for it hopes to regain the likeness.[72] Many have become lovers of this beauty even as many have become lovers of the beauty of a woman.[73] And even when they are lovers, the tem-

69. Origen discusses the benefits of "bringing oneself into" prayer in *Or.* 8.2. See also PS67H2.4 above.

70. Ps 77.61b.

71. Gn 1.26.

72. See *Princ.* 2.10.2 and 4.6.1. Origen distinguishes between the image, *eikōn*, of God in Gn 1.26, which all human beings retain (see PS15H1.3 above), and the likeness, *homoiōsis*, which must be gained. We find this distinction already in Irenaeus (*Haer.* 5.6.1), who identifies likeness with the presence of the divine spirit. Origen identifies the divine likeness with the human spirit and the image with the soul. God says, "Let us make a human being in our image and likeness" (Gn 1.26) but, according to Origen, God did not complete that creation in the beginning, because the next verse leaves out the "likeness" and says only, "he made him in an image" (Gn 1.27). Like Clement of Alexandria before him (see *Strom.* 2.131.5), Origen agreed with Plato (*Theaetetus* 174a) that the "likeness" is something yet to be achieved and that can be achieved only by the practice of virtue. Plotinus's treatise on the virtues of the soul, which cites and expands on the same passage in Plato, concludes with a contrast between "image" and "likeness"(*Enn.* 1.2.7): "But likeness (*homoiōsis*), on the one hand, to them [good human beings] is as an image (*eikōn*) that resembles another image of the same thing. But the likeness to a different being [a god] is as to a pattern (*paradeigma*)."

73. Origen thus nods to the concept of the desire for the beautiful as a path to transcendence in Plato's *Symposium* and in his *Phaedrus,* which ends with Socrates's prayer: "O dear Pan and all other gods as are in this place, may you grant that I may be beautiful inwardly, and that outwardly all I have may be on friendly terms with what is within" (279b). In Origen's day this found expression in the first treatise Plotinus wrote, *On Beauty* (*Enn.* 1.6). There, for example, alluding to Socrates's prayer, Plotinus states: "And seeing your own inward beauty, what do you experience? And how, being in a Bacchic frenzy and stirred up, do you even desire to collect yourselves away from the body? For these things those who are really lovers caperience. But what is it, concerning which they experience these things? It is not form, it is not color, it is not some magnitude, but it concerns a soul, itself colorless [*Phaedrus* 247c], but having colorless moderation

perate soul does not give in; the sexually immoral and the licentious soul are taken either by licentiousness or by some pleasure or by some profit. In the same way every soul of a human being for the sake of its own logos and the formation just mentioned is a beautiful creation, although not every soul employs that beauty in the same way, but it is possible for some soul to be employing it badly.

And I suppose that Solomon was saying this in Proverbs when he said, "Like a ring in a pig's snout, so is beauty in a woman thinking badly."[74] In a woman thinking badly the beauty of the soul is bad, for the very soul surrenders itself in quest of her lovers, and she walks in quest of them. Who are the lovers? The spiritual adversaries are recorded as lovers also in Ezekiel.[75] And the rulers are lovers, the authorities, the cosmic powers of this darkness; the spiritual things of wickedness are lovers. When, then, they love and do not succeed with the soul they love, then they become enemies to the one they love, and instead of their wanting to deceive, they become enemies. And it is said, not to all human beings, but to the just: "Our wrestling is not against blood and flesh, but against the rulers, against the authorities, against the cosmic dominators of this darkness."[76]

You will find these secrets as riddles in the prophets, especially represented in Ezekiel. For there God threatened, as it appears—and I suppose that appearance was true—it is promised that "your lovers will make war on you."[77] This is said in relation to that Jerusalem: *"and he consigned his people to a sword*

---

and the other radiance of the virtues, when you behold in yourselves or in someone else some magnitude of soul; a righteous way of life; courage having a shaggy face; and dignity and modesty advancing in a resolute, calm, and undisturbed disposition, the godlike mind shining on all these." Sarah Coakley writes of this tradition: "… it is God who is basic, and 'desire' the precious clue that tugs at the heart, reminding the human soul—however dimly—of its created source"; *God, Sexuality and the Self: An Essay on the Trinity* (Cambridge: Cambridge University Press, 2013), 10.

74. Prv 11.22.

75. See Ezek 16.33–37, 23.5, 23.9, and 23.22. See also *Hom. Ezech.* 7.6.

76. Eph 6.12.

77. See Ezek 16.37–42. Because Ezekiel uses figurative language, this "appears" to be a threat.

and overlooked his inheritance."[78] When we sin he consigns us to a sword. What sort of sword? The sword of one making war against us. For there is a certain sword by which sinners become wounded.

"*And he overlooked his inheritance. Fire consumed their youth.*"[79] If you see a soul set on fire, either of a youth in an intelligible sense[80] or of a youth in a bodily sense, do not hesitate to say that "fire consumed the youth of Israel." If you see a youth loving a prostitute and gripped by desire for a woman, do not hesitate to say concerning that person that such are the youth concerning whom the Scripture says, "*Fire consumed their youth.*"[81] The same applies to "*and their virgins were not commended.*"[82] For so it must be read, as all the other versions hold as well as the Hebrew and some reliable copies.[83] For there is blame to a virgin, whenever she is not commended, for virginity must be a commendable activity—through modesty; through dignity; and through beauty, not of the body, but of the soul.

"*Their priests fell by the sword.*"[84] The logos is speaking against us, if we are not sober, for we believers are the priesthood.[85] If we sin, the Scripture, "*their priests fell by the sword,*" pertains to us.

78. Ps 77.62.

79. Ps 77.62b–63a.

80. Someone who acts immature at any age.

81. Ps 77.63a.

82. Ps 77.63b.

83. *Antigraphois,* "copies," that is, of the Septuagint text used by the Church. Only one letter differentiates the Greek words "bewailed" and "commended." Most Septuagint texts read, "their virgins were not bewailed." By consulting his *Hexapla* and giving the Hebrew priority, Origen substitutes the reading "their virgins were not commended," found in a few "reliable" copies of the Septuagint. Scribes early in the transmission of the Septuagint probably found the Hebrew inappropriate or incomprehensible and "corrected" it by substituting "not bewailed" for "not commended." Origen restores a more accurate reading. Apparently, however, Origen did not understand that young women would ordinarily be "commended"—or "praised"—when they were married. The NRSV translates the Hebrew as "and their young girls had no marriage song" (because the enemies of Israel have killed their potential husbands).

84. Ps 77.64a.

85. For Origen, as in the New Testament, "priesthood" applies to believers in general, not exclusively to elders or bishops. See 1 Pt 2.5 and 2.9 and Rv 1.6 and 5.10.

Furthermore, if we also see the widowhood of the Church not ornamented by a beautiful pattern of conduct, it is said concerning this: "*and their widows will not be bewailed.*"[86] Therefore, the judge is awake to them; since God does not prefer anyone's persona,[87] he punishes all sinners rightfully for any action.

To be sure, we know this: that the nobler and superior believing soul, when it sins, will not be punished in the same way as a lesser believing soul. The daughter of a priest has committed fornication; a lesser offender would be stoned, but she is burned with fire.[88] By the measure that a person who has sinned is nobler, that person has sinned to a greater extent; he has a greater and fuller punishment. These things turn out otherwise than they occur in this cosmos. For a noble and a common person commit the same sins, and on account of nobility the noble is sentenced by a worldly law that respects persons.[89] But the law that does not prefer anyone's persona powerfully scrutinizes the powerful.[90] For it knows that "the least are allowed mercy."[91] But let us offer a prayer, having come to a great and holy calling, not to tread the Son of God underfoot or to regard as profane the blood of the covenant by which we have been made holy,[92] nor to abuse such a great secret, but rather to adorn[93] it, so that we

86. Ps 77.64b.

87. See Acts 10.34.

88. See Dt 22.21 and Lv 21.9.

89. What Origen says about "worldly law" is not just an observation that the legal system can be distorted by social inequality, as has been the case in most societies, including our own; it is also a timely observation about Roman law. During his lifetime, the distinction between the *honestior*, his "noble" (*eugenēs*), and the *humilior*, his "common person" (*agenēs*), was formalized, with fewer rights and severer penalties prescribed for the latter. In contrast to Scripture, where higher status brings a more severe penalty, Origen's hearers would have known that a *humilior* could be sentenced to be burned alive, but a *honestior* could not. *Honestiores* were also favored in civil suits. See G. E. M. de Ste. Croix, *The Class Struggle in the Ancient Greek World* (Ithaca, NY: Cornell University Press, 1981), 453–62. Jill Harries sets forth a more positive evaluation of late Roman legal theory (but not necessarily practice) in *Law and Empire in Late Antiquity* (Cambridge: Cambridge University Press, 1999), 135–52.

90. See Lk 12.48 and PS81H.3.

91. Wis 6.6.

92. See Heb 10.29.

93. Greek, *kosmēsai*, the verbal form of *kosmos*.

may become the light of the cosmos,[94] but also of the earth,[95] in Christ Jesus, to whom is the glory and the might to the ages of ages. Amen.

94. Jn 8.12, Mt 5.14. Becoming holy by accepting the divine logos into our hearts enables us to be truly what Jesus is himself and calls us to be, the light of the cosmos. See PS67H1.7 above and PS81H.1 below.

95. Christ, the Sun of Justice (Mal 4.2), will shine through us. See PS80H1.6 below and PS36H1.6 above.

HOMILY 9 ON PSALM 77

E ASK TO receive wakefully the logos from God concerning, "*And the Lord has awakened as from sleep*," and we intend to speak about "*as a powerful man and befuddled with wine*,"[1] if God, who is sober for those who are deserving and maintains himself in the dignity of his greatness for those who are close to him, should give us the ability. Let us then be governed by the logos here; Paul, as great as was his progress in God and in speaking the truth—"let as many of us as are mature think this"[2]—was so powerful as a mature person as even to say, powerfully, "I can overcome all things in Christ Jesus my Lord, who empowers me."[3] But, being powerful, he saw that the weak did not need him to be powerful. Therefore, he became weak for the weak, so that he might gain the weak.[4]

Out of love, then, Paul, who could overcome all things, became weak for the weak, because his weakness was more needful to the weak than the power that, had it been kept, would have preserved his dignity intact, but the weak would not have been redeemed. Thus Paul saw that some, because they were without the law, were unable to hear him as someone conformed to the law and to accept the explanation that the law consisted of the shadow of good things to come.[5] And he saw that to such persons he did not need to transmit the heavenly aspects of the law, but he needed to be conformed to them; not being at all lawless as far as God is concerned, but in every way a law-abiding follow-

---

1. Ps 77.65.
2. Phil 3.15.
3. Phil 4.13.
4. 1 Cor 9.22.
5. See Heb 10.1.

er of Christ Jesus,[6] he put on an act of being someone without the law.[7] For putting on an act[8] of lawlessness produces salvation for the lawless, so that they may no longer be truly lawless. Therefore, for the lawless, Paul became, not "lawless," but "as one lawless, not being lawless as far as God is concerned but law-abiding as far as Christ is concerned," so that he might gain the lawless.[9] For Paul was confident that Christ had redeemed him from the curse of the law, becoming a curse on his behalf and on behalf of all believers, so that he might put an end to the curse of all those under the law.[10]

Aware of these things, Paul imitated those under the law, having as his goal the freeing of those under the law by imitating them. And just as my Lord Christ Jesus, when the fullness of time came, was sent out by the Father to be born from a woman, to be born under the law,[11] not so that he might be a slave to the law—for the Son of a Human Being is lord of the Sabbath[12]—but so that he might provide freedom from the law,[13] so Paul, imitator of Christ,[14] came to be as one under the law to those under the law, so that he might gain those under the law.[15] But seeing others acting like Jews and turning away from sharing in the common life of human beings, and wishing to act

6. See 1 Cor 9.21. In a fragment from his *Homilies on 1 Corinthians*, Origen gives Paul's behavior at Athens, as recounted in Acts 17, as an example of this behavior. See Judith Kovacs, *The Church's Bible: I Corinthians Interpreted by Early Christian Commentators* (Grand Rapids, MI: Eerdmans, 2005), 154–55.

7. For a more detailed justification of this behavior on Paul's part, see *Comm. Jo.* 20.7. Origen believes that God also puts on an act for our benefit. See *Hom. Jer.* 18.6, which describes God's "putting on an act," coming down to our level of speaking and understanding as a parent treats an infant.

8. *Hupocrisis*, which gives us "hypocrisy," is putting on an act. Here and in the previous sentence, where Origen uses the corresponding verb, it is used in a neutral sense. Origen considered deception something that God engages in for our benefit and that we can also practice when God is working through us to help those who would be harmed by the full truth. See *Hom. Jer.* 20.

9. 1 Cor 9.21.

10. See Gal 3.13.

11. See Gal 4.4.

12. Mk 2.28.

13. See Gal 4.5.

14. See 1 Cor 11.1.

15. 1 Cor 9.20.

like Jews, imagining that they were maintaining Judaism, to such persons, then, Paul even became a Jew. For if, as he thought, he had appeared and presented himself as one who dined and conversed with gentiles, he would not have gained Jews. And to the extent that he fell in with Jews, he was an observant Jew with them, that he might obtain Jews: he circumcised Timothy; he cut his hair and offered an offering at the altar.[16] For this seemed profitable to the Jews, so that he might gain them.

If, with me, you have understood Paul accommodating himself to such persons for no other purpose than to be useful to other human beings, seek with me Paul's model, for Paul did not do these things imitating you. Paul's model, then, was Christ; "for become imitators," he said, "of me as I am of Christ."[17] Before Paul, you will find Christ becoming weak, so that he might gain the weak.

For he was crucified out of weakness and "becoming under the law," as I have just said from the Epistle to the Galatians, but it is also evident in the Gospels. For he was in the gatherings,[18] even gathering himself with the Jews.[19] If he had not gathered, on the grounds that it was not worthwhile to gather, he would not have gained those he gained by gathering. And he himself kept other things of the law, so that those under the law might not turn away from him but approach and be benefited. What must one say, but that he was a Jew to the Jews? For he was such a Jew to the Jews, that the Samaritan woman said, "How is it that you, being a Jew, ask [for something] to drink from me, being a woman of Samaria? For Jews do not have dealings with Samaritans."[20] But Christ also became such a lawless person for the lawless, that he was reckoned among the lawless.[21]

Besides, we shall ascertain that Christ had become lawless

16. See Acts 16.3 and 21.26. Paul's willingness to accommodate himself to the extent of concealing his actual position is a common theme in Origen's writings. See also *Cels.* 2.2. Paul accommodated himself to three groups: gentiles, Judaizing Christians, and Jews. This is the practice of *oikonomia.*

17. See 1 Cor 11.1. See PS15H2.4 above.

18. Or "synagogues."

19. See, for example, Mk 1.21, Mt 4.23, Lk 4.15, Jn 6.59.

20. Jn 4.9.

21. See Is 53.12, Lk 22.37.

for the lawless from the Gospels, because, before Paul, contrary to the custom of the Pharisees and the Jewish way of life, he ate and drank with sinners and tax collectors, "lawless among the lawless, not being lawless as far as God is concerned but law-abiding as far as Christ is concerned, in order to gain the lawless."[22] Everything that Paul did in imitation of Christ, Christ did in imitation of the Father. For the God and Father of the universe also, if he did not suffer along with nature[23] that comes to be, the human race and the substance of other rational living beings would not have been benefited. Therefore, accordingly, God becomes for each whatever each, insofar as depends on his own choice, makes himself. If you neglect God, God says to you, "You have abandoned me, and I shall abandon you."[24] If you are still hearing, you would not give sleep to your eyes or slumber to your eyelids;[25] when you are asleep, God does not supervise you, but, even as he is awake to creation, he falls asleep to you alone and those like you.

22. 1 Cor 9.21.

23. *Sumpathēsēi tēi genētēi phusei.* Origen taught that God "suffers along with" us and seeks us out. *Hom. Ezech.* 6.6: "The Father himself, also, the God of the Universe, patient and abounding in mercy [Ps 102.8] and one who has mercy, does he not in some manner suffer? Or are you unaware that, when he plans human affairs, he suffers a human suffering? Your Lord God has borne with your behavior, as a man does who bears with his son [Dt 1.31]. Because God bears with our behavior, in the same manner the Son of God bears with our passions. The Father himself is not impassible. If he is petitioned, he is merciful and shares our sorrow. He undergoes the passion of love and for our sake puts himself in situations incompatible with the grandeur of his nature and bears sufferings for us human beings." The distinction Origen implies here between being and becoming is fundamental to any Platonic outlook on reality. God, identified as being, is changeless (see, for example, PS67H1.3 above), but the cosmos itself and all who inhabit it belong to "the nature that comes to be," the realm of becoming. Attributing to God an active concern for the welfare of human beings distinguishes Origen from his fellow Platonist, Plotinus. Plotinus taught that the divine is always present and accessible to us by contemplation, but not that God seeks us out. Thus, for example, "it appeared to us and our logos showed that **those realities** [those of the realm of being] **do not look toward those here** [those coming to birth in the realm of becoming], but that these [here] depend upon those and imitate them" (*Enn.* 6.7.7).

24. 2 Chr 12.5.

25. See Ps 131.4.

Thus he himself is also without wrath, for an inner disturbance[26] does not attach to God. But when you commit many
sins, you enkindle for yourself a wrath called "wrath of God."[27]
When God is provoked to wrath, he speaks logoi of one provoked to wrath, for a father, provoked to wrath, can pronounce
logoi to a son, as if from wrath, without undergoing any inner
disturbance, so he might direct an infant, so that he might discipline the child; but, if we require threatening logoi, cannot
God, without wrath, speak logoi of one provoked to wrath? Thus
God never undergoes a change of heart, and his gracious gifts
and all his actions are without regret, but when he is having a
change of heart, the change of heart that has been recorded is
yours.

Whenever you sin, God is estranged from you. But if you
change, he says, "I have regretted concerning this people, saying
that it is no longer rightfully under Saul, but now to be reigned
over by David."[28] And such a consideration accounts for, "I
have changed my mind about anointing Saul as king."[29] Never
make the assumption, then, when you notice the ascription of
human mental disturbance to God, that God is truly subject to
mental disturbance. For if, as I have already said, no one should
assume that Paul was truly weak when he said, "Who is weak and
I am not weak?"[30] or that he truly burned with the burning of
those who lust, when he said, "Who is offended and I do not
burn?"[31] you ought all the more to think that God is not in any
manner subject to mental disturbance. Nonetheless, when you
sin, God sleeps to you, and when you have a change of heart,
"the Lord has awakened as from sleep."[32]

2. I must prepare for the wording to follow, so that *"the Lord
has awakened as from sleep"*[33] may become still clearer. I say that,

26. *Pathos.* See PS77H7.7, n. 83 above.

27. On wrath, *orgē*, see PS75H.8 and PS77H7.7 above.

28. See 1 Sm 15.11–16.13.

29. 1 Sm 15.35. In *Princ.* 4.2.1 Origen mentions this as a text that heretics
cite in order to discredit the God of the Old Testament.

30. 2 Cor 11.29.

31. Ibid.

32. Ps 77.65a.

33. Ibid.

when God wakes up for you, he is unable to be an enemy to you, but if an enemy is empowered against you, God is sleeping for you. Just as contrary winds were able to do nothing, waves were able to do nothing, the sea was able to do nothing when Jesus was awake, but when he was asleep, the contrary wind blew, and the waves rose up, and the boat was in danger of sinking beneath the waves, until the sailors who were watching in prayer aroused Jesus, and when he arose, he rebuked the sea, he stopped the contrary winds, and he made calm.[34] So understand with me about enemies, the adverse powers, which are empowered when you are asleep, and, because you are asleep, God is put to sleep. But when you arise, he awakens "*as the Lord does from sleep*" and "*strikes your enemies in the rear.*"[35]

For who rightly renders propitious the one "sweetened," if I may use the term, by him? There is someone embittering the Lord, and someone sweetening the Lord; living my life in a certain way embitters the Lord, but certain activities sweeten the Lord. For example, the prophet says, "May my estimate be sweetened to him,"[36] and again, "Lord, they have made you bitter."[37] But God does not just "*awaken as one sleeping*" but also "*as a powerful man and befuddled with wine.*"[38]

For what do we not make God? If I myself had said that God was "*as a powerful man and befuddled with wine,*" which of my fault-finders would not have taken it upon himself to say, "You ascribe drunkenness and befuddlement to God; are not we human beings taught that human beings who are drunk do not inherit the kingdom of God?"[39] But nonetheless the Holy Spirit, taking the authority to speak freely, says that God was once roused "*as a powerful man and befuddled with wine.*"[40] For perhaps,

34. See Mk 4.37–40, Mt 8.23–27, and Lk 8.22–24.

35. Ps 77.65a.

36. Ps 103.34.

37. Ps 5.11.

38. Ps 77.65b.

39. See 1 Cor 6.10.

40. Ps 77.65b. The ascription of authorship to the Holy Spirit does not rule out the agency of human authors. This is especially clear in PS76H1.1 above, where Asaph, who, as a prophet, speaks by the Holy Spirit, composes a Psalm to suit the character of Jeduthun, who will recite it. Here Origen reminds his listeners

as it were, we carouse and make God drunk, as we make him fall asleep, get angry, and so on,[41] so that God is not sober to us, but he becomes "*as a powerful man and befuddled.*" But if we turn around so as to live soberly, in keeping with what the Apostle said about someone, "sober, moderate, generous, seemly,"[42] if we become mindful, God wakes to us "*as a powerful man and be-fuddled with wine.*"

3. As he is punishing, he is like one befuddled with wine, but when he halts his wrath, he is roused "*as a powerful man befuddled with wine.*" And what does God do, when he is awakened "*as one sleeping, as a powerful man befuddled with wine*"? "*And he struck,*" it says, "*their enemies in the rear, he gave them age-long reproach.*"[43] It said, "*He struck their enemies.*" Why does it need the addition of "*in the rear*"? But, let us see, the one fleeing God gives his back to him. Such a one was the snake, which we have mentioned earlier, the fleeing serpent that was destroyed by the holy and great sword of God.[44] When, therefore, his enemies flee God, the divine justice pursuing them does not strike them in the front. Those who see God face to face standing in his presence are not struck, but when someone flees God, then he is struck, being an enemy as well as putting God behind him. Therefore, God, having been put behind, strikes "*in the rear*" the one who puts him behind.

Do you want to learn who puts God behind? Hear the Forty-ninth Psalm say here: "You have put my logoi behind."[45] The one who puts logoi behind, puts Christ behind, and, by putting him behind, will be wounded by him in the rear. But who is

---

that, although the wording is surprising, it must be taken seriously. Compare *Hom. 1 Reg.* 5.4, where Origen ascribes to the Holy Spirit the narrative voice that recounts how a medium raises the soul of the prophet Samuel from hell.

41. Origen is teaching his hearers how to read Scripture on their own. He has just spoken about God's wrath and counts on them to remember what he had said at other times about God's sleeping, as in PS36H1.1, which also discusses wrath, and PS67H1.3 above. He now addresses another stumbling stone, God's drunkenness.

42. 1 Tm 3.2. All believers should have the qualifications of a bishop; see *Cels.* 3.48.

43. Ps 77.66.

44. See Is 27.1. The reference is to PS77H5.8 above.

45. Ps 49.17.

not struck in the rear as one fleeing God, but is honored as a friend of God? The one who takes up the cross and follows behind Christ[46] cannot be struck in the rear, for your rear is guarded even though there is no one behind you, but your rear is guarded by Jesus—for you also see the rear of Jesus—and you are healed and watched and walled in. A shield strengthens your back and you are free from care, I say, to the extent that you walk behind the Lord your God and to the extent that you follow behind Jesus, because no one will wound you in the rear.

4. And what else does God do to his own enemies? "*He gives them age-long reproach.*"[47] For we also know Daniel saying about the resurrection that, "some will be raised up to age-long life, but others to reproach and age-long shame,"[48] not first to shame and then to reproach, but to reproach and then to shame. For when you are shameless about your sins, one who intends to guide you to turn around reproaches, but when, on being reproached, you hear the reproach, you will be made ashamed of what you were shameless about earlier, when you were insensible to your vices. Therefore, beautifully also in Daniel, the order is maintained of what is going to happen on account of sins, first in reproach, but second in shame.

That it is the work of the Savior to reproach a holy person is written in the Gospel: "He began to reproach the cities, in which there had occurred many deeds of power, because they did not undergo change of heart."[49] Well, "he began to reproach" so that by beginning to reproach he might forewarn them not to be worthy to suffer reproach. Here, then, Jesus begins to reproach, and when you undergo change of heart, the reproach stops when it begins, and the beginning is the same thing as the end. But if you do not undergo change of heart when the logos begins to reproach you for your sins, your reproach is maintained even to the resurrection, and an age-long reproach is given then to those who did not undergo change of heart when Jesus first reproached them. Thus the sinners will

46. See Mt 16.24.
47. Ps 77.66b.
48. Dn 12.2.
49. Mt 11.20.

receive age-long reproach; but the just, age-long glory. Just as some are reproached because they did not undergo change of heart about their sins, so also others hear themselves praised. And perhaps in the age to come a holy one is maintaining and nourishing the holy one, the one from God who is praised continually, age-long, on account of good deeds over a short period, for it is not, let us say, as if he did well for thirty years, so that he might receive praises for thirty years, but he enjoys praises eternally.[50]

I have put forward these understandings as a logical opposite from "*I have given them age-long reproach.*"[51]

5. And "*he rejected the tents of Joseph, and he did not choose the tribe of Ephraim, and he chose the tribe of Judah.*"[52] According to the statement, Jeroboam claimed the rule of the ten tribes in the division, and, after him, his son; "and there did not lack a ruler from Judah and a leader from his parts,"[53] until Christ came, for whom the age-long, royal throne was laid up. According to the statement, then, "*he rejected the tents of Joseph, and he did not choose the tribe of Ephraim*": this amounts to saying that he did not intend for there to be a king from Joseph or a ruler from Ephraim. For he chose the tribe of Judah, so that from Judah he would reign over the people. Shall we stand, then, by the narrative alone, or do we also say that this statement is a prophecy that occurred about things that were to come about in the times of Solomon— for this Psalm is by Asaph, and I suppose that it is older—or that there is also some token evident in these things?[54]

---

50. Origen appears to be suggesting that the continuing assistance of the logos, "a holy one who maintains and nourishes," accounts for the disproportion between the actual conduct of the redeemed, a human life in which thirty years or so may have been passed in holiness, and its eternal reward.

51. By drawing out its logical implications, a warning becomes a promise.

52. Ps 77.67–68a.

53. Gn 49.10.

54. The logic of this paragraph is partially implicit. The words of Ps 77.67–68 constitute a "narrative" (*historia*) of God's rejection of Ephraim. This is a problem because no such rejection had taken place when Origen believed that Psalm 77 was written, the reign of David. He resolves that problem by setting the "statement" (*rhēton;* see introduction, pp. 31–32) of the passage beside the putatively much older "statement" of Gn 49.10, the Patriarch Jacob's blessing of his son Judah. These two, taken together, generate a further "statement," a prophet-

I dare say, indeed, that the division of the people then was a prophecy of the divisions and sects of the genuine Jerusalem, God's Church. For as those of the tribes of Israel did not remain then to be reigned over by the seed of David, but those who could not bear the harshness of Rehoboam had said, "There is not for us a portion in David nor an inheritance in the son of Jesse,"[55] so, even now, those who depart from the Church with various pretexts, blaming either bishops or sins among the people, fleeing, as if they themselves were free from sins, say, "There is not for us a portion in David nor an inheritance in the son of Jesse." Some of them say it nakedly, so that there is no need for its interpretation.[56]

Inquire of the Marcionites, then, "Is there actually a portion for you in David and an inheritance in the seed of Jesse?" He replies, "There is not for us a portion in David nor an inheritance in the seed of Jesse." For they deny the one "born of the seed of David according to the flesh."[57] And inquire of a Valentinian, "Is there actually a portion for you in David and an inheritance in the seed of Jesse?" And that person replies, "I am one who knows another God, better than that God Jesse worshiped." Nonetheless, the Valentinians also clearly say, "There is not for us a portion in David nor an inheritance in the son of Jesse." So go to Basilides; he will tell you the same things, and the overwhelming majority of the heretics will say the same thing and conform with the wording and say what was said then by those of the division, "There is not for us a portion in David nor an inheritance in the seed of Jesse." For all of them are, then, just like those of Jeroboam and from the tribe of Joseph.

---

ic warning that the separation of the tribes would not accord with God's will. Origen then asks if this further statement refers only to the schism under Rehoboam after the death of David's son, Solomon, or is also a "token" (*sumbolon*) of an ongoing reality.

55. 1 Kgs 12.16. See PS77H2.1 above.

56. Origen may be recalling actual encounters, in which he brought up this verse and asked Marcionites and Valentinians if they agreed with it. By "nakedly" using the actual words of Scripture to make their case, the heretics shamelessly condemn themselves out of their own mouths.

57. Rom 1.3. Marcion deleted this statement from his edition of the letters of Paul.

Why it is from the tribe of Joseph and from the tribe of Ephraim, this is possible to see rightly by means of figurative interpretation. Let it be plain, should Christ give it, from the presentation of a statement in Ezekiel and from the interpretation that we have reached in the prophetic passage. It is said to Jerusalem, "Your father was an Amorite, and your mother a Hittite."[58] And I have heard a tradition[59] about the passage that says that Abraham, in his life before the promises, was of the Amorite race, and Sarah, analogously to Abraham, was once of the Hittite race. And they were from those gentiles living around them, the very ones that the Lord later destroyed. Those, then, who have handed down the tradition say, it is as if someone said to an ordinary man born as the son of a man who was first a gentile, but later a believer, "Your father was a gentile, your father was an idolater," but because he underwent a change of heart, said, "Your father was a holy person, your father was a just person"; he would not be referring to two different fathers, but to the same father before and after he believed. And someone saying this would not be lying. So, since Jerusalem had become sinful, she heard, "Your father Abraham was an Amorite before he believed, who had no dealings with God," and about Sarah, that Abraham's wife, "she was a gentile too." "When you are a sinner, you are not the son of Abraham the just. When you are unfaithful, you are not a son of the faithful Abraham."

6. If the statement in Ezekiel has been understood by you along with the traditions—not easily dismissed in my opinion—that explain it, come also to, "*He rejected the tents of Joseph, and he did not choose the tribe of Ephraim.*"[60] "*The tents of Joseph*" are of his sons, who are Ephraim and Manasseh, and these sons of Joseph, Ephraim and Manasseh, are also the sons of Joseph and of the Egyptian woman, Asenath.[61] When, then, God rejected the tents of Joseph, he rejected the children of the Egyptian woman, for

58. Ezek 16.3.

59. On Abraham, see Kugel, *Traditions of the Bible*, 245–55. Perhaps Origen knew a tradition that inferred Sarah's ancestry from the purchase of land from the Hittites for her grave (Gn 23).

60. Ps 77.67.

61. See Gn 41.45. Jewish interpreters also found Asenath problematical. See Kugel, *Traditions of the Bible*, 435.

in rejecting the tribe of Ephraim, he did not reject the son of the just Joseph, but children of the Egyptian woman, Asenath. And each of us is liable to be some son of a vulgar person, remembered sometimes as being a vulgar person before he became cultured, sometimes as being a just person when later he became cultured.[62] So I would be bold, and I would say that one who is a persecutor of those who have been taught the logos is a disciple of Paul the persecutor, but he who imitates Paul's life and mission is a disciple of Paul the apostle.

"*And he chose the tribe of Judah*"[63] on account of Christ, indicating ahead of time that our Lord would arise from Judah. Accordingly, when you hear "*he rejected the tents of Joseph,*" hear concerning the heresies. When you hear "*and he did not choose the tribe of Ephraim,*" hear something spoken concerning the heterodox, as we have maintained in the passage we have dealt with in our commentary on Hosea.[64]

"*Mount Zion, which he loved.*"[65] Is this in fact the inanimate one or that concerning which it is often said, "But you have arrived at Mount Zion and the city of the living God, heavenly Jerusalem"?[66] "*And he built its sanctuary as of unicorns.*"[67] The other versions have "and its sanctuary is high," showing that "*of unicorns*" has been placed there instead of "lofty." And now perhaps "*unicorns*" figuratively designates those in God, goring enemies with one horn and saying, "In you we shall gore our enemies,"[68] and, "He has lifted the horn of his people";[69] God lifts one "horn," not "the horns" of his people.

"*He has laid its foundation on the earth,*" namely the tribe of Judah, from which Christ came, "*to the age, and he has chosen David his servant.*"[70] It has often been demonstrated by us that David

62. Origen seems not entirely satisfied with "they took after their mother" as an explanation for God's rejecting the sons of the righteous Joseph.

63. Ps 77.68a.

64. This has disappeared, but see Ps77H2.3 above.

65. Ps 77.68b.

66. Heb 12.22.

67. Ps 77.69a.

68. Ps 43.6.

69. Ps 148.14.

70. Ps 77.69b–70a.

is named in place of Christ. For whenever David, servant of God, is prophesied in Ezekiel to be about to shepherd the people and to turn around the stray and to seek out the lost and to treat the oppressed,[71] it must not be considered to be spoken about the man David, but about our Savior. For God chose him as a servant, being his own son and servant.

"*And he took him up from the flocks of sheep, he took him from behind those in labor.*"[72] The logos did not have anything else to mention about David as a shepherd than attending sheep in labor, but in order to praise David serving as midwife to the sheep and receiving the offspring, it mentions him in this way. For the holy person is such; he serves as midwife to the offspring of the just.[73] For example, when "the midwives feared God,"[74] he made households in them. Those who fear God are midwives, serving as midwives to the offspring so that the works of virtue, good activities, may be perfect.

It is the work of a good shepherd to be behind those in labor from which the offspring are received. I spoke a little earlier about those who stand behind.[75] Do you see that he is in front of you, that you may follow, and he is behind you? For he can be both here and there, since he does not happen to be a body only in one place. He is behind you, when you are labor, when you are in labor pains and give birth. Why are you in labor pains, and how are you in labor except when you say, "Lord, from your fear we have conceived in the belly and have been in labor pains and have given birth; we have made a spirit of your salvation on the earth"?[76] If you have thus conceived in the belly from the fear of the Lord, if you have thus been in labor pains until you have

71. See Ezek 34.16.

72. Ps 77.70b–71a.

73. Origen generalizes from David to state that any holy person whose teaching brings forth virtue in others exercises the function of a midwife. His discussion calls to mind Plato, *Theaetetus* 149–51, where Socrates ascribes the function of a midwife to himself. The student of Origen who delivered the *Address of Thanksgiving* to him describes Origen as following a Socratic teaching method, which includes the use of wonder as recommended in *Theaetetus* 155.

74. Ex 1.17.

75. Ps 77.71b–c. See section 3 above.

76. Is 26.17–18.

given birth, seek the midwife. Christ comes, whom God "*takes from behind those in labor to shepherd Jacob his servant and Israel his inheritance.*"[77] This is not vain repetition, where the people is spoken of by the more human name, "Jacob," but the inheritance by the greater and more divine name "Israel." For we know that the name "Israel" had been given as a prize for his having wrestled well.[78]

"*To shepherd,*" then, "*Jacob his servant and Israel his inheritance. And he shepherded them*"—not David, but Christ—"*in the innocence of his heart.*"[79] Only Christ is entirely innocent; anyone else has every vice, "for he did not commit sin, nor was guile found in his mouth."[80] The other versions have put "in the perfection of his heart." Thus, then, Christ shepherds us "*in the innocence of his heart*"; and "*in the understanding of his hands,*" it says, "*he guided them.*"[81] For those whom he shepherds, "*in the innocence of heart*" fits the word "*innocence,*" in which he shepherds;[82] but "*in the understanding of hands*" fits those whom he plans, guides, and shows the road. Blessed are those who are worthy of being guided in the understanding of Christ's hands, for they are guided by him to reach the Father and God of the Universe, to whom is the glory and the might to the ages of ages. Amen.

77. Ps 77.71b–c.
78. See Gn 32.25–29.
79. Ps 77.71b–72a.
80. Is 53.9, 1 Pt 2.22.
81. Ps 77.72.
82. Christ is "shepherd" for simple Christians, who obey without understanding. See PS73H1.3 above.

HOMILY 1 ON PSALM 80

RAYERS IN a holy spirit are entirely fulfilled, and, "even as" the one praying "is speaking," God stands by and says: "See, I am here."[1] A request concerning the vine was made in prayer prophetically in a holy spirit in the preceding Psalm: it said: "God of powers, turn, please, look down from heaven and see and visit this vine and arrange it and make ready what your right hand has planted."[2] So, in fact, as the prayer request was being made, God looked at the vine. When he saw it, he visited it; he shaped it; he gathered its fruits; the fruits went into the vats. Therefore, the next Psalm after the prayer for the vine is inscribed, "*concerning the vats.*"[3] And if, in fact, according to the Savior's words, "I am the genuine vine, you are the branches, my Father is the farmer,"[4] we are branches who have grown together[5] with Jesus Christ and are made one with him; then we are husbanded by the Father and God of the Universe, and we are pruned, so that we may bear more fruit. We must expect that, because our grapes are ripe, that is, our good works,

---

1. Is 58.9. Origen frequently cited this testimony to the immediate efficacy of prayer. Thus he stated, in *Or.* 10.1, "Even if there should be no other result for us when we pray, we gain the best things when we have understood how we ought to pray and accomplish that prayer. But it is evident that the one thus praying will be hearing 'even as he speaks,' observing the efficacy of the one who listens, 'See, I am here.'"

2. Ps 79.15–16.

3. Ps 80.1b. Origen interprets the inscription to indicate that this Psalm deals with a further step in the process of wine-making once prayers for the vine have been answered. "Concerning the vats" is the Septuagint translation of a Hebrew term no longer understood.

4. Jn 15.1–5.

5. See Rom 6.5.

the fruit of the spirit,[6] our fruit will reach the heavenly vats. Because the Psalms *"concerning the vats"* refer, not to just one vat, but to many, we are told these things about us and about our fruit.

But, just as in vineyards, there is a variety of fruits of the vine, and there are, for example, dark fruits that produce a dark variety of wine and white fruits producing white wine, fruits that produce sweet wine and others partaking of different properties. By the same token, if you consider the variegated Church of God and the variegated manners of life—I am not speaking about objectionable ones, but commendable ones—you will find an abundant variety of commendable customs when it comes to practice, to contemplation, to teaching, to oversight, to common life in marriage, and to those who love chastity.[7] One must not blend these fruits. For just as, in vineyards, it turns out that each vine and each kind of grape goes into its own vat, in the same way, if you understand the spiritual vats, you will see in what manner each will be resurrected in its own order,[8] and according to the proportion of its achievements and courageous deeds it will be consigned to a particular vat. And perhaps just as there is a noble wine and a wine fit for slaves, and among noble wines, one fit for the emperor and one not so good, but inferior, so there would be found also among the many fruits of the Church someone who, on account of the spirit of slavery "into fear," does not accept the spirit of adoption,[9] bearing a fruit, as it were, servile but drinkable, but another bearing fruit through the spirit of adoption, not servile but freeing, having been made for the great banquet that the master of the household makes to honor the marriage of the son.[10]

But some are *"concerning the vats,"* and these are *"into the end,"*[11] for the vine is still cultivated and increases the fruits. For I am bold and say, just as "when the harvest takes place, it is

6. See Gal 5.22.

7. The explicit inclusion of varied states of life, including the married and the single, is also found in Ephrem, *Hymns on Paradise* 7.

8. 1 Cor 15.23.

9. See Rom 8.15. On the "spirit of slavery" see PS77H8.8, n. 63 above.

10. See Lk 14.16 and perhaps also Rv 19.6–9.

11. Ps 80.1a.

the end of an age,"[12] so the gathering of grapes is the end of an age. This takes care of the inscription.

But because in vintage songs what is declared must be happy, seeing that the harvesters are glad and are gathering wine that "gladdens a human being's heart,"[13] therefore the things in the Psalm are very sweet, as in a vintage, and marvelous, not just here but in the other vintage Psalms, specifically the Eighth Psalm and the Eighty-third. And these express happy things, such as, "Lord, our Lord, how marvelous is your name in all the earth, so that your greatness is exalted above the heavens; from the mouths of infants and nurslings you have crafted praise,"[14] and the rest. And again in the Eighty-third, itself one that is "concerning the vats,"[15] the oracles proclaimed are of happiness, for "how lovely," it says, "are your tents, Lord of powers; my soul longs and languishes for the courts of the Lord."[16]

2. So, then, here, understand such things as are always said as in the vintage Psalms: *Exult to God our helper.*[17] To the extent that the fruit remains on the vine, I am struggling, and I am not rejoicing at all—for I do not know when heat may burn up the vine and dry it out or some other mishap may occur, so that it may be said, "What the caterpillar left behind, the locust consumed, and what the locust left, the blight consumed"[18]—and the vine is endangered before the harvest. But when the season of harvest arrives and the grapes are borne off by the angels to the heavenly vats, it is said, *Exult to God our helper.* Since there are varieties of exultation, the supreme exultation is when one is exulting to God, to exult in a way analogous to "rejoice to God." Therefore, it does not simply say "exult," but *exult to God.* It is a blessed thing to dedicate all movements to God. If, then, your fruits go into the vats, hear, *Exult to God our helper.* But if you sin and need a change of heart and turning around, you do not exult, but are sorrowful. I would say about that sorrow,

12. See Mt 13.39.
13. Ps 103.15.
14. Ps 8.2–3.
15. Ps 83.1.
16. Ps 83.2–3.
17. Ps 80.2a.
18. Jl 1.4.

"Be sorrowful to God your helper," for a sorrow directed to God accomplishes a change of heart leading to salvation, not to be regretted.[19]

And make everything to God! It is possible to make [something] not to God. Do you love? Love to God. For if you love anything apart from what is divine, you do not love to God. For example, if you love money, you do not love to God. If you love fame, you do not love to God. If you cherish your children in a fleshly way and with fleshly affections, you do not love to God, but if you love children as did that blessed mother of the seven in the written accounts of the Maccabees,[20] you love children to God. So it is possible to have love for one's husband[21] to God, and to love one's husband, but not to God. So it is possible to work the earth to God, to be forbearing to God, and to have these things to God.

This on "*Exult to God our helper.*" For it was necessary to say in what way also we must exult to God and we must make all things to God. Having been helped by God, it says, I bore fruit, but also, having been helped by God, I will make a harvest of fruits for the holy vats. Do not, then, forget God, seeing that he has become your helper.

3. For this reason it says, "*Exult to God our helper*"; whatever you might say is less than the graces of God toward you, and you seem to be at a loss for logoi worthy of being returned to God in a thanksgiving.[22] Therefore, I want you to "*ululate to the God of Jacob,*"[23] that is, with a sound without signs of a heart that has cried out,[24] stepping beyond things signified—being at a loss[25]

19. See 2 Cor 7.10.

20. See 2 Mc 7. See *Mart.* 27.

21. *Philandrein,* "loving a husband," is an early attestation of this verb. Origen probably had in mind Ti 2.4, where older women (or, conceivably, female elders) are to teach young women to be lovers of husbands (*philandrous*) and lovers of children (*philoteknous*).

22. In *Or.* 1.1–2.6 Origen describes how we require God's help, supplied by the Spirit present to us in our hearts, in order to say what we should as we should in prayer.

23. Ps 80.2b.

24. See Rom 8.26.

25. "Being at a loss when it comes to the wordings," *aporousēs tōn lexeōn. Aporia* is the philosophical term for a problem to be investigated through dialectic.

when it comes to the wordings, and, by being at a loss when it comes to the wordings, saying unspeakable things,[26] so you are thus enabled to *"ululate to the God of Jacob."*

Do you want to see what a great thing the ululation is, if it is produced for God? Consider: "Blessed," it says, "are the people who know a ululation."[27] If, then, someone is blessed by nothing that happens at random, it is necessary to receive the knowledge of the ululation. And perhaps, if you use things said as a step, if you step over things reported, things given voice by the mouth, if you step over the sonorous voice and you were enabled to hymn God with a mind only, one at a loss for means to add its own movements by logos, even as the logos in you is unable to bear up under the unspeakable and divine things of the mind, for whose sake do you ululate but to the God of your patriarch Jacob? And for this reason, I suppose, you ululate to the God of Jacob: because you have become Jacob, and "the one who trips."[28] And you tripped him,[29] you first took hold of the heel;[30] next you took the birthright;[31] and, third, you take the blessing.[32] Whenever, then, these three things occur in relation to you, you also ululate as a son of Jacob and an imitator of Jacob, the one who trips.[33]

Here Origen suggests that, when our human efforts fail to solve a problem with a biblical text (*lexis*), the divine logos enables us to express "unspeakable things."

26. See 2 Cor 12.4 on saying the unspeakable.

27. Ps 88.16.

28. One who has risen above the normal human condition moves from his family of birth into the family of the covenant people, of which Jacob is patriarch. Being adopted into divine sonship (see, e.g., Eph 1.5) entails belonging to the patriarchal line. We find this idea already in Clement of Alexandria, *Strom.* 6.7.60.3, along with the interpretation of Jacob as "one who trips" (*pternistēs*), as in n. 33 below: "On the one hand, the seed of Abraham are still servants of God—are the called—but the sons of Jacob are his chosen, those who trip up [or 'those who supplant': *pternisantes*] the performance of evil."

29. Grammatically, "him" should refer to Jacob. The text may be corrupt.

30. See Gn 25.26.

31. See Gn 25.31–34. Philo interprets the conflict of Jacob and Esau as a wise person (*sophos*) overcoming mental disturbance (*pathos*): "And Jacob will not relax his hold on the heel of his antagonist, mental disturbance, until it has surrendered and confesses that it has been tripped and defeated twice, in the matter of the birthright and in the blessing" (*Laws of Allegory* 3.68.190).

32. See Gn 27.

33. Hos 12.4 states that Jacob "tripped" or "supplanted" (*pternisen*) his brother

4. Let us see what follows. What is it that the prophetic logos enjoined on us by the Holy Spirit? "*Take a Psalm and give a drum and a pleasant psaltery with a harp.*"[34] The logos gives one thing, but it asks me for three. It gives me a Psalm and asks from me first "*a drum,*" then "*a pleasant psaltery,*" then "*with a harp.*" We must understand the "*drum*" and prepare it, so that, when we receive the Psalm, when the logos says to us, "*Take a Psalm and give a drum,*" let us give a drum, but giving a drum so that we give a "*psaltery,*" not simply a psaltery, but a "*pleasant*" one. For perhaps there is some "*psaltery*" that is not pleasant and a "*pleasant psaltery*" joined with a "*harp.*" For it is written, "*psaltery with a harp.*"

"Do not interpret figuratively and do not allegorize," they say, "but keep to the wording!" Shall we actually prepare a drum, such as they have who are strangers to the faith? But how can we human beings, unless we have been taught either to play the harp or to pluck on a psaltery, pluck on this instrument as those do who have been taught to do this since childhood, so that we may make ready a pleasant psaltery with a harp (since this is what the logos says according to them)?[35] "*Take a Psalm*"? But

---

in the womb. The image Origen is calling to mind is that of a wrestler tripping his opponent to make him fall. Hippolytus (*On the Antichrist* 14) speaks of the devil as having "tripped" Adam. Origen found wrestling a particularly good image for the struggles involved in Christian life; see especially PS36H4.2 above. He also seems to assume that his hearers, or some of them, would understand what it means to do these three things as an imitator of Jacob. Origen discusses the story of Jacob's relationship to Esau, as it is told in Genesis and alluded to in Malachi and Romans, in several other places in his writings. In *Princ.* 3.2.5 he states what he probably assumes here, that when Jacob wrestled with an angel, the angel was not wrestling against him but assisting him against a demonic adversary. (See also Kugel, *Traditions of the Bible,* 386–87.) A cryptic discussion of the birth of Jacob survives in *Hom. Gen.* 12.3–4 (in Rufinus's translation). There Jacob and Esau symbolize, respectively, potential for the virtue and vice in the human heart. *Hom. Num.* 3.2 also refers to the passage to indicate that being firstborn before God has to do with disposition of mind rather than birth order. In *Princ.* 3.1.22 he ascribes God's preference for Jacob over Esau in Mal 1.2–3 to "older causes" that would explain their different dispositions before they were in Rebecca's womb.

34. Ps 80.3.

35. The position of those who do not allow allegory involves the absurdity of telling people who have never learned to play an instrument to pluck on a psaltery.

we take a Psalm and we prepare these things when we understand what is being said.

When, therefore, God's grace gives me the ability to discourse about God, so as to be able from the discourse about God to understand God and to know him and to exalt his name and to magnify him, it gives me a Psalm. And it is a gift of Christ—who said: "No one knows the Father except the Son and the one to whom the Son reveals him"[36]—and giving a Psalm about our God is to reveal the Father.[37] And if someone actually knew the Father, having been devoted to learning according to, "Be devoted to learning and know that I am God,"[38] he knew God; he took the Psalm. But if you take a Psalm,[39] give back also what is asked. You are composed of three things—a spirit, a soul, and a body—and the logos asks of you complete consecration, so that you may be sanctified completely in spirit, soul, and body according to what was said by the Apostle in the Epistle to the Thessalonians.[40] Perhaps, then, you should understand "*drum*" to refer to the body,[41] "*psaltery*" to refer to the spirit, and "*harp*" to refer to the soul.

Why is the body a drum? For this reason: a drum is wood[42] that has a skin[43] that has been put to death, and you also must,

36. Mt 11.27.

37. The Psalms themselves are a gift from Christ, who speaks through them, revealing God to us so that, using their language, we can speak intelligibly about God.

38. Ps 45.11. The LXX translates a Hebrew word meaning "do nothing" as *scholasate,* a word that can mean either "be at leisure" or "devote yourself to learning." (It gives us "school" and "scholastic.")

39. "Taking a Psalm" is what each member of Origen's congregation is doing as they listen to him. He is using the second-person singular here to speak to each of them individually about their responsibility to act in accordance with what they are hearing.

40. See 1 Thes 5.23.

41. See PS67H2.4 above.

42. "Of the cross" understood.

43. Adam and Eve received garments of skin from God after they sinned, before being expelled from Eden (Gn 3.21). In the late fourth century, Epiphanius of Salamis, seeking to discredit Origen, accused him of identifying these "garments of skin" with the fleshly nature (*sarkōdes*) of the body or the body itself (*Anchoratus* 62). This passage may explain the second charge, inasmuch as the skin is understood as "sinful flesh" in Pauline terms. In *Hom. Lev.* 6.2 the "garments of skin" are human mortality and frailty.

on the cross, put to death your constituent parts upon earth.[44] And in the One-hundred-fiftieth Psalm we are taught to praise God in various manners, and it is said there: "Praise him, in the drum and dance."[45] The person who puts to death the constituent parts on earth praises God in the drum. Hear, if you like, the names of the constituent parts: "sexual misconduct, uncleanness, passion, bad desire, and avarice." Whenever these things are put to death in you, they have been put to death through the cross of Christ, and your flesh is put to death, so that you arrive at the ability to say, "If we have died with him, we shall also live with him."[46] When you do these things, you have made a drum. For to the extent that your flesh and the mindset of your flesh are alive,[47] your flesh has not been put to death and you cannot hymn God.

I consider that the order is well stated here: "give a drum" first, then "a psaltery with a harp." First a drum, then, after this, a psaltery with a harp. For first we must concentrate on putting to death the parts of the body on earth, and on killing the sin in us, so that we may no longer be activated by sin. Then, when sin is defeated and put to death and we have been empowered to give the drum, then we shall be empowered to make harmony of spirit with soul or, in the words of the Apostle, spirit with mind, so that I say, "I will make music with the spirit, but I will also make music with the mind,"[48] and I will, on the one hand, give the spirit, a psaltery, and, on the other, the soul or mind, a harp. But I give both, "*a pleasant psaltery with a harp*" to be joined with the drum. But if I speak of spirit, I am speaking of the human spirit about which Paul says: "No one knows the things of a human being, if not the human spirit that is within."[49]

5. The wording resumes. He[50] has given a Psalm; he requests from me "*a drum and a pleasant psaltery with a harp*." After these

---

44. See Col 3.5 here and for constituent parts named below.

45. Ps 150.4.

46. 2 Tm 2.11.

47. See Rom 8.6–7.

48. 1 Cor 14.15.

49. 1 Cor 2.11. The human spirit is that aspect of a human being that is in relation to God.

50. The logos speaking through the *lexis,* "wording."

things he commands me to sound a trumpet[51] and to take up
a great sound. For it is said that of all the sounds made by human beings for other human beings—sounds made by any instruments whatsoever—the greatest is the trumpet. And servants
of music say that there is no resonance in music greater than
that of the trumpet. Therefore it is employed in awakening the
fierceness of those who make war and to prepare for their best
efforts those who struggle over cities. The law of Moses employs
trumpets in two manners: to mobilize Israel's armies so that they
employ them for war, and in the feasts of the Lord, as it is written in Numbers.[52] And we are enjoined to sound a trumpet with
a great sound: "Ascend upon a high mountain, you who give
good news to Zion; lift up the sound with strength, you who give
good news to Jerusalem; lift up, do not fear."[53] And in the last
Psalm, "Praise him in resonance of a trumpet."[54] Who can praise
God "in resonance of a trumpet" unless it is Paul, resounding in
resonance of a trumpet? For he was eloquent, and if any others
among the holy ones of God want to be so, they should be such
a one as he.

Do you want to see how great this spiritual trumpet is, even
if the lovers of the letter do not want to? The angels also use a
trumpet: "The trumpet will sound, and the dead shall be made
to arise incorruptible in Christ,"[55] and, "the Lord himself in the
word of command, in the voice of an archangel, and in God's
trumpet will descend from heaven."[56] Actually, when we hear
these things, do we suppose that there is a brass section in heav-
en or some trumpets on supply for the angels,[57] so that the blessed angels may sound a trumpet and the dead may arise through
the sound of the trumpet? Or are great and divine teachings and

51. See Ps 80.4. The same Greek word, *phōnē*, means both "sound" (as of a
trumpet) and "voice." The word Origen uses here in connection with the trumpet, *megalophōnia*, can mean either the "big sound" of a trumpet or human "eloquence."

52. See Nm 10.2–10.

53. Is 40.9.

54. Ps 150.3.

55. 1 Cor 15.52.

56. 1 Thes 4.16.

57. See PS77H4.5 above for a similar argument.

eloquence betokened by the sound of the trumpet, and were the angels to be sounding a trumpet vaguely, would no one be in battle array for war?[58]

Therefore, let us pray that we may have trumpets that do not make an announcement indistinctly, but, as it is possible in the trumpet, let us make everything clear. But the Revelation of John is filled with many trumpets. "An angel sounds a trumpet," and something has come about; then a second, and something has come about.[59] And it is possible to see a multitude of heavenly and divine trumpets, which the angels of God sound. And if the law has the shadow of heavenly things and speaks as a model,[60] and the aforementioned trumpets are spoken about there, take the trumpets to a higher level, recognizing more openly in the books by John or in some other Scripture by Paul, the angelic heavenly trumpets and their eloquence.

6. But when do you "*sound a trumpet*"? "*At a new moon.*" For, it says, "*Sound a trumpet at a new moon with a trumpet.*" And when? "*On a propitious day of our feast.*"[61] At a new moon, there is a conjunction of the sun and moon and they come to be in alignment. If that is what a new moon is—see with me—the moon, the Church illuminated by the sun. The sun—see with me—is the sun of justice,[62] my Lord Jesus Christ. Should it occur that the Church and Christ are aligned, a new moon occurs, of which the law of Moses has a shadow. "Let no one," it says, "judge you in food and in drink or in being part of a feast or of a new moon or of sabbaths, which are shadows of things to come."[63] Therefore, the logos about the new moon has a shadow of things to come, but of what sort of things to come? Listen. There is a new moon again there, and there is a full moon again there, but there it is not a new moon on account of this sun—for this one will have been delivered from the "bondage of corruption" according to the things written[64]—or from this moon; but from

---

58. See 1 Cor 14.8.
59. See Rv 8.7–8.
60. See Heb 10.1 and 8.5.
61. Ps 80.4.
62. See Mal 4.2.
63. Col 2.16–17.
64. See Rom 8.21. See especially *Princ.* 1.7.5 for Origen's discussion of this

the sun, Christ, comes about also the new moon of the Church. Then we are empowered to sound a trumpet, and then we are empowered to employ divine secrets with eloquence.[65]

Who, in fact, is worthy to reach that new moon and that propitious day of our feast (in place of "*on the propitious day of our feast,*" the other versions have "in the full moon," but one also makes it "in the half moon"), so that trumpets may be best employed?[66] In each of these, a conjunction occurs of the moon with the sun, both when the moon appears to be bright, full, illuminated by the sun, and when, from the perspective of those on earth, it has been illuminated and is in conjunction, even though it is not illuminated in such a way that its illumination can be known—but in the full moon it is illuminated and its illumination is known; when, then, the Church is illuminated by me and I have been empowered by it, receiving the light of the sun of justice known to the rest, including those not from the Church, there also comes about a full moon, the genuine and heavenly feast.[67]

And then it will be necessary to sound the trumpet on the

---

verse. Origen believed that the sun was a rational being endowed with a body. By using a participle, *gegrammena,* "the things written," Origen emphasizes that Paul has partially disclosed a secret. He has taken a risk by putting it in writing. See *Cels.* 7.6 on the need not to write certain things down, a view famously expressed by Plato in *Epistle* 7, 341d.

65. Origen discusses learning divine secrets as an eschatological promise in *Princ.* 2.11.

66. The obvious answer: "I am." "That new moon" is when the Church, the moon of which our moon is the shadow, is fully illuminated by the sun of justice, Christ. At the new moon, the entire moon is actually illumined by the sun, but we cannot see it from our perspective on earth. At the full moon, the entire moon is illumined again, and we can see it. Origen, relying on Heb 10.1 and Col 2.16–17, regards the law of Moses, including provisions for festivals and new moons, as the "shadow" of things to come.

67. Origen probably expected those who had studied extensively with him to catch an allusion to ideas set out in more detail elsewhere. *Or.* 27.14 sees the recurring cycles of festivals as foreshadowing recurring world ages. The use of the word "knowable," rather than "seen," which might have been expected, points to a connection with 1 Cor 13.9–12, a key text for Origen. The new moon, whose illumination is not "knowable," refers to our present existence; and the full moon, whose illumination is fully "knowable," to its eschatological fulfillment. See *Comm. Cant.* 3.5.13–19.

propitious day of our feast, and to do these things for this reason: "*because it is an ordinance to Israel and a judgment by the God of Jacob.*"[68] All these things—to take the Psalm, to give a drum and so on, and to do what has been said already—are ordinances to Israel, to the one seeing God.[69] And it is a judgment, pronounced by the God of Jacob: "*he set it as a testimony against Joseph.*"[70] He made this ordinance "*a testimony against Joseph.*" What is the testimony, and to whom was it made? Not to the Patriarch Joseph, but to the one from Joseph, the one from Ephraim, to Jeroboam, who divided the people.[71] These oracles become a testimony against that man. This has often been interpreted by us against those who are dividing from the Church, because they are heterodox; thus the oracles and ordinances of God become a testimony against that person.[72]

7. After these things, a secret is spoken concerning the whole people that has not been written in Exodus but has been dared by the spirit in the prophet.[73] For it is said, "*When going out of the*

68. Ps 80.5.

69. This Hebrew etymology comes from Philo. See *Life of Abraham* 57.

70. Ps 80.6a.

71. See above PS77H2. The story is in 1 Kgs 12.

72. Again addressing the question, "Who is worthy?" Origen states that, to refute heretics in advance, the prophet reveals what should otherwise remain secret, namely that Hebrew, the language of the Old Testament, is actually the language for speaking to God. In rejecting the Old Testament, by implication, heretics are rejecting God. In his homily, Origen's own speech falls into alignment with Asaph. By the logic of Origen's interpretation so far, someone such as he with fuller access to divine mysteries—things not known to, or knowable by, simple Christians—may disclose them in the restricted circumstances symbolized by the new moon. Thus Origen, like Asaph, may share secrets about the beginning and end of creation with those who deny the goodness of the creator-god because those secrets testify to the goodness of the creator. Such secrets should ordinarily be withheld from simple Christians who still need to be motivated by fear, so sharing them entails risk. In *Cels.* 5.15 we see this principle applied to similar criticisms from a Platonist. On the way in which Jeroboam's schism prefigures Christian heresy, see esp. PS77H2 above.

73. The empowerment by the spirit, the divine element originally and potentially present in the human composite, constitutes a prophet. Moses had not been willing to consign this secret to writing, but Asaph took the risk, perhaps because, as his name suggests, he had a gift for expressing himself obscurely. Origen claims the right to take the same risk, knowing that his homily is being transcribed.

land of Egypt, he heard a tongue that he did not know."[74] When, it says, Israel was in Egypt, they did not hear Hebrew, but when they went out of Egypt, "*a tongue that he did not know*"—for, he did not know Hebrew—"*he heard.*" And this secret is unspeakable: for understand, with me, Hebrew to be the tongue announcing foreign things, things above the cosmos, so that the very word "Hebrew" is interpreted as "foreign," and the tongue as "foreignese."[75]

When, then, we learn what is beyond bodies, what is beyond the cosmos, when we discuss these things spiritually, we discuss in Hebrew. When do we discuss spiritually in Hebrew, except when we go out of the land of Egypt? Insofar as we are involved in bodily things and do not go out of Egypt, but work in mud[76] and straw,[77] we cannot hear the tongue "*that he did not know.*" And if anyone who is still in Egypt in his way of thinking should hear logoi beyond, should he hear loftier logoi, he would not pick up on them, but only someone who has gone out of Egypt does so. The one who learns to abandon bodily things and to be wholly in heavenly things, the one who has a treasure in the heavenly places, that person has gone out of the land of Egypt, and a tongue that he did not know when he was in Egypt, he hears. "For the soulish[78] human being does not receive the things of the spirit of God: they are foolishness to him, and he cannot know [them], because they are discerned spiritually."[79]

8. "*He relieved his back from burdens; his hands slaved in the basket.*"[80] When you leave Egypt and bodily affairs behind, then it will be the task for the angels to relieve your back of burdens. For heavy loads are placed on your back from sin, and to the ex-

---

74. Ps 80.6b. This passage partially discloses an eschatological "secret," *mustērion*, comparable to Paul's allusion to the deliverance of the cosmos in Rom 8.21.

75. *Peratisti,* a word Origen made up. Origen's life-long struggle to comprehend Hebrew becomes an image for striving to understand at a higher level. Origen probably knew Jewish traditions that identified Hebrew as the original human language, spoken before the confusion of tongues at the Tower of Babel; see Kugel, *Traditions of the Bible,* 235–36.

76. See Ex 1.14.

77. See Ex 5.10.

78. See PS67H1.5, n. 80 above.

79. 1 Cor 2.14.

80. Ps 80.7a.

tent that you are in Egypt, the loads placed on your back are all the heavier. When you go out of Egypt and leave behind bodily things and already consider heavenly things and make the heavenly your goal, then the angels attending God's logos will take care to relieve your back from burdens, so that you may lighten your back and you will be enabled, when you have put off the heavy yoke of Nebuchadnezzar,[81] to take up the light yoke of Christ.[82]

"He relieved his back from burdens; his hands slaved in the basket."[83] Israel, when he is in Egypt, slaves, carrying mud in a basket, gathering straw in a basket. Israel, if he were to go out of Egypt, his hands would no longer slave in the basket, but they would be empowered to become hands such as those that gather Jesus's loaves left over by those who are fed and that, with the apostles, deposit them in a basket,[84] so that the hands that had once been enslaved in the basket in Egypt, these hands later take in the basket what is in excess and came to be multiplied.

But at the same time, who would not seek also, while reading, according to the Gospel, that there was a great crowd in the desert hearing the teacher and bread was not to be found, except for five loaves with a boy[85] and a few fish?[86] And how, where bread was not to be found, were twelve baskets filled?[87] But let the one who has ears hear[88] the logos worthily, and let him seek to be worthy of first reclining[89] and eating the loaves that are not yet left over, so that when there are some loaves left over, given to the apostles, he may, having proved worthy of the first loaves, ascend to those that are left over and found in the baskets.[90]

81. See Jer 27.8. Subjection to Nebuchadnezzar in Babylon, like subjection to Pharaoh in Egypt, symbolizes the soul's captivity and service to sin and Satan.

82. See Mt 11.30.

83. Ps 80.7.

84. See Jn 6.13.

85. Jn 6.9.

86. See Mt 15.34.

87. See Jn 6.13.

88. See Mt 11.15.

89. See Mt 14.19. Reclining is the normal posture for eating.

90. The summons to those who "have ears to hear" indicates that Origen knew that his cryptic discussion of baskets was difficult and that he intended it to be so. Like Jesus in Mt 11.15, Origen is presenting a doctrine that is intended

"*In distress you called upon me,*" God responds to him, and says, "*In distress you called upon me, and I rescued you.*"[91] When, in him, we are in a trial, then let us pray, for then the prayer is heard. For example, the body of a son, husband, wife, father, mother, or friend is lying dead; do not be idle about prayer then, when you are distressed, but arise and pray! Demonstrate to God that you have preferred prayer to sorrow, to grief, to lamentation, so that God may say to you: "*In distress you called upon me, and I rescued you.*" But if anything else takes place about which you are distressed—illnesses, thefts, irrational false witnesses, and anything that happens to human nature—then especially pray, so that you may hear, "*In distress you called upon me, and I rescued you.*"

"*I listened to you in a hidden place of a whirlwind.*"[92] How is "*In distress you called upon me, and I rescued you*" akin to "*I listened to you in a hidden place of a whirlwind*"? How are they akin? Listen. We know that, bodily, a whirlwind is a wind that is great and violent, that often even overturns houses and uproots trees. A whirlwind is a terrifying thing. When, then, a difficult test comes upon us, it comes on us like a whirlwind, and then the spirit[93] is a whirlwind entrusted to us as a test. But where a whirlwind of great testing comes, call upon the Lord, and he will say to you: "*I have listened to you in a hidden place of a whirlwind.*" I am in the hidden place of a whirlwind and present to testing, so that I may stop it at your request from testing you; "*I have listened to you.*" "God is faithful,

---

only for those who "have ears" for it. The ears listening to Origen would recently have heard in PS77H4 how Origen associated the manna in the wilderness with Jesus's feeding of the five thousand and, at a higher level, with Jesus's teaching. We already see these connections in the New Testament, especially in Jn 6, and it is a connection Origen makes consistently throughout his work, often in contexts where one might have expected a reference to the Eucharist, as in PS15H1.9 above. The baskets with "left over" bread thus suggest teachings that go beyond the needs of ordinary Christians. These are teachings Jesus gave that were not written down by the apostles. In this way, Jesus is like Moses. See Kugel, *Traditions,* 657–62. See *Princ.* Preface 3, where Origen remarks that the apostles knew much more than they stated forthrightly and left deeper matters for gifted teachers who would come after them to arrive at on their own. These are probably the people who "deposit in a basket" the food left unconsumed when the apostles taught.

91. Ps 80.8a.
92. Ps 80.8b.
93. *Pneuma* means both "spirit" and "wind."

who will not allow us to be tested beyond what we are able, but will make with the testing also an escape so that you can bear it."[94]

Once these things have been taken care of, we have yet to deal with, "*I approved you in the water of contradiction.*"[95] Then he gave the people the water of contradiction from a rock, so that Moses said, "Hear me, you who are unconvinced, shall we not bring water out of a rock?"[96] And there is now a "*water of contradiction*" among human beings, not by my interpretation, but by that of a far greater authority: "The rock was Christ," and, "They drank from the spiritual rock that was following."[97] Just as there was there, in the narrative, a water of contradiction, so there is here a water of contradiction.

But how is Christ the "*water of contradiction*"? Hear. If you see the heresies concerning him, if you see the discord, when this person says one thing about him and someone else understands him another way, each of them understanding something, you will see that he is "*water of contradiction*." This water is "for falling and standing up,"[98] this water is "so that those who do not see may see, and those who see may become blind."[99] This is "a cornerstone, chosen, precious"[100] to believers. This is "a stone of stumbling" and "rock of offense"[101] to unbelievers. We are proved, then, by the water of contradiction. How are we proved by the water of contradiction? "There must be heresies among you, so that those who are approved may be apparent."[102] If there were not a multitude of opinions, we would not be apparent as adherents to the Church, not led astray by clever explanations, by plausibility, by confounding of texts, by those who explain the Scriptures badly. And we are proved by this in the midst of the heresies. Having become adherents to the Church, let us pray to inherit the holy things of God in Christ Jesus, to whom is the glory and the might to the ages of ages. Amen.

94. 1 Cor 10.13.
95. Ps 80.8c.
96. Nm 20.10.
97. 1 Cor 10.4.
98. Lk 2.34.
99. Jn 9.39.
100. Is 28.16, 1 Pt 2.6.
101. Is 8.14, 1 Pt 2.8.
102. 1 Cor 11.19.

HOMILY 2 ON PSALM 80

OME MUSICAL instruments are tuned. Some are out of tune. A trained and skilled musical performer selects a psaltery,[1] a lyre, a harp that is in tune, and, having chosen it, makes a powerful display of his musical skill. But he absolutely runs away head over heels, if the psaltery, the harp, or the lyre is out of tune, because such an instrument will embarrass him, giving the impression that the performing artist is lacking in skill.

Why, then, mention this, if not because all human beings are, as it were, harps, psalteries, and lyres? And God, as a performing artist, seeks a lyre musically in tune, a harp well-tuned, a psaltery on which the strings have been tightened as they need to be, and God, after distinguishing where he can find such instruments, performs heavenly music. But if God lacks instruments to use, not by his own fault, but on account of a lack of such instruments, he is silent.

The blessed prophets became God's instruments. Just as someone hearing a lyre's tone and resonance does not hear the instrument, but hears the musician playing music on an instrument ready for his use, so someone hearing a prophet does not reckon that he is hearing a human being, but God, who has found a ready instrument and is making use of him as needed. Asaph, to be sure, was also an instrument of God, and, hearing God the musician speaking through Asaph's strings, saying, *"Hear, my people, and I will indict you, Israel,"*[2] and the reference of what is said I do not refer so much to the instrument as to God, who is employing the instrument.

---

1. *Psaltērion,* "plucked instrument," from the same word that gives us "Psalm."
2. Ps 80.9a.

I congratulate the instrument because he has ordered himself and made himself ready for the approval of God, who is playing his own instruments. It is even possible for God to use the tongue of a just person as his own tongue and for God to use the mouth of a holy person, so that it is possible to say, "The mouth of the Lord has spoken these things."[3]

But I say[4] that a god is also employing the eyes of a just person, eyes dim so as not to see iniquity,[5] but wide open so as to see heaven and the cosmos, because God is using them as instruments of understanding to see how whatever God made is very good.[6] So God makes use of the ears of the just person and the hand, so that through the ears of the just person a holy logos may be received, but a specious one rejected. And if you ever see the hand of a believer stretched out in generosity, do not reckon that such well-doing has come about from a human being so much as from God, who is making use of the just person's hand to relieve those who need relief from God. Thus

3. See Is 40.5. While Origen stresses the divine element in inspiration, the human element is not eliminated. It makes a difference which instrument is chosen and what condition that instrument is in.

4. This is an example of Origen's reasoning from Scripture. Since God is incorporeal and the words are those of the prophet, when Isaiah speaks of "the mouth of the Lord," the prophet is speaking through his own mouth. Scripture itself, by this reasoning, ascribes a human mouth to God. "But I say" introduces logical extensions of this language. If God has a human mouth, God may also be said to have human eyes, ears, hands, and feet by inference from other scriptural passages. See also PS76H1.1 and PS76H4.4 above.

5. See Hab 1.13.

6. See Gn 1.31. God "sees" the beauty and order of the cosmos through our eyes and understands them and makes them understood through our minds. A student of Origen, traditionally identified as Gregory Thaumaturgus, the Apostle to Pontus, spoke of how Origen awakened him, through natural philosophy (what we now call science), to a rational appreciation of the beauty and order of the cosmos. See *Address of Thanksgiving* 9. Origen's designation of the eye as an instrument (*organon*) of seeing echoes Greco-Roman science. Lehoux points out that the greatest scientists of the second century, Galen in medicine and Ptolemy in astronomy, shared with each other a heightened interest in careful and systematic observation of natural phenomena. Like Origen, both speak of the eye as the instrument (*organon*) of observation. See Daryn Lehoux, *What Did the Romans Know? An Inquiry into Science and Worldmaking* (Chicago: University of Chicago Press, 2012), 106–32.

from God, using the beautiful feet of the one who proclaims good news,[7] the feet of those who preach good news of good things have become beautiful. And blessed is that person, who entirely becomes, in all the parts of the body, through the entire faculty of sensation, an instrument of Christ, an instrument of God's logos, in such a way as to say: "I no longer live, but Christ lives in me."[8]

2. Let us hear, then, what God says in his own instrument, Asaph, for the Psalm is his: "*Hear, my people, and I will indict you, Israel; if you will hear me, there will not be among you a recent god.*"[9] He does not say this to them only, but to you who are hearing it, for in the place where you were called "not a people," you have become a people of the living God,[10] and perhaps God honors you before that Israel. Therefore, when he speaks, he does not begin with "Israel" but with the "people": "*Hear, my people, and I will indict you, Israel.*" See, the word "Israel" has been set in the second position, but the one in the first is not being referred to as "Israel" but, rather than "Israel," bears the title "God's people."

Why, then, does God tell you that he is going to indict you? "*If you will hear me, there will not be in you a recent god.*" Let us see first how God indicts; accordingly, what he says: he speaks with witnesses and calls witnesses; this time he calls heaven and earth;[11] this time he even calls a song;[12] this time he calls a hearing stone. "For this stone," it says, "will be the one hearing the things said."[13] But thus you will find even thousands of other witnesses called by God to give testimony: for example, when Christ, speaking in Paul,[14] says, "I bring an indictment before God and Jesus Christ and the chosen angels, that you keep these things without prejudice."[15] Do you see? Christ also, in Paul, has

7. See Is 52.7.

8. Gal 2.20. Origen thus ties this key Pauline text to the deification of the body.

9. Ps 80.9–10a.

10. See Hos 1.10 and 2.23 and Rom 9.25–26.

11. See Dt 4.26, 30.19, 32.1.

12. See Dt 31.19 and 31.21.

13. See Jos 24.27.

14. See 2 Cor 13.3.

15. 1 Tm 5.21.

brought an indictment before the chosen angels, before God, and, to be sure, before Christ Jesus, as Paul brings an indictment. These indictments, then, will last until the day of judgment, in the mouth of two witnesses[16] or three or more, so that those who sin may be condemned; therefore, they are witnesses in the day of judgment; if the sinner is to be lost, the creations are witnesses; heaven witnesses against the one lost; the earth, the angels witness against the one who has done evil.

I fear that Christ Jesus may witness against someone—"for," it says, "the logos itself that I have spoken will condemn" you[17]—and through the witnesses we are put in fear of sinning. The sins of the people, then, insofar as they were condemned, and were condemned on the basis of witnesses, were heard by witnesses and seen by witnesses. For example, witnesses came forward saying, "We saw this man walking around in an unseemly manner with a woman and closeted with her," and the eyewitness testimony by witnesses condemns the one accused. When it comes to things we do, in case other human beings are unaware of them, human beings are not going to come and condemn us. Everywhere is full of angels; every household and every land is full of the powers of God. Where is Christ not present? "He stood in the midst of you."[18] If any sin, say to them, "What you do not know is that God is everywhere."

"Where shall I go from your spirit, and from your persona where do I flee?"[19] And if a human being should see something that we are ashamed of, we do not dare to speak a logos from which we might be recognized by that person or to do anything blameworthy, but we despise the eyes of God, the presence of Christ always present to the cosmos; we despise the Holy Spirit, the chosen angels, not knowing that all these, as if they were assaulted by the shameless things that meet their eyes, condemn us and say: "This person sinned under our eyes," for "against you only," it says, "I sinned and I did evil in your sight."[20] This

16. See Dt 19.15 and 2 Cor 13.1.
17. Jn 12.48.
18. Jn 1.26.
19. Ps 138.7.
20. Ps 50.6.

is what it means to sin when God indicts, but the one who confesses will testify to his sin and say: "I did evil in your sight."[21]

3. "*If you will hear me, there will not be in you a recent god.*"[22] I know a simpler way to hear what is said: if someone would hear God, he will not worship idols, nor will there be for the one hearing "*a recent god,*" nor will the one hearing the logoi of God prostrate himself to "*an alien god.*"[23] But explaining more diligently and wishing to hear the divinity of the Holy Spirit, I am bold and I say that all human beings have in them either the genuine God or a recent, alien god. For example, "all the gods of the nations are demons";[24] the person who receives activation of something demonic, the one sinning by the inspiration of an evil spirit—let it be posited that in him an evil spirit is the object of prostration as a god, some demonic unclean thing. But I would say that those so-called but nonexistent gods are in those who are enslaved to sins. Whenever they deify and lift up money as a god, there is in them a demonic object of idolatry, which is why covetousness is called "idolatry" by Paul.[25] So if you are overcome by the thinking of the flesh,[26] it is a spirit of sexual immorality for you, and you have become a temple[27] of the spirit of sexual immorality; in the same way someone else is a temple of the spirit of anger and of the rest of the sins.

If, then, you want there not to be in you a made-up god, a recent god, one not truly God, hear God: "*If you will hear me,*" it says, "*there will not be in you a recent god.*" In ordinary idolatry, it is not the wooden image, the silver one, or the gold one in itself that is the object of idolatry, when this logos says that a recent god is not to be in you. The holy person says, "or do you

---

21. Though framed in terms of the divine judgment described in such passages as Dn 7 and Mt 25.31–46, Origen and his hearers would have been familiar with criminal court procedure in Caesarea, the seat of the Roman governor, who was also the chief judge for the province of Palestine. On confession, see also PS36H1.5–6 and PS73H3.7–9 above.

22. Ps 80.9b–10a.

23. Ps 80.10b.

24. Ps 95.5.

25. Col 3.5.

26. See Rom 8.6–7.

27. See 1 Cor 6.19.

seek the proof of Christ speaking in me?"[28] and in other vices it is possible to hear the voices of demons using, as if they were prophets of their demonic condition, those available for the service of demonic logoi.[29]

And if we read the old narrative, that there were certain priests of idols, prophets of idols, prophets of abhorred things, and prophets of Baal,[30] or others comparable, it is likely that we despise those prophesying by Baal, not seeing that we also are sometimes prophets of anger, and say, "Anger says these things," and instead of, "The Lord God, ruler of all, says these things,"[31] we say, in effect, "Anger says these things." For just as, in that case, the Spirit of the Lord, the Almighty, would fill the prophet with the appointed prophecy, it is possible to hear a prophet saying what the Spirit says; the same is true of the opposite. When we are angered, the spirit of anger employing us as prophets speaks what it has to say. Whenever we calm down, so that we become different from what we had been, we no longer say these things, for the spirit activating us has departed. The same applies in the case of the rest of the sins. Therefore, "keep your heart guarded with care."[32] These things we have explained on account of "*there will not be in you a recent god.*"

4. "*You shall not prostrate yourself to a foreign god.*"[33] Everyone who values a thing prostrates himself to it. And to show that everyone who values a thing prostrates himself to that thing, we will say this: the idol worshipers do not prostrate themselves before idols so much on account of the idols, as on account of what they value, so that they might have those things for the sake of which they prostrate themselves to idols. For they prostrate themselves to idols in order to get rich, imagining that the idols offer them this. And they prostrate themselves to idols in order, let us say, to be famous. They value those things on account of which they prostrate themselves to the idols more than they value the idols.

---

28. 2 Cor 13.3.

29. Just as Christ speaks through the holy person, the sins speak through those who are enslaved to them.

30. See 1 Kgs 18.

31. 2 Sm 7.8, 1 Chr 17.7.

32. Prv 4.23.

33. Ps 80.10b.

Thus when each one of us, because we are not hearing, "You shall prostrate yourself to the Lord your God and him only shall you worship,"[34] does a different thing and assents to a different thing, he prostrates himself "to a foreign god" and does not hear the one who says: "*I am the Lord your God, who led you up out of the land of Egypt.*"[35] Do not suppose that he led only them up out of the land of Egypt, but he does not lead you.[36] Look at where you were when you were a gentile, when you thought in your reasoning about nothing except clay[37] and the affairs of the cosmos and the empty things of life that you considered good, and you will see that you were in Egypt. Your Lord your God, then, taking you away from bodily things, brought you up from Egypt and led you onto the mountain of God, onto faith in Christ Jesus. Therefore, it is said both to you and to those honoring idols, whenever, by virtue of a new power, you do not prostrate yourself to these things any more than those, but on account of them, "*I am the Lord your God who led you up out of the land of Egypt.*"

5. Next let us see what God commands us. For he speaks a wording, concerning which I beg him that I may understand why he says: "*Widen your mouth, and I will fill it.*"[38] Let those who want us not to allegorize gain a deep understanding and not allegorize, but let them put their minds to how God says, "*Widen your mouth, and I will fill it,*" and let them say how one must open the mouth. For does the logos actually want us to open it and make the lips wider? And how is it not shameful to reckon that God said such things? How, then, is someone going to explain this passage without using figurative interpretation? How can what is said be suspected to befit God? And the promise that says, "*and I will fill it,*" urges us to seek, so that we may under-

---

34. Dt 6.13, Mt 4.10. At issue is the use of prayer for instrumental purposes rather than as a means of personal transformation. See *Or.* 14–17 on the proper object of prayer.

35. Ps 80.11a–b.

36. Throughout his writings, not least in the homilies on Psalm 77 above, Origen applies Paul's principle (see especially 1 Cor 10.1–12) that God's dealings with Israel are the same as God's dealings with each individual soul. See also PS76H2.3 above.

37. Clay was often used for making images of gods.

38. Ps 80.11c.

stand widening the mouth, for when the mouth is widened, God will fill it.[39]

Accordingly, as someone writing a few things, and not intending that on which he writes to hold many letters, does not widen that on which he writes, but writes compactly, but someone wanting to write more seeks something larger, that will hold more, on which to write; in the same way, perceive with me, the mouth of our soul is widened by practice in paying attention to the holy letters, but we are narrowed because we do not know any Psalm, because we do not know any gospel statement, nor anything else from the holy letters. Thus we widen our mouth by practice with the holy letters. And when we do not know in the beginning what the letters say, if we deal with them, we will begin to fill the mouth, by practice with the letters, intending to remember the law and the prophets, the Gospels and apostles. You have a promise: "If you widen your mouth, I will fill it." All these things, whatever we have done for the acquisition of the holy letters—and if it is possible for one confessing with thanksgiving and thanking God to say: "But I know truly that the one speaks truth who says, 'Widen your mouth, and I will fill it'"— for the more I widen my mouth, the more I make that my concern, the more it shall be filled, and when I make my concern nothing except the statement [of Scripture, my mouth] is filled with the mind of the divine letters.[40]

And as I am praying, while you are working together and joining in the struggle, for my mouth to be filled, so that I may not lack things to say, you see the helpfulness that is produced from

39. The Christian "opens wide" to receive the logos who is the bread of life. See Marguerite Harl, «La 'bouche' et le 'cœur' de l'Apôtre,» in *Le déchiffrement du sens: Études sur l'herméneutique d'Origène à Grégoire de Nysse* (Paris: Études Augustiniennes, 1993), 151–76, esp. 174.

40. The "divine letters" are the actual words of the Bible. Origen recommends "acquiring" them, as he clearly did, by memorizing them. On the vital importance of memory in the classical world, see Frances A. Yates, *The Art of Memory* (Chicago: University of Chicago Press, 1966), 1–49. Just as it is up to us to be a well-tuned instrument for God's use, so, if God is going to fill our mouth with words, it is up to us to have our mouth widened, that is, to have a wide store of Scripture in our memory. Knowing Scripture by heart provides words for God to speak through us and provides us ways to come up with our own words by extending through logic the implications of the logos in the Bible.

the text. I am then persuaded (and I recommend and beg that you be persuaded by the one saying,[41] "Widen your mouth, and I will fill it"), if, in order to establish further what has been said, I might add something that has happened among the brothers. Often someone comes seeking to understand concepts laid up in the Holy Scripture, and laid up in a way that has been hidden, but not knowing an evangelical statement, nor remembering an apostolic logos, nor knowing what a prophet says or why it is written therefore in this very book.[42] Someone might in a timely way say to that person, "Widen your mouth, if you intend for your mouth to be filled, by learning these things about which you inquire." If, then, someone is going to understand the holy Scriptures, let there be no other preparation except the memory of the Scriptures, for we speak divine things not in logoi taught by human wisdom, but in those taught by the spirit, comparing spiritual things with spiritual things.[43]

6. On the one hand, God says, "*Widen your mouth, and I will fill it.*" But, on the other hand, God brings a charge against those who are not hearing and says: "*And my people did not hear my voice, and Israel did not pay attention to me.*"[44] In common usage[45] one must hear this concerning the sinners among the people, either in this one or in that one. For this has been said concerning all sinners: "*My people did not hear my voice,*" and concerning all who fall, "*and Israel did not pay attention to me.*" But if you want Christ to be the one speaking, you will not be mistaken, for he prophesies and says concerning the people, "*My people did not hear my voice, and Israel did not pay attention to me.*" The Son of God was present; Christ visited, and Israel did not pay attention, but "*they went the wrong way according to the customs of their hearts.*"[46]

41. That is, the divine logos.

42. The phrasing implies that Origen, at this point, held up the codex of the Psalms from which he was reading.

43. 1 Cor 2.13.

44. Ps 80.12.

45. *Koinoteron,* "commonly" or "in common usage." The statement might be interpreted to imply that all the people did not hear God's voice, but the statement is an example of a common figure of speech, synecdoche, in which a part stands for the whole, or, as here, the whole stands for a part.

46. Ps 80.13a. Besides referring to a familiar phenomenon at any time,

And it is possible to add something else in connection with the statement—as often as it comes up in confronting those who misconstrue Scripture—that I consider appropriate to bring up just as we are dealing with "*My people did not hear my voice.*" Such-and-such a logos of the Savior has been written in the Gospel according to John: "You have never heard his voice, nor have you seen his form; and you do not have his logos abiding in you, because the one he sent, that one you do not believe."[47] What is said is unexceptionable and well said. But followers of Valentinus and of Basilides[48] have seized on the wording and say, "Thus he introduces another god besides the god of the law and the prophets. Jesus Christ is speaking against the Jews, to whom the law and the prophets are well known: 'You have never heard his voice, nor have you seen his form.' Therefore, the Jews have not heard the genuine God ever at all, the one different from the god of the law, but the Lord Jesus has introduced a new god different from the god of the Jews."

A naïve and simple soul heard that it was said, "You have never heard his voice, nor have you seen his form," and it hears them avowing that the Jews did not see the form of the genuine god (although, in fact, God was seen by Abraham or by Moses), and it goes away and leaves the Church, and it abandons this logos[49] as something stupid. It flees to heresy as if to knowledge and wisdom. Since the wording in the Gospel is misconstrued that says, "You have never heard his voice, nor have you seen his form," we are rebuking those who misconstrue and take in a bad sense what has been written.

And, right here, to the people hearing the law and the prophets is said: "*The people did not hear my voice.*"[50] It is said instead of

---

namely that some people pay no attention to God, this statement also refers prophetically to the failure of many Jewish people to pay attention to Christ during his visitation (*epidēmia*).

47. Jn 5.37–38.

48. Marcionites are not included. They taught much the same thing, but they rejected the Gospel of John. In his *Commentary on John* Origen refuted the interpretations of Heracleon, a follower of Valentinus.

49. "This logos" could be the preaching of the Church, in which Origen is engaged, or it could be the Psalm, since it belongs to the Hebrew Scriptures, which the heretics reject.

50. Ps 80.12a.

"it did not perceive or understand my words," and, not at all for the reason that the prophets were not speaking, they did not hear nor had they done what was requested. Likewise, in the Savior's rebuke of the Jews of his time who did not understand what was written in the prophets, it had been said, "You have never heard his voice, nor have you seen his form, and you do not have his logos abiding in you, because the one he sent, that one you do not believe."[51] For if you had heard the voice of God prophesying, you would have entirely accepted Christ, whom God sent; but, not accepting the one whom God sent, "you have neither heard his voice, nor have you seen his form."[52]

And you will not be mistaken in saying to the Jews who read the Hebrew Scriptures and care—as they suppose—for the law and the prophets, you will not be mistaken in saying to the Jews, "You have never heard his voice, nor have you seen his form; and you do not have his logos abiding in you, because the one he sent, that one you do not believe." They say also that they believe Moses, but my Lord Jesus Christ rebukes them as unbelievers, saying, "If you were believing Moses, you would be believing me, since he wrote about me, but if you do not believe his writings, how will you believe my utterances?"[53]

"*And Israel did not pay attention to me.*"[54] Everyone who sins does not pay attention to God; for it is impossible for sin to come when the soul is paying attention to God,[55] but sin is alive

---

51. Jn 5.37–38.

52. Origen takes the opportunity presented by preaching on Psalm 80 to disarm a seemingly potent weapon in the hands of the Valentinians and Basilideans. They misconstrue Jn 5.37–38 to say that the God and Father of Jesus never spoke to the Hebrew people. But, Origen says, here in the Old Testament the God who spoke through the prophets says the very same thing about the response to Jesus that Jesus himself did. Jesus was not speaking about some god whom the prophets did not know about; the God and Father of Jesus is the God of the prophets.

53. Jn 5.46.

54. Ps 80.12b.

55. The manuscript reading is unclear here. The manuscript says, "when sin is paying attention." Perrone suggests that the text should read "when sin is not paying attention." On the benefits of continual prayer, see PS76H1.2 and PS76H4.4 above. Compare *Or.* 8.2: "If, for the sake of argument, no usefulness other than this should come to the one devoting his disposition to prayer, it

and productive through lack of attention to God and establishes its kingship among us; so that we must hear the words, "Do not let sin reign in your mortal bodies."[56]

7. And he sent them away from the altar of sacrifice, from the Temple, "*according to the customs of their hearts*"—he returned to them things worthy of the customs of their hearts—and they went their way in the customs of their hearts, not in the customs of the commands of God and of his logoi. "*If my people heard me, Israel would have walked in my roads; in no time I would have humbled their enemies.*"[57] If enemies ever are empowered against the people and not humbled, it is because the people have not heard God or have not come to be walking in God's roads. Such things as this are said to them and to us. For if we will hear God, if we will walk in his roads, hearing the secrets in the Scriptures, in no time God will humble our enemies, to be sure, not without our toil, not without struggles, but he will humble our enemies, coming to be among us, so that through us he might humble the enemies.

"*And on those who oppress them I would have struck with my hand.*"[58] For he will strike the oppressors with his chastening hand, be they the angels of the evil one, the evil one himself, or human beings motivated by the evil one against us. God strikes with his hand; "*the enemies of the Lord lied about him.*"[59] If someone is an enemy of the Lord, such a person completely lies about

must be borne in mind that someone who reverently harmonizes himself in a time of prayer receives no casual benefit; when this comes about often, how many sins it prevents and how many achievements it promotes those who continually give themselves to prayer know by experience." Greco-Roman Stoics, such as Epictetus, whom Origen admired (see *Cels.* 6.2), recommend the practice of continual attention, *prosochē*. Pierre Hadot describes this as "the fundamental Stoic spiritual attitude," for which he gives Epictetus's definition, "concentration on the present moment" (Epictetus, *Discourses* 4.12.7, cited in Pierre Hadot, *Philosophy as a Way of Life*, ed. Arnold I. Davidson, trans. Michael Chase [Oxford: Blackwell, 1995], 84). See also Pierre Hadot, *The Inner Citadel: The* Meditations *of Marcus Aurelius*, trans. Michael Chase (Cambridge, MA: Harvard University Press, 1998), and *Plotinus or the Simplicity of Vision*, intro. Arnold J. Davidson, trans. Michael Chase (Chicago: University of Chicago Press, 1993).

56. Rom 6.12.
57. Ps 80.14–15a.
58. Ps 80.15b.
59. Ps 80.16a.

God; that is, he does not say true things about God, he does not say true things about God, and "*their time will be to the age*."[60]

"*And he fed them from the fat of wheat*";[61] so that those who have become God's enemies should not give up hope for themselves, it announces the provision of kindness also toward those who have become God's enemies. And we were God's enemies, but his kindness reached us. For hear "God was in Christ, reconciling the cosmos to himself,"[62] and, "we beg you on behalf of Christ, be reconciled to God."[63] And how else, but if Christ Jesus came to loose "the enmity in his flesh, abolishing the law of commands in teachings, so that he might make the two, by a new creation in him, into one new human being, making peace."[64] And, being enemies, we were reconciled to God. Very well, we were enemies; "*the time*," then, of those "*enemies is to the age*."[65]

And rescuing the enemies, God "*fed them*," it says, "*from fat of wheat*."[66] I seek one wheat, so that I may see the fat of the wheat and comprehend how God feeds us from the fat of wheat: "If the kernel of grain falling into the earth does not die, it will remain alone, but if it dies, it bears much fruit."[67] My Lord Jesus Christ himself was the wheat, was he not? He was the kernel of grain, the glorious flour was his fat. In him and by his death we were delivered, for because he fell—but he fell, I say, when he was delivered and crucified for us—the fat of his wheat became our nourishment. Concerning this fat of wheat Moses prophesies in Deuteronomy, saying, "He mounted them on the power of the earth, he fed them increase of fields, they sucked honey from a rock, and oil from a dry rock, butter of cows and milk of

60. Ps 80.16b. That is, their time is temporary. See n. 65 below.

61. Ps 80.17b.

62. 2 Cor 5.19.

63. 2 Cor 5.20.

64. Eph 2.14–15.

65. For Origen, "to the age" refers to the end of a cosmic period. At the end of an age, another age follows, so the hope of redemption for God's enemies is never cut off. Our own redemption through Christ is proof that those who have been God's enemies can be reconciled. As our enmity was temporary, so will theirs be.

66. Ps 80.17a.

67. Jn 12.24.

sheep with fat of lambs and rams, of the sons of bulls and goats with fat of kidneys of wheat and blood of grapes."[68] All this is our genuine nourishment, Christ, the genuine cup.

And he himself *"fed us from the fat of wheat and supplied honey to us from a rock,"*[69] but the rock is Christ.[70] "He mounted them on the power of the earth, he fed them increase of fields, they sucked honey from a rock." We, those who believe in Christ, are those who suck honey, for how can anything be sweeter than God's logoi? We, then, suck honey from the rock. Therefore, the rock itself gives us this logos, which is honey, concerning which we say, "How sweet to my throat are your oracles, beyond honey and honeycomb."[71] Concerning this honey, which we suck from a rock, Solomon spoke in Proverbs: "Finding honey, eat enough,"[72] and elsewhere, "Eat honey, son, for this is a good thing."[73] And does he command me to eat honey, on the grounds that eating honey by itself is this good thing?

I am allegorizing again; again, some are going to be irritated at the allegory. Again, as a matter of fact, the one stumbling over what is said, "Eat honey, son, for this is a good thing," says this: "Eating honey is a good thing, and God by the Holy Spirit commands us to eat honey." But is the sweet thing not, rather, the logos, the one from the rock? The logos commands us to eat, so that, always loving to be nourished by the holy logos, we may eat both milk and honey[74] in Christ Jesus, to whom is the glory and the might to the ages of ages. Amen.

68. Dt 32.13–14.
69. Ps 18.17.
70. 1 Cor 10.4.
71. Ps 118.103.
72. Prv 25.16.
73. Prv 24.13.
74. See Ex 3.17. Continually attending to God is to eat the milk and honey of the Promised Land, the nourishment of God's presence.

HOMILY ON PSALM 81

HE GOAL FOR a disciple is to become like the teacher, and the ideal of a slave is to become like the lord; and it is sufficient for the disciple that he become like the teacher, and for the slave that he become like the lord.[1] And the teacher aims for this, that he may, to the extent that he can, make the disciples like him; and the lord has visited, not so as to keep the slaves, but so that the lord might make the slaves to be as he is. But our teacher, Christ Jesus, is a god, and if it is sufficient for the disciple that he become like the teacher, the ideal of the disciple is to become a christ from Christ and a god from a god, and to learn from the light of the cosmos. For everything at all that the Savior is, he calls also his disciples to be: "You are the light of the cosmos,"[2] he says to them, having already said, "I am the light of the cosmos."[3] And, being a christ, he says: "Do not touch my christ, and among my prophets do not do evil."[4]

1. Origen states this principle elsewhere in his work, notably in *Comm. Jo.* 32.10.118–119: "And this is the teacher's purpose for the disciple, should he be a teacher: to make the disciple like himself, so that he may no longer need the teacher, insofar as he is a teacher, though he may need him in some other way. As the purpose of a physician—whom those doing poorly need, but the strong have no need for a physician [see Mt 9.12, Mk 2.17, Lk 5.31]—is to stop those who are doing poorly from doing poorly, so that they may no longer need him, so the purpose of the teacher is to bring about in the disciple the 'enough' in 'It is enough for the disciple to become as his teacher is [Mt 10.25].'" Origen follows this principle in his own teaching, seeking to assist his hearers to come to sound conclusions on their own.

2. Mt 5.14.

3. Jn 8.12.

4. Ps 104.15. Origen explains how there can be more than one "christ" in *Comm. Jo.* 6.6.42: "But perhaps thus one must also seek 'Or do you seek proof of Christ speaking in me [2 Cor 13.3]?' For Christ is found, as it were, in each holy person, and through Christ there come to be many 'christs' who are his

This gathering, when we genuinely are gathered, if we do not walk in a human manner, if we do not sow in the flesh what God speaks about in "You harvest corruption,"[5] and if we do not do the works of the flesh but the fruits of the spirit,[6] it is not a gathering of human beings, but a gathering of gods; the devil can do nothing; but God visits, and he visits standing in the midst of the gathering of gods. Therefore, it is said, "*God stood in the gathering of gods.*"[7] But what makes us human beings, so that, having fallen from divinity, we might destroy the legacy calling us to become gods? What makes human beings?

Hear Paul speaking about very small sins:[8] "for when there is among you jealousy and strife, are you not fleshly, and do you not walk in a human manner?"[9] And he adds, "Are you not human beings?"[10] Does he not all but cry out there and say:[11] "The logos has called you, so that you may be gods, but, for this reason and that, you are human beings"? And here he says well, "'*I have said, "You are all gods and sons of the highest," but you*'—I see us practicing such things not worthy of divinity"—he adds and

---

imitators and who are transformed into his image, so that God says through the prophet, 'Do not touch my christ.'" Here Origen cites Psalm 104 as a saying of Christ, since he understood the Psalmist as having written in the persona of Christ.

5. Gal 6.8.

6. See Gal 5.19 and 5.22.

7. Ps 81.1a. On "gathering" see also PS67H1.4–6, PS76H2.5, and PS77H8.2–3 above.

8. Even sins that seem "very small" to us can make all the difference in the world.

9. 1 Cor 3.3.

10. 1 Cor 3.4. Paul, in 1 Cor, makes exactly the same point as Psalm 81. It may be that Paul had the Psalm in mind as he wrote his epistle or simply that the same divine logos speaks through both Asaph and Paul.

11. Although the homilies give the impression of impromptu speaking, they are more artfully composed than they may seem. As Lorenzo Perrone has pointed out (in an address to be published with the proceedings of a colloquium dedicated to Origen's newly discovered homilies at the Catholic University of America on May 22, 2017), Origen characteristically composes like a musician who subtly introduces a theme that he will develop more fully later. Later in the homily he will talk about the way in which believers assume personae. From here on, most of this paragraph is in one set of quotation marks (not trying to nest quotations within quotations) because, having assumed Paul's persona, Origen speaks it as a quotation from Paul.

says, "see, in fact, '*you die as human beings and you fall as one of the rulers,*'[12] and God's legacy coming to us, making us gods, which ought to be received with the whole soul, we sinners do not accept, but throwing away and eliminating divinity, we accept the flesh's ways of thinking, accomplishing works of the flesh,[13] not putting to death by spirit the deeds of the flesh,[14] which we ought to do."

For when the deeds of the body are put to death,[15] so that there are no longer deeds of the body in us, then we have been made gods. A god-logos, if it is produced in the soul, makes the soul that receives it a god. For if a small leaven leavens the whole lump,[16] what is to be said, not concerning a small and insignificant leaven, but about the god-making logos,[17] but that it, having come to be in the soul, leavens the whole lump of a human being into godhood and the whole human being becomes god? For "the kingdom of the heavens is like leaven, which a woman took and hid in three measures of meal until the whole was leavened."[18] Are not, then, the three measures the spirit, the soul, and the body of a human being? The leaven came from the woman, the Church that has received Christ, and the leaven itself, preaching[19] to the three measures, leavened that whole, the lump, and has made the human being from the whole to become a god.

That the spirit in us was divinized is no marvel; it has kinship[20] with a god, since the incorruptible spirit is also in all, but it is a marvel that the soul has been divinized; since it would no longer sin, it would no longer be mortal, for the soul that sins,

12. Ps 81.7.

13. See Gal 5.19.

14. See Rom 8.13 ("flesh" replaces "body").

15. See ibid.

16. 1 Cor 5.6.

17. Ignatius, *Magnesians* 10.2, identifies Jesus Christ as the "new leaven" of 1 Cor 5.7–8 and Gal 5.9.

18. Mt 13.33, and see Lk 13.21.

19. Greek, *homilēsasa*, "preaching" or "discussing," the same root as *homilia*, "homily." Origen describes what he is doing as he does it, inserting the leaven, the preaching logos.

20. *Suggeneia*, see PS73H2.1 above.

that soul will die.[21] But what is more marvelous than all of these is that the body has been divinized, so that it is no longer flesh and blood,[22] but it becomes conformed to Christ Jesus's body of glory;[23] and, having been divinized, it is received into heaven[24] according to the saying, "We shall be taken in the clouds to meet the Lord in the air, and thus we shall forever be with the Lord,"[25] having become gods, with a god standing in the middle of our gathering, Jesus Christ.

2. God judges those outside, but God does not judge those inside; but he does something better than judgment for those inside, when they are found to be gods. What is that better thing? Hear the prophet say, "*God stood in the gathering of gods; in the midst he distinguishes gods.*"[26] And just as when an emperor on a glad day wants each of those worthy to receive an honor corresponding to their dignity, we term, strictly speaking, such a person not as "judging" but as "distinguishing"; so, for example, he says: "These hundred are worthy of honor from me, but these first two of the preeminent consulates, these eight or so of the second-rank consulates, these subordinates of the procuratorships, these still more subordinate of second-ranking procuratorships." And thus he descends through the honors to the one worthy of the lowest honor, not to receive those honors, but to be rewarded by an honor and a subordinate favor.

Such a thing, perceive with me, on the glad day of the recompense of the chosen angels, when God rewards them. After the judgment, perceive with me, after the sentence, after the sinners are punished, when all these things have occurred to them, God will invite the gathering of gods, and, after inviting them, he will make distinctions: who is worthy to arise in the resurrection as a sun; who is worthy of standing up in the resurrection as a moon; who are worthy of resurrection as the brightest and most preeminent stars; who are worthy of resurrection as subordinate and less perfect stars; and who are stars worthy of heaven itself, but not to

21. Ezek 18.4.
22. See 1 Cor 15.50.
23. Phil 3.21.
24. As Christ was first, see PS15H2.8 above.
25. 1 Thes 4.17.
26. Ps 81.1.

rise up in the dimmest and most inferior resurrection in comparison with the rest of the stars. When that occurs, "*God stood in the gathering of gods; in the midst he distinguishes gods.*"[27]

3. It is the custom for the god-logos, whenever it lifts us up and exalts us with promises, to rebuke us in return for our sins and to remind us that "these things are said as a promise for those who are worthy, but you are base." Thus, for example, it might be said to me, "You are unworthy of the promises, so I will rebuke you for this or that sin." Such a thing occurs here; after "*God stood in the gathering of gods; in the midst he distinguishes gods,*" those who are not gods, but "*die as human beings,*"[28] are rebuked in the midst of the gathering of gods, and these are the ones worthy of rebukes.

Shall we hear, then, that we are those who are not gods in the midst of the gathering of those who are blessed and behaving well as gods with us, and it is said to us, "*How long will you judge unjustly and receive the personae[29] of sinners?*"[30] Why does it say that when you judge, you judge unjustly, and, judging unjustly, you receive the personae of sinners? When, in fact, there are two people being judged, a rich sinner and a poor just man, you, taking the persona of the sinner because of his wealth, prefer the sinner to the one who is just, but poor. And this sin is frequent among us wretched human beings. It has become our custom to give preference to those who are exceptional, not according to God, but according to the cosmos, and to exclude and despise those who are exceptional according to God. To us, then, to the extent that we sin these sins, God says, "*How long will you judge unjustly and receive the personae of sinners?*"

It is possible, besides what has been said, that there is also some recondite logos in "*receive the personae of sinners.*" Just as those on the stage for plays receive personae that they have practiced, now that of a king, now that of a household slave, now of a woman, now of whoever it might be, and it is possible to see in theatrical performances the performers receiving

27. Ibid.
28. Ps 81.7a.
29. *Prosōpa;* see introduction, pp. 13–14.
30. Ps 81.2.

personae; such a thing, I think, also occurs on the stage of the world.[31] For all the performers always receive personae; if we would be blessed, we should receive a persona like that of God and say: "I have begotten sons and exalted them, but they have rejected me."[32] Again, if we would be just, we receive the persona of Christ, and, while still human beings, we say: "The spirit of the Lord is upon me, for which reason he has anointed me; he has sent me to announce good news to the destitute."[33] But in this way a just person receives an unjust persona according to what is written, so the Holy Spirit says: "Today, if you harden your hearts."[34] But the one who is god-possessed also receives the persona of a holy angel from the angelic power, as does the one saying, "The angel of the spirit speaking in me."[35]

These considerations concern the better category, but it is also possible to see the opposite, someone receiving the persona of the devil, someone else the persona of the antichrist, another receiving the persona of a demon. Or does not someone who is crazy seem to bear an alien persona? But thus also there are activities related to mental disturbances activating anger, sorrow, bad desire, and the rest of the sins. We receive, then, now if we are angels, the persona of God; otherwise, the persona of sorrow, and otherwise, the persona of the spirit of sexual immorality. And always human beings switch personae, sinning after the images of sins, but straightening out and acting better according to the value of what comes about. These considerations lead me to say what? Because "*you receive the personae of sinners.*"[36] If you

31. Origen testifies to a sophisticated understanding of acting. Although long despised, Greco-Roman theater is now being reevaluated. See Ruth Webb, *Demons and Dancers: Performance in Late Antiquity* (Cambridge, MA: Harvard University Press, 2008).

32. Is 1.2.

33. Is 61.1, Lk 4.18.

34. See Ps 94.7–8.

35. See Hermas, *Mandate* 11.9: "Whenever, then, the human being who has the divine spirit comes into a gathering of the righteous having a faith in the divine spirit, and a supplication occurs to God from the gathering of those men, then the angel of the prophetic spirit sitting on him fills the human being, and, when he is full of the Holy Spirit, that human being speaks to the whole as the Lord wishes."

36. Ps 81.2.

want to receive a persona, receive the persona of a god, receive the persona of a christ. Say, "Or do you seek proof of Christ speaking in me?"[37]

4. Seeing that we are blamed for our sins, what was said to those before is also said to us: "*Judge orphan and destitute, and give justice to humble and poor, deliver from the hand of a sinner.*"[38] You see, even the apostles, when they were giving each other right hands, because the human race feels a certain contempt for the destitute, they made this the condition for giving their right hands: that they would remember the destitute, as it is said in the Epistle to the Galatians.[39] Unremittingly, then, Scripture is saying to us, "Judge for an orphan and give justice to a widow, and come and let us be rebuked,"[40] anywhere it says, "*Judge orphan and destitute, and give justice to humble and poor.*"[41] For example, when you apportion something just to the humble and poor, "*Release the poor and destitute.*"[42] If you ever see a poor person being harmed, do something about it. When that person is harmed, stand by him. He is despised because of poverty; the just person is at his side. Often he has property, and the property is lost by our hesitation to stand by him when we can do so.

It says about such persons, "*Give justice to humble and poor, release the poor and destitute, deliver them from the hand of a sinner.*"[43] Therefore, it is a good thing, because "in the measure that we measure out, in that measure it will be measured in return for us";[44] we also will deliver the poor and destitute from the hand of a sinner. For he will say, "Because you did this for the poor person, I will also do it for you; because you did this for the humble person, I will also do it for you.[45] Next to me, all human beings and the rest of the powers are humble and all are desti-

37. 2 Cor 13.3.
38. Ps 81.3–4.
39. See Gal 2.9–10.
40. Is 1.17–18. On "let us be rebuked," see PS67H1.2 above.
41. Ps 81.3.
42. Ps 81.4a.
43. Ps 81.3b–4.
44. See Lk 6.38.
45. Origen extends the logic of Mt 25.31–46 as he does in PS15H1.3 and PS36H3.12 above.

tute." It is a good thing to stand by the helpless, so that in this you may become children of God.[46] Referring to him, the very wise Judith said in her prayer, "You are God of the humble, helper of the least, upholder of the weak, protector of the forlorn, Savior of the hopeless, yes, yes, Lord God."[47] Insofar as possible, because these things are ascribed to God, be zealous to become God's imitator,[48] so that you may become a child of your Father, who is in the heavens.[49]

5. Next it is said concerning sinners, "*They have not known, nor have they understood. They go about in darkness.*"[50] On the one hand, those who go about in sensible darkness, for example, at night or in an unlighted house, have darkness outside them, for, if they happen to be just, they are internally enlightened but externally darkened. But sinners go about in darkness. What sort of darkness? There is an internal darkness in them. If, then, the light in you is darkness, how great a darkness is that?[51] Do you see that the Savior also knew that there was someone having in himself the darkness that is darkened light, much more than the darkness of darkness? One must then expel the darkness within; we expel darkness from the soul when we hear Jesus saying, "Stand with your loins girded and your lamps burning."[52] If the lamp in me is burning and I place it on a lampstand of the tent of witness in me, in the place where access is denied to human beings, where only the high priest has authority to enter,[53] the darkness will flee. And it occurred in the tent of witness, that there was darkness then. "For kindle," he says, "the lamp at all times, from dusk to dawn,"[54] so that there may never be darkness in the tent. And you have a tent—"we groan as we are weighed down in the tent."[55] Take pains, then, that this tent be always

46. See Mt 5.45.

47. Jdt 9.11–12.

48. See Eph 5.1.

49. See Mt 5.45.

50. Ps 81.5a.

51. See Mt 6.23.

52. Lk 12.35.

53. See Heb 9.11–12.

54. Lv 24.3. Note that we are God's tent or tabernacle; when we are enlightened, God is present within us.

55. 2 Cor 5.4.

illuminated, and receive the five virgins in you, the five senses in you; give them oil, kindle their torches,[56] so that you may not walk in darkness as the sinners do, about whom it is written, "*They have not known, nor have they understood. They go about in darkness.*"[57]

6. But if we turn back, it is said, "*all the foundations of the earth will be shaken.*"[58] There is a certain foundation that is a foundation not on earth or of earth, but, if I can term it such, a foundation of heaven, for no other foundation may be laid except the one laid down, but a foundation of heaven: "God in wisdom founded the earth; he prepared the heavens in thoughtfulness."[59] We have in Scripture that God even founded the heavens.[60] There are, then, foundations, of earth on the one hand, of heaven on the other; Christ Jesus is a foundation of heaven, and those who are his imitators are foundations of heaven. Concerning those it is written, "built upon the foundation of the apostles and prophets, its cornerstone being Christ Jesus"[61] our Lord. Let these things, then, be said about the logos of truth and of the secrets of salvation.

If you want to see what the foundations of the earth are, see with me the logoi of the heretics and those outside the Church; see with me the logoi of the Jews who do not accept Jesus Christ. All their foundations are on earth, and, because they are on earth, they speak from the earth;[62] therefore, the heavens do not hear them. "*All the foundations of the earth will be shaken,*"[63] for all will be overthrown, all will be uprooted. And who is it who shakes the foundations of the earth but the one receiving God's logoi? Let God also say to me, "See, I have given my logoi into your mouth."[64] And may he say, "I have said this," and the rest, "See, I have established you today over nations and kings to

56. See Mt 25.1–13.
57. Ps 81.5a.
58. Ps 81.5b.
59. Prv 3.19.
60. See Ps 8.4.
61. Eph 2.20.
62. See Jn 3.31.
63. Ps 81.5b.
64. Jer 1.9.

uproot and to overthrow and to build and plant,"[65] to uproot every plant that the heavenly Father did not plant, to overthrow the foundations of the earth, to plant God's farm, to build God's building. All the foundations of the earth will be shaken and shivered and shattered.

7. When these things have been said, he rebukes us yet again with the one logos alone that is also said to those worthy, and says,[66] "I did not call some of you to be gods without calling others; are not bishops, presbyters, and deacons to be God's, but I want you from the people[67] to be gods; but *I have said, You are gods and children of the highest*—not some of you to the exclusion of others—but you *all.* Next I have said this—and the Scripture cannot be dissolved—that the one for whom God's logos is produced, that one is a god and becomes a child of the highest, but you die in the sins of human beings."[68]

Therefore, it is said, "*but you die as human beings.*"[69] What sort of death? It is not speaking about the common death, but the death that we die when we activate death. Just as there are some who make for themselves a bodily death (for example, as Judas

65. Jer 1.10.

66. Having earlier adopted the persona of Paul, Origen interprets as he quotes Ps 81.6–7 in the assumed persona of Asaph (or God). Origen often cited these verses in his writings to make it clear that the privilege of divine status has belonged to some, is intended for all of us, and is provisional. Thus we read in a homily that survives only in Latin translation (PS37H2.3): "If we were such persons as the divine logos (*sermo*) intends us to be, we might speak to God, as Elijah did, 'may he give rain,' and it would rain [1 Kgs 18.41–45]; like Samuel we might ask that it might rain during the days of harvest, that he might provide an abundance of rain from the heaven, and he would hear [1 Sm 12.17–18]. But now, however, how would God hear us, we do not hear him? God intends for us to be such that we speak to God as gods. He intends us to be children of God, so that we may become sharers and coheirs of God's son and that we may say to the Father as he does, 'Father, I know that you always hear me' [Jn 11.42]. We know because God said to us, 'I have said, You are gods and all children of the highest' [Ps. 81.6]. But we, on the basis of our merits, are more deserving of (and may expect) what follows: 'You,' truly, 'die as human beings, and you fall as one of the rulers' [Ps 81.7] ...."

67. *Ek tou laou,* "from the people," is an early use of "people" to distinguish Christians who do not belong to the three orders of clergy.

68. See Ps 81.6–7.

69. Ps 81.7a.

hanged himself or as some throw themselves off cliffs or take lethal drugs), so they engineer the death for themselves. But in that case it is a death that comes even to those who do not engineer it, but this death of the soul never occurs involuntarily; but if we ourselves do not make the death, death does not come, "for God did not make death, nor does he delight in destruction of the living, for he created all things so that they might be."[70] And just as Judas hanged himself, so all sinners bring death upon themselves.

No one forces you to commit sexual immorality so that you die, but through sexual immorality you die. No one forces you to commit fraud so that you die, but by doing this and taking another's belongings and not returning what you owe, you bring death on yourself. No one makes you die, but on account of wrath you destroy yourself even when you are thoughtful.[71] He warns you, then, that you are bringing death on yourselves on account of sins, and says, "*but you die as human beings.*"[72] For when you are called to be gods, you yourselves die as human beings; whenever, after this teaching and guidance, you again imitate the gentile way of life, what else have you done but to die as human beings?

And would that the bad things stopped there, at our dying as human beings! The sin was moderate, but now we commit a worse sin. He adds what is worse and says, "*and you fall as one of the rulers.*"[73] That ruler was once in heaven; that one was once a god. But as soon as he sinned, he fell from heaven, as the Savior, even our Lord, makes clear, saying, "I watched Satan falling from heaven like lightning."[74] And you, then, just as that one has fallen from heaven, also yourselves fall from heaven, for you are in heaven when you believe in Christ, and in heaven when you recognize God; you are in heaven when you receive the Holy

70. Wis 1.13–14. There is such a thing as suicide, when we voluntarily engineer for ourselves the "common" death that would occur in any event; when we sin, however, we voluntarily commit, as it were, spiritual suicide and make for ourselves a preventable death.

71. See Prv 15.1. Wrath causes us to be out of our minds.

72. Ps 81.7a.

73. Ps 81.7b.

74. See Lk 10.18.

Spirit. Whenever, then, with these teachings and a discipline of moderation, you exercise citizenship in heaven, you may fall and you may sin, imitating the ruler who fell from heaven.

But if such things come about and you die as human beings and fall as one of the rulers, it is your care, as the one who says these things,[75] to beseech God, that he may stand back up those who have fallen, that he may make alive those who have died and not allow them to be in a state of demise. For that very reason it prays and says, "*Arise, God, judge the earth, because you will make a bequest in all the gentiles.*"[76] It says this on account of Christ's visitation, for previously God did not make a bequest in all the gentiles, but his bequest was in Judea alone. But when my Lord, Christ Jesus, made a visitation, then he made a bequest in all the gentiles, and we are drawing them into the allotted portion of the holy ones, those who are on hand to be drawn by God toward our Lord Christ Jesus. Therefore, let us also beseech God, let us say if we also fall, let us say even if we have died, "*Arise, God, judge the earth, because you will make a bequest in all the gentiles,*"[77] through Jesus Christ, to whom is the glory and the might to the ages of ages. Amen.

75. That is, those who say the Psalm.
76. Ps 81.8.
77. Ibid.

INDICES

GENERAL INDEX

Abraham: and beginning of Jewish people, 183, 413n28; being a child of, 134, 174, 263, 305; divinized, 261; faith of, 324; first "elder," 130; followed the law by nature, 30; has spiritual fathers, 192; imitating, 263; marriage of, 257; once an idolater, 173–74, 405; saw God, 454; secret concerning, 257; still living, 53–54; taught angels, 336n73; wealth of, 110, 374

accommodation (*sugkatabasis*): angels', 326–27; God's, 145, 323n26; Paul's, 144–45, 307n16; 395–97. *See also* biblical interpretation

acting, 13, 108, 176n111, 396n8, 443–45

Adam: received garments of skin, 415; secret concerning, 257; the devil tripped, 413n33; why God rejected, 179

Address of Thanksgiving. See Gregory Thaumaturgus

adoption (*huiothesia*): freedom through, 41n26, 109n41, 389; fruit through spirit of, 89, 410; kinship through, 143, 192

Aëtius Amidenus, 54n117

affliction (*thlipsis*): being forsaken, 132–35; God's power in, 59. *See also* desert, testing

age (*aiōn*): heretics make up, 306–7; implies a long duration, 235, 251, 323, 402–3, 411, 437; more than one, 17, 182, 329, 419n67; possible participation in timelessness, 82, 113, 136–37, 210, 215, 227, 285, 358–359, 365, 406; this, 63, 93, 108–10, 113, 115–16, 237, 310–11, 315–16; to come, 164, 294. *See also* eschaton; time or occasion

age of life (*hēlikia*), spiritual, 129–32. *See also* elder

Alexandria, 11

allegory. *See* figurative expression

Ambrosius, Origen's patron, 6–7

Ammonius Saccas, 16

anathemas of the Second Council of Constantinople, 282n35

angel, angels: bread of, 338; fed by Abraham, 336n73; nourished, 329–331; of Great Counsel, 44–45, of nations, 5; oversee churches, 304n6; protecting, 44, 132; using trumpet, 354, 417. *See also* Cherubim; Seraphim

anger. *See* wrath

anthropology. *See* human being

antichrist, 174, 309, 311, 444

Apelles, 201

Apocryphon of John, 317n89

apokatastasis. See restoration

aporia, 13, 335n65. *See also* problems and solutions

apostles, 58–59, 222–23, 423n90, 447

Apostolic Tradition, 239n8

Aristeas, Letter to, 24

Aristotle: cardinal virtues, 243; depravity voluntary, 95n30; grammar from, 10; heart seat of intelligence, 67n58; on logical

Plotinus: (*cont.*)
    likens human body to a lyre, 165n39; music of the spheres, 163n32; on beauty, 390n73; on being and becoming, 393n23; on circular motion, 281n34, 282n35; on the cosmos, 276n1; on flying in dreams, 312n49; on image and likeness, 390n72; on intelligible being, 384n37; on virtue, 177n115; philosophy kin to the divine, 192n2; sculpting one's own statue, 38n10
Plutarch, 247n54
Pohlenz, Max, 374n83
polutropos (multiple) vs. *monotropos* (single), 176–77
poor (*penēs*), 32. *See also* destitute
Porphyry, 16n16
Pradel, Marina Molin, 1–2, 33
prayer (*euchē*): fulfillment of, 409; in homilies, 22; must be made through Christ, 41; nourishment of our souls, 54; Origen requests, 59; Savior teaches us to, in Psalms, 40, 95, 140, 213; use of Psalms in, 21, 197; we do not know how to, 203
preaching: evidence of, in CMG 314, 22; Origen's, 6–10; power of, 441
precipitousness (*propeteia*): for secrets, 286, 313; to blame God, 273–74; to emend text, 279n17, 289
preexistence. *See* soul
presbyter. *See* elder
priest (*hiereus*): Aaron figurative, 286; Christ as, 41, 68, 209, 446; each believer is potentially, 52; leads songs, 238; of idols, 430; the noble and superior soul, 392–93
Prinzivalli, Emanuela, 4, 29–30
problems and solutions (*problēmata kai luseis*), 13, 59, 291, 297–301, 335n65, 403n54, 412. *See also* *aporia*

Prochnik, George, 281n30
progress (*prokopē*), 21, 121–24, 131, 254–55
prophet and prophets: angels speak in, 327; apostles consistent with, 69; arrows, 104; bees, 153; Celsus criticized, 279n20; Christ prays through, in Psalms, 41; dedication to studying, 86; foundations of heaven, 447; God's instruments, 230, 425; heavenly powers learn from, 71; heretics slander and delete, 196, 374; Jews know, 434; Jews no longer have, 114, 194, 204, 434–35; Job was a, 134n81; mercifully sent to sinners, 352; need to identify persona in, 291; need to memorize, 452; of idols, 430; only, compose psalms, 238; progressed in prayer, 203; riddles in, 391; rivers of living water, 272; sent at dawn, 349; should be lent out, 119; speaks what is worthy of God, 158n2; spirit prays in, 293; spiritual, 179
prosōpon. *See* persona
Psalms: inscriptions or titles of, 37–38, 178–79, 220, 238–39, 287, 409–10; numbering of, 33; presents humanity in favorable light, 181–82; prophetic character of, 20, 28, 40, 41, 56, 60, 69, 91, 116, 131, 138, 168, 178–79, 203–4, 208, 213, 214, 218, 228, 238, 243, 245, 247, 251, 264, 287, 293, 354, 359, 362, 376, 383–84, 400, 403, 405, 409, 414, 429, 433, 440n4, 442; reading, liturgical, 20–21, 139; use of, as prayers, 21–22, 41, 139, 197, 200, 213, 320, 409
Pythagoras, likens human body to musical instrument, 165n39

Rehoboam, 288, 288–89n12, 303–4, 306, 404
repentance. *See* change of heart

Apocryphal/Deuterocanonical Books